America's Bishop

Also by Thomas C. Reeves

*Freedom and the Foundation: The Fund for the Republic
in the Era of McCarthyism*

(ed.) *Foundations Under Fire*

(ed.) *McCarthyism*

Gentleman Boss: The Life of Chester Alan Arthur

The Life and Times of Joe McCarthy: A Biography

(ed.) *John F. Kennedy: The Man, the Politician, the President*

A Question of Character: A Life of John F. Kennedy

(ed.) *James Lloyd Breck, Apostle of the Wilderness*

The Empty Church: The Suicide of Liberal Christianity

Twentieth-Century America: A Brief History

America's Bishop

The Life and Times of Fulton J. Sheen

THOMAS C. REEVES

ENCOUNTER BOOKS
San Francisco

First edition published in 2001 by Encounter Books, an activity of Encounter for Culture and Education, Inc., a nonprofit tax exempt corporation.

Encounter Books website address: www.encounterbooks.com

Manufactured in the United States and printed on acid-free paper.

The paper used in this publication meets the minimum requirements of ANSI/NISO Z39.48–1992 (R 1997)(*Permanence of Paper*).

Library of Congress Cataloging-in-Publication Data

Reeves, Thomas C., 1936–
  America's bishop : the life and times of Fulton J. Sheen / Thomas C. Reeves.
    p.   cm.
  Includes bibliographical references and index.
ISBN 1-893554-25-2 (cloth : alk.)
1. Sheen, Fulton J. (Fulton John), 1895–1979.   2. Catholic Church—United States—Bishops—Biography.   I. Title.
BX4705.S612 R44 2001
282'.092—dc21
[B]   2001033375

10   9   8   7   6   5   4   3   2   1

For John C. Kubeck

Contents

Introduction

*A*s the twentieth century wound to a close, there was speculation about who had been the greatest, the most popular, the most significant, and the most influential Catholics of the preceding hundred years. In a poll taken by the Internet *Catholic Daily*, with 23,455 people casting ballots, the top four Catholics of the century were Pope John Paul II, Mother Teresa, Blessed Padre Pio, and Archbishop Fulton J. Sheen.[1] The *Catholic Almanac* for the year 2000, published by Our Sunday Visitor, described Sheen as "perhaps the most popular and socially influential American Catholic of the 20th century."[2]

A strong case can be made for the accuracy of these evaluations. In the first place, Sheen was the best and most popular public speaker in the Church. Millions, in the United States and around the world, listened to his *Catholic Hour* radio programs from 1930 to 1952, and millions received printed copies of these talks. Journalist Gladys Baker observed that in 1949, Sheen was "the name priest in America," adding that "By members of all faiths, Monsignor Sheen is conceded to be the most electric orator of our times."[3] In 1979, Billy Graham called Sheen "one of the greatest preachers of this century."[4] In 1983, the noted Catholic historian John Tracy Ellis labeled him "the twentieth century's most famous Catholic preacher."[5]

When Sheen went on television in February 1952, his *Life Is Worth Living* programs became extremely popular, competing effectively against shows starring "Mr. Television" Milton Berle and singer-actor Frank Sinatra. A television critic remarked, "Bishop Sheen can't sing, can't dance, and can't act. All he is ... is sensational."[6] In

1

his first year on television, Sheen won the Emmy Award for Most Outstanding Television Personality, beating out media giants Lucille Ball, Arthur Godfrey, Edward R. Murrow, and Jimmy Durante. He was on the cover of *Time* magazine. The following year, the bishop was featured on the covers of *TV Guide, Colliers,* and *Look.* A journalist remarked, "No Catholic bishop has burst on the world with such power as Sheen wields since long before the Protestant Reformation."[7] By early 1955, the Sheen programs were reaching 5.5 million households a week.[8] Between 1952 and 1956, according to the Gallup poll, Sheen was one of the nation's ten most admired men.[9]

No record can be made of the thousands of sermons, speeches, and retreats Sheen gave over the decades, often to huge audiences. When he was scheduled to preach at St. Patrick's Cathedral in New York, 6,000 people regularly packed the church. On Easter Sunday, 1941, 7,500 worshippers were jammed into the cathedral, while 800 waited outside, hoping for a chance to get in. On Good Friday, Sheen's sermons were broadcast outdoors to the thousands standing outside St. Patrick's. "For three hours," a journalist wrote, "the heart of Manhattan's most congested midtown area became a miniature St. Peter's Square. The phenomenon is repeated for the evening service."[10] Many of Sheen's television shows, sermons, and speeches are still available on videocassette and tape.

In addition to establishing himself as a philosopher and theologian, Sheen was one of the American Church's most prolific writers. Over a period of 54 years he authored 66 books and published 62 booklets, pamphlets, and printed radio talks. The number of his readers can only be imagined. A single radio talk of 1934 was in its eleventh edition in 1948, a printing of 54,000 copies.[11] Sheen wrote countless magazine and newspaper articles, and numerous book introductions and chapters.[12] In the early 1950s he was writing two regular newspaper columns; his syndicated column in the secular press ran for thirty years. He also edited two magazines, one for sixteen years.

Sheen's expertise encompassed a wide variety of topics, from Aristotle, Augustine, and Thomas Aquinas to Karl Marx, Sigmund

Freud, and John Dewey. In his *Philosophy of Science*, he revealed a sophisticated knowledge of the literature of physics and mathematics. Sheen's academic credentials were excellent; he was the first American to be awarded a rare postdoctoral degree from the prestigious University of Louvain. His linguistic achievements were admirable: he read Greek, German, Italian, Latin, and French, and spoke the last three fluently. (It was said that he "thought in Latin.") Three of Sheen's books, published between 1925 and 1934, were major contributions to scholastic philosophy, earning widespread applause from scholars and exhibiting a breadth of knowledge that was truly exceptional.

Sheen's popular works were often as appealing as those of the great Anglican apologist C. S. Lewis, and consistently less pedantic. "Bring big ideas down to the level of Second Year High," he told an interviewer in 1947. "No idea is too abstract for anyone to understand. Most people don't digest thought, they assimilate it. Be simple, not complex. Write the way you feel; write self-expressively."[13] In a 1948 book he observed: "This is indeed an oversimplified explanation of Hegel, so simple that if Hegel heard it he would turn over in his grave, but it is often the business of philosophers to complicate and obscure the simple things of life."[14] At times Sheen created lengthy sentences that glittered with wisdom and wit. In 1948, for example, he wrote on death and judgment, when "each man will have to learn for himself that narrow is the gate and strait the way to Eternal Life, and few there are who enter therein":

> *There will be no attorneys to plead his case; no alienists to plead that he was not in his right mind because he did wrong; no Freudians to plead that he was not responsible because he had an Oedipus complex; all the masks will be taken off; he will step out of the ranks, away from the crowd, and the only voice he will hear will be the voice of conscience, which will not testify in his behalf, but will reveal self as he really is; its X rays will penetrate beyond all moods and phantasies, gestures and schemes and illusions; no loud orchestra will play to drown his conscience; no*

opiates will be served to make him forget or waft him off into the delightful irresponsibility of sleep; no cocktails will be served at heavenly bars with angelic barmaids to make him deaf to the voice of conscience; no Marxist will arise to defend him and say that he was determined by economic conditions under which he lived and, therefore, was not free; no book of the month will be read to prove that since there is no sin, there can be no judgment.[15]

More than a dozen of Sheen's books remain in print, and fourteen anthologies of his writings and talks have been published, four of them in the 1990s. What Sheen wrote about a single book of his, *Way to Happiness,* might be said to summarize virtually everything he published: "The purpose will be to bring solace, healing and hope to hearts; truth and enlightenment to minds; goodness, strength and resolution to wills."[16]

❧

FULTON SHEEN WAS ONE of the Church's great missionaries. In 1979, the Jesuit magazine *America* called him "the greatest evangelizer in the history of the Catholic Church in the United States."[17]

He lavished personal attention on those who elicited his special interest or sympathy, both rich and poor. A reporter observed in 1952: "The bishop's official date book, listing names of those he plans to see ('I will see *anybody* with a spiritual problem'), regularly bulges with eight hundred to a thousand entries."[18] Thousands attended his convert classes. No one, of course, could count the vast numbers who came into the Church, wholly or in part, as a result of Sheen's publications and media and personal appearances.

As national director of the Society for the Propagation of the Faith from 1950 to 1966, Sheen raised more money for the poor than any other American Catholic, an effort that was augmented by the donation of more than $10 million of his personal earnings.[19] Not long before his death, he declared, "My greatest love has always been the Missions of the Church."[20]

Decades ahead of others in his opposition to racism, Sheen

raised funds and donated very large sums of personal income to help build a hospital and churches for blacks in Alabama. In the late 1920s, while Klansmen were riding through the streets of hundreds of American cities, Sheen was giving speeches stressing racial equality and brotherhood.[21] In 1944, a time when America's armed forces were segregated, Sheen pointed to Christ's "explicit command to love all men, regardless of race or class or color."[22] He also declared, "For a Catholic to be anti-Semitic is to be un-Catholic."[23]

Frequently outspoken, Sheen stirred controversy with forceful statements on such topics as communism, socialism, the Spanish Civil War, World War II diplomacy, psychiatry, secularism, education, and the Left in general. He often attacked the growing secularity of liberal Protestantism, declaring that "Satan's last assault was an effort to make religion worldly."[24] And yet the bishop defied efforts to place him politically on the left or the right. He was equally critical of monopolistic capitalists, irresponsible labor union leaders, and idealistic advocates of the welfare state. This stance was a reflection of his total devotion to Church teaching:

> *If by capitalism is meant, not diffused ownership of property, but monopolistic capitalism in which capital bids for labor on a market, and concentrates wealth in the hands of the few, then from an economic point of view alone, the Church is just as much opposed to capitalism as it is to communism. Communism emphasizes social use to the exclusion of personal rights, and capitalism emphasizes personal rights to the exclusion of social use. The Church says both are wrong, for though the right to property is personal, the use is social. It therefore refuses to maintain capitalism as an alternative to the economic side of communism. Monopolistic capitalism concentrates wealth in the hands of a few capitalists, and communism in the hands of a few bureaucrats, and both end in the proletarianization of the masses.[25]*

Sheen in fact eschewed all forms of earthly utopianism. "It is man who has to be remade *first*," he wrote in his best-selling book

Peace of Soul, "then society will be remade by the restored new man."[26] Still, he often supported reform movements, eager to help create a world rid of inequality, insensitivity, hatred, crime, and corruption. In 1967, he fell under attack from the right for publicly opposing the Vietnam War. He was the first American bishop to attempt to implement in a diocese the full teachings of the Second Vatican Council, prompting severe criticism from conservatives and radicals alike.

Sheen had a few secrets, and his ambition, vanity, and luxurious lifestyle embarrassed him in his old age, yet there were few among the Church's intellectuals who tried harder to be a model for others. He was ever the defender of the Catholic faith. In his old age, he replied to a question by television interviewer Bill Moyers, "I'm never haunted by doubts about essentials, no; but by nonessentials. No, as regards the gospel and Christ and the Church I have a certitude that is absolute. About other things, I don't care so much."[27]

Although he was a major figure in the Church by the early 1930s and lived until 1979, Sheen will always be remembered as a man who helped set the tone of the 1950s. In the *Time* magazine story of 1952, he was lionized as "perhaps the most famous preacher in the U.S., certainly America's best-known Roman Catholic priest, and the newest star of U.S. television." The article quoted a spokesman for the Archdiocese of New York exclaiming, "He's telegenic. He's wonderful. The gestures, the timing, the voice. If he came out in a barrel and read the telephone book, they'd love him." And it cited Harriet Van Horne of the *New York World-Telegram & Sun:* "It's quite possible that he is the finest Catholic orator since Peter the Hermit."

The *Time* story provided biographical data, emphasizing the bishop's humble background in rural and small-town Illinois. It remarked upon his many publications, sniffing slightly that the most popular books, such as *Peace of Soul* and *Lift up Your Heart,* "were designed for the middle-brow reader." It presented photographs of Sheen's most prominent converts: automobile magnate Henry Ford II, leftist writer Heywood Broun, author Clare Boothe

Luce (wife of *Time* owner Henry Luce), former Communist editor Louis Budenz, and famed violinist Fritz Kreisler. And it presented excerpts from Sheen writings, the first being:

> *America, it is said, is suffering from intolerance. It is not. It is*
> *suffering from tolerance: tolerance of right and wrong, truth and*
> *error, virtue and evil. Christ and chaos... The man who can*
> *make up his mind in an orderly way, as a man might make up*
> *his bed, is called a bigot: but a man who cannot make up his*
> *mind, any more than he can make up for lost time, is called tol-*
> *erant and broad minded.*[28]

This celebration of religious certainty that characterized Sheen and much of the 1950s in this country has no doubt been responsible in part for the bishop's neglect at the hands of more recent historians and journalists. Especially since the upheavals of the 1960s and 1970s, it has become decidedly unfashionable in intellectual circles to talk, as he did, about objective moral standards or to proselytize for one religion or denomination over another. In recent years religion itself has been virtually banished from public education and the public square, and rendered nearly invisible in the media (except, of course, for lurid reports on clerical malefactions).

Sheen's staunch anticommunism undoubtedly also contributes to his lack of appeal for many modern intellectuals. Donald F. Crosby's *God, Church, and Flag: Senator Joseph R. McCarthy and the Catholic Church, 1950–1957* devotes a page to Sheen, noting that he "poured forth a gushing stream of books, articles, pamphlets, sermons, and speeches" attacking the theory and dynamics of communism and emphasizing its opposition to Roman Catholicism.[29] David Caute's *The Great Fear: The Anti-Communist Purge under Truman and Eisenhower* observes that Sheen "played the leading role" in drawing ex-Communist informers into the Church, an action the leftist author greets with scorn.[30] Historian Ellen Schrecker, who mourns the virtual disappearance of the Communist Party in America, takes the same position.[31] Richard Gid Powers, in *Not Without Honor: The History of American Anticommunism,* notes

Sheen's radio sermons attacking communism and cites an anti-communist speech he gave before the American Legion's All-American Conference in 1950.[32]

Yet despite such controversies, which are perhaps as much about the 1950s as about Sheen himself, steps have been taken in recent years to beatify the archbishop. On the twentieth anniversary of Sheen's death, John Cardinal O'Connor of New York formally initiated the lengthy process. In the spring of 2000, Paul Cicarelli of St. Petersburg, Florida, launched a Web site to build public support for Sheen's canonization.[33]

This book is not an effort to bolster or defeat that effort. Long ago I was taught that "Hero worshipers make poor biographers as do also those who delight in 'debunking' or are careless in their search for facts."[34] Although it is perhaps an unfashionable commitment today, I still believe that the best history is written with accuracy and objectivity as the highest goals, and it is in this spirit that the following is presented.

ONE

A Successor of the Apostles

B etween 1846 and 1851, over a million people fled the Great Famine in Ireland and came to the United States. The typical Irish emigrant was under thirty-five, unmarried, poor and unskilled. Although they started at the bottom of the socioeconomic scale, the Irish worked hard, saved their money, bought property, and enjoyed rapid social mobility. By the turn of the century, there was a sizable Irish middle class.

Many Irishmen went into politics, eventually running many of the nation's cities. For others, social mobility was achieved through the Roman Catholic Church, the faith of the great majority of Irish immigrants. While the Church in America was cosmopolitan, encompassing worshipers who spoke twenty-eight languages, the Irish quickly moved into positions of authority. In 1900 they constituted no more than 50 percent of the Catholic population in the United States, yet they contributed 62 percent of the bishops. One study showed that from 1850 to 1930 in the Diocese of St. Paul, Minnesota, 45 percent of all the clergy were of Irish heritage. In the Diocese of St. Louis, Missouri, where the clergy of German descent outnumbered the Irish, eleven of twelve priests elevated to the episcopacy between 1854 and 1924 were Irish. Some who resented this ecclesiastical domination, like the Germans (who comprised about 25 percent of the Catholics in America by 1900) and the Poles, described the Church in the United States as "One, Holy, Irish, and Apostolic."[1]

Most of the Irish stayed in the cities, but some moved to the Midwest, choosing to farm the fertile soil they found there. Stephen

Patrick McCarthy, for example, was born in Tipperary County, saved his money while toiling as a farmhand in Livingston County, New York, and bought a farm near Appleton, Wisconsin. He cleared the land, built a log cabin, married a local girl from Bavaria and taught her to speak English. They had ten children and the family prospered. The third child, Tim, would start his own farm in the mid-1890s on 142 acres purchased from his father. The fifth child born on that farm would be named Joseph Raymond McCarthy, the future senator.[2]

Many Irish farmers could also be found in neighboring Illinois. Peter Sheen, born three miles south of Dublin, came to the Midwest before the Civil War. He married Melissa Robinson, who was born on a farm in Rising Sun, Indiana, on the Ohio River, and was probably of English extraction. The couple owned their own farm by the time the eighth of their eleven children, Morris Newton Sheen, was born in Peoria County, Illinois, in 1863.[3]

Newt, as he became known, was short and slim, usually rather quiet, friendly, strong-willed, highly intelligent, hard-working, and extremely frugal. He had only three years of formal schooling, but his native abilities and a fierce determination to succeed soon led to modest prosperity.[4]

A son described him as "an agriculturist and inventor, a farmer with a pronounced mechanical bent."[5] One of his later inventions was a "shocker," a machine that would pick up bales of oats and stand the shocks on end.[6]

Peter Sheen had given up the Catholicism of his ancestors when he came to the United States, and Newt did not join the Church.[7] A brother, Daniel Sheen, would become a law partner of the famous agnostic Robert G. Ingersoll. (Fulton J. Sheen said later that while Daniel was not himself an agnostic, he was not a Catholic either.)[8]

In his early twenties, Newt married Ida Clara Von Buttear, a Protestant of German descent and a native of Newark, Ohio. At nineteen, in 1886, she gave birth to a daughter, Eva Natalie Sheen.[9] A few years later Ida died, and subsequently Newt, who now owned a farm near the tiny agricultural town of Minonk, Illinois, married Delia

Fulton. The twenty-nine-year-old bride had been raised on a farm in Kickapoo, Illinois, slightly to the northwest of Peoria. Newt joined the Church in order to wed Delia, and he quickly absorbed much of her intense piety and devotion to the Catholic faith.[10]

Ida's Protestant parents then went to court to protect their granddaughter from "popery." They won their case and legally adopted Eva. The girl appears in a few early Sheen family photos, but was soon virtually forgotten by the family in the Peoria area. Raised by Newt's brother Andrew, she eventually married and had five children.[11] Few outside the Sheen family would ever know that Fulton had a Protestant half-sister. He never mentioned her or her mother publicly. Mary Baker, a close friend of Sheen's for fifty-one years, learned about Eva from one of Fulton's brothers.[12]

Delia was the third oldest of seven children and the only girl born to Irish immigrants John and Mary Fulton. (Delia's mother and grandmother were from County Roscommon.) The young woman, plain and dark-haired with deep-set eyes that her firstborn would inherit, had finished the eighth grade, and she devoted herself almost entirely to domestic pursuits. A nephew would later describe "Auntie Dee," as she became widely known, as "laid back, cordial, quiet, sociable" and an expert cook who made "fabulous meals."[13] A cousin would remember her as "quiet, wonderful, reserved.... She was close to a saint and much loved."[14] A granddaughter recalled a dignity and elegance about Delia, who was articulate and carried herself well. "She was very, very saintly."[15] Neighbors later remembered Mr. and Mrs. Sheen with great fondness; said one, "Everybody in El Paso loved them."[16]

By the time their first child arrived, the Sheens had moved from the farm to the nearby town of El Paso, where Newt and his brother Andrew ran a hardware store at 25 Front Street, in the heart of the main business block. The family lived in a small apartment over the store with a view of the street, paved with red bricks, and the single-track railroad that ran parallel to it. There on May 8, 1895, Peter John Fulton was born, and named after his two grandfathers.[17] Four days later, he was baptized at St. Mary's Church in El Paso.[18]

The infant Peter quickly distinguished himself by his almost incessant crying; a babysitter later recalled that "he really had a pair of lungs." One Sunday when Peter was about two, he started to cry while the family, accompanied by the babysitter, was riding in a surrey. The din became such that Newt said to the babysitter, "Marie, take him out of the surrey and prop him up against that tree over there and we'll pretend to drive off without him to see if that won't stop him." The trick worked—temporarily.[19] For years, relatives and the family doctor, when referring to Peter, would say, "Oh, this is the boy who never stopped crying." Sheen later learned that he had suffered from tuberculosis as an infant, no doubt the cause of his perpetual misery.[20]

The hardware store, along with much of the business section of El Paso, burned down when an errand boy, seeing his father come down the street, ditched his lighted cigarette under the stairs and ignited a fifty-gallon can of gasoline. Newt then moved his family to a farm he inherited from his father. When Peter was five, the family moved to Peoria in order that the youngster might be enrolled in St. Mary's, the local parochial school; both Newt and Delia were committed to giving their children as much education as possible.[21] Newt made a living by managing two farms, each about thirty miles from the city.[22] Peter's first brother, Joseph, arrived in 1898. Then came Thomas in 1902 and Aloysious in 1908. The family's first home in Peoria, at 111 Seventh Street, had eight rooms, to provide space for the boys and for Delia's parents, who visited and lived with them on occasion.[23]

No matter where they lived, the Sheens were devout Catholics. Regular church attendance, parochial schooling, grace before meals, the nightly Rosary, and frequent visits by clergy were part of the family routine. "Our family life was simple and the atmosphere of our home Christian," Sheen recalled.[24] A relative remembered Delia reading the family Bible, inherited from her mother, to young Peter.[25]

Such everyday observances were not at all unusual. The family Rosary was a practice held up as an ideal for Catholics throughout the nineteenth and early twentieth century, and was especially prevalent among the Irish, whose homes were often decorated with holy pictures and statues as perpetual reminders of their Catholic faith. The mother's role as religious educator and moral guide, a role Delia eagerly embraced, was a common theme in the literature, both Protestant and Catholic, of the nineteenth century.[26]

The religious atmosphere in the Sheen home made a profound impact on the oldest son, particularly his mother's veneration of the Virgin Mary. He later wrote, "When I was baptized as an infant, my mother laid me on the altar of the Blessed Mother in St. Mary's Church, El Paso, Illinois, and consecrated me to her. As an infant may be unconscious of a birthmark, so I was unconscious of the dedication—but the mark was always there. Like a piece of iron to the magnet, I was drawn to her before I knew her, but never drawn to her without Christ."[27]

When Peter was five and a half years old, he enrolled in the first grade at St. Mary's School, operated by the Sisters of the Sacred Heart. This is when his first name was changed. Whether his grandfather did it, as described in Sheen's autobiography, or whether he himself was responsible, as other accounts have it, Peter became Fulton.[28]

He later explained that his crying as a baby had so irritated his mother that she often sent him to her own mother's home, "where I got to be known as Fulton's baby." Then Fulton as a first name stuck.[29]

While no school records for the time exist, Fulton would be remembered at St. Mary's as exceptionally bright and studious. In fact, all of the Sheen boys were intellectually gifted. Tom had a photographic memory, Fulton's was at least semi-photographic, and Joe and Al were thought by family members to be highly intelligent.[30] A woman who knew the Sheens well said about Fulton, "Seems to me, he was always reading." He excelled in arithmetic and strove to be a leader in his class.[31] A fellow student recalled that Sheen was not only "a little better than the rest of us in his studies" but also "just a little more devout."[32]

In Fulton's first year at St. Mary's, a nun suggested that students put at the top of every page the initials J.M.J., standing for a dedication to Jesus, Mary, and Joseph. For the rest of his life, Fulton Sheen would inscribe those letters at the top of most of the pages of his writings and always on the blackboard during his television programs.[33] (This was by no means a novel practice. In Poland, Karol Wojtyla, the future John Paul II, would use the same initials on pages throughout his life as a student and writer.)[34]

When he was about eight, Sheen began serving regularly as an altar boy at massive St. Mary's Cathedral, not far from the school, where his family regularly worshiped.[35] He was often at the side of Bishop John Lancaster Spalding, the dynamic first bishop of Peoria who presided over a diocese that embraced 18,000 square miles and, at his consecration in 1877, a Catholic population of 45,000. During his tenure in office, which ended in 1908, he built 140 churches, 58 schools, numerous charitable institutions, and St. Mary's Cathedral. He tripled the number of priests in the diocese in order to meet the needs of a Catholic population that had also increased threefold. Spalding was a founder of the Catholic University of America and leader of the Irish Catholic Colonization Association (which encouraged Irish immigrants to settle on farms in the West). A great orator and intellectual, he was a major figure in the American Church during the Gilded Age and Progressive Era.[36]

When confirmed at age twelve, Fulton dedicated himself to the Blessed Virgin Mary. At the end of his life, he wrote, "My first Communion book with its mother-of-pearl cover contained the Litany of the Blessed Virgin, which I began reciting every night as a boy and have continued to this hour."[37] By the time of his confirmation, Sheen said, he had "a very conscious vocation" to the priesthood.[38] He did not mention it to his parents, but later learned that they had long been praying for his vocation.[39] Even as a small boy Fulton, at his proud mother's request, would entertain relatives with spiritual talks he had prepared. His brother Joe later wrote, "To my knowledge Fulton never announced his decision or intention to become a priest. It seemed to be an accepted fact by our family."[40] Fulton later remembered that as a boy he was shocked at the dinner table when a relative dared question the wisdom of a position taken by the Pope.[41] He wrote in his autobiography that his spiritual calling "emerged in the earliest recollections of childhood."[42]

Fulton was clearly influenced toward the priesthood by the priests and nuns he encountered in church and in the schoolroom, and by his experiences as an altar boy; but vital to the decision was the love and discipline he experienced at home. Of Newt, Fulton once wrote simply, "My father was the head of the household as I grew up."[43] Newt sometimes spanked his boys for good cause, and later Fulton would often opine, "There is nothing that develops character in a young boy like a pat on the back, provided it is given often enough, hard enough and low enough."[44] In *Children and Parents,* he wrote with a smile that "factors contributing to juvenile delinquency have been safety razors which have dispensed with the razor strap, and garages which have done away with the woodshed. To borrow shipboard terminology, spanking is known as 'stern' punishment. It is a form of depressing one end to impress the other end. It takes much less time than reasoning and penetrates more quickly to the seat of wisdom."[45]

Delia, for her part, provided the family's sense of order. Joe Sheen later wrote, "My mother, very humble and never speaking ill of anyone, saw to it that we'd always be on time for Mass."[46] But Delia's influence went far beyond that for Fulton: she provided him with a lifelong model of Catholic motherhood. As he wrote in *Way to Inner Peace,* "The best influences in life are undeliberate, unconscious; when no one is watching, or when reaction to the good deed was never sought. Such is the long-range influence of a mother in a home; fulfilling of daily duties with love and a spirit of self-sacrifice leaves an imprint on the children that deepens with the years."[47] In the same book, Sheen explained his understanding of the difference between a Christian mother and father, making undeclared but unmistakable reference to his own family:

> ... *a man governs the home, but the woman reigns in it. Government is related to justice and law; reigning, to love and feeling.*

The orders of the father in a home are like written mandates from a king; the influence of the woman, however, is more subtle, more felt and less aggressive. The commands of the father are more jerky and intermittent; the quiet pervading radiance of the mother is constant, like the growth of a plant. And yet both are essential for the home, for justice without love could become tyranny, and love without justice could become toleration of evil.[48]

In her own way, Delia too provided her boys with discipline. She made Fulton return a geranium he had stolen from a grocery store and pay the grocer fifty cents from his piggy bank for the plant that cost a dime. "My act of dishonesty thus punished by restitution taught me for life that honesty is the best policy," Fulton wrote in his autobiography. "In any case, when I took the money to Mr. Madden, he gave me two pots of geraniums."[49]

Both Newt and Delia preached by word and deed the value of hard work. Delia often headed for the kitchen when in a relative's home to take on more than her share of the labor. When visiting his tenant farmers, Newt "would help them build barns, reap the harvest, and do anything to keep himself busy." Fulton later observed, "Not only because it was parental training but perhaps because it was already ingrained in me, the habit of work was one I never got over, and I thank God I never did."[50] (Years later, commenting on his schedule of nineteen-hour days, seven days a week, a niece described Fulton as "a driven person." But her father, Joe, and her uncle Tom were the same way. "It was a Sheen thing.")[51]

While he rarely spoke about his parents in public, Fulton loved them deeply. He once wrote, "No one can ever take the place of a mother, a father or a best friend. When they are gone, the niches remain empty for the rest of life."[52] On a television program, he said, "Mothers in the animal kingdom care only for a body; mothers in the spiritual kingdom must care also for a soul, a mind, and a heart. The soul comes from God and must go back again to Him. God sets the target, the parents are the bow, and their vocation is to shoot the arrow straight."[53] In his autobiography he praised the goodness of God for giving him "the gift of Christian parents."[54]

Fulton would often reveal his fond remembrances of growing up by writing about the supreme value of the family as a training ground for such vital elements of character as self-discipline, self-sacrifice, industriousness, reverence, compassion, fidelity, and loyalty. In 1948 he remarked, "It is the home which decides the nation. What happens in the family will happen later in Congress, the White House and the Supreme Court. Every country gets the kind of government it deserves. As we live in the home, so shall the nation live."[55]

Evidence suggests that there were mild tensions in the Sheen home, however. Al, the youngest boy, felt isolated from his siblings and neglected by his parents. Delia had apparently not wanted a fourth boy so late in life, and a measure of regret may have surfaced in her treatment of her youngest son. Al dropped out of high school and road the rails for a time before settling down with a job and a family. He was never to be very close to his brothers and, while capable of great charm, would lack their strength of character and Christian commitment. One of Al's daughters, Catherine, later described him as a cold and bad-tempered alcoholic who often frightened her, saying, "There was much anger in him."[56] Al never talked about his past, and thus the precise source of his bitterness eludes the historian. (Tom, good-natured, happy, and professionally successful, also never talked about his youth.) The distance between Fulton and Al extended to Al's family; Catherine Sheen said, with a touch of bitterness, that she barely knew her famous uncle.[57]

Fulton was reportedly closest to his brother Joe. Tom and Fulton would remain friends for the rest of their lives, both living in New York for many years, and seeing each other on a fairly regular basis; but they were not exceptionally close. Perhaps it resulted from the egotism that almost inevitably flows from brilliance. Perhaps it was simply that their careers diverged sharply and they lacked mutual interests. However that may be, this coolness also reflected something deeper, an inner reserve that, as Fulton would later reveal, isolated him on the deepest level from almost everyone including his siblings, a reserve that stemmed in large part from his priesthood and the Divine call to lead an extraordinary, otherworldly life.

By all accounts, the formative years of Fulton Sheen were happy and healthy. Reeda Eibeck, a cousin who saw much of the Sheens during her youth in Peoria, remembered Newt and Delia as "pleasant, happy people," and described Fulton as "a delightful young man" with a great sense of humor.[58] The very young Fulton appears to have been intellectually precocious, deeply religious, good-natured, consistently positive, self-confident, happy, and popular. The vanity that would plague him throughout his life would first appear shortly.

～

IN 1909, FULTON ENTERED all-male Spalding Institute in downtown Peoria near St. Mary's Cathedral. The large high school, built by Bishop Spalding and opened in 1899, was operated by the Brothers of Mary, whom Sheen recalled as "excellent teachers, given to discipline, yet much beloved." A classmate was Jimmy Jordan, later to become famous as radio star Fibber McGee. (Across the street, in the Academy of Our Lady, was the young girl who would become Fibber's wife, Molly, in real life and on the radio. A block away, at Peoria High, was Charles Correll, who would later be renowned as Andy on the famous *Amos and Andy* radio show. Thus, four of radio's biggest stars in the 1930s and 1940s grew up as neighbors in Peoria.)[59]

That Fulton was sent to a Catholic high school again illustrates the resolve of his parents to equip him with the best available religious education. Catholics had been slow to organize high schools; the fashion was college preparatory academies, often calling themselves colleges, for men and finishing schools for women. Church leaders, seeking to compete effectively against the public school system, opened the first parochial high school in 1890 in Philadelphia. It would be some time until such schools were popular with Catholics. In 1912, 60,000 students were enrolled in the parochial schools of Philadelphia, yet the high school had an enrollment of only 394.[60]

Classmates called Sheen "Spike" because his hair was combed straight back in the style that would later be called the "pompadour." For a time he worked for the O'Brien-Jobst haberdashery in Peoria, where he learned much about clothes and how to wear them. A classmate remembered him as "a very careful dresser. His suit always looked neat as a pin and his hair was always in place." Perhaps this was the beginning of the vanity that would later emerge and admittedly be a serious personal problem. Fulton didn't ignore local girls, but he did not seem particularly interested in them. "I remember his telling me on more than one occasion that he was going to become a priest. That's the way we had him figured out, too."[61]

Most noticeable were Sheen's scholastic achievements. During his freshman year, studying religion, English, German, Latin, science, and mathematics, he placed second in his class. He was first in his sophomore, junior, and senior years. His general grade point average, on a 1–100 point scale, was 93.6 in his junior year and rose to 95.1 during his senior year. He again excelled in mathematics, having a perfect mark in trigonometry as a senior.[62]

In his senior year, Sheen was given one line in the annual school play because, he said, "my father paid for the program." His beaming parents were in the audience for the performance, so popular that it ran for two nights instead of the usual one.[63] He did not turn out for sports; he was smaller than many of his classmates, weighing no more than 115 pounds. Fulton played a little handball and tried to run a hundred miles around a small track set up in the gymnasium in order to qualify for membership in the Century Club. Classmate Ralph Buchele said later, "I don't know if he ever made that 100 miles, but he gave it a good try." What Buchele remembered most was the fact that Spike Sheen "was more of a student than the rest of us."[64]

Sheen graduated as valedictorian of the seven-member class of 1913. Buchele, the class salutatorian, still remembered Sheen's speech at graduation exercises forty years later. "It was a real humdinger and the people at the graduation loved it."[65] Edwin Kneer, also a top student, said of Fulton, "he had a wonderful memory and he could talk."[66]

In Fulton's sophomore year at Spalding, his parents moved to a farm in Stark County, near the town of Dunlap, about thirteen miles from the city limits of Peoria. Three years later, Newt sold his two farms outside Peoria and purchased a larger farm near Wyoming, Illinois, thirty-five miles north of Peoria. Fulton stayed with Delia's brother, Arthur, and his family in Peoria while attending high school. At one point he went door to door in Peoria selling subscriptions to the *Cathedral Messenger*. Richard Bradley, a local tailor, later remembered giving the boy some tips on salesmanship and trying, unsuccessfully, to persuade him to charge double for the subscription and pocket the balance.[67]

During the summers Fulton lived, and worked, on the farm. The Sheen farmhouses lacked running water, electricity, and a telephone.[68] For years Delia cooked on a huge iron stove, a "corncob stove," named after the dried corncobs that were used as fuel.[69] Kerosene lamps, a chore to clean, provided light. Newt, a recreational reader, had a gas lamp that when pumped up (like a modern camp lantern) and with the mantles ignited would glow with a bright light; young relatives sometimes stole the mantles just to irritate him.[70] Joseph Sheen Jr. later remembered Newt sitting on the family porch singing songs like "Billy Boy" and "My Darling Clementine" to his grandchildren. "He was no great singer, but his voice had a Burl Ives quality."[71]

The other Sheen boys tolerated life on the farm, but Fulton hated it, not only for the long hours but also for the nature of the work. On the farm, he "plowed corn, made hay while the sun shone, broke colts to harness, curried horses, cleaned their dirty stalls, milked cows morning and night and in cold, damp weather shucked corn, fed the pigs, dug postholes, applied salve to horses cut by barbed wire, fought potato bugs on the day that a circus came to town, argued with my father every day that farming was not a good life and that you could make a fortune on it only if you struck oil."[72]

Fulton's distaste for farming was such that he later told a few people, with tongue in cheek, that he chose the priesthood in order to escape it. His cousin Merle Fulton would recall, "He told me one time that probably the thing that made him decide to become a priest was when his dad started him plowing around an 80-acre field with three horses and a sulky plow. After two days, he could still jump across what he had plowed, so he decided that surely there was something in this world he could do better than that."[73]

Taking care of chickens gave Fulton a lifelong aversion to eating chicken dinners—staples of the "rubber chicken" banquet circuit. "In the course of my young life," he later wrote, "I wrung the necks of about 22,413 chickens. At night, I do not have nightmares; I have 'night-hens.' That childhood experience ruined me for what many consider a delicacy."[74]

Fulton's shortcomings as a farmer were evident to all. One day a neighbor told the elder Sheen, "Newt, that oldest boy of yours, Fulton, will never be worth a damn. He's always got his nose in a book."[75] Indeed, to Newt's disappointment, not one of his sons chose to remain on the farm.[76] Joe would become a lawyer, Tom a physician, and Al a corporate executive. Still, he remained proud and supportive, providing funds to help three of them with their education. (Al, the youngest son and a reportedly "wild" youth, dropped out of high school and chose not to go to college.)[77]

～

IN THE FALL OF 1913, eighteen-year-old Fulton entered St. Viator College in Bourbonnais, Illinois, fifty-one miles south of Chicago and three miles north of Kankakee. Bourbonnais was founded by French-speaking immigrants from Quebec in the 1830s and 1840s. The tiny town (population 600 in 1940) was inhabited almost entirely by Catholics.[78] The Viatorian Fathers who ran the college belonged to an order founded in France in 1835 to enhance the country's religious literacy after the revolution. Following the suppression of religious schools in France in 1903, most Viatorians emigrated to Belgium or Canada, and some found their way to Illinois.[79]

St. Viator College, in the Archdiocese of Chicago, opened in 1868. The campus was nearly destroyed by a fire in 1906, but by 1913 there were four nearly new stone buildings, lighted by electricity and heated by steam. St. Viator had grade school, high school, collegiate and seminary faculties on campus, along with a commercial department that taught business office skills and a two-man music department. Most of the young men on campus were high schoolers. This was not uncommon: a study of 84 colleges in 1916 showed high school students on college campuses outnumbering college students two to one.[80] Such figures were a major reason, in fact, why Catholic high schools were slow in developing.

St. Viator had twenty-five college students and forty-five seminary students when Fulton entered. Newt sent Joe at the same time to complete his high school classes at St. Viator, and the brothers roomed together. (Room, board, and tuition added up to $250 a year.) Tom entered a year later and completed high school, at age fifteen, as Fulton was finishing college.[81]

The author of a senior class biography wrote of Fulton: "His favorite pastime is the devouring of endless treatises on philosophy, art, and a hundred other kindred topics with which we ordinary mortals have hardly more than a passing acquaintance."[82] Indeed, in his four years at St. Viator, Fulton raced through the almost entirely prescribed courses, completing four years of English; two years of Greek, economics, Latin, philosophy, and sociology; two and a half years of French; and courses in religion, logic, English composition, psychology, biology, and chemistry. His grades were almost all in the 80 and 90 range (66.67 was required for passing) and his highest marks were scored in psychology and chemistry.[83]

In his freshman year, Fulton turned out for the varsity debating team. Membership, he said, was "the pinnacle of scholastic honor" on campus, and there was "the keenest competition and rivalry" among the young men to be selected. He made alternate as a freshman, and became a star of the team in the next three years. One of their victories was over powerful Notre Dame, the second such victory for St. Viator in four years and the equivalent for the small school of a triumph on the gridiron.

The debate coach was Father William J. Bergan, who taught Latin and philosophy. Sheen would come to consider him "one of the greatest inspirations of my life." Before the Notre Dame debate, Father Bergan called Sheen aside and told him bluntly, "Sheen, you're absolutely the worst speaker I ever heard." He stood Sheen in a corner, took a paragraph from his prepared speech and made him repeat it for an hour. Then he said, "Do you know what's wrong with you?" After pondering the question for a moment, Fulton replied, "I'm not natural." He was right, and it was a lesson he never forgot.[84]

Fulton later recalled the exact day he first felt comfortable on stage. In May 1917, he was chosen to lead students in the daily Rosary service in the gymnasium. As he did, he looked over at a stage prepared for a debate with undefeated Morningside College of Iowa, and became so distracted he could not finish the Rosary. "I believe that all the nervousness of my whole existence must have been concentrated in those few moments, for I was never seriously nervous again in my life before an audience."[85]

Sheen and his partner defeated Morningside College, a Methodist institution, and many at St. Viator considered it a victory of Catholic over Protestant education. Fulton wrote in the campus magazine, "An intellectual combat of this sort is the real test of any system of education.... The secret of it all is the rigid insistence by the Catholic instructors on a rigid philosophical training which is at the root of all intellectual progress." Sheen thought that the greatest competition the debate team experienced came from Catholic colleges. "Only one conclusion can be drawn from these facts and that is the absolute superiority of the Catholic system of education which cares not for the frills and fads of which modern education is so fond, but insists on the deep fundamental principles which underlie great problems of our social, civic, religious and educational life."[86] This was no mere youthful Catholic chauvinism. Sheen would expound this view of education for the rest of his life.

Charles A. Hart, a classmate known for his academic and debating prowess, wrote of "Fult" in 1917, "On the debating platform of St. Viator's there has not been known his superior if ever his equal, in any point that constitutes effective debating." The campus magazine declared, "No one has shed greater 'sheen' upon the Class of 1917 than this golden-tongued fiery young Demosthenes, who has shown his quick wit, versatility and power of mind so often on the debating platform. In stature he is rather abbreviated, slight of build, quick, business from the word go, with shining eyes that catch you and flood you with his striking personality."[87]

Although he had reached his full height of five feet, seven inches, Fulton remained thin (he would never weigh more than 142 pounds) and wisely chose not to try out for the varsity football team. He appeared in plays in his junior and senior years, including *The Taming of the Shrew*, presented at Homecoming Day, 1916. He was a class officer as a freshman, and served as class treasurer for the next three years. He gave orations during Irish Celebration his junior year and at Class Day and graduation as a senior. (Charles Hart was the valedictorian.)[88]

In his graduation day address, entitled "Immortality of the Soul," Fulton showed his promise as a thinker and writer. It was obvious that he had devoted considerable thought to the subject at hand and was not simply parroting professors. Citing Rousseau, Newton, and Shakespeare, among others, the young orator put together a logical and compelling talk.

> *Was it not God who implanted this insatiable craving in our hearts for illimitable happiness, love, and truth and beauty? And is God therefore to be conceived as urging us on irresistibly to an end which we can never attain? Must I who feel made for happiness and truth by virtue of the nature which he has given me, sink back into nothingness after this life of trouble and turmoil is over? Is it possible that of all living beings on earth man alone— and in his highest powers—is to be aimlessly disproportioned and mis-adapted to his environment? Is this highest of rational*

instincts destined to be universally frustrated? Are the loftiest
and best yearnings of the noblest and best work in the rational
universe to be forever vain and illusory?[89]

In his last three years of college, Fulton had his own column in
the campus magazine and published twelve articles. Subjects
included "Alexander Pope with the Mantle of Thomas à Kempis,"
"Hamlet, the Man," "The Short-Story," and "The Book of Nature."
The brief article on Pope, published in 1916, revealed Sheen's deep
devotion to Thomas à Kempis and an appreciation of Samuel Johnson, Shakespeare, Lord Byron, and Cardinal Newman. The 1917
essay "The Book of Nature" was an argument in favor of natural
law and an Intelligent Designer of the world and of man. This was
standard Catholic teaching, and perhaps reflected material he studied in such courses as "Evidence of Religion" and "Ontology and
Natural Theology." Still, the young author revealed his logical mind,
his wide reading, and his engaging writing style.[90]

There was a lighter side to Fulton Sheen that his classmates also
appreciated. In his senior class profile there was a reference to the
"stunts" he and other students pulled on campus. In a history of
the "War Class" of 1917, the author noted that Sheen and another
student were so genial that they received off-campus invitations to
Bourbonnais homes while the other students were forbidden to
leave campus on Sunday evenings during Lent. The author of the
senior class profile also appreciated Sheen's perpetually sunny dis-
position: "he came into our midst in the autumn of 1913 with the
fire and enthusiastic optimism of a ray of light.... There may be
rarer optimists on this side of the sun, but we doubt it."[91]

During holidays and all through the steamy Illinois summers,
Fulton wearily submitted to life and labor on the Sheen farm. Joe
Sheen later wrote of a time when all the local farmers were shelling
corn in the huge valley of coal black soil between Camp Grove and
Wyoming, Illinois. Fulton drove a team of horses and a loaded
wagon to the corn shelling machine set up on one of the farms, and
tried repeatedly but unsuccessfully to manipulate the wagon into

its proper position. Other farmers waited impatiently in line with their wagons as the young man struggled. One of the farmers reported to his family that night, "That eldest Sheen boy is never going to amount to nothing. He can't even back a wagon into the corn shelter!"[92]

Every Sunday, the family rode to St. Dominic's Church in Wyoming, six miles away, where Fulton still served as an altar boy when home. They traveled in a special carriage, a sign of their prosperity, which the family called the Klondike. Instead of curtains, which most carriages had, the Klondike displayed three panes of isinglass, both on the right and the left sides. Joe Sheen recalled, "Newton Sheen, our father, wearing a stiff hat held the reins from the inside and from there guided the two horses. The seats faced one another. I think the children in Wyoming got as much a thrill out of it as if the circus had come to town."[93]

In his senior year, Fulton took a national examination to win a three-year, all-expenses-paid scholarship for graduate work. Informed during the summer that he had won one of the coveted awards, he immediately went to Fr. Bergan, his debate coach and now a close friend, to share the news. To Fulton's shock, Bergan told him to reject the award. "You know you have a vocation; you should be going to the seminary." Fulton protested, saying he could always attend seminary after he earned a Ph.D., while obtaining a graduate degree after seminary might prove impossible. "Tear up the scholarship," Bergan said again. "That is what the Lord wants you to do. And if you do it, trusting in Him, you will receive a far better university education after you are ordained than before." Fulton took the advice, saying later that it was a turning point of his life, and adding, "I have never regretted that visit and that decision."[94]

Sheen would later write books and articles about the priesthood, in which a common theme was his own unworthiness. It must have seemed overwhelming to him as he prepared for seminary. Vocation begins, he wrote in his autobiography, when one "is confronted with a presence, not as dramatic as Paul when he was converted, but with a sense of the unworldly, the holy and the tran-scendent." Fulton had felt the call his entire life.

The second stage is the individual's reaction, "which is a pro-found sense of unworthiness." God is holy; the candidate is not. This awareness is tempered, however, by the prayerful realization that God calls men, not angels, to be his priests. "He did not make gold the vessel for his treasure; He made clay. The motley group of Apostles that He gathered about Him became more worthy through his mercy and compassion." If God so blessed the Apostles, He would surely offer the same grace to their successors, that they might become, if not perfect or even saintly, at least more worthy. "God can do something with those who see what they really are and who know their need of cleansing," Sheen believed, "but can do noth-ing with the man who feels himself worthy." The purgation begins in seminary "and continues through life in the form of physical suf-fering, mental anguish, betrayals, scandals, false accusations—all of which summon the one called to become more worthy of the treasure."

The third stage in the call is response. "After the purging, Isa-iah heard the voice of the Lord asking: 'Whom shall I send?' And Isaiah answered: 'Here I am, send me.'" Fulton Sheen entered sem-inary seeking the purgation and praying for the grace to be sent.[95]

ॐ

THE DIOCESE OF PEORIA, now led by Bishop Edmund M. Dunne, sent nine men to St. Paul Seminary in St. Paul, Minnesota, in Sep-tember 1917. The list included both Sheen and Charles A. Hart, the two top scholars in St. Viator's senior class. The diocese covered seminary costs, which amounted in Sheen's first year to $120 a semester.[96]

The seminary was the brainchild of dynamic John Ireland, the first archbishop of St. Paul, and was largely funded by railroad mag-nate James J. Hill in honor of his Catholic wife. The six-building facility, opened in 1894, was designed to educate men from the entire

Upper Midwest. Ireland sought qualified faculty who were parish priests to serve on the faculty in order to help Catholics feel "at home" in American culture. He thought a priest should be "a gentleman, a scholar, and a saint." By 1912, seminary enrollment had reached two hundred. Before World War I, thirty-five dioceses were represented in the student body.[97]

Sheen would not feel out of place at the seminary. A majority of seminarians throughout the nation at the time no doubt came from lower-middle-class and working-class origins. A survey in the Diocese of Hartford showed that fewer than 2 percent of local seminarians had fathers in the professions. Historian Kenneth J. Heineman has noted, "Of America's twenty-one thousand priests and one hundred bishops in 1921, most had humble origins." This was due to the working-class status of most Catholics as well as a strong anti-Catholic bias in many universities and professions, which limited the socioeconomic mobility of those whom many still scornfully labeled "papists."[98]

Several theological developments during the nineteenth century point to the nature of the education Sheen received in St. Paul. One was Pope Pius IX's definition, in 1854, of Mary's Immaculate Conception as dogma: the mother of Jesus was "preserved from all stain of original sin" and was predestined by God to be the *Theotokos* (God-bearer). This doctrine, expanding on the idea held by most Fathers of the Church that Mary was free from personal sin, intensified a reverence that was rooted in the first and second chapters of St. Luke's Gospel and discernible in the very early Church.

Historian Ruth Harris has called the nineteenth century the "age of Mary." In southern France, for example, there were forty shrines dedicated to the Virgin within an area of twenty-five kilometers.[99] At Lourdes in 1858, fourteen-year-old Bernadette Soubirous, who was illiterate and did not know her catechism, said that Mary had appeared to her and declared, "I am the Immaculate Conception." The very year Fulton entered the seminary, another reported Marian apparition, to three shepherd children in Fatima, Portugal, solidified belief in Mary's powerful role in the Church and in the world.

Another key development was the enhancement of papal supremacy. The hierarchical structure of the Church and the duty of obedience to that hierarchy were things every seminary student learned by heart. Catholic teaching made clear that however revered America's form of government might be, the Church was not, and never had been, a democracy. In recent years, the authority of the papacy had grown, and priests and laity alike were expected to heed the commands of the Vatican.

The principal figure in the rise of modern papal authority was Pius IX, whose pontificate ran from 1846 to 1878, the longest in history. He increased papal involvement and control throughout the world, in part by assuming the responsibility of appointing all bishops. Reacting to hostile actions by secular governments in Italy, France, and Prussia, he opposed liberalism and the separation of church and state, which he assumed meant the confiscation of all Church property and authority and the persecution of clergy and religious. The First Vatican Council's decree in 1870 of the dogma of papal infallibility in faith and morals strengthened the power of the papacy and kept the Church from being divided into national bodies, which was the Eastern Orthodox experience. Jesuit theologian Avery Dulles said in 2000 that the reforms of Pius IX allowed the papacy to become a moral voice for humanity.[100] Critics of papal supremacy have made less flattering comments over the years.

Pius IX's successors, Leo XIII (1878–1903), Pius X (1903–14), and Benedict XV (1914–22), in office during Sheen's seminary years, were staunch protagonists of papal authority. Leo XIII, who would tolerate no disagreement, once silenced his secretary of state by snapping, "I am Peter!" Those granted a papal audience were expected to kneel during the interview. In his first pastoral letter, Pius X wrote, "When we speak of the Vicar of Christ, we must not quibble, we must obey: we must not . . . evaluate his judgments, criticise his directions, lest we do injury to Jesus Christ himself. Society is sick . . . the one hope, the one remedy, is the Pope."[101]

American Catholics learned initially about papal authority and other Church teachings from the Baltimore Catechism, produced in 1884 by the Third Plenary Council of Baltimore and memorized by Catholic schoolchildren for the next seventy-five years. In the chapter titled "The Church," the catechism asserted the traditional teaching that the Catholic Church was the only true Church of Christ, and described Apostolic Succession, an indispensable feature of Catholic authenticity.

The catechism also spelled out the traditional requirements for salvation. Membership in the True Church was paramount, although Protestants theoretically could be saved if they were baptized, believed their church to be authentic, and died without "guilt of mortal sin." Lacking the Sacrament of Penance, however, their chances were dim. (Catholics were prohibited from entering a Protestant church, and children of a mixed marriage were required to be raised Catholic.) Non-Christians, according to the catechism, were without hope. Renegade Catholics, as well, had no chance of reaching heaven: "All are bound to belong to the Church, and he who knows the Church to be the true Church and remains out of it cannot be saved."[102]

The necessity of evangelism, then, was pounded into the minds and hearts of catechumens and seminarians. Fulton had heard the message from infancy and continued to hear it at St. Paul's: every soul lost to the Church might well be lost forever. All earthly events existed in the shadow of that moment described in Matthew 25, when Jesus Christ would return and divide the sheep from the goats, the faithful from the unbelieving, sending some to everlasting bliss and others to eternal fire and pain. What could be of more importance than eternity? Every priest, indeed every Christian, had the obligation to save souls. Some, like Fulton, took the duty with high seriousness.

Seminarians also learned of the Church's hostility toward communism and socialism. Pius IX condemned communism in 1864, less than three months after Karl Marx created the First International. Pope Leo XIII issued an encyclical against socialism in 1878. The founding of the Socialist Party in 1901 greatly concerned America's bishops, one of whom wrote that it "denies the existence of

God, the immortality of the soul, eternal punishment, the right of private ownership, the rightful existence of our present social system, and the independence of the Church as a society complete in itself and founded by God."

The fear of socialism prompted many American bishops to be initially hostile toward labor unions, but this attitude tended to change as parish priests increasingly became involved in labor disputes on behalf of their people. Such "labor-priests" often cited *Rerum Novarum,* issued by Leo XIII in 1891, which upheld the right of workers to organize and stressed the need for state intervention to protect the interests of working people. Catholics, Sheen was taught at St. Paul's, had to have a social conscience as well as a concern for souls.[103]

And yet the Church, which was eternal, could not be expected to acknowledge all the needs and desires of a particular period, nation, or civilization. That was the message of the "Americanism" controversy that wracked the late nineteenth century. Several bishops, among them both Spalding of Peoria and Ireland of St. Paul, argued that the Church should adapt its doctrine to the religious ideas of modern culture, that human culture revealed God, and that human society was progressing toward the Kingdom of God. This theory of cultural adaptation, which many American Protestants endorsed, was condemned in 1899 by Leo XIII. Out of this clash, liberal and conservative wings of the Church began to form, the one eager to be "in step" with the popular culture, to get along with Protestants, to seek accommodation with the public schools; and the other stressing exclusivity and the supremacy of revealed and historic Catholic truths. Sheen was no doubt taught that Leo XIII's dictates were paramount—and in any case, that would have been his inclination.

A similar clash a few years later, originating in France, became known as the Modernist controversy. St. Joseph's Seminary in Yonkers, New York, and Catholic University in Washington became American centers of the idea that the Church should reexamine its teachings, including the authority of the Magisterium, in light of

modern thought. Again, the Vatican refused to yield. In 1907 Pope
Pius X issued an encyclical against efforts to transform Catholic
theology, pursuing what has been called "nothing less than a reign
of terror" against liberal scholars and clerics at all levels. Moreover,
the Pope soon required all priests and candidates for the priesthood
to sign an "Anti-Modernist Oath" to insure hyperorthodoxy. (The
oath remained in force until the 1960s.) Historian Eamon Duffy
has observed that "Obedience, not enquiry, became the badge of
Catholic thought."[104]

The Catholic standard throughout the Church when Fulton
entered seminary was neo-Thomism or neo-Scholasticism, a view
of the world and its Maker defined by the writings of the thirteenth-
century genius St. Thomas Aquinas. The neo-Thomistic revival was
a sign of the Church's alienation from the modern mind. It had its
Romantic side, emphasizing continuity and tradition and things
medieval. And yet like the Enlightenment thinkers, it had a profound trust in the power of reason. Theologian William M. Halsey,
leaning on Thomist philosopher Jacques Maritain, has written,
"Thomism was the ideological vehicle used in the construction of
an 'objective rational system' in order to save spiritual, intellectual,
and human values 'in the face of contemporary aspirations and per-
plexities.' "[105] Thomists were to be both conservative and creative,
tradition-minded and yet forward-looking. Their philosophy was
designed to provide the Church with a system that held certainty,
objectivity and optimism in a world increasingly reliant on science
and inclined to materialism, immorality, cynicism and despair.

Pope Leo XIII championed the return to Thomism in 1879 as
part of an effort to limit the boundaries of individual reason. When
the School of Philosophy was established at the Catholic University in 1895, it was dedicated to Aquinas, and its faculty quickly
became leaders of the Thomistic revival. In 1907, the encyclical *Pas-
cendi Dominici Gregis* made Thomism the only orthodox Catholic
mode of thought. In 1914, Pius X warned Catholic theologians and
philosophers not to deviate from Aquinas. Three years later, the
revised Code of Canon Law required that all professors of theol-

ogy and philosophy "shall adhere religiously to the method, doctrine and principles" of Thomas Aquinas.[106] Fulton Sheen was schooled rigorously in Thomistic thought, as were all priests for the next half-century.

St. Paul Seminary no doubt also taught the importance of the "Communion movement." Devotion to Jesus in the Eucharist had been stressed in the nineteenth century, and Benediction and Eucharistic Adoration services were commonplace. In 1905, Pius X urged frequent Communion, a mandate closely tied to frequent use of the Sacrament of Penance. Instead of going to Confession and taking the Eucharist once a year, as many did to keep their membership intact, Catholics were now expected to step up their devotional activity and take the Church and its teachings more seriously. Before long, retreats were held for lay men and women seeking intense periods of prayer and devotion.[107] Fulton Sheen was caught up in this intensification of the religious experience.

The growing spirit of self-confidence among Catholics no doubt also inspired Sheen during his seminary training. The Catholic population in America had tripled between 1860 and 1890, to more than 7 million, and Catholicism became the nation's largest religious denomination, encompassing about 12 percent of the population and more than a quarter of the churchgoers.[108] By 1916 the Catholic population had reached almost 16 million. Four years later there were close to 18 million Catholics, some 21,000 priests, more than 16,000 churches, and 5,000 parish schools.[109] Many if not most Catholics were convinced that they were the future in America and already the superior guide in theology and morals. As early as 1876, Catholic scholar John Gilmary Shea declared,

> *As things are now tending around us, in the decline of morals and religion, the substitution of secret societies for churches, in the war of natural science on faith, it is not rash to assert, that, fifty years hence, the Catholic Church will be on this soil almost the only compact Christian body, battling for the Scriptures and the revealed Word of God, or recognizing Him as the Creator*

*and moral Governor of the Universe, a rallying point for all who
shall claim to be Christians.*[110]

Bishops did not hesitate to appeal to the nation's conscience by
speaking out boldly against contraception, divorce, and morally
suspect movies. A group of educators declared, "The Catholic College will not be content with presenting Catholicism as a creed, a
code, or a cult. Catholicism must be seen as a culture."[111]

Sheen would also have been keenly aware of the Catholic commitment to American patriotism. For generations, Protestants had
condemned Catholics for their allegiance to the Vatican and to an
authoritarian form of religion. But as early as 1825, Bishop John
England of Charleston, South Carolina, assured members of the
House of Representatives that the Church was not a threat to the
civic freedoms of Americans, confining its authority to the area of
religious truth and its own internal discipline. Fifty years later,
Bishop Spalding wrote of the importance of the separation of church
and state and religious freedom. Catholics in Maryland had led the
way in establishing religious liberty, he stated, and Catholics were
deeply committed to this fundamental principle.[112]

In World War I, Catholics had firmly supported the war effort.
"Dioceses sponsored war bond drives, held victory masses, designated days of prayer for soldiers, and led celebrations of progress
at the front," wrote Charles R. Morris. "Army statistics used for chaplain assignments showed that Catholics accounted for more than
their fair share of American soldiers." America's bishops created the
National Catholic War Council in 1917 to coordinate Catholic efforts
during the war. Father Francis Duffy of New York earned the Distinguished Service Order and Medal and the Croix de Guerre for
his war exploits. To many American Protestants the word "Catholic"
began to be associated with the likes of Duffy and to bear unprecedented positive overtones.[113] To Catholics themselves, the war and
their response to it symbolized their "arrival" at the gates of American middle-class respectability. As William M. Halsey observed, "It

heightened their optimism while deepening their attachment to the American way and to things Catholic."[114]

Academic records for St. Paul's during this period are spotty, but we know that in his first year in seminary, Sheen won third prize in apologetics (his high school classmate Charles Hart tied for second place), tied with Hart for third prize in moral theology, and took second prize in Church history (Hart placed third). In "Prizes for General Excellence" in the Department of Theology, Sheen and Hart tied for third place. In the third year, the best students, those having an average of over 85, were permitted to participate in one of five seminars for advanced work. Sheen and Hart were members of the seminar on Holy Scripture. Both men were also listed as presenting sermons in their third year, Sheen's topic being "Thy Kingdom Come."[115]

Sheen later remembered the courses at St. Paul's as "extremely good," especially those classes in which he excelled: Sacred Scripture, history, and moral theology. He had a difficult time performing Gregorian chant because "I was among those who could hardly carry a key on a ring." Sheen often laughed about his lack of musical ability. "They say singing is every man's birthright but it certainly never was mine. I didn't sound good even in the shower."[116] In fact, he could and did sing on key, in what a musical expert later called "middle register baritone," and eventually became rather sophisticated in his musical taste.[117]

While in seminary, Fulton suffered from a severe case of ulcers and was sent to the infirmary. The following year, he went to the Mayo Clinic, where a portion of an intestine was removed.[118] For the rest of his life, Sheen ate little, often living for days at a time on cookies, candy (he especially loved chocolates) or ice cream bars. At banquets and dinners he would stir the food on his plate, a process he called "rolling the carrot," to pretend he had eaten a good quantity of it.[119] In 1919, he may well have regarded the stomach pain he endured as part of the purgation process he had expected in seminary.

At one point in his seminary years, Sheen had an extraordinary mystical experience. It occurred at 5:30 in the afternoon while he was listening to a conference led by the spiritual director. "My mind seemed to be suffused with light," he recalled, and he no longer heard the conference speaker. In retrospect he could not remember how long the vision lasted, only that "there came to me an illumination of soul, a light that suffused my intellect, bringing with it an overwhelming conviction of the certitude of the Faith.... I was momentarily possessed of the absolute and irrefutable character of Faith." The vision forever quelled any doubts he may have had. "My faith centered not just in the Creed, but in the Church, and it became personalized in the Pope as the Head of the Church and the Vicar of Christ."[120]

At St. Paul's, Sheen began the practice of spending a continuous hour every day "in the presence of our Lord in the Blessed Sacrament." The idea came to him one evening in 1918 as he paced back and forth outside the locked campus chapel. He began his Holy Hour observance the next day and maintained it for the rest of his life, usually early in the morning before Mass.

Over the years Sheen would give many reasons for keeping the Holy Hour: Growing closer to the Lord ("We become like that which we gaze upon. Looking into a sunset, the face takes on a golden glow. Looking at the Eucharistic Lord for an hour transforms the heart in a mysterious way as the face of Moses was transformed after his companionship with God on the mountain"), reverence for the Eucharist, self-discipline, reparation, the absorption of spiritual truths ("Theological insights are gained not only from the two covers of a treatise, but from two knees on a prie-dieu before a tabernacle"). "Even when it seemed so unprofitable and lacking in spiritual intimacy," he remarked, "I still had the sensation of being at least like a dog at the master's door, ready in case he called me."[121]

There would be times in his busy life when keeping the Holy Hour proved difficult. A friend would recall Sheen, in the midst of a frantic daily schedule, trying to get rid of him in order to spend the next hour before the Blessed Sacrament.[122] Sheen enjoyed telling the story of how, while waiting for a train to take him to Lourdes, he entered a Paris church and promptly fell asleep before the Blessed Sacrament. "I woke up exactly at the end of one hour. I said to the Good Lord: 'Have I made a Holy Hour?' I thought His angel said: 'Well, that's the way the Apostles made their first Holy Hour in the Garden, but don't do it again.'"[123]

Sheen would become a lifelong advocate of the Holy Hour, persuading many to emulate his practice. After World War II, he produced a booklet containing readings and prayers for a daily hour of meditation. The opening line declared that the purpose of the publication was to "aid souls in securing an inner peace by meditating one continuous hour a day on God and our immortal destiny." Sheen explained,

> *Very few souls ever meditate; they are either frightened by the word, or else never taught its existence. In the human order a person in love is always conscious of the one loved, lives in the presence of the other, resolves to do the will of the other, and regards as his greatest jealousy being outdone in the least advantage of self-giving. Apply this to a soul in love with God, and you have the rudiments of meditation.*[124]

Sheen and his friend Charles Hart completed their work at St. Paul Seminary on the first day of June in 1919. They did not take degrees, but transferred their credits to the Catholic University of America in Washington, D.C., where they would continue their studies toward doctorates in philosophy. (St. Paul's had an affiliation with CUA that went back to 1894 and permitted this arrangement.)[125] That summer the two young men completed additional work at St. Viator and each received the M.A. degree. Their academic abilities recognized, Sheen and Hart were clearly following paths to become Church scholars.

Bishop Dunne ordained Fulton Sheen at St. Mary's Cathedral in Peoria on September 20.[126] On the day of his ordination—the day when, he later said, he reached the pinnacle of happiness—Sheen made two silent promises: to keep the Holy Hour and to offer a Mass every Saturday in honor of the Blessed Mother "to solicit her protection on my priesthood."[127] He spoke of the "deep ecstatic sense of love that comes with ordination and spoils us for all other love.... It's like opening a new world." Then comes the realization that "you are a successor of the apostles. It's a wonderful but frightening moment."[128] The day after his ordination, the new priest sang his first Mass in St. Mary's.[129]

TWO

The Taste of Champagne

In November of 1889, the Catholic University of America formally opened its doors in Washington, D.C. There had long been talk among Catholics about founding such an institution; a council of American bishops had favored it a few years earlier, as had Pope Leo XIII. The foremost proponent was John Lancaster Spalding, the bishop of Peoria, who has been called "the leading Catholic educator in the period between the Civil War and the World War." The idea was to match or surpass the great universities being advanced after the Civil War such as Cornell, Harvard, Columbia, and Michigan. The opening of the Johns Hopkins University in nearby Baltimore, the first attempt to create a primarily graduate university, was also a stimulus.

After the Civil War, there were seven Catholic institutions with university charters, and by 1875 there were seventy-four Catholic colleges. All of them, however—including Georgetown, the oldest American Catholic university—were small and generally considered incapable of achieving greatness in the area of graduate studies. Many Church leaders thought the time right for creating a truly distinguished institution with a special dedication to advanced work for the clergy. They saw the Catholic University of America as an effort to establish a major voice for Catholic truth in a nation that was becoming consciously secular.

There was another motive for building a great university, one that often lurked in the minds of the "brick and mortar" bishops who filled the land with beautiful and sometimes spectacular churches and cathedrals. As one priest put it, the university "means a *status* in this country which, to be frank, Catholics have not yet attained."¹ Still sneered at for being the church of the lowly immigrants, despite all their recent socioeconomic gains, Catholics were telling the Protestant majority that they themselves were just as good, if not better. "Noble and dignified buildings are a sign of a noble and dignified people," wrote a California priest, who wanted for his parish "a church building better than the best."²

The pontifically chartered university soon became the center of graduate Catholic education in the United States, the first of its kind to offer doctoral work on a significant scale.³ But the funding was not sufficient to realize the dream of a campus among the top research institutions of the country. Internal problems and struggles between the Vatican and the university also helped cripple the grandiose dreams of the campus founders. Still, as the ranks of the faculty expanded in the new century and more buildings went up, CUA had much to offer on both the undergraduate and graduate levels, and was especially strong in theology and philosophy.

When Fulton Sheen and Charles Hart enrolled in the fall of 1919, the campus had been enlarged to 144 acres. There were eight buildings, and a new gymnasium was under construction. Seven religious houses of men were in the vicinity. Campus life was racially segregated, in large part due to the tensions culminating in the riots that swept across the country in the summer of 1919.⁴ (Ironically, the first CUA degree in the social sciences, awarded in 1896, had gone to an African American.)⁵ Only men were permitted to matriculate, although CUA had a thriving off-campus teachers' college for nuns, which offered its first two doctorates in 1914.⁶

CUA's most notable professor was John A. Ryan. Born in rural Minnesota on the family farm, Ryan had graduated from the St. Paul Seminary and received his S.T.D. (doctorate in sacred theology) from Catholic University in 1906. He taught at his alma mater in St. Paul for a time, returning to CUA just before Sheen arrived at the seminary. In 1919, he was elected dean of the School of Sacred Theology.

Ryan was actually a sociologist rather than a theologian, known for his commitment to the reforms of the Progressive movement that flourished between the 1890s and the First World War. He helped write a minimum-wage law in Minnesota, spoke widely to reform groups, and in 1916 wrote the second of two major books on the distribution of wealth in America. He was also the author of a highly acclaimed social action policy statement released in 1919 by the National Catholic Welfare Conference, the organization of American bishops. (Ryan would later become the first director of the Social Action Department at the NCWC.) The "Bishops' Program for Social Reconstruction" endorsed a lengthy list of economic reforms including a minimum wage, child labor laws, equal wages for women, strict antitrust enforcement, and federally sponsored health and old-age insurance.[7]

Ryan's career showed the extent to which Catholics were now officially advocating what was called the Social Gospel, a focus, first adopted by Protestant clergy, on improving living conditions as well as saving souls. Despite the Vatican's condemnation of efforts to wed Catholic theology to the needs of the day, the current wave of Progressive social reforms, led on the national level by Presidents Roosevelt, Taft and Wilson, had proved irresistible. Catholic reformers often cited *Rerum Novarum,* the 1891 encyclical of Leo XIII, as the authority justifying their commitment.

Sheen greatly admired John A. Ryan, referring to him later as "a leader in this country in the field of social ethics."[8] He would also pay special tribute to Dr. Edward A. Pace, a pioneering professor of psychology and a longtime professor of philosophy and administrator at CUA. His psychological laboratory, established on campus in 1899, was the second of its kind in the United States. In 1925 he would be elected to the presidency of the American Council of Education.[9] A leader in the Thomistic revival, Pace would become the first president of the American Catholic Philosophical Association in 1926.[10]

The doctorate in philosophy sought by Sheen and Hart required three years of residence and study, years that Fulton enjoyed. While a full-time student at Catholic University, he served as chaplain at St. Vincent's Orphan Asylum, celebrating Mass every morning at six o'clock for the young girls and the sisters. On weekends, he made himself available to the local parishes. With his slight build and youthful face, he was mistaken for an altar boy when he first appeared at St. Paul's Church. During Holy Week in St. Patrick's Church, the young priest sang a highly complex Alleluia as part of the Holy Saturday liturgy. When he was finished, the elderly pastor in attendance shouted in front of the congregation, "Sing it again!" Fulton complied, and then the pastor made the same demand, only louder. When he had struggled through the forty-nine-note Alleluia a third time, Fulton realized sheepishly that the Latin directive contained the word *ter,* which meant three times.[11]

During this period, Sheen made his first convert. In September an aunt asked him to visit an ailing relative, warning that the woman was hostile toward Catholics. When the priest knocked at the door, the woman spat in his face and told him to leave. Fulton begged God during the Mass every morning thereafter to give the woman the grace of conversion. In February the woman telephoned, saying that a physician told her she had only two weeks to live, and that she was deeply concerned about the fate of her two children. Sheen assured her that she was not going to die, and told her of his prayers for her conversion. "The Lord, I believe, is frightening you into the Church." He began instruction the following day and baptized the woman in May. She recovered, and the two stayed in touch for many years. That first conversion, Sheen wrote later, "illustrates how much Divine Light in the soul, rather than the efforts of the evangelist, produce the harvest."[12]

On graduation day, June 16, 1920, Sheen was one of sixteen graduates, including Charles Hart, to receive two CUA degrees. They each received the Bachelor of Canon Law (J.C.B.) and the Bachelor of Sacred Theology (S.T.B.), the latter degree resting largely on the transferred credits they had earned in St. Paul. Both young men now had four higher education degrees.[13]

Hart would stay at CUA for the rest of his life. He joined the faculty as an instructor in 1921, earned his doctorate in philosophy in 1930 under Edward A. Pace, and taught in the philosophy department until his death in 1959. He would have a distinguished career as a philosopher, writing four books, lecturing on the *Catholic Hour* radio series, founding the Catholic Evidence Guild of Washington, and serving as national secretary of the American Catholic Philosophical Association for twenty-eight years. He would direct forty doctoral dissertations and more than a hundred master's theses.[14] Over the years, Hart would remain Fulton's colleague and friend.

SHEEN WAS MORE AMBITIOUS. He studied at Catholic University for another year, and then decided to go elsewhere to complete his doctorate. In his autobiography, Fulton admitted that as a young priest he was praying to become a bishop. There was nothing unusual in this, of course; priests often long to wear purple, to have the authority, the power, the glamour, and the burdens of the episcopacy. But ascent in the Church usually required the candidate to have an assortment of credentials, beginning with a European, preferably Roman, doctorate. Fulton wanted such a diploma for the mobility it would give him.[15]

Moreover, Sheen wanted to further his studies in neo-Thomism. Neo-Thomists, it will be recalled, countered the various forms of empiricism, positivism, pragmatism, and materialism intellectually popular at the time by arguing that rational arguments for the existence of God complemented revealed truth. Sheen would often say that "faith *depends* on reason. People who try to get to religion without using their brains usually end up believing that some crackpot is God, because he says so. The Church won't take you without your thinking things through to the full extent of your ability."[16] Beyond emphasizing reason, neo-Thomist thought also stressed the existence of objective rights and wrongs (natural law), free will (making one responsible for one's actions), and the importance of personal moral virtue. Students of Aquinas were intensely involved in historical studies, as well as theology and philosophy, and were usually distinguished by their theological orthodoxy and the assortment of distinctions, definitions, and categories at their command.[17]

This was not everyone's favorite approach to the Catholic faith. Joseph Cardinal Ratzinger, a major figure in the Church during the 1980s and 1990s, would confess that as a seminarian he had "difficulties in penetrating the thought of Thomas Aquinas, whose crystal-clear logic seemed to me to be too closed in on itself, too impersonal and ready-made."[18] Protestants, especially Lutherans, rejected the whole of it, arguing that human reason, as Luther put it, was "Frau Jezebel" whereby Satan had deluded so many Catholics. Salvation was by faith alone, Scripture was the sole authority of Christian truth, and divine predestination reigned in place of man's free will.

The leading European center for Thomistic studies was the University of Louvain in Belgium. At some point in 1921, Rector Thomas A. Shahan recommended Louvain to Sheen.[19] The combination of the right sort of training and the right sort of degree seemed irresistible, and Fulton decided to make the move. The bishop of Peoria approved but was unable to provide funds. Newt and Delia pledged their continued financial support, and also sent brother Tom, who had graduated from Notre Dame at nineteen, to Europe with Fulton.[20] (In 1922, when both Fulton and Tom found themselves broke, Fulton wrote privately, "We need money. Wrote home.")[21] Tom would be studying medicine at Louvain for the next seven years, as well as surgery in Paris and psychoanalysis in Vienna.[22]

In the summer of 1921, Fulton went to the University of Paris to expand upon his college French. He lived in a boarding house in the Latin Quarter along with several other Americans. About a week after he moved in, the landlady, Madame Citroen, came to Fulton brandishing a bottle of poison and threatening suicide because of her tragic family life and the financial failure of the boarding house. Fulton had two Boston schoolteachers help him piece together what the emotional woman was saying, and in halting French he persuaded her to delay her action for nine days. He then began a novena (nine days of public or private devotions and special prayer for a particular intention) at the Church of Notre Dame des Champs. And every evening he tried, with the aid of his pocket dictionary, to instruct Madame Citroen in the rudiments of Christianity. On the ninth day, Fulton brought the woman into the Church and even persuaded her Catholic maid, impressed by the young priest's efforts, to resume her worship. Eventually, he also reconciled Madame Citroen with her husband.[23]

Many hearing and reading this story over the years have no doubt attributed Sheen's success to his radiant personality and perseverance when faced with someone in spiritual trouble. There is some truth in that, of course, but in Sheen's eyes he was merely opening doors for the grace of God; the supernatural aspect of conversion was paramount. He would often tell those interested in the Church, "Pray for the Light and that you will be strong enough to reach the Light." As for Madame Citroen, he gave all the credit for her conversion to the power of prayer.[24]

That fall, Fulton and Tom headed for Louvain. The university had been founded in 1425, and in the sixteenth century it was one of the capitals of humanism. By the late nineteenth century it enjoyed international fame, and its Institute of Philosophy, founded in 1882 at the instigation of Pope Leo XIII, was famous for its neo-Thomism. World War I left deep scars on the campus. In 1914 German troops had destroyed the library, along with 300,000 books, 1,000 or more manuscripts, and all of the university archives. (In 1928 a new library opened, a gift of the United States government.) The campus was closed for four years, reopening in 1919 with 3,180 students.[25]

On reaching the university, Fulton recalled, he was jolted by a childhood memory. One day when he was an eight-year-old altar boy serving with Bishop Spalding, he accidentally dropped a cruet of wine, which sounded like an explosion when it hit the cathedral's marble floor. After Mass, rather than scold the trembling boy, Spalding put his arms around him and asked where he was going to school when he got big. Fulton managed to sputter out, "Spalding," the high school named after the bishop. The bishop tried again: "I said 'when you get big.' Did you ever hear of Louvain?" Fulton had not.

"Very well, you go home and tell your mother that I said when you get big you are to go to Louvain, and someday you will be just as I am." (Spalding had earned two degrees at Louvain and was ordained there.) Delia later explained to her son what Louvain was. She no doubt pondered at length and with considerable pleasure the bishop's prediction about Fulton's future position in the Church.[26]

All of Fulton's courses at Louvain were required, and the lectures were in French and Latin. He studied metaphysics, experimental psychology, rational psychology, cosmology, modern space and time, and was "drenched" in Aristotle, Plato, and the ancients, and "immersed" in Aquinas. "No assigned reading was ever given, but it was always assumed that any book which a professor suggested to be read could be brought up in the final oral examination."[27] He later remembered spending at least a hundred hours studying the theory of relativity.[28]

The young scholar loved the intellectual challenge and maintained a rigorous daily devotional schedule. He also had personal advancement constantly on his mind. He admitted in his autobiography that every day on his way to class he said a Hail Mary before each of seven paintings of the Blessed Mother on the walls of the Church of St. Michael in the hope of becoming a bishop.[29] But he kept his ambition to himself, undoubtedly realizing that it was a province of pride, the deadliest sin.

Fulton often traveled during his years of study. In London for the first time, after a Benediction service at Notre Dame Church in Leicester Square one cold November evening, he came upon a five-year-old girl named Ann O'Connor, waiting to be taken home. Sensing that she was Irish, he asked the youngster her name. The two chatted a bit about herself and her family, and the girl invited him to her home for tea the next day. Fulton accepted the invitation. When Ann told her parents about the priest she had talked to, dressed in "a fur coat" (actually, a coat with a fur collar), they thought it one of the precocious girl's "frequent imaginations."

The next afternoon, Ann paced nervously on the frigid balcony of the flat, wondering if the priest would appear. Promptly at

3:00 P.M., Fulton arrived, carrying what Ann later described as "the biggest box of sweets I had ever seen." Fulton quickly became attached to the O'Connor family. Ann later recalled her father saying after the initial visit that the young man "will be Pope one day."

Thereafter, for the rest of his life, whenever Fulton Sheen arrived in London the O'Connor flat was his "first port of call." Ann O'Connor would visit the United States a half-dozen times to meet Sheen and an assortment of staff members, converts, relatives, and others close to him. She later mentioned in particular his generosity in the early 1920s—tossing a half-crown to a street singer, giving candy to the children who flocked about him, bringing baskets of food he had been given by well-wishers when departing from the United States by ship. At eighty-four, Ann recalled many stories of Fulton's kindness and encouragement over the years, both to herself and to her older brother, Hugh. She described Sheen as "magnetic, wonderful, amusing, extremely humble." She has in her possession some two hundred Sheen letters, cherished relics of a delightful friendship.[30]

In February of 1922, Sheen went to Paris to preach. At the hotel he met an Englishman and invited him to dinner. That evening the man told Fulton sorrowfully that he had yet to encounter a good person, and that he was having woman trouble. Fulton took him to the Basilica of the Sacred Heart, and the two prayed all night with a thousand others (including philosopher Jacques Maritain) before the Blessed Sacrament. But this time the attempt at conversion failed. Sheen later observed that not everyone can accept the free gift of grace, and not everyone instructed in it remains faithful. He wrote of the man in Paris, "I have always had hopes that the good inspiration that he received during the night he spent with the men of prayer will eventually save his soul."[31]

From January 5 to August 4, 1922, Sheen kept a diary describing his daily schedule (up at 5:00 A.M.), his studies (which included being tutored in French and German), his travels, the local weather (which he largely detested), the state of his health, his meals (of which he often complained), and the many worship services he attended. During Christmas vacation, for example, he went to Brussels, where he met his brother and the two of them enjoyed *La Boheme* (which may have been the first opera Fulton ever attended). He also spent time visiting the poor in Louvain, whom he assisted financially from time to time. In early February he was in Paris, where he preached, said a private Mass at Notre Dame Cathedral, visited friends (including Madame Citroen), and took in *Madama Butterfly* and *Faust.* From April 22 to May 1 he toured Germany with Tom, seeing an assortment of historical landmarks, visiting great churches (of the Lutheran Cathedral in Berlin he wrote, "'He is not here'—empty tomb—very appropriate"), and attending numerous operas including Bizet's *Fair Maid of Perth* and Verdi's *Masked Ball.* In late May, Fulton was in Paris briefly, sightseeing, preaching, and taking in Wagner's *Lohengrin.*[32] At the conclusion of his diary, he listed the twenty-one operas he had seen in the previous eight months. Life was not quite so exciting in Peoria.[33]

In addition to high culture and religious passion, Sheen's experience of Europe included moments of American humor. Once, Thomas K. Gorman (later the bishop of Dallas–Fort Worth) had a bellboy move a piano several floors in one of Europe's finest hotels because he overheard a fellow priest say he wanted to play. When it came time to tip the exhausted bellboy, Gorman had what amounted to one cent in his pocket. Sheen and the others present, no doubt roaring with laughter at their embarrassed classmate, had to bail him out.[34]

During June and early July, Sheen's diary entries often said simply "Study"—the final oral examination was scheduled for July 11. Even before this hurdle, Fulton was offered a professorship in philosophy at Sacred Heart Seminary in Detroit, a prospect he liked, but Bishop Dunne did not, saying he needed Sheen in Peoria.[35]

In the day-long examination for the doctorate at Louvain, about twenty candidates at a time were admitted into a large hall, where twenty professors were seated at twenty desks. A student could choose any desk, and the questioning continued until the student could no longer answer. Then the young man moved to another desk with another interrogator until he had worked his way through all twenty. Each professor assigned a grade, and then all the professors would come together to give a general score. Sheen later remembered that one of his favorite professors (and later thesis adviser), Dr. Leon Noel, asked him, "Tell me how an angel makes a syllogism." The question was designed to test how thoroughly the candidate had read Aquinas.[36]

In his diary, Sheen wrote simply: "Took exams today. Passed with distinction."[37] Now he had qualified to write a doctoral dissertation. He selected as his topic, "The Spirit of Contemporary Philosophy and the Finite God."

∽

AFTER A BRIEF STINT in London and Oxford, and on the recommendation of the rector of the School of Philosophy, Sheen accompanied the distinguished French novelist Emile Baumann in the summer of 1922 on a trip tracing the journeys of St. Paul, about which the novelist was planning a book. Sheen was particularly impressed by Damascus, where Paul was converted. In Athens, he repeatedly climbed Mars Hill and read the famous speech of St. Paul in Acts 17:

> *Men of Athens, I perceive that in every way you are very religious. For as I passed along, and observed the objects of your worship, I found also an altar with this inscription "To an unknown god." What therefore you worship as unknown, this I proclaim to you. The God who made the world and everything in it, being Lord of heaven and earth, does not live in shrines made by man, nor is he served by human hands, as though he needed anything, since he himself gives to all men life and breath and everything.*

The failure of that speech to win significant numbers of converts, Fulton concluded, resulted from Paul's neglect to mention the name of Christ and point to His Crucifixion. In Ephesus, now a wilderness, Sheen reflected on the architectural glories that once graced the city and on the mobs that railed against the great Christian saint.[38]

In Rome, Sheen had his first private audience with a Pope—evidence of having high connections in the Church. Pius XI had succeeded Benedict XV on February 6, an event marked in Fulton's diary. During the audience, the Pope, who had once been a librarian, asked Sheen about his university studies, wondering at one point if Fulton had read Taparelli (Jesuit Aloysius Taparelli, 1793–1862). The twenty-seven-year-old priest admitted that he had not, and "dissolved into an emotional crumble" as he answered. Surprised and disappointed, Pius XI made him promise that he would immediately buy Taparelli's two Latin volumes and read every line. Fulton carried out the assignment, no doubt acknowledging that he still faced much hard work in his pursuit of academic excellence.[39]

During the following academic year, Fulton labored on what would become a 186-page dissertation. On July 13, 1923, he received his Ph.D. from Louvain with greatest distinction. His work had been so outstanding that he was invited to continue on to achieve a rare postdoctoral degree, the *agrege,* which meant that the degree bearer would become aggregated to (i.e. eligible to join) the faculty at Louvain. To attain the honor, one had to receive an invitation, pass a public examination before professors of other universities, and write a distinguished book. If Sheen could win the degree, he would be the first American to do so. He readily accepted the invitation.[40]

An *agrege* student was not obligated to remain in Louvain while preparing for the examinations, and Fulton elected to go elsewhere. Soon he was in Rome. The libraries were excellent, the churches were splendid, and the climate was not at all like the gray, damp and cold weather he detested in Belgium. Fulton was also mindful of the value to his career of studies in Rome. A Louvain doctorate, let alone the *agrege,* might be sufficient to make one eligible to become a bishop, but it would be good insurance to add some Roman credentials.

Fulton decided to spend the academic year 1923–24 in Rome, studying in two of the Church's great universities; two would look more impressive than one on his curriculum vitae. He attended theology classes at the Angelicum for a period of time a school official later described as "briefly."[41] While there, he said, he read through every line Thomas Aquinas had ever written.[42] He then moved over to the Jesuit Gregorian University, where, admitted as an "extraordinary student," he did not take a single examination.[43] Sheen was not working toward a degree in either institution and, according to official records, none was awarded.

While in Rome, Fulton took voice lessons, the only formal instruction in public speaking he would ever have. He was given deep breathing exercises and told to talk with his diaphragm full of air. He said later, "That was the best training I have ever received, and I'm glad I never had any other. Because that, after all, is the key—the key to resonance."[44] Rome was a sort of finishing school for Fulton, deliberately preparing himself for leadership in the Church.

But the spiritual side of Fulton Sheen was dominant, easily capable of pushing aside the pride and vanity that lay deep within the young priest. That summer, Sheen made his first trip to the Shrine of Our Lady of Lourdes. He had barely enough money to get there, and he depended upon the Blessed Mother to find a way to pay the rest of the bills. He checked into a hotel and began a novena. When nothing happened and he was faced with washing dishes to pay his bill, Fulton went to the grotto at about 10:00 P.M. There he met an American who asked him if he would come to Paris with his wife and daughter and instruct them in French. He also paid the hotel bill. For more than twenty years thereafter, whenever Sheen was in New York he would visit the couple, enjoy their friendship, and be reminded of the love he believed the Virgin Mary had for him and for all who sought her aid.[45]

From September 1924 to July 1925, Sheen was in England teaching dogmatic theology at St. Edmund's College, Ware, the seminary of the Archdiocese of Westminster.[46] At about this time he also began six or seven years of summer service as a curate at St. Patrick's Church in Soho, where he became famous in the region as a preacher.[47] He later referred to the "hell hole area" in which the parish lay, and told how he brought a very troubled actress, appearing in a nearby play, back to the Church by literally pushing her into the confessional after having promised not to "ask" her to go to Confession. Two years after that experience, the leading lady entered a convent, where she remained the rest of her life.[48]

At St. Edmund's, Fulton became friends with Father Ronald Knox, a notable scholar, wit and Catholic convert whose father was the Anglican archbishop of Birmingham.[49] He also met and very favorably impressed the great English literary critic and author G. K. Chesterton. Gilbert Keith Chesterton had published the Christian masterpiece *Orthodoxy* in 1908, converted from Anglicanism to Catholicism in 1922, and then wrote the classic apologetic *The Everlasting Man.* C. S. Lewis was among those deeply influenced by his religious writings. Now fifty-one, Chesterton must have given the young American priest considerable scrutiny at their initial meeting, pondering the weight of his knowledge and the power of his intellect. While impressed, he could not know that in time Sheen would become an equally celebrated Catholic apologist, widely known in fact as "the American Chesterton."

Sheen also became initiated into the art of teaching while at St. Edmund's. The young scholar knew little about dogmatic theology, but he plunged into relevant sources—"I spent hours reading Bonaventure, Aquinas, Suarez, Billot and other theologians"—and managed to produce some lectures. At one point he heard a student say to another, "Oh, Dr. Sheen is a most extraordinary lecturer, most extraordinary." Sheen asked him what he had said in the lecture. The British deacon replied, "I don't quite know." Sheen answered, "Neither do I." He learned that day, as he later wrote, "that sometimes when you are confusing, you are mistaken for being learned."[50]

While teaching, Sheen studied for his examinations and worked on his dissertation, entitled *God and Intelligence in Modern Philosophy: A Critical Study in the Light of the Philosophy of Saint Thomas Aquinas.* During a visit to the famed philosopher Samuel A.

Alexander at the University of Manchester, he discovered that Alexander had scheduled a public debate with him on the nature of God. Sheen had read Alexander's books, was prepared, and handled himself admirably.[51]

In the spring of 1925, the time arrived for the *agrege* examination, conducted by professors from France, England, and other European countries, with three hundred people on hand to observe. A poor family Sheen had befriended and aided financially during his years at Louvain walked more than twenty miles to the Shrine of Our Lady of Montaigu and back again to pray for his success in the examination.[52] The questions began at 9:00 A.M. and concluded in the late afternoon. A board of visiting professors then met to determine the final grade: Satisfaction, Distinction, Great Distinction, or Very Highest Distinction. A dinner was scheduled that evening for the successful candidate. "If you passed with Satisfaction," Fulton later wrote, "only water could be served; if with Distinction, beer; if with Great Distinction, wine, and if with the Very Highest Distinction, champagne." Then he added, "The champagne tasted so good that night!"[53]

Sheen received the degree of *Agrege en Philosophie* on July 16, 1925. He soon transformed his dissertation into a book, and *God and Intelligence* was published by the distinguished Longmans-Green and Company, both in England and in the United States. G. K. Chesterton, greatly impressed by the young scholar and his work, wrote the introduction. The following year, Louvain awarded Sheen the Cardinal Mercier International Philosophy Award for the book; he was the first American to win the prize, awarded only once a decade.[54]

God and Intelligence was a major contribution to neo-Thomism. The two great problems confronting modern philosophy, Sheen argued, were the immanence, or essential nature of God in the universe, and the subjectivity of human thought, which Sheen branded as the "anti-intellectualist assault" upon reason, logic, proof, and truth. "All religion hangs on the first, and all science on the second." The answer to both problems, Sheen contended, was the philosophy of Thomas Aquinas. "Thomistic Intellectualism is the remedy against anarchy of ideas, riot of philosophical systems and breakdown of spiritual forces."[55]

Sadly, Sheen wrote, Thomism had been neglected by modern thinkers. "That vast literature of proofs for God's existence drawn from the order of nature, which a century ago seemed to be so overwhelmingly convincing, to-day does little more than to gather dust in libraries, for the simple reason that our generation has ceased to believe in a kind of a God that must be argued for."[56] In place of reason had come "religious experience," instinct, intuition, and "felt contact." Over the past half-century "men have been learning to find God within rather than without."[57] Modern systems, Sheen wrote, contained a threefold interpretation of religious experience:

1. *According to the needs of the individual.*
2. *According to the spirit of the age.*
3. *According to the evolution of the world.*[58]

Along with many other orthodox Catholic thinkers, Sheen would wage war against these pillars of liberal religion and philosophy for the rest of his life.

Sheen's mastery of Aquinas, amply displayed in *God and Intelligence,* is most impressive. Scores of other thinkers falling under his careful examination include Henri Bergson, William James, Immanuel Kant, August Comte, Alfred North Whitehead, Samuel Alexander, and H. G. Wells. Many, often massive, footnotes in four languages (English, Latin, French, and German) buttress the text in revealing the author's wide-ranging study and extraordinary intellectual prowess. His grasp of history is often evident, as in this passage:

> *The Greeks had their James and Dr. Schiller in Protagoras; they had their Bradley in Parmenides; they had their M. Bergson and M. Le Roy and Professor Alexander and the whole School of Becoming in Heraclitus. They had all their Dynamists and their Atomists. In a word, they saw all philosophy from its highest*

reaches in Aristotle to its shallows in the Sceptics. All modern aberrations were foreshadowed in the Greeks.[59]

In *Commonweal,* the recently established American journal of Catholic thought, a reviewer wrote that *God and Intelligence* "may safely be called one of the most important contributions to philosophy which has appeared in the present century."[60] The Jesuit magazine *America* called it "not merely critical and scholarly, but brilliant."[61] The book is at times repetitive, abstract and difficult, and it contains some breathtaking generalities. (There are several pages on angels, surely enough to satisfy his thesis adviser, Dr. Noel.) Being a dissertation, *God and Intelligence* was written for an extremely limited audience consisting largely of philosophers and theologians. Still, it was a timely and welcome contribution at a time when Catholic philosophers and theologians were keenly interested in Thomism.

For example, in 1925 *The Modern Schoolman* appeared, the first journal exclusively dedicated to the neo-Scholastic philosophy in America. Its editors declared that they wanted Thomism to reach the "American mass mind" and be reconciled with modern science and popular thought. A year later, the American Catholic Philosophical Association was formed "to promote study and research in the field of philosophy, with special emphasis on Scholastic philosophy."[62] Another Thomistic journal, *The New Scholasticism,* was launched in 1927. Articles in less technical magazines such as *America* stressed the compatibility of American political principles with the teachings of Aquinas. Historian Philip Gleason has noted that in the 1920s the Scholastic Revival attained the status of a popular ideology among American Catholic intellectuals.[63]

This optimistic development stood in sharp contrast to the philosophical conceptions most popular at the time among non-Catholics: Bertrand Russell's angst about man's desperate struggle in a meaningless universe and Alfred North Whitehead's similar but somewhat less pessimistic view of man's encounter with an unintelligible world. William Halsey has observed that in the postwar years, outside the Church, "the quest for truth which supplied the emotional and intellectual underpinning of the philosophical and scientific apparatus of modern American thought was predicated on the assumption of the uncertainty of ever finally attaining it."[64] In 1935, Marquette University professor John O. Riedl would declare, "Outside scholasticism there seems to be nothing but intellectual chaos and despair."[65]

∽

IN THE SUMMER of 1925, Sheen was a thirty-year-old published scholar with extraordinarily distinguished academic credentials, an invitation to participate in a summer conference at Westminster in London, and two invitations to teach: one from Oxford and the other from Columbia University.[66] Moreover, he was popular and highly respected for his preaching and pastoral concern. In short, Fulton Sheen was a young man on the fast track in the Church, obviously destined for a position of considerable authority. The bishop of Peoria's reaction to the fame and promise enjoyed by his young priest was to send him a letter telling him in no uncertain terms to "come home."

Bishop Dunne assigned Sheen to St. Patrick's Church, a parish in the "lower end" of Peoria, an area lacking sidewalks and populated by the poor. Many years later, Fulton described the parish as the worst in the diocese: "It was the off-scouring of the earth. Only 20 percent of the parish could speak English."[67] He was to be a lowly curate there. Fulton also had duties at St. Mark's Church on the west side, where he said his first Christmas Mass.[68] It was a test: Dunne had been kept fully apprised of Sheen's successes and had actually summoned him home to test his willingness to be obedient; but two years earlier he had quietly promised Catholic University officials that they could add Sheen to their faculty.

Could the news of the promise to Catholic University have leaked to Sheen? It is hard to believe that, with his academic credentials, connections and burning ambition, he could have accepted his bishop's decision with grace if he thought there was no hope of escaping the slum parish. On the other hand, Fulton was an extraordinary person, deeply committed to the supernatural, always struggling with himself to become humble and obedient to the will of God and his Church superiors. Moreover, during the previous summer, Fulton had returned to Lourdes, receiving what he later described as another miraculous assurance that he was favored by the Blessed Mother. He had asked in his prayer for a sign: "that after I offered the Holy Sacrifice of the Mass and before I would reach the outer gate of the shrine, a little girl aged about twelve, dressed in white, would give me a white rose." According to Sheen, that is exactly what happened, an experience that left him trembling.[69] What, then, was there to fear in being sent to Peoria?

Yet Sheen always said that he was wholly unaware of Bishop Dunne's intentions, and there is no evidence to the contrary. In his autobiography he wrote, "I had to forget my desire to follow a more intellectual vocation, and was resigned to being a curate. This gave me a great peace of mind."[70] In any case, Fulton passed this latest test with flying colors.

The young curate quickly became friends with the elderly pastor, Monsignor Patrick O'Connor Culleton, and threw himself into his duties with a passion and without a word of complaint. (He urged his parents to say nothing negative about Bishop Dunne.)[71] His Lenten and Advent sermons packed the church. He visited every house in the parish, administered the sacraments, and continued his successful efforts at winning converts and bringing people back to the Church.

Knocking on doors proved difficult at times. In one tumbledown house, a mechanic threw a wrench at the young priest the minute he saw him. Sheen spent fifteen or twenty minutes talking to the assailant about Hudson automobiles until he calmed down. Eventually, the man and his family became devout members of the parish.[72]

Another afternoon Sheen found himself talking to an elderly man who said he had been a robber and murderer, and had spent thirty years in jail. Fulton asked if he would like to confess his sins.

The man scoffed, saying he had not been to Confession in seventy years. The young priest then said he would return the following morning with the Blessed Sacrament. Fulton heard the man's confession and gave him Communion; and the next day, the man died. Sheen remarked, "He was not the first thief the Lord saved on his last day."[73]

Another conversion occurring during this period was made famous by the journalist Fulton Oursler in a piece called "A Bargain in Brimstone," published in 1950 in his best-selling *Why I Know There Is a God.* It is the story of Sheen's encounter outside a confessional with a prostitute who admitted having made a pact with the devil in order to be released from a reformatory. After the angry young woman rejected the priest's arguments and pleas and fled the church, Sheen enlisted the prayers of parishioners and stayed up alone into the early hours of the morning praying for her. As he predicted to her, the woman, weeping and repentant, came back and was reconciled to the Church. "If I had not waited for her," Sheen told Oursler, "she would have found the doors locked and would have turned away, perhaps never to come back. Agatha is a wonderful girl today."[74]

Monsignor Culleton remarked, "The thing I remember best about Bishop Sheen is his terrific energy. He ate like a bird. The rest of us would be having our dinner and he'd be satisfied with a glass of milk and a few graham crackers. Sometimes he took a small piece of chocolate for extra energy." Culleton also remembered Sheen's humor. "Bishop Sheen was always quick with the quip, and we had our own little private jokes." When asked to evaluate Sheen's overall performance at St. Patrick's, Culleton said, "He was a wonderful curate."[75]

Whenever Fulton returned to Peoria in later years, he would head for St. Patrick's, borrow Culleton's car, visit relatives, and then return to the rectory for the night. In 1951, when Bishop Sheen came to town wearing a miter, everyone assumed he would be saying his first Pontifical Mass in the cathedral. Instead, he came to St. Patrick's. "It was like the old days," Monsignor Culleton exclaimed, and Fulton was kept busy for almost an hour after the service shaking hands.[76]

After eight months at St. Patrick's, Sheen learned from Bishop
Dunne that he was to be sent to teach at Catholic University. He
was also told why he had been recalled to Peoria: "everyone said
you'd gotten so high-hat in Europe that you wouldn't take orders
any more. But you've been a good boy, so run along."[77] In April,
Sheen was appointed to the Chair of Apologetics in the School of
the Sacred Sciences.

During that summer of 1926, Fulton went to Europe to prepare
his courses, and made a third trip to Lourdes. (In his lifetime he
would make some thirty journeys to the shrine.) He asked the
Blessed Mother again for a sign, this time "some kind of trial and
suffering or a splinter from the Cross to help a soul." When nothing had happened, and he was in a hurry to leave for Paris, he
encountered in his hotel a Dutch woman of about twenty-one, rac-
ing after him. When she calmed down, she declared herself an atheist and seemed to be spiritually troubled. Sheen stayed three days
longer at the hotel until the young woman made her confession
and was restored to the Church.[78]

Whatever his future, at Catholic University or anywhere else,
Fulton was totally confident that there was a Woman, the most
highly favored and the most holy who ever lived, the Woman to
whom he had dedicated his life at age twelve, who cared and played
a direct and active role in life. Later, when designing his coat of arms
as a bishop, Fulton Sheen would choose as his motto *da per matrem
me venire*—Grant that I may come to Thee through Mary.

THREE

A Catholic Philosopher for the New Age

*W*hen Fulton Sheen joined the faculty at Catholic University, Bishop Thomas J. Shahan was coming to the end of a long and successful tenure as rector of the university. After assuming his duties in 1909, he had expanded the number of buildings, beefed up the quality of the faculty, and increased the endowment threefold, to just over $3 million.[1] Still, the financial situation of the campus was weak; in 1931 the actual unencumbered productive endowment consisted of only $20,000, while the average endowment for members of the Association of American Universities at the time was $38 million.[2]

Yet CUA was in all respects other than financial very much a going concern when Sheen arrived in 1926. The university had 848 male matriculates, of whom 278 were graduate students, 468 were undergraduates, and 111 were special students. Almost half of the on-campus students were registered in the School of Philosophy. There were another 2,400 CUA students in affiliated programs. In June 1926, 373 degrees would be granted, including 33 doctorates. There were 111 professors and instructors on the faculty. The new John K. Mullen of Denver Memorial Library, nearing completion, had well over a quarter-million volumes.[3]

In the mid-1920s, it remained unclear whether CUA was to be predominantly a research or teaching institution. There were also fears among the clergy that CUA would fall into the hands of the laity, whose numbers among the faculty grew steadily. A church historian grumbled, "Priests form but 30% of the staff, yet do 90% of the work."[4]

Sheen was one of seven new faculty members.[5] His "super doc-torate" at Louvain entitled him to a full professorship in the School of Philosophy at the Belgian university, and thus he assumed that at Catholic University he would start at the top, the equal of the finest and most experienced scholars on campus. Promises appear to have been made to that effect when he was hired. (Rector Sha-han hired Sheen directly, ignoring a new campus constitution that called for faculty consultation on all academic levels.)[6] Instead, Sheen found himself at the bottom of the status and pay scale as an instructor, a routine starting point for new faculty.[7]

Catholic University had long paid notoriously low salaries, requiring many faculty to seek off-campus employment.[8] While the university will not release Sheen's salary figures, he probably made about $1,500. (A colleague, also an instructor, was earning $1,800 in 1931. A professor of homiletics received $1,650 that year, up from $1,500 seven years earlier. James H. Ryan, the new rector in 1928, would be paid only $6,000 a year.)[9] Full professors normally taught five hours per week, and others in lower ranks might have up to ten.[10] In 1929, Fulton taught six hours, but was facing a jump to fourteen. He complained to Edward A. Pace, his former professor and now a vice-rector at the university, saying he was physically incapable of teaching more than six hours, and noting his rigorous schedule of writing.[11]

In 1928, Sheen brought out *Religion Without God,* a sequel to his dissertation, and likewise published by Longmans-Green. Very sim-ilar to *God and Intelligence,* it is a scholarly study of contemporary philosophy, decrying attacks on the traditional Christian understanding of God and employing the works of Thomas Aquinas to argue the truths of the Catholic faith. It displays, again, Sheen's breadth of read-ing, his powers of analysis, and a facility for finding just the right pas-sages to illustrate what he saw as the foolishness of philosophers like Bertrand Russell. Better written than his first book and less deliber-ately pedantic, it is, however, far too long and repetitive, and Sheen later expressed dissatisfaction with it. Still, a brief review in the *Jour-nal of Religion* found in it "evidence of wide and careful reading."[12]

The young instructor quickly became an active and popular figure on campus. In March 1927, he gave the sermon at the Feast of St. Thomas Aquinas as part of a Solemn Pontifical Mass in the National Shrine of the Immaculate Conception. A student reported in the campus newspaper, "Doctor Sheen's panegyric combined a beautiful literary style with remarkable precision and clarity of thought and his remarks made a great impression on all of his hearers."[13] He gave lectures on campus to an assortment of campus groups and soon became the adviser to the Abbey Club, a student group devoted to "the full development of the college man's character."[14] Ten years later, the secretary of the Abbey Club wrote that Sheen's "goodness, fineness, and manliness impressed every member."[15]

Sheen was drawn to professional activities, becoming involved, for instance, in the newly formed American Catholic Philosophical Association. He traveled to the University of Notre Dame in 1927 for a meeting with the organization's founders, philosopher James H. Ryan and Vice-Rector Pace.[16] In 1929 he succeeded Ryan as secretary of the association, and in 1941 became its president. Fulton had little interest, however, in what would today be called faculty governance, then as now often the refuge of the least productive professors. Always bored by meetings, committee work and administrative detail, Sheen would never become a CUA faculty insider.[17]

～

SHEEN QUICKLY BEGAN building a reputation off campus as a public speaker. In 1926 and for the next five years, he served as the Lenten homilist at the Paulist Church in New York City. In January 1927, after a series of talks in Pittsburgh, the diocesan newspaper acknowledged him as standing "in the front rank of Catholic preachers."[18] The following year, he went on the radio for the first time, displaying his wealth of knowledge, his extraordinary talent for oratory, and his splendid voice. The young CUA professor was soon receiving additional requests to be on the radio.[19]

Invitations for personal appearances began to pour into Sheen's office. He reported to a cousin in early 1928, "The pressure of writing a Lenten course, preparing two books at the same time, doing research for lectures, and preaching retreats every weekend has kept me from doing justice to my correspondence."[20] In the autumn of the following year he told his cousin, "Last week I traveled 3,000 miles, which I ask you to take as symbolic of the pressure that I have been under for some time."[21]

Of course, Fulton could have simply rejected the invitations and concentrated on his university work, but he obviously loved the excitement and the challenge of his public appearances, and no doubt also the considerable fame they brought. He was becoming a nationally known figure in the Church, a prelude for higher things than the classroom at CUA. Then too, Sheen saw these activities in a missionary context. Wherever he went, there were souls to convert and feed. And he relished the opportunity to do so.

Fulton saw no conflict between his personal ambition and his passion for souls, although he was far more likely to talk and write about the latter than the former. He was serving the Church exactly as he had been trained, in total conformity with its teachings and to the best of his considerable ability. He enjoyed his priesthood immensely, and it was clear that vast numbers of people appreciated his talents.

In early 1928, Sheen offered a retreat at the newly founded Rosemont College outside Philadelphia, filling in for a Jesuit writer who cancelled at the last minute. When Fulton arrived, the nuns thought he was an altar boy. He made a great impression at the retreat, however, again no doubt because of his charm, orthodoxy, and powers of persuasion. He became good friends with Mother Mary Cleophas of the Sisters of the Holy Child Jesus, who founded the women's institution. Fulton soon funded an annual scholarship, and later sent two favorite nieces and a friend through the college. Between 1928 and 1973 he would visit the campus almost annually, offering retreats and delivering speeches and commencement addresses.[22]

In the summer of 1928, Sheen was again in England, attending the Pax Romana, the international union of Catholic university students' societies. There were over a hundred delegates from twenty countries in meetings that began in Cambridge, moved to Oxford, and wound up in London. Hillaire Belloc, the celebrated historian and novelist, was one of the speakers at Cambridge, and so was Sheen. After Fulton's address, the local Catholic newspaper referred to the young professor-priest as the one "who has often been alluded to as the new Catholic philosopher of the age."[23] Fulton would use that phrase in biographical statements and press releases for several years.

In 1928, Sheen hired a newspaper clipping service to document his activities. He was proud of the impression the farm boy from Peoria was making in Catholic circles and desired to keep a permanent record of his accomplishments. His simultaneous efforts to crush his own pride may have had only limited success, as he continued to employ the clipping service for the rest of his life. (The thousands of clippings remain the best source of information on Sheen's travels.)

The following year, Sheen delivered the Advent sermons on Sunday mornings at St. Patrick's Cathedral in New York, gaining attention in the New York press.[24] Later in 1929, he earned major headlines by blasting Prohibition as "pharisaism" in an address before the National Council of Catholic Women. The dry crusade, he said, was "an externalism which identifies religion with puritanical prohibitions, with the result that when exaggerations are brought into disrepute, real religion is dragged down with it."[25]

The eighth anniversary of the coronation of Pius XI was celebrated in early 1930 by a Mass at the National Shrine of the Immaculate Conception. The celebrant was Rector Ryan, and Sheen delivered the sermon. He spoke before a huge crowd that included the Most Reverend Pietro Fumansoni-Biondi, the Vatican apostolic delegate, and Archbishop Michael J. Curley of Baltimore.[26] Sheen also preached at the annual celebration of the Feast of the Holy Name, at the Cathedral of the Holy Name in Chicago, proving so effective that Bishop Bernard J. Sheil set a precedent by asking him to return the following year.[27]

For all the fanfare, Sheen was keenly aware of his personal failings, such as vanity and ambition, and of his need to seek the prayers of others to be a holy and useful priest. (He told the prostitute he met at the church in Peoria that she was not, as she claimed, "the worst girl in this town," as that award went to "the girl who thinks she is the *best* girl in town.")[28] One source of spiritual strength was a group of Carmelite nuns in New Albany, Indiana. Sheen was deeply attracted to this order, which had an extremely severe rule, and in a series of letters he saved all his life he begged the mother prioress for her prayers. "Your prayers and sufferings do more good than all our preaching and our hectic actions. We make the noise; we get the credit; we enjoy the consolation of a victory seen and tasted. You are responsible for it and yet you cannot see the fruits—but you will, on that day when the Cross appears in the heavens and everyman is rewarded according to His works." Sheen raised funds for the Carmelites, and visited them in late 1926. He wrote to the mother prioress, "I want to cling on to Carmel for I love its love of Jesus. I refuse to give it up and like the blind man of Jericho I shall go on shouting out to you continually to cure my blindness and my ills." The prayer he sought above all: "Make Father Sheen a priest burning with love for Thee alone."[29]

∾

SHEEN CONSTANTLY SOUGHT fulfillment in the wider world not only because of the excitement and challenge but also because he found life at Catholic University less than pleasant. The fifteen-man theological faculty consisted of many quarrelsome and unproductive professors who were moonlighting off campus to compensate for their low salaries and routinely defying the administration. The reputation of the theology program at CUA had slipped badly.[30]

In January 1927, Sheen became involved in a bitter struggle over a proposal to offer undergraduate seminary classes for some two hundred members of the thirty-two religious houses attached to Catholic University. The idea came from Rector Shahan, and the main purpose was to boost enrollments. Many campus theologians grumbled about the proposal, and the chancellor, Archbishop Michael J. Curley, privately called it "a very advanced form of lunacy," inasmuch as the Sulpicians had a well-established seminary across the street.[31]

When face to face with the elderly rector, however, the theologians voted in favor of the seminary courses. Sheen alone voted no, upsetting his less principled colleagues. Shahan threatened to fire the instructor for his independence; colleagues told Sheen he was an outcast.[32] Hoping to escape the wrath of his peers, Fulton requested a transfer to the School of Philosophy. This was approved in April by the full professors of theology, but the actual transfer was delayed.[33]

In his second year of teaching, Fulton no doubt saw a bleak future for himself at CUA. His colleagues were often hostile, probably due in part to the young instructor's prominence, and the administration had shown no desire to promote him. He might remain an instructor for years, slowly creeping his way up the academic ladder. (His old friend Charles Hart was promoted to full professor twenty-two years after receiving his doctorate, thirty-one years after he joined the faculty.)[34] Sheen believed he deserved better and had been promised more. He was in demand, becoming nationally, even internationally, famous.

So he did something, perhaps with great reluctance, that was highly uncharacteristic, and shocking to anyone who knew him—something that would become his darkest secret. Fulton invented a second doctorate for himself.

Initially, the new degree listed was an S.T.D., a doctorate of sacred theology. The rector and the vice-rector each had an S.T.D., which is an earned degree, as required by the campus constitution.[35] (Vice-Rector Edward A. Pace also had a Ph.D.) Old Testament scholar Franz J. Coln, dean of the School of Theology, had a Ph.D. but no S.T.D. Many of the theologians held doctorates of sacred theology. The S.T.D. first appeared under Sheen's name in the *General Information* catalogue for 1927–28, on a list of the School of the Sacred Sciences faculty. But on the faculty listings that required dates and places of degrees, no second doctorate appeared that year.[36] In the *Courses of Study* catalogue for 1928–29, Sheen for the first time declared publicly, "S.T.D., Rome, 1924."[37]

The second doctorate appeared on the title page of Sheen's second book, *Religion Without God,* published in 1928. It also appeared in a document from Sheen's personnel file, apparently typed by Sheen himself (in his hunt-and-peck style) in the late 1920s. The document lists the source of the S.T.D. as "Rome," in the year 1924.[38]

Sheen had indeed studied at the Angelicum and at the Gregorian in Rome in the fall and spring of 1924; but he had not received a degree of any kind from either institution. No doubt this is why he first cited the source of the S.T.D. as simply "Rome." Giving the name of the city alone would serve to ward off those who might ask the name of the institution granting the degree. Because of his public persona of spiritual prowess and high personal character, few if any would even think of challenging Fulton Sheen's integrity by asking such a question—though he could never be certain.

As it happened, the issue was never raised. The S.T.D. was listed on the title page of a 1929 book, *The Life of All Living,* and appeared in a campus newspaper article of the same year and in an article published in the *New York World.*[39]

Sheen also began switching from S.T.D. to D.D. at times. (They were never listed together.) In the nineteenth and early twentieth century, the Doctor of Divinity degree had been earned as well as honorary.[40] By this time, however, the D.D. was usually an honorary degree, often bestowed upon bishops and other dignitaries. The first reference to a D.D. appeared in Sheen's application for early promotion (the typing appears to be his), where he listed his doctoral credentials as "Ph.D., D.D."[41] The *Catholic Who's Who* from 1930 and the Marquis *Who's Who in America* for 1930–31 both listed the D.D. and cited its origin as the University of Rome, evidently assuming that "Rome" after D.D. meant the campus in the Eternal City that Sheen never actually claimed to have attended.[42] In 1934, in an interrogatory for a dispute on campus, Sheen listed D.D. rather than S.T.D.[43] A year later, in Sheen's handwriting, we see the second doctorate listed as "D.D. Rome 1924."[44]

In 1937, the S.T.D. degree reappeared on the title page of the book *Communism Answers Questions of a Communist.* Publications and biographical sketches would list one or the other of the second doctorates for the rest of Sheen's life.

It is interesting to note that the S.T.D. was listed under Sheen's name, along with his Ph.D., in every CUA catalogue from 1927 until he left the campus in 1950. He never cited the D.D. in the official campus publication; but then, no one else on the faculty listed that degree either. A few other honorary degrees were listed—Sheen himself cited an honorary LL.D. beginning in 1931—but not the D.D.[45]

In 1942, Sheen claimed that the D.D. had come from the Angelicum.[46] Five years later, in a curriculum vitae that appears to have been typed by Sheen, we see the same claim.[47] In his annual reports to CUA officials in mid-1947 and in mid-1949, there was no mention of a second doctorate.[48] Nor was a second doctorate reported in the *Time* magazine cover story of 1952, but the S.T.D. appeared on the title page of the 1952 reprint of *God and Intelligence.* On the official program of the luncheon following Sheen's installation as bishop of Rochester in late 1966, he was listed as D.D.[49] On his official vita from the Diocese of Rochester, written at about the same time, Sheen listed an S.T.D. from Rome in 1924.[50]

No one asked how an S.T.D. could be earned in a brief stint in "Rome," perhaps because of Sheen's remarkable academic achievements elsewhere. No one asked why the Angelicum would give an honorary doctorate to a twenty-nine-year-old priest without publications, and whose highest degree was a year away. The issue wasn't questioned above all because no one dreamed that Fulton J. Sheen was capable of such a deception. His invention of a second doctorate, a device undoubtedly designed to enhance his reputation as a scholar and elevate him from the lowest depths of the campus status system, would remain a secret until twenty years after his death.

On the more general level, perhaps there was some laxity about credentials at CUA during this period, the assumption being that only wholly honorable men would teach at the pontifical institution. In 1930, Rev. William J. DesLongchamps, a full professor who had been named dean of the proposed School of Liturgical Music, resigned after the discovery that his "Mus.D. Rome" was fraudulent. This was unearthed not by the faculty but by the wealthy woman, Mrs. Justine Ward, who offered funding for the school. Indeed, when the administration hesitated to suspend Des-Longchamps immediately, Mrs. Ward withdrew her financial offer.[51]

The reason behind Fulton's creation of the D.D. for himself remains puzzling.[52] The same is true of Fulton's switching back and forth, for the rest of his life, between the S.T.D. and the D.D. when listing his academic credentials. There appears to be no pattern in the usage. Both degrees were theological. The S.T.D. carried the most prestige, but Fulton more often than not chose the D.D. Why use either? A world-famous author, speaker, and television star with a legitimate Ph.D., the highly coveted *agrege* from Louvain, and a bevy of honorary doctorates did not need to continue citing the two bogus degrees. But he did.

Perhaps Fulton could not overcome a Peoria farm boy image that lurked somewhere deep in his mind, and having two doctorates made him seem twice as important as having only one, at least to himself. On rare occasions, he would lump together his earned and honorary degrees. The *Time* cover story of 1952 noted his Louvain doctorate and added, "he has eleven others."[53] Perhaps Fulton could never be sufficiently important in his own eyes. If so, we can be sure that this very human and common failing grieved him often.

In his autobiography, which is strongly confessional, Sheen said only that he had studied at the two Roman universities; he did not mention the awarding of any degree. That was as far as he could go toward admitting the falsification. Even as an archbishop and world-renowned churchman, Fulton could not, at the last, completely rid himself of the vanity he recognized in his old age as one of his most abiding sins.

༄

THE BRIEF ACCOUNT Sheen gives of his years at CUA in *Treasure in Clay* also glosses over the young instructor's role in the struggles within the CUA theology and philosophy faculties. Two incidents appear in the autobiography, each portraying the author in a highly positive light. The first, as we have seen, involved the proposal, in Fulton's first year on campus, to introduce an undergraduate program for seminary students in the School of the Sacred Sciences. Sheen objected, and was censured and later forgiven by Rector Shahan. This story is partially documented in the School of the Sacred Sciences Minutes.

The second incident concerned the rector's rejection of Francis J. Haas as professor of moral theology because his doctorate was not in theology. When the theologians passed around a petition to protest the move, Sheen wrote, he alone refused to sign, on the ground that the rector had not been given a hearing; Sheen then found his classes cancelled, and the rector had to move him to the philosophy department.[54] The primary sources, however, tell a different story. Sheen's account is again most likely the product of a faulty memory. It also, surely, reflects the author's clearly stated desire not to offend anyone or reopen old wounds.[55]

What Sheen failed to say in his autobiography is that in 1929 he prompted controversy among the theologians and administrators by claiming that he could not teach the undergraduate, graduate, and postgraduate courses in apologetics he was assigned. (His was one of a chorus of complaints from the theologians; for instance, John A. Ryan, professor of moral theology, refused to teach in the seminary, contending that he had been employed to teach graduate students exclusively.)[56] Sheen preferred to teach second-year philosophy courses, especially metaphysics and cosmology.[57] He also complained, as we have seen, about the proposed increase in his course load. Instructors were expected to be obsequious, and Sheen was not playing the part.

Of more importance was the case a year later of Father F. L. Brockmann, a Franciscan who submitted a doctoral thesis written under Sheen that was rejected unanimously by the three full professors who were official referees. Brockmann went directly to the rector, along with his provincial leader, charging unfair treatment by the senior theologians and alleging that the faculty had acted out of jealousy toward his adviser, Fr. Sheen.

Rector James H. Ryan, who had been battling the theologians for some time over their lack of productivity and their belligerent attitude, berated them at a meeting with Dean Franz J. Coln from the School of Theology. Ryan claimed that Coln and his colleagues had long held an "unfair attitude" toward himself and Sheen, and that he knew about their "secret conventicles" and was informed about all they did. (Coln may well have suspected that Ryan's friend Sheen was the informant.) He said the theologians were even charging Sheen with heresy in order to get him removed from the faculty. Ryan informed the dean that he would appoint two objective faculty members outside the school to see that Fr. Brockmann was treated fairly.

Dean Coln, long an ardent foe of the rector, soon called for a formal investigation. Senior faculty criticized the Brockmann dissertation harshly, one calling it "a hopeless mass of confusion and superficiality," another saying that it abounded in "wild and meaningless statements."

In a prepared statement, Fulton sounded humble, saying he would abide by the decision of the readers and denying that he was involved in Brockmann's appearance before the rector. Still, he noted that he had advised his student that one of his readers, Church history professor Patrick J. Healy, would be helpful "provided he eliminated the personal element" and read the thesis objectively. The jealousy charge was very much on Fulton's mind, as well as his student's.[58] John A. Ryan said later that "the charge of jealousy, etc. all emanated from Dr. Sheen's very vivid imagination" and that "he made them quite generally known around the university and off campus."[59]

The senior faculty voted to create a special committee to help Brockmann rewrite the dissertation. This of course was a direct slap at Sheen. They also declared that "until Father Brockmann apologizes to the Faculty for his unfounded accusations of injustice and jealousy, the Faculty will not consider him as a prospective candidate

for the degree."[60] The rector countered by appointing two unidentified readers, who promptly approved the thesis. Dean Coln threatened legal action by the Academic Senate.[61] The senate rejected the
thesis.[62]

After the Brockmann case, a heated controversy emerged in fall
1930 over the constitutionality of the new seminary, which was
designed to be under the authority of the university, not the School
of the Sacred Sciences. Chancellor Curley later sighed, "Every Department in the University is in the finest kind of shape and going ahead
with the utmost harmony except the one unblessed and unholy
spot where only priests are gathered."[63] The following spring, the
theology faculty signed a statement leveling lengthy and personal
attacks on the rector—a statement Fulton refused to sign. It was
printed and leaked to the press. Dean Coln appealed to Rome.[64]
The Board of Trustees was in an uproar.[65]

The tumult triggered a full investigation of the relations between
the theology faculty and the rector, authorized by the Board of
Trustees. The three-member special committee of bishops was
headed by Archbishop John T. McNicholas of Cincinnati. Rector
Ryan moved his friend Sheen away from the field of fire to the philosophy department, where he had been trying to be reassigned for
three years.[66]

Hearings opened on May 11, 1931, and lasted five days. Faculty
members complained bitterly about low salaries, about the seminary, about allegedly illegal and insensitive conduct by the rector,
and especially about what they considered to be his war against the
theology faculty. Sheen was not called upon to testify because he
had not signed the statement against the rector. The way in which
he was hired, without faculty advice and consent, was noted, however, and Vice-Rector Pace most probably had him in mind as he
described the reluctance of theological faculty to teach in the seminary. When Professor John A. Ryan testified, McNicholas asked
him why Sheen had been transferred from theology to philosophy.
He replied, "I don't think he was very happy with our Faculty because
he did not feel that he was quite fitted for this work. Dr. Sheen

thought that we were to blame for this trouble with the Rector. The main reason was academic, because he felt that he was not prepared for the classes which we wished him to teach."[67]

In its report to the Board of Trustees, the McNicholas committee sided strongly with the rector. Dean Coln and another senior faculty member, New Testament professor Heinrich Schumacher, were permitted to resign. Documents alleging immoral conduct by both men emerged and hastened their departure.[68] John A. Ryan became the new dean of the School of Theology.[69]

McNicholas wrote a cordial letter to Sheen, who emerged from this battle on good terms with administrators, trustees, and the philosophers. Still, McNicholas expressed a great concern to Fulton that he should devote more of his time and energy to the university. Ryan, who talked with Sheen several times about this, wrote to McNicholas, "Dr. Sheen has the best will in the world but he's become so accustomed to the feverish life of a public speaker that it is going to be extremely difficult to tie him down to the more or less drudgery of preparing men for the kind of work he is doing."[70]

Fulton paid little attention to such pleas, and from this point on he and the CUA administration enjoyed an amicable relationship—on his terms. Sheen was permitted to continue his frantic life as a writer, public speaker, retreat director, preacher, and spiritual director for untold numbers of converts, and the campus basked in his fame.

❧

IN 1934, SHEEN BROUGHT out *Philosophy of Science,* the third of his scholarly books. It was an effort to align modern science, in particular the fields of mathematics and physics, with Thomist philosophy. The 191-page study is another example of Fulton's voracious reading and rigorous thinking. Given the pace at which he lived, it was remarkable that he could have mastered such a breadth of knowledge in academic fields he had only been introduced to in his undergraduate education. Sheen's principal purpose in writing the book was clear: Science, the authority most widely trusted and respected in the modern world, needed the peerless and timeless philosophy of St. Thomas to explain the deeper meanings of its findings.

> Science deals only with an aspect of reality based on an abstraction, *and therefore can never give us reality as such. Only the science which is disinterested in aspects and interested only in the intelligibility of things can completely satisfy the mind, and that science is metaphysics, which treats of the* whole *of reality*—being as being—*whereas the particular sciences treat only of an aspect of that whole.*[71]

Fulton was granted tenure and promoted to associate professor in early 1935. His salary was no doubt still extremely low; as the Depression bottomed out, the faculty had taken a 10 percent pay cut in 1933 and had been requested to make financial pledges to help the campus survive the hard times.[72]

Sheen usually taught in the same small classroom, McMahon 112, often in the afternoon to maximize enrollments.[73] In 1934 he taught "Modern Idea of God in the Light of St. Thomas," "Modern Idea of Religion in the Light of St. Thomas," and "Philosophy of Science and Religion." In 1935 he offered two courses a semester, which would remain his standard teaching load.[74] His schedule and course offerings were little affected by the philosophy department's transformation into the School of Scholastic Philosophy in 1936.[75] In 1939 he had thirty-four students in a course on "Natural Theology" and a graduate seminar of eight.[76] The graduate students often came to his home for private tutorials rather than meet as a formal class.[77]

The classroom could not have taken too much of Fulton's time during the school year; he was usually on campus only two days a week. Every weekend he was in New York, where he did radio broadcasts, preached regularly at St. Patrick's Cathedral, and taught convert classes (and worked through the four-hour train ride each way).[78] He spent summers abroad and traveled at almost every opportunity. A highly complimentary article in *Time* in 1940 noted that Sheen filled 150 speaking dates a year while teaching full-time at CUA.[79] Fulton later recalled, "I was constantly warned by my fellow professors at the university that I was shortening my life. It was universally agreed that I would never live to reach the age of forty-five."[80]

Even so, Sheen took a strong interest in CUA and in 1935 submitted a statement to a five-bishop special committee of the Sacred Congregation of Seminaries and Universities, summoned in response to continued turmoil on campus. In his statement, he sided with those who argued that CUA should not be the Catholic Harvard that Rector Ryan was trying to achieve. He called for "primacy of the spiritual," saying that "The task of integrating the supernatural with the natural, of infusing human knowledge with the divine, of complementing our knowledge of things with our knowledge of God, of making all things Theocentric, is the business of a Catholic University." To Sheen, Catholic University "is to education what the Catholic Church is to religion, namely, the *leaven in the mass.* The Church is not one of the sects; it is the unique life of Christ; the Catholic University is not one of the American Universities; it is their *soul.*"[81]

Ironically, Sheen's statement probably bolstered a sentiment among members of the Board of Trustees, in particular Bishop McNicholas, to replace his friend and protector James H. Ryan with someone more inclined to make CUA an outstanding teaching institution and a beacon of Catholic truth, wholly unlike the many notable state and private institutions throughout the country. Ryan, a bishop since August 1933, was transferred to the Diocese of Omaha on August 6, 1935.[82]

Sheen's promotion to full professor was very slow in coming. He reached that distinction in the fall of 1947, twenty-one years after joining the faculty. By that point he had published 33 books, 3 booklets, 13 pamphlets, and 34 volumes of radio broadcast talks. The philosophers at CUA must have quietly fumed over the years as their colleague became increasingly famous, and their major recourse was to deny him entry into their highest rank. A graduate student later recalled that the vice-rector in the 1940s was a Sheen critic, and that there was a general feeling on campus that Sheen was not pulling his weight, that CUA seemed to be a sideline for him.[83] The rift is further evidenced by the fact that from 1932 Sheen had his office apart from his colleagues, in spacious quarters in the basement of the library. From 1934 until he left CUA, Fulton lived across town from the campus, in the fashionable northwest part of the District of Columbia, where few if any philosophers were to be found.[84]

Still, Sheen enjoyed teaching, which he called "one of the noblest vocations on earth, for, in the last analysis, the purpose of all education is the knowledge and love of truth." Sometimes he entered class laughing, a result of the funny stories he heard from a Dominican priest as they walked together toward their adjoining classrooms. At Louvain, Cardinal Mercier had given him two suggestions that he followed throughout his professional career. The first was: "always keep current: know what the modern world is thinking about; read its poetry, its literature; observe its architecture and its art; hear its music and its theater; and then plunge deeply into St. Thomas and the wisdom of the ancients, and you will be able to refute its errors." The second suggestion was to tear up one's lecture notes annually. Sheen vowed early in his teaching career never to repeat a course. (He did, but probably approached it in a different way with new material.)

Meanwhile Sheen was doing well as a public speaker, as he reported to Mary Baker in 1930: "It would delight your soul to see the crowds that flock to hear your cousin. I tell you this because I know you delight in such tributes. Over five thousand heard me yesterday in the Cathedral and tickets are already sold out for tomorrow's lecture."[85]

Wherever he spoke, in the classroom and outside, Sheen felt a moral responsibility to his audiences to be thoroughly prepared. He spoke without notes, and he always spoke standing—"my first rule was *never sit. Fires cannot be started seated.*" He regularly brought humor into his presentations. Lectures and sermons usually began with a display of self-deprecating wit. "An audience ... does not like to be made to feel inferior to the speaker. That is why a story in which the speaker is humbled gives them a feeling of equality." An example, which Fulton said was a true story: "On a crossing of the Atlantic before the days of airplanes, a deck steward came to me and said: 'Are you the priest who preached the Mission Sunday sermon at St. Patrick's last year?' 'Yes.' 'I enjoyed every minute of that hour and a half.' 'My good man, I never talked an hour and a half in my life.' He said: 'It seemed that long to me.'"

Fulton wanted always to be fresh, relevant, demanding, exciting; and that required preparation. "It is very easy for a professor to turn into a kind of dried-up intellectual without constant stimulation and study," he reflected.[86] Much of his summers in London were spent in study. He read virtually everything, with the exception of fiction, but enjoyed reading book reviews in that area of literature. He liked poetry, especially from *The Oxford Book of Mystical Verse,* and in particular the work of Francis Thompson and Studdert Kennedy.[87] He had a file of favorite poems, many of which he memorized, and often left audiences gasping at his command of long passages. Sheen loved browsing in bookstores, often emerging with a dozen, perhaps twenty books. All would be quickly and thoroughly digested. (A priest who worked for him later in life tested Sheen's breakfast conversation about a book he had started to read upon retiring for the night, and found the volume thoroughly marked.)[88] At Sheen's funeral, a close friend said of him, "He always had to have new books, he loved meeting interesting and informed people, the latest scientific discoveries and technological devices fascinated him." Sheen had "an intellectual curiosity that never deserted him."[89]

All this enhanced Sheen's effectiveness in the classroom, to which many would testify. "He worked his students!" exclaimed one CUA graduate. "His required reading lists were awesome, but we knew that he had read all the works he recommended and we realized that if we were to get anything out of his courses we should do the same."[90] Said another, "You'd no more think of raising a hand in one of his classes than of telling the sun to stop shining for a minute. Nor can I honestly say you'd want to. He was that spell-binding a teacher."[91] Robert Paul Mohan, who studied under Sheen for three years as a graduate student, called his mentor a "masterful communicator," a "man of great faith with fiery energy," and "a real gentleman" who was always positive and helpful. Sheen could be sharply critical of positions, but not of people.[92] Sister Ann Edward, as a graduate student at CUA, was one of many young people who would drop by to watch Sheen in action. "I joined them several times to hear and enjoy this remarkable, appealing priest. Inspiration, beauty, wit—these and other virtues, plus a melodic voice, explained why corridors around his classroom always bulged with people."[93]

◞◟

WORD OF SHEEN's powers as a teacher and public speaker quickly spread, and the medium of radio became an outlet for his talents soon after he joined the CUA faculty. Fulton went on the radio in 1928, delivering a series of Sunday evening Lenten sermons over New York's station WLWL.[94] He was not the first Catholic priest to go on the airwaves. Father Charles Coughlin, a fiery right-winger, had made his debut in October 1926, and for years thereafter was called the "radio priest." Fundamentalist and mainline Protestants were broadcasting even before Coughlin. The very first religious program in the United States emanated from Pittsburgh in 1921, a vesper service conducted by the Reverend Edwin J. Van Etten at Calvary Episcopal Church.[95]

In 1930, following an uproar over the controversial nature of programs aired by Coughlin and a number of fundamentalists, the National Broadcasting Company and the Columbia Broadcasting System, under pressure from the mainline Federal Council of Churches, decided to donate free time to major, nonfundamentalist groups of Protestants, Catholics, and Jews. (Fundamentalists and evangelicals were even denied the right to purchase air time on these networks.) NBC made its stations available to "recognized outstanding leaders" who were to "interpret religion at its highest and best." For a Catholic expression of Christianity, studio executives turned to the National Catholic Welfare Conference (NCWC) and the National Council of Catholic Men.[96]

The Catholic Hour made its debut on March 2, 1930, over station WEAF in New York City. After Cardinal Hayes, archbishop of New York, made a short introduction to the series, Bishop Joseph Schrembs of Cleveland delivered the talk. Future programs were promised to feature outstanding speakers and "the best music in the liturgy of the Church, Ancient, Medieval, and Modern" sung by the Paulist Choristers and accompanied by different orchestras. "The purpose of the National Council of Catholic Men in sponsoring this series is to promote a better understanding of the Catholic Church and its doctrines and to contribute to the growth of friendly relations among the several religious groups in the United States." On the next Sunday evening program (broadcast from 6:00 to 7:00 P.M. Eastern Standard Time), the speaker was Fulton J. Sheen.[97]

Sheen was known to the leadership of the Washington-based National Council of Catholic Men (an arm of the NCWC) not only because of his reputation at nearby Catholic University and his previous radio experience, but also because he was writing newspaper articles for the NCWC news service in early 1930.[98] A series on the "New Paganism" won the praise of the Vatican's *L'Osservatore Romano.*[99] Sheen was gaining the attention of the highest Church officials.

Sheen's twenty-minute talks on the *Catholic Hour,* written and delivered from a script and pre-approved by Church officials, were immediately well received, and he became a regular speaker.[100] In late 1933 and early 1934, his radio addresses covered fifteen weeks, beginning on Christmas Eve and concluding on Easter Sunday. Nearly half a million of the printed versions of these talks had already been distributed.[101] When a new NBC studio opened in Radio Center in 1933, Sheen gave the opening address.[102]

Sheen said he worked forty to sixty hours preparing for each of his broadcasts, always asking himself two questions: what is the purpose of the program, and what will non-Catholics think of it?

The answer to the first was "I will preach Christ and him crucified." And to the second: "The bigoted American Catholic, and some non-Catholics, too, think that we are antiquated, medieval, shallow. It will be my purpose, not to tell them directly that we are refined and intelligent, but to present our picture and our program in such a way as to brush aside their preconceived ideas."[103]

Radio was a perfect outlet for Sheen's talents. His ability to think clearly, his desire always to reach beyond clichés and say something meaningful, his flare for persuasive speaking, his orthodoxy, his charm and wit, and his extraordinary voice made his popularity inevitable. Those in the studio audience were probably even more captivated by his good looks, ever-present smile, and impeccable attire. Fulton often reached out personally to individuals in his audience after the programs, paying special attention to those who attended regularly.

For several years the format of the *Catholic Hour* included questions and answers, with questions provided by members of a live audience in New York, and responses by several experts including Sheen. His replies were delivered impromptu, revealing his splendid facility with words and ideas. When asked about evolution in April 1930, for example, he replied, "It is not absolutely and intrinsically impossible that the body of man could have evolved from a lower organism. Secondly, if it could be proved, it would not conflict with any official teaching of the Church." On the other hand, he also pointed to the paucity of evidence, citing the Smithsonian Institution. He concluded his lengthy remarks by saying that "man is not an evolution but a revolution."

> He may be an animal, but he has also a soul. He is the only animal in the world that is not a domestic animal. Every other animal in this world seems to belong to this world and is content with it. Man is the only wild animal in the sense that he is not domestic to this earth. On account of his soul he has an infinite reach toward the infinite life, love, truth and beauty, and therefore his home is with God in heaven.[104]

The Catholic Hour was carried on fifty-four NBC stations by May 1933, some three thousand letters a month were pouring in to the National Council of Catholic Men, and more than 1.3 million copies of broadcast talks had been distributed. The program was rebroadcast over a General Electric Company station and transmitted all over the world. The Catholic press reported on a woman who was converted by Sheen's talks, and whose husband was brought back to the Church after an extended absence.[105] The general press carried the story of how Colonel Horace A. Mann, a campaign manager for Herbert Hoover in the election of 1928, was converted to Roman Catholicism after hearing Sheen's radio sermons. This was especially newsworthy because Mann had been charged with anti-Catholic activity in the South during the Republican effort to defeat Catholic Al Smith. Sheen provided personal instruction for Mann and his wife, who also converted.[106] In 1936, Sheen told a Boston reporter that his radio talks were resulting in some fifty conversions a week.[107]

Sheen's reputation was soaring, both nationally and internationally.[108] In the summer of 1932, he addressed the International Eucharistic Congress in Dublin.[109] Then he went to London for the balance of the summer, again preaching at Westminster Cathedral and no doubt enjoying a drawing of himself and G. K. Chesterton that appeared in a London newspaper. It was quite an honor, for Chesterton was the mightiest Catholic apologist in the English language; and Sheen, according to the caption, was "the American Chesterton."[110] At Catholic University, where the student newspaper often featured stories on their most famous professor, a writer noted that "Dr. Sheen is generally considered the ablest Catholic pulpit orator in America."[111]

By 1933, Fulton was sufficiently well known in New York to preside at the lavish wedding of the daughter of Nathan L. Miller, a former Empire State governor, to a groom who had bloodlines to both the Roosevelt and the Astor families.[112] Sheen was probably the only one of the hundreds of high society people present that day in East Norwich, Long Island, who had ever been to El Paso, Illinois.

Fulton was also a personal friend of Al Smith, the 1928 presidential candidate who now ran the Empire State Building in New York. Sheen and Smith often appeared together in newspaper stories and photographs, and they sailed together to Europe in 1937.[113] In 1935, both addressed 43,000 pilgrims and an international radio audience at the National Eucharistic Congress in Cleveland.[114] Bishop Joseph Schrembs of Cleveland informed Sheen privately that all twelve bishops on the congress planning committee mentioned him as their choice for a speaker. Afterwards, Schrembs was lavish in his praise of Fulton's performance: "Hundreds of thousands were swept away with the force of your logic and your beauty of expression. Your deep sincerity made your words reach the very souls of men."[115]

∽

UNTIL 1952, WHEN he went off the *Catholic Hour,* Fulton based a large number of his books on his printed radio addresses. *The Seven Last Words and the Seven Virtues,* for example, became *The Seven Virtues. Light Your Lamps* became *Communism and the Conscience of the West. The Modern Soul in Search of God* became *Peace of Soul. The Fullness of Christ* became *The Mystical Body of Christ.* Sometimes Sheen and his publishers would list the radio books and the books from commercial publishers as distinct volumes, making a truly imposing list of publications. Even pamphlets were sometimes cited as books.[116]

Sheen's publications continued to display his Thomistic knowledge, but also increasingly showed a willingness to move beyond scholasticism and talk to the literate general public about extraordinarily important topics. In *The Life of All Living: The Philosophy of Life* (1929), one such topic was the "religion of humanitarianism," later to be further secularized into "secular humanism," which holds that mankind is all that matters and that man, by employing his reason, can attain paradise on earth. Is it not a strange paradox, Sheen asked, "that men who most wildly disclaim against religion are those who wish to make a religion out of irreligious humanity?

Humanity can never be the object of religion for the very reason that a self-centered humanity would be just as chilling as a self-centered individual." Sheen observed that in fact there was no such thing as "humanity," simply individual men and women, whose religious cravings can never be met by science or service to humanity. "What then will that food be which will satisfy the cravings of a spiritual soul which is ever haunted by infinity?" God gave man food enough, wrote Sheen. "Jesus Christ is the Bread of Life; He promised He would be and He fulfilled the promise." And He gave the people of this globe his Church, Sheen wrote, the mystical body of Christ, which since the beginning has held the Real Presence of Jesus Christ to be in the Eucharist. "It has been only since the beginning of the sixteenth century that the world has devitalized religion, made the Church a structure, and the Bread of Life only a figure and a symbol."[117]

Sheen took a similar shot at Protestantism in his Lenten sermons at St. Patrick's Cathedral in early 1934. The Catholic Church, he argued before his huge congregation, was the only institution standing between civilization and chaos. (This was familiar language to those who listened to Father Coughlin on the radio.) He described what he considered to be the degeneration of the Western churches, pointing especially to the liberal, mainstream Protestant bodies.

> *In the sixteenth century, Western civilization spent its belief in earthly fatherhood and the necessity of authority. In the seventeenth century it spent its belief in the authenticity of Sacred Scripture as the Word of God. In the eighteenth century, it spent its belief in the divinity of Christ, the necessity of grace and the whole supernatural structure. In the nineteenth century it squandered the capital of belief in the existence of God as the Lord and Master and the supreme Judge of the home and the dead.*

Sheen concluded, "And in our own day, it has spent its last penny—a belief in the necessity of a religion or obligations to a personal God."[118] In another Lenten sermon, he charged that mainline

Protestantism was now obsessed with economics, social service, humanism, and sociology, "and a thousand and one things foreign to the spiritual side of the Father's house."[119] Contemporary Protestantism was "an empty husk," he said, but "By the grace of God, Western civilization is beginning to look back toward the Father's House."[120]

Later in the same Lenten series at St. Patrick's, Sheen challenged critics of the Catholic Church to prove that it limited the freedom of the individual. "If we do not accept the authority of the Church, we must accept the authority of public opinion, and that is what most of those outside the Church accept—the dictates of the day. For the life of me, I cannot understand how a man can accept the authority of George Bernard Shaw and refuse to accept the authority of the Son of God." Sheen defined Catholic dogma as "the result of the Church's clear, consistent thinking for over 2,000 years."[121]

Such bold and partisan rhetoric, reported in the press, elicited a swift reply from Protestant clerics. The rector of nearby St. Bartholomew's Protestant Episcopal Church decried Sheen's "untrue and cruel accusation" and defended the Reformation as "esteemed among our choicest blessings." The Reverend Norman Vincent Peale of the Marble Collegiate Church on Fifth Avenue declared angrily, "It must be increasingly evident that the Protestant Church needs a Martin Luther to drive another nail in the famous theses he tacked on the church door at Wittenberg; to tell the world that we believe in Protestantism and it is here to stay until the gates of St. Peter rust on their hinges."[122]

Undaunted, Sheen replied in another Lenten sermon that the Reformation was needed but that it should have been a "reformation of discipline not of faith." "We must remember that those who are outside the Church are not there through any fault of their own. They were brought up in prejudice and have accumulated a mass of ignorance. If we believed what they believe about the Catholic Church we would hate it ten times more than they do." Only the Catholic Church, he concluded, can save a pagan society that "knows no more about Christianity than the man in the moon."[123]

Sheen's fearless preaching and writing attracted the attention of a great many Catholics. In the spring of 1934, Marquette University granted him an honorary doctorate.

The list of Sheen admirers also included top officials in the Vatican. In the summer of 1934, just before Fulton sailed for Europe on his annual excursion, Pius XI named him a papal chamberlain, a member of the papal household, with the title of "Monsignor."[124] (A year later, Sheen was elevated another step, being named a domestic prelate with the title "Right Reverend Monsignor.") This was a distinction he accepted with joy, admitting later that he found the title in front of his name "mellifluous."[125] Cardinal Hayes of New York, who may have nominated him, sent his personal congratulations: "No one among your many friends is more delighted than I am. Your exceptional service to the Church not only in your chair at the University but also in the pulpits of our churches as well as the radio made such recognition inevitable."[126] Cardinal Pacelli, the Vatican secretary of state and later Pope Pius XII, sent his congratulations as well.[127] (Sheen was now sending copies of his books to leading Vatican officials, and on Christmas of 1934 he sent a personal photograph to Cardinal Pacelli. Cardinal Hayes also received Sheen publications.)[128] Hereafter, when preaching and lecturing, Fulton would usually wear his full monsignor's regalia, including a flowing scarlet ferraiolo and sash, looking as well as sounding like what he had become: a major spokesman for the Catholic Church in America.

At about this time (as Sheen later revealed in his autobiography), Bishop Francis C. Kelley of Oklahoma City asked Fulton's permission to submit his name to Rome as a candidate for bishop. After some deliberation, Sheen rejected the offer, saying he preferred "a gift from above" rather than a "push from below." By this he meant "an appointment by the Holy See under the inspiration of the Holy Spirit and without the influence of men."[129] He knew that his time would come, and the prize would be greater than Oklahoma City.

In his second Lenten sermon of 1934 at St. Patrick's Cathedral, Sheen had called Pope Pius XI a "great man" whose authority was becoming more widely recognized. "Today the world is beginning to realize that the only hope for us all to escape from this depression lies in the recognition of some authority who speaks with the voice of God. Pius XI is beginning to be recognized as that authority."[130] These comments, reported in the *New York Times,* were surely remembered a few months later when Fulton met the Pope in Rome. In a special audience (again revealing Sheen's high Church connections) granted on July 23, Pope Pius XI commended the thirty-nine-year-old priest for his apostolic work on the *Catholic Hour* and commended his latest book, *The Philosophy of Science.* The Pope stressed the importance of ideas found in the volume, especially the necessity of fixed and immutable principles of reason to illumine the findings of physical scientists.[131]

Pius XI gave Fulton a silver crucifix inlaid with ebony. He cherished it and used it frequently—until eleven years later, when he thought it would help a desperately ill woman, writer Gladys Baker, who was wrestling with conversion. He gave it to her, saying, "When you are tempted to think your sufferings are too hard to bear, all you have to do is look at the crucifix and remind yourself, 'God let *that* happen!' But always bear in mind that Our Lord never spoke of His Crucifixion without His Resurrection. This was to teach us the glorious mystery that behind each private crucifixion is the seed of our own resurrection." Fulton quietly gave Baker three months of weekly private instruction in her hospital room. She entered the Church and lived more than a decade. Of Sheen, she later wrote, "There was my instant recognition in Monsignor Sheen of the quality I had so rarely met with in the most worthy men of the cloth—pure spirituality, untarnished by the faintest breath of worldliness."[132]

The evaluation, however sincere, was inaccurate. But it was widely shared by those who enjoyed the lavish attention and concern that Fulton was often eager to spend on people in trouble, in need, and especially those preparing to enter the Church.

∽

SHEEN ONCE CONFIDED to a close priest friend, Edward T. O'Meara, that Pius XI had told him to study Karl Marx and communism, and never to speak in public during his pontificate without exposing their fallacies.[133] Fulton took the charge to heart and began an intensive study of Marxist literature. On the radio, in the pulpit, and in his publications of the 1930s, Sheen dealt often with the Great Depression and the efforts to end it, frequently pointing to communism as the worst of all possible alternatives for Americans or anyone, anywhere to adopt.

In a 1935 Lenten sermon at St. Patrick's, Sheen spoke out against critics such as philosopher C. E. M. Joad of Cambridge University who charged that Christianity sided with the rich and told the poor to bear their burdens silently. "There is nothing of that attitude in Christianity," he said. "Our Lord does not stand for resignation to destitution. The Gospel poor were not destitute. Christianity is not a glorification of the rich as such, or the poor as such, but of the poor who are poor voluntarily and of the rich who are rich unselfishly." Communists and others who would "confiscate, disperse and annihilate" the property of the wealthy were not poor men but "rich men without cash," Sheen declared.[134]

A week later, Sheen devoted most of his Lenten sermon to communism, warning that it was a parody of religion, "the ape of Christianity in its divine and historical forces." Its primary appeal was religious, not political or economic. "New Deals or fascism will not kill it because they can never summon forth sufficient zeal and fervor to do so," he said. The Church would have to oppose it in a different way than it had employed against any other force it had confronted over the last few centuries. "The duty of Catholics at the present time is to go down to the disinherited group and form a Catholic proletariat culture just as vigorous and just as zealous as a Communist proletariat."[135]

From the same pulpit the following year, Sheen defined communism as "capitalism gone mad" and declared that the atheistic state is "always a slave state" because it deprives people of their souls as well as their economic freedom. "Why can't the modern mind see there is nothing new in communism? It is a groan of despair, not the revolution that starts a new age. It is the logical development of civilization which for the last 400 years has been forgetting God."[136] In further talks in the Lenten series, Sheen called Russia "the most anti-Christ nation on the face of the earth," whose emblem of unity was, fittingly, "a rotted corpse, the body of Lenin—a perfect symbol of that to which all communism must lead us all, unto dust, unto dissolution, unto death."[137] Communism, Sheen declared, had replaced heresy as the chief enemy of the Church. Still, he expressed admiration for communist "ideas of justice and service to our fellow men." These were Christian goals as well, he reminded his huge audience in St. Patrick's Cathedral.[138]

Sheen had little to say in the way of specific solutions to end the economic misery he described often and eloquently. In late 1937, he advocated a program of trade unionism based on papal encyclicals. Business and labor should no longer struggle against each other, he said. Employers and employees of the same industries should join together to work for economic justice, in a guild system that "would give to labor a share in the profits, as opposed to the two theories now prevalent: That capital should have all the profits or that labor should. Today labor receives too small a share for its work and none for its social contribution."[139]

There was nothing new or daring in Sheen's sermons opposing communism; the Church had recognized its mortal enemy from the start. Popes and theologians in recent years, using Thomas Aquinas, had anchored private property to natural law in their condemnations of socialism and communism. The Spanish Civil War, as we shall see, intensified warnings about the Reds in this country and elsewhere.[140]

Nor was there anything unusual in Sheen's call for higher wages and an end to strife between capital and labor. American bishops had been endorsing progressive economic reforms since 1919, and an entire generation of priests had read John A. Ryan's pamphlets published by the NCWC Social Action Department. In 1931, Pope Pius XI issued *Quadragesimo Anno,* published on the fortieth anniversary of *Rerum Novarum* and affirming, in a general way, the Church's support for labor and the "law of social justice" as the equalizer of society's wealth. Catholic University was a stronghold of clergy who preached the Social Gospel and the rights of labor. Catholics in general, who had moved strongly into the Democratic Party with Al Smith's race in 1928, were now highly supportive of Franklin D. Roosevelt's New Deal efforts to end the Great Depression. Maurice Sheehy, assistant rector of Catholic University and the president's political link to the Church, estimated that in 1936 three-fourths of the priests and most of the bishops in America supported the administration.[141]

In the early 1930s, Father Charles E. Coughlin devoted his highly popular radio programs to the need for reform. He preached a populist message decrying "want in the midst of plenty," a message that was both anticommunist and anticapitalist, and he swayed millions to back New Deal reforms. (He received more mail than FDR, and at times needed more than a hundred secretaries to handle it.) Coughlin broke with the New Deal in 1936 and soon lost his credibility by falling into a flamboyant anti-Semitism that obscured one part of his legacy: a strong Catholic commitment to reform. Historian David J. O'Brien observed that Coughlin helped Catholics "to relate their economic and social problems to their faith. In that period, he made constructive contributions, opening the minds of his listeners to the possibility of an active and dynamic government seeking to realize the ideals of justice and equality. Even more than Ryan, he succeeded in communicating to his listeners the basic immorality of the old order's concentration of wealth, low wages, and social insecurity."[142]

There was no unified Catholic reaction to the Great Depression. The Pope had called for "Catholic Action," stressing lay participation in an effort to return society to its Christian foundations; but this call could be interpreted in a wide variety of ways. In the United States, the major example of official Catholic Action in the 1930s was the Legion of Decency, which prevented the production of morally objectionable movies. This effort was highly popular among Catholics but anathema to many others who thought it stifled free thought and creativity.[143]

Radical idealist Dorothy Day won some applause among Church members, especially in New York City, for her selfless activities on behalf of workers, black and white, during the Depression. The Catholic Worker movement stressed the inherent dignity and worth of all people, and expressed itself by supporting organized labor, creating hospitality houses to feed and educate the masses, advocating pacifism, and promoting agricultural communes. Day and her mentor, French philosopher Peter Maurin, rejected bourgeois values and attempted to create a Catholic society without greed, hatred and materialism. A former Communist, Day was far less critical of Marxism than many Church leaders of the period, saying at one point that "often the Communist more truly loves his brother, the poor and oppressed, than many so-called Christians." The *Catholic Worker* newspaper, while opposed to John A. Ryan's dependence on the state to bring about reform, was generally sympathetic toward the early New Deal.[144]

Sheen was deeply concerned about the plight of workers and the poor, yet not attracted to the Catholic Worker movement. His firm grounding in the Christian doctrine of original sin and his strong views on socialism and communism left him without any worldly utopianism. All efforts and plans to create heaven on earth, in his eyes, were sinful folly, detracting from the essential reason God placed man on this globe: to accept or reject God and His Son, to be judged accordingly, and to spend eternity in pure love or torment.

Nor was Sheen very friendly toward the New Deal. In *The Eternal Galilean* (1934), he criticized the "new religion" that ceases talking about the Kingdom of God and talks primarily about the republics of earth. "All its energies and zeal must be directed to support governmental policies such as liquor control, gold standards, and labor codes; there must be a swing away from the stress on eternity, prayers, and the communion of saints; for the world problems, in need of a solution, are not religious, we are told, but economic and political." Sheen had liberal Christianity primarily in mind, but the allusion to the New Deal was unmistakable.[145]

Sheen met Franklin D. Roosevelt in 1936 at the White House. He later described the president as bristling with hostility toward Catholics in general and toward Sheen in particular. "There is one thing that I will not tolerate in this country," Roosevelt said, "and that is giving speeches such as you gave last night in Constitution Hall." When Sheen asked what had offended him, the president read from a newspaper article. Realizing instantly that Roosevelt was reading from an account of another meeting in Washington, Sheen asked to see the article. The president recognized his mistake, crumpled up the newspaper and threw it into a wastebasket. "You must take my word when I say anything," he declared.

Roosevelt then said, "You think you know a great deal about the Church's attitude toward communism, don't you? I want to tell you that I am in touch with a great authority, and he tells me that the Church wants the Communists to win in Spain."

Sheen replied, "You are referring to Cardinal Mundelein, and I know that Cardinal Mundelein never made the statement that you have attributed to him."

Roosevelt then changed the subject and began attacking the archbishop of Baltimore for criticizing the Spanish ambassador to the United States, and also a local priest for allegedly telling parishioners to join a protest against the president "who is in favor of sending arms to the Communists in Spain." Referring to the priest, FDR shouted, "That man is a liar." He then realized that he had just condemned the archbishop of Baltimore for using the same term, and laughingly said, "You know how it is, we men in public life become a little excited now and then."

Roosevelt concluded the interview by promising a job for a friend of Sheen's, which was the reason for the visit. Sheen, however, immediately informed the third party that he wouldn't get the job—and he didn't.[146]

Sheen discussed the wrongs of monopolistic capitalism as well as communism and socialism in *Seven Pillars of Peace* (1945). He added another political category that should be avoided: "A third solution is Bureaucracy, or Capitalistic Fascism, which normally,

instead of diffusing profits by giving some of it to the workers, col-
lects profits in the form of taxes from industry, passes it through a
thousand government offices, and then gives the residue as dole."
Ultimately, he added, "Bureaucracy by a slow evolution ends in the
abduction of personal dignity." Sheen called for a golden mean,
"one in which the property rights are diffused through co-
partnership, instead of being concentrated either in the hands of
Capitalists or in the hands of the State. The State must *guarantee*
the social security of its citizens, but it must not *supply* that security. Freedom from want must not be purchased by freedom from
freedom, in which a Bureaucratic State becomes the world's
caterer."[147]

In a later book, Sheen seemed to be describing Franklin D. Roosevelt when he wrote: "By entering politics, the rich man is subcon-
sciously defending his wealth by rendering a public service. He is
less thought of as an accumulator of wealth; he now is pictured as
one benefiting humanity. But how does he benefit humanity? By the
spending of public funds. A study of wealthy men in politics will
reveal that national and state debts always increase in greater pro-
portion under wealthy men who have gone into politics than poor
men who have gone into politics." The wealthy man has a need to
justify himself, wrote Sheen. "He is the 'friend' of the downtrodden,
the forgotten man, the poor, the slum dweller, the unfortunates of
the world. But the money that is touched is not in his own vaults
nor in his own pocket but comes out of the pockets of the people."[148]

While sometimes indulging in oblique political commentary of
this kind, Sheen considered himself apolitical and he never participated in political campaigns. He told his radio audience in early
1941, "The reactionary wants things to remain as they are; the liberal wants change though he is little concerned with its direction. . . .
There is a golden mean between the reactionary and the liberal,
and the word that seems to fit best is 'Catholic.'" Both the terms
"liberal" and "reactionary" change their meanings over time, he
said, but "The ideas of the Church are like her vestments; always
well dressed but never the slave of passing fashion." He concluded,

The Church knows after 1900 years' experience that any institution which suits the spirit of any age will be a widow in the next one. The Church, therefore, will never please either the reactionary or the liberal. She will please only the relatively few who can understand how a house built on an immutable rock with an abiding proprietor, Peter, has a key that admits strangers. The reactionaries want the rock without the keys; the liberals want the keys without the rock; and we who believe in Christ, who gave both to Peter, want both.[149]

The creation of Social Security might be useful and just, but it would not answer the cravings of the heart or save one single soul. To Sheen, the gospel message and the Church were all—the purpose of man's being. He expounded eloquently upon the concept of the Church in *The Mystical Body of Christ* (1935), which contains some of his most powerful writing. "All misunderstandings come from regarding the Church as an organization. It is not an organization like a club; it is an organism like a body.... The Church was in existence before Peter or James or John or the other apostles became believers. It was in actual existence the very moment when the Word was made flesh and dwelt among us.... The written Gospel is the record of His historical life. The Church is the living Gospel and record of His present Life." Were it not for the Mystical Body of Christ, the Church, "where would Christ find lips with which to speak forgiveness to penitent thieves? If it were not for this Body, where would He find hands to lay on little children, feet to receive the ointment of other Magdalenes, and a breast to receive the embrace of other Johns? Were it not for this Body, where would Christ find a visible Head to articulate His voice and draw all souls into the unity of one Lord, one faith, one Baptism?"[150]

And what did the Church mean to Sheen himself? "I answer that it is the Temple of Life in which I am a living stone; it is the Tree of Eternal Fruit of which I am a Branch; it is the Mystical Body of Christ on earth of which I am a member. The Church is therefore more to me than I am to myself." The Church could live without

Sheen, but he could not live without the Church. "So absorbing does she become that her thoughts are my thoughts; her loves are my loves; her ideals are my ideals. I consider sharing her life the greatest gift God has ever given to me, as I should consider losing her life the greatest evil that could befall me." No longer was he a moral speck, a wanderer without a home. "My life is her life, my being is her being, she has my love, my service, as I myself have the entire devotion and service of my hand. She is the living organism, I am but an organ; she is the body, I am but a member; she is Life, I am a living thing; she the Vine, and I the branch."[151]

FOUR

Battle Lines

In the 1920s, many Catholics were deeply concerned about the rise of Fascism in Italy. Having seen the Church persecuted by leftist governments in the Soviet Union and in Mexico, leaders feared similar treatment at the hands of right-wing extremists. Tensions eased in 1929 when Pope Pius XI and Benito Mussolini signed the Lateran Treaty and Concordat. Just as his predecessors, for the sake of survival, had been forced to coexist with every sort of ruler and government, the Pope now made the best of a difficult situation.

The 1929 agreement was praised by many American Catholics, including John A. Ryan and Fulton Sheen, who thought it meant the preservation of the Church's independence and freedom to preach the gospel.[1] At no time was Sheen attracted to Mussolini or Fascism; he was thinking above all, as always, about the best interests of Catholicism.[2]

At first there was no internal terror in Italy under Mussolini, and no racial laws or deportations. (In 1933, forty-three American Jewish publications selected Mussolini as one of a dozen Christian leaders who had "most vigorously supported Jewish political and civil rights.")[3] Still, when the Italian leader violently attacked the Pope's Catholic Action movement, which encouraged laity to become active apostles in world affairs, Pius XI responded, in June 1931, with an encyclical letter *Non Abbiamo Bisogno*, attacking Mussolini and the Fascist Party. (Monsignor Francis Spellman, an American who was assistant to Vatican secretary of state Pacelli, smuggled the letter out of Rome and took it to France to be published.)[4]

When Hitler assumed power in Germany in 1933, many Church leaders, along with others in the West, quickly understood that he was something quite different from Mussolini. Nazism's hostility toward Christianity was deep. As Norman Podhoretz has reminded us,

> *both communism and Nazism were forms of social engineering based on supposedly scientific foundations. The communists who took over in Russia in 1917 explicitly saw themselves as "scientific socialists," carrying out the hitherto hidden laws of History as unearthed by the mind of Karl Marx and creating as they went along the "new Soviet man." As for the Nazis, they justified their slaughter of Jews and others as part of a program of putatively scientific eugenics that would purify the human race and create the higher breed foreseen by Nietzsche in his vision of the superman.*[5]

Many Americans on the left in the years of the Great Depression, while eager to condemn Hitler and Mussolini, remained stubbornly convinced that Stalin was a benevolent dictator and that the Soviet experiment would in time create the earthly utopia that Karl Marx predicted. British journalist Malcolm Muggeridge, in Russia during the early 1930s, has given us an amusing and revealing account of leftist tourists and their relentless credulity on visiting what they saw as the emerging heaven on earth.

> *They are unquestionably one of the wonders of the age, and I shall treasure till I die as a blessed memory the spectacle of them travelling with radiant optimism through a famished countryside, wandering in happy bands about squalid, over-crowded towns, listening with unshakeable faith to the fatuous patter of carefully trained and indoctrinated guides, repeating like schoolchildren a multiplication table, the bogus statistics and mindless slogans endlessly intoned to them.*[6]

Americans who read the *New York Times* received a wholly false account of life in Russia from reporter Walter Duranty. Muggeridge, who knew him, said later that he thought no one else followed the party line with such rigor. "I always enjoyed his company; there was something vigorous, vivacious, preposterous, about his unscrupulousness which made his persistent lying somehow absorbing." *The Nation* and numerous other magazines and newspapers on the left, in America and Europe, saw the Soviet Union through the same tinted glasses.[7]

What accounts for the unwillingness by often well-educated and well-meaning people to see things clearly? In large part this failure involves the intense idealism of those who join the Communist Party, more often than not in youth. Douglas Hyde, a prominent member of the party in England for twenty years, argues that idealism provides "the dynamism of the Communist movement." He notes, "Communism becomes the dominant thing in the life of the Communist. It is something to which he gives himself completely. Quite obviously it meets a need, fills a vacuum at the time when he is first attracted to it. More significant is that it normally continues to be the dominant force in the life of the Communist for as long as he remains in the movement." The extreme self-sacrifice demanded by the party—time, money, thought, and if necessary life—reinforces the idealism, producing a single-minded devotion, an impenetrable zeal, that knows no bounds.[8]

The True Believer is, of course, a familiar character in history. It is important to observe that he is capable of great good as well as great evil. There is nothing intrinsically bad in seeking meaning to life and trusting wholeheartedly in an institution or book or philosophy that claims to have the whole truth. By the same token, cynicism, doubt, indifference, and selfishness are not always, as some believe, evidence of enlightenment and goodness. In the case of the Communists, it was the object of their passion rather than the passion itself that proved destructive. A great many of the youth who became Reds did so with the highest intentions, believing that utopia was in their immediate grasp. Like Lenin, their hero, they were willing to do what was necessary to bring it about.

Two Communist parties had been created in the United States in 1919. Members of both led strikes, waged terror, and harangued belligerently during the nervous postwar years. The result was the First Red Scare of 1919–21, which saw hundreds of Communists arrested and more than a thousand alien radicals deported. The two parties merged in 1921 and soon fell under the authority of Stalin.

The Communist Party of the United States of America (CPUSA), as it became known in 1929, was part of a worldwide effort, directed by the Communist International (Comintern), to foment revolution. During the early years of the Depression, CPUSA members opposed the New Deal and organized demonstrations and strikes. In 1935, with the USSR facing the challenge of Hitler, the Comintern changed gears, proclaiming a Popular Front against fascism, endorsing the New Deal, making friends with liberals and socialists, joining labor unions, and attempting to enter mainstream politics. Party membership increased four- or fivefold during the late 1930s, reaching a high point of some fifty thousand in 1939. Thousands more were fellow travelers who supported the Communist Party without formally joining it. Still, the number of Reds and their associates was tiny relative to the general population and to membership in the two major political parties. And not until the 1930s were a majority of American Communists native born and English speaking.

The influence of the Communists surpassed their numbers, however. Many of the nation's most prominent intellectuals, especially in and around New York City, were CPUSA members, and they had an impact on the influential media and in many of the nation's most prestigious colleges and universities. They also had strong allies in Hollywood. Being obsessed with the "proletariat," they often out-worked others in attempting to seize control of labor unions. They also made an impact on politics. In New York, they were prominent in the American Labor Party, and in Minnesota, a Popular Front faction dominated the Farmer-Labor Party.

To Communists, the Catholic Church and the fascists were equally evil and deserving of destruction. Thus it was common in the mid and late 1930s to hear charges from the left that the Vatican embraced fascism. Both the Pope and Hitler were mortal enemies of those who found truth, beauty, and goodness in the famines, purges, and gulags of Stalin's Russia, where millions died for the putatively "higher" cause of the International Soviet and the building of a better world for the masses.

How many millions died? In the 1930s, the West knew about the great famines caused by Bolshevik policies, although not in detail. The press covered three public trials in the 1930s in Moscow, as Stalin purged the last of his political opponents. Stories swirled, especially within the Catholic press, of Soviet barbarism. We now know that the butchery was beyond even the most lurid accounts. According to the authoritative study of the issue, created in part from Soviet files made available after the downfall of the Soviet Union, some five million died from famine in the early 1920s, and another six million in the famine ten years later. Between 1937 and 1938, there were 720,000 executions. About seven million entered Soviet concentration camps and Gulag colonies between 1934 and 1941, and some 400,000 died in the camps from 1930 to 1940.[9] The dire warnings of Church authorities about the terrorist activities of the Soviets appear, in retrospect, almost understated.

Msgr. Sheen opposed communism and fascism with almost equal fervor. He told his radio audience, "In both fascism and communism the tendency is to absorb the individual into the state; to make the citizen the virtual slave of a wealthy, highly-centralized government, to strip him of his freedom and rights to individual action, one by one." Most of his attention, however, turned to communism, the very faith that was beguiling so many American intellectuals blinded by ideology and sick at heart over the misery that surrounded them in the Depression. The reason for this emphasis was clear: as Sheen put it, "Fascist Italy recognizes the freedom of religion. Nazi Germany annoys religion; Communism destroys it."[10]

Before an audience of forty-three thousand in Cleveland in September 1935, standing on a white stage in the middle of a brilliantly lighted stadium, Fulton raised his arms to the sky and predicted an almost apocalyptic struggle with communism.

> *In the future there will be only two great capitals in the world: Rome and Moscow; only two temples, the Kremlin and St. Peters; only two tabernacles, the Red Square and the Eucharist; only two hosts, the rotted body of Lenin and the Christ Emmanuel; only two hymns, the Internationale and the Panis Angelicus— but there will be only one victory—if Christ wins, we win, and Christ cannot lose.*

A hush fell over the huge crowd for what one reporter thought was a full minute before the thousands stood and cheered.[11]

When the Spanish Civil War broke out in 1936, the Loyalist, or Republican, side enjoyed the backing of the Soviets and many American liberals and Communists (as well as the governments of France and Mexico). Since the Church supported General Francisco Franco, who was backed by Hitler and Mussolini, it was declared by many on the left that Catholics were, as long suspected, fascists. The connection was explored and supposedly confirmed in a six-part series published in the *New Republic.* The assertion, however, was simplistic and inaccurate, and it ignored what had actually happened in Spain.

In the late eighteenth century, Spain had become two contending camps, one traditionalist and orthodox, the other founded on the Enlightenment. Both sides remained Catholic, but the chasm between them grew larger over time. After Napoleon, Spain was roughly divided into two extremes, "Catholic conservative" and "socialist revolutionary." Privileged aristocrats tended to support the former, and landless peasants and the working class the latter. As in Russia, the country lacked a large educated and landed middle class that would have served as a moderating influence. The union of church and state remained in place, as it had for a thousand years.

In 1931 the monarchy of Spain was toppled, the king fled the country, and a democratically elected government assumed power. The assortment of quarreling leftists who headed the Second Republic (after defeating conservatives by less than two percentage points) began killing clergy and burning churches. A right-wing counter-movement sprang up, including one faction willing to work with the government and another, the Falange, that declared its opposition to republican government, capitalism and Marxism in a 27-point manifesto of 1934, and called for a strong military and imperialist expansion.

By early 1936, Spain was in an economic crisis and ripe for civil war. General Francisco Franco, commander of Spanish forces in Morocco and long a national hero, entered the country with the backing of the Falange and many military leaders. Serious fighting broke out, killing nearly a hundred thousand people within one month and prompting large-scale foreign intervention. Nazis and Soviets saw the bloody conflict as shadow boxing for World War II, and both delighted in savaging the people of Spain who opposed them.

Many Catholics, in the Iberian peninsula and around the world, saw the civil war as a contest between a Catholic or a communist future for Spain. Nationalists pointed to the murder of some seven thousand bishops, priests, monks and nuns, and thousands of churches burned to the ground. On the other hand, many Catholics were less than enthusiastic about Franco, who could be as ruthless as his opponents; and the Pope protested his bombing of cities. One fact was certain: with a Nationalist victory the Church would survive; without it, Catholicism would be subjected to a bloody purge. (Pope John Paul II would beatify 238 martyrs of the Spanish Civil War during his tenure. Not one of the victims of "hatred against the faith" had participated in the political rivalry.)[12]

In America, the Left tended almost reflexively to support the Loyalists, arguing that they were backing democracy and all of the highest ideals of modern life. In early 1937, a group of young Americans, composed largely of Communists, traveled to Spain to help the Loyalists. As members of the Abraham Lincoln Battalion, they were part of the seven International Brigades recruited, organized and orchestrated by the Soviets. The French sent the largest contingent, numbering some 28,000. Altogether some 3,300 Americans fought in Spain or served with American medical units, and about 900 were killed in action. (One member of the battalion, Morris Cohen, would go on to found the spy ring that stole atomic secrets for the Russians from the Manhattan Project. He was later convicted of espionage in England as part of a spy ring that penetrated the British navy.)[13]

The Left in America often dismissed the wave of terror against Catholic clergy in Spain as "alleged atrocities." The media on the whole, led by the nation's major newspapers, took the same approach. In Hollywood movies, including *Blockade, The Fallen Sparrow,* and *For Whom the Bell Tolls* (based on Ernest Hemingway's famous pro-Loyalist novel), the Republicans were portrayed as heroes and their opponents as villains. Fulton Sheen, among others, expressed considerable anger about this partisanship in the mass media.[14]

A majority of the Catholic hierarchy, almost the entire Catholic press, the National Catholic Welfare Conference and all of its subsidiary organizations, the Knights of Columbus (whose monthly publication had a circulation in the neighborhood of half a million), Holy Names societies, and a great many prominent Catholic laymen favored Franco. The general Catholic population in America, on the other hand, was less enthusiastic. A public opinion poll taken in 1938 indicated that only about 39 percent of Catholics in the United States favored Franco, 30 percent were pro-Loyalist, and 30 percent were neutral.[15] (A Gallup poll taken that same year revealed that 83 percent of Protestants favored the Loyalists.)[16]

Why did so many Catholics disagree with the Church on this issue? Undoubtedly many were influenced by the major media. The Great Depression was still paramount in the minds of many working-class Catholics, and a struggle in Spain was remote and outside their range of interest. Isolationism was powerful throughout the United States at the time, and the public, both Catholic and Protestant, wanted to keep hands off the struggle in Spain. Both houses of Congress passed near-unanimous resolutions to embargo arms shipments to the country. Moreover, as John David Valaik has observed,

The anti-Semitic tone of some Catholic reporting, the callous and intemperate, even un-Christian, references to the fate of Loyalists and their supporters, the constant emphasis on the Communist menace to the virtual exclusion of the Fascist aspect of the struggle to be noted in many Catholic papers, and an inherent American devotion to democracy in opposition to dictatorship anywhere, certainly drove some Catholics away from Franco.[17]

In 1938, as the Loyalists began to falter, American politics divided between those on the left who sought to lift the embargo that President Roosevelt had imposed on shipments to the Republic, and those on the right who wanted to keep it. The Catholic clergy and press, including Sheen, were almost unanimously in the latter camp.[18] Sheen spoke out often on the Spanish Civil War, consistently defending the Church's position. In an October 1936 article for *The Tablet,* a conservative Brooklyn diocesan paper, he displayed a detailed knowledge of the crisis in Spain and documented Soviet efforts, in part from the Russian press itself, to turn the nation into a communist state.[19] In November of the following year, Sheen recited gruesome statistics on atrocities against Catholics in Spain and lashed out at liberal intellectuals and mainline Protestants who were backing Loyalists.[20] He felt deeply the torture and murder of priests and nuns, and once told a potential convert about a priest who gave his Red tormentors a blessing after they had chopped off his hands.[21]

Like many Catholic leaders, Sheen backed Franco because he was the Church's hope for survival in Spain. He was guilty of some rhetorical excesses early in the war, for instance saying in 1937, "Franco is saving western civilization by keeping the barbarians out of Europe."[22] But he later tried to backtrack: "I never defended Franco. I always defended Spain against the attack of the Communists ... he was the lesser of two evils. I hold no brief for Franco."[23] He wrote later, "Had the Communist-Republicans maintained neutrality toward religion as did the popular front in France, the Vatican would have remained neutral."[24] Sheen didn't have to support the Falange with such fervor. Several major churchmen, including George Cardinal Mundelein of Chicago and Edward Cardinal Mooney of Detroit, had been reticent in endorsing Franco.[25] But he was closer to those, like Archbishop Francis Spellman of New York, who had a glowing view of Franco as a self-sacrificing man of God, confronting enemies who were inspired by "hatred of religion."[26]

In March 1937, Pope Pius XI issued the encyclical *Mit Brennender Sorge* ("With Burning Anxiety"), denouncing Nazism and dispelling the notion that he was a fascist. Five days later, he issued *Divini Redemptoris*, a more strongly worded encyclical condemning communism and detailing attacks on the Church by communist regimes in Russia, Mexico, and Spain.

Meanwhile, the Catholic hierarchy in the United States stepped up its war against communism. The Social Action Department of the National Catholic Welfare Conference published and widely distributed the pamphlet *Communism in the United States,* summarizing the history of the Communist Party in America, estimating its membership, describing its front organizations, and calling attention to the influence that Communists wielded in all walks of American life, including organized labor and the media. Each diocese was to create a committee of priests to help the bishop keep tabs on local Communists and to transmit the information to the NCWC. Catholic schools, study groups and clubs were requested to join in the fact finding. Catholic youth organizations were to be kept fully informed about the Communist "party line," and were warned against working with Reds in united front organizations.

That same year, Cardinal Hayes of New York approved the creation of the Association of Catholic Trade Unionists, an organization designed to carry the Church's war against communism directly into the unions. Chapters were soon formed in New York, Detroit, Cleveland, Newark, Pittsburgh, Saginaw, Trinidad, San Francisco, Milwaukee, Chicago, South Bend, and Seattle. "Actu," as it was known, promised to neutralize or destroy Communist control of unions wherever it existed.[27]

In 1938, Sheen told a rally in New York's Carnegie Hall that Americans had been too patient over the past twenty years with man's inhumanity toward man:

> *We were silent before when 2,000,000 kulaks met death and 60,000 churches were closed by an atheistic government in Russia; we were silent before when 20,000 churches and chapels were desecrated, burned and pillaged and when 6,000 diocesan clergy were murdered in Spain; we were silent before when eleven Mexican Bishops were exiled and 131 churches in the State of Tobasco alone were taken down, stone by stone, and when Socialist education was made compulsory; but now the secret is out; those who cannot pull God down from heaven are driving his creatures from the face of the earth.*

That silence in the face of atrocity was at an end, he declared. "Now we shall let the broad stroke of our challenge ring out on the shields of the world's hypocrisy; now we shall with the sword of justice cut away the ties that bind down the energies of the world. Now we shall lift up our voices and say to all persecuting nations, 'This is not the first of your persecutions, but it shall be the last.' "[28]

Sheen's bold pronouncements won him widespread applause in Catholic circles. The Marquesa Anderson de Ciefuegos (formerly Jane Anderson), an American-born war correspondent who had been imprisoned by the Loyalist government in Madrid, called Sheen "the world's greatest authority on the techniques of communism." In 1938 she told an audience in New York that radicals had placed Sheen on a blacklist similar to one that resulted in the death of six thousand civilians in Malaga, Spain. "Loyalist Spain is loyal only to murder and to Moscow," she asserted, warning, "If communism is not stopped in Spain, it will sweep the world."[29]

In January 1939, Sheen spoke before a huge rally in Washington's Constitution Hall, sponsored by the "Keep the Spanish Embargo Committee." He shared the platform with several speakers, as well as Senator David I. Walsh of Massachusetts and the heads of the National Catholic Welfare Conference and the National

Council of Catholic Women. Sheen argued that he did not advocate assistance to Franco but stood squarely for American nonintervention in the war. "There is entirely too much hate in the world now," he said. "Let us dignify the glorious traditions of our country by keeping our hands free from blood." Many understood that the continuation of America's neutrality was actually spelling the end of the Loyalists, as Stalin was losing interest in Spain; so for Sheen to pretend that he was not backing Franco and his cause was disingenuous. Red Cross worker Aileen O'Brien, also a speaker, told of being in Spain and finding half-burned bodies of priests, partly burned fragments of nuns' robes, desecrated holy relics, and other evidence of "the most unparalleled religious persecution in history." Surely no one at the rally was truly neutral.[30]

Sheen's partisanship soon flared up when he learned from the press that he had been invited by a Loyalist leader to come to Spain and see for himself that religious freedom existed. He sarcastically rejected the overture, saying he would accept the invitation only if those Church leaders who had already been murdered would add their names to the bid. "The massacred can write no letters; the crucified can never invite; the slain can extend no hand of welcome."[31]

Franco's victory on March 29, 1939, brought great relief to Church officials and to most of the people of Spain. As German scholar Peter Berglar has written of the conflict, "Begun as a revolution, it ended as a liberation, since the overwhelming majority of Spaniards vastly preferred an authoritarian Franco regime to a totalitarian communist one."[32] Franco was sworn into office with his hand on the Bible, in front of a crucifix, surrounded by priests and bishops. He restored many privileges of the Church, even giving it control over motion picture censorship. The Pope praised the new government with a special Christmas blessing, but noted in his official declaration that "excess" could sometimes be committed in the defense of God and religion.[33] Half a million people had died in the ferocious struggle.[34]

Father Charles Coughlin told his millions of radio listeners that Franco had "put to flight the Communist hypocrites. No longer will Spanish Democrats burn churches; tie nuns together in kerosene-soaked pits; massacre bishops, priests, and ministers; mow down hundreds of thousands of men and women and children just because they are Christians." He had nothing but scorn for the pro-Loyalist leftists in the United States. "No longer need the American columnists, kept newspapers, paid Red agitators, or Washington Internationalists weep for 'Spanish Democracy,' for it is now only a dark red spot in history."[35]

In December, Sheen delivered a sermon in New York in which he gave thanks to the Blessed Virgin: "We need no defense now for the stand we took in Spain. Supposing the forces of evil had triumphed, where would France and England be today?"[36] The Second World War had broken out in Europe, and Nazis and Reds, through their Mutual Non-Aggression Pact, were united in an effort to conquer not only the Church but the West.

∽

THROUGHOUT THE 1930s, Sheen continued to preach regularly to millions over the *Catholic Hour*. His major competitor in the first half of the decade was Coughlin. When asked to compare his radio addresses to those of the "radio priest," Sheen said there was no conflict. "There is a difference in the two, however. Father Coughlin chooses to confine himself largely to the material. My sermons are confined to spiritual values. Which of the two is of the most benefit is, of course, a matter of opinion, but I will always assert the spiritual will out-weigh and out-last the material."[37] After Coughlin was silenced by his bishop following Pearl Harbor, Sheen and the other *Catholic Hour* speakers had the field to themselves.

During the ten years of Coughlin's highly popular broadcasts, many of the tens of thousands of letters that poured into his office contained donations of one to five dollars. The money covered the cost of broadcasting—in 1931 his independent network of twenty-six stations cost $12,000 a week—and a great deal more. A single mailing could bring in as much as $400,000, enabling Coughlin to build a magnificent church called the Shrine of the Little Flower and create his own national political party in 1934.[38]

By comparison, Sheen and the others on the *Catholic Hour* struggled. The National Council of Catholic Men raised funds for the program in a number of ways, including the sale of copies of the radio addresses. But as the minutes of the Catholic Hour Executive Committee reveal, during the 1930s funds were always tight. In 1933, for example, program leaders contemplated asking the National Broadcasting Company for a $10,000 loan.[39]

Some listeners sent donations, along with pleas for personal advice and copies of talks, directly to Sheen. Since he was far and away the most popular speaker on the program, many listeners assumed that he and the program were one and the same thing. In 1937, a Catholic newspaper in Providence, Rhode Island, trumpeted Sheen's arrival by declaring, "His keen mind, his tireless energy, his peerless eloquence have been devoted to the great apostolate of the radio ever since the inception of the popular Catholic Hour. Indeed, for most, Monsignor Sheen is the Catholic Hour."[40] This would be true throughout the more than two decades Fulton was on the radio.

Mary Dunn worked for Sheen full-time for six months in 1949–50, and one of her principal jobs was to open the mail that arrived at his home. Dozens of letters appeared daily, many containing cash. Dunn typed Sheen's Dictaphone responses to people writing in with questions and personal problems (some of the replies were based on form letters), and supervised the mailing of "tons" of Sheen's books to letter writers, mostly the booklets and pamphlets containing radio speeches.

Dunn later recalled that Sheen "didn't handle money well." The cash received in the mail was placed in drawers all over his house. He never refused a request for funds; cash from the drawers was put in the return mail to supplicants, and no records were kept. Sometimes checks were sent, but Mary didn't handle those.[41]

Letters came to Sheen from as far away as India requesting all sorts of material assistance. When a man from Brooklyn asked for an overcoat, Fulton told the Catholic Charities in Brooklyn to buy one for the man if he needed it, and forward the bill. Catholic Charities reported that the man didn't need an overcoat and was simply testing Sheen.[42] A niece said later that one of Fulton's favorite maxims was "Always have things with a detached spirit."[43] One winter during a train ride, he gave away a new camel hair overcoat to a poor priest who genuinely lacked a coat. It was an action he would repeat over the years.[44]

Sheen was always giving money away—on the street, in shops, after the *Catholic Hour* broadcasts, to anyone who asked. He carried a lot of cash about with him and spent it liberally, never bothering to keep an account. Wealthy people often gave him cash and left him things in their wills, his niece Joan Sheen later recalled, and he would often recycle the cash and the monies from the sale of furniture and other donated items into new gifts. One regular supplicant, an indigent woman named Pearl who attended the *Catholic Hour* broadcasts, documented her poverty by showing Fulton a hole in her dark stocking that she had tried to conceal by putting ink on her leg. Joan Sheen questioned her uncle about the authenticity of the woman's need, and voiced doubts about many of the others who flocked about him seeking financial assistance. His answer always was, "I couldn't take a chance and not give them the money. They might truly be in need." He would be handing out cash for the rest of his life to any and all.[45]

Marlene Brownett, a close personal friend, recalled the Carney family of New York, whom Sheen often encountered on the street. The father drove a garbage truck. Mrs. Carney did not get along with her husband. One of their little boys had bad teeth. Fulton helped to heal the Carney marriage and paid the orthodontist.[46]

If Sheen could not help someone directly, he often asked wealthy friends to lend a hand. When a woman whose husband could not find work in Philadelphia wrote to Sheen, he forwarded the letter to Mrs. James McGranery, wife of a federal judge in the area, asking that she regard the appeal as an opportunity for Christian charity.[47]

Brownett said that if you admired something in Sheen's apartment, he often just handed it to you. She once presented him with a fine clock, suitably engraved, and urged him not to give it away.

He remembered the admonition, but eventually returned it to the donor when she forgetfully admired it many years later. "Things didn't matter to him," she recalled.[48]

By 1940, the *Catholic Hour* was being broadcast over 106 radio stations.[49] The National Council of Catholic Men had mailed out almost five million reprints of program addresses, including 1,750,000 copies of Sheen's 140 radio talks. In his first address for 1940, Sheen offered listeners a free, tiny pocket prayer book; more than 300,000 were soon mailed. The tenth anniversary broadcast attracted many prominent clergy, including Archbishop Francis J. Spellman.[50]

Sheen had two secretaries to handle personal mail and a staff of twenty clerks, employed by the National Council of Catholic Men, to handle the bulk of the mail, which amounted to between 3,000 and 6,000 letters a day. He dictated some 200 replies daily. Only one in a hundred letters, said Sheen, were from critics of the priest or the program. He told of answering one such missive from a Communist, who wrote back a week later saying he would send his children to a Catholic school.[51]

By this point, Sheen was reported to have brought hundreds of converts into the Church. He was spending about ten hours a week on personal instruction. The process was slow, each neophyte requiring from forty to a hundred hours of lessons, depending on his or her ability to absorb theology. One convert, socialist writer Heywood Broun, took ninety hours because of his desire to be thoroughly informed.[52]

Broun, fifty years old in 1939, was a columnist for the *New York World-Telegram* and other Scripps-Howard newspapers, and president of the Newspaper Guild. Brought up an Episcopalian, he had lost his faith and during the Depression had become a socialist champion of the working class. Broun was often given to attacking clergy, Sheen among them, and his critics called him anti-Christian and Communist. In fact, however, Broun was married to a Catholic, and he faced a crisis of meaning in his life. The day after the election of Pius XII, Broun approached Fr. Edward Dowling, a priest-journalist friend, and asked him if it was possible for a social and political progressive to be Catholic. Dowling replied, "Don't you realize that you're a little naïve, Heywood? You like to call yourself a radical, but the doctrines of the Church to which I belong imply so many deep changes in human relationship that when they are accomplished—and they will be—your own notions will be nothing more than an outmoded pink liberalism."[53]

Sheen approached Broun at the suggestion of the famed religious novelist, editor, journalist and playwright Fulton Oursler. When he telephoned, he told Broun that he wanted to see him about his soul. Broun was ready for the invitation, replying, according to Sheen: "Yes, I am interested in the Church for the following reasons: I am convinced that the only moral authority left in the world is the Holy Father; second, I made a visit to Our Lady of Guadalupe in Mexico and was deeply impressed by the devotion to the Mother of Christ. Finally, and most important, I do not want to die in my sins." Sheen led the gruff and rumpled newspaperman through instruction over a period of two and a half months, and Broun completed the sessions asking for Sheen's blessing. A celebrity convert, Broun was the first person to receive Confirmation from Archbishop Spellman when he came to New York from Boston.

A month after his conversion, Sheen asked Broun for his reactions, and remembered him mentioning three. "The first was great peace of soul and a feeling of being home at last; the second, a realization that much liberalism was extremely illiberal. Some of his friends, he said, who were loudest in shouting for freedom were also loudest in protesting against him because he acted freely." Broun said, "I discovered that freedom for them meant thinking as they did." A third reaction also involved his former leftist colleagues. "It has dawned upon me that the basis of unity in radicalism is not love, but hate. Many radicals love their cause much less than they hate those who oppose it." Fr. Dowling's general observation had proven true: "As regards radicalism, I have also discovered that no social philosophy is quite as revolutionary as that of the Church."[54]

The once hard-bitten and cynical journalist died of pneumonia six months later. Sheen delivered the funeral eulogy, which was then published.[55]

In the late 1930s Sheen kept publishers busy. From 1936 through 1939, he published seven books, eight pamphlets, and eleven volumes of radio speeches. Even acknowledging that the books and radio speeches were often very similar, it was a remarkable output for a full-time professor who traveled the country giving speeches, commencement addresses and retreats, and went to Europe every summer.

Sheen seemed to be everywhere. In June 1936, for example, he was in England for Chesterton's funeral and he lectured in Ireland.[56] In 1937 he was in Windsor, Ontario, lecturing on communism at Assumption College.[57] A few weeks later he was in Berkeley, California, to lecture on the immortality of the soul.[58] In early 1938 he introduced a radio series that was carried on a hundred radio stations in the United States and Canada.[59] Soon he was in Pittsburgh speaking on organized labor.[60] In April 1938 he was in Duluth, Minnesota, where he kept an audience spellbound for more than two hours.[61] In late 1938 he talked the president of a corporation into giving 4 percent of his net earnings from the business to his employees, and Sheen himself made the distribution of the funds on the night before Christmas Eve.[62] In March 1939 he introduced an NBC program on the coronation of Pius XII.[63] The following month he was in Nashville, Tennessee, lecturing before the Nashville Diocesan Council of the National Council of Catholic Women.[64] He gave the baccalaureate address in 1939 to the University of Illinois.[65] That summer, he traveled to France, Belgium and Rome with several relatives and his secretary, and had a private audience with the Pope.[66] On March 24, 1940, he was the preacher for the first Catholic television program in the world, broadcast from the NBC studios in New York.[67] And at the same time, he was making headlines with his sermons at St. Patrick's Cathedral and his speeches on the Spanish Civil War. Adding to his activities, Fulton served as treasurer of the American Catholic Philosophical Association and national chaplain for the Ancient Order of Hibernians.[68]

In 1937, Sheen asked his ten-year-old niece, Joan Sheen, his brother Joe's oldest daughter, to come to New York and be his companion. Fulton was close to Joe and his family. Joan adored her uncle, and Fulton greatly enjoyed being around the bright young girl. He paid for her schooling in New York (later paying her way through Rosemont College), and she joined him on the weekends. She attended all of his radio broadcasts and traveled with him during the summers. Joan would remember in particular a trip to California when she was twelve, staying with actress Irene Dunne and attending a dinner party given by movie star Loretta Young. She often made the arrangements for dinner parties following clergy retreats.

Joan later acknowledged that it might have seemed odd to some for a young girl to be traveling with the famous priest, but people accepted her warmly and she had a splendid time. Joan Sheen, later Mrs. Jerry Cunningham, would enjoy a close relationship with Fulton for the rest of his life. "Family members will tell you that he was my second father," she said. And through all the decades she loved him dearly.[69]

Despite the adulation of millions, the frenzied trips, the ceaseless activity, the countless invitations to dinners, parties and rallies, there was in Fulton Sheen a quiet loneliness that may well account for his desire to have Joan (and later a second niece) with him. He had no intimate friends, not even his brother Tom, who lived in New York and might have been consulted regularly. Later, Fulton's youngest brother, Al, also worked in New York, but the relationship between the two men was never close.

A very few familiars, mostly clergy, sensed Fulton's loneliness. Yet his own personality, his tendency to keep aloof, increased his isolation. "I don't think he ever knew my first name," said a priest long associated with him in the media.[70] Fr. John Tracy Ellis, who lived with Sheen for three years and served as his secretary, recalled, "We were never what one might call close friends, even if our relationship was never other than cordial."[71] Sheen assistant D. P. Noonan wrote, "Sheen can be charming, sympathetic, brilliant, beguiling, entertaining, and companionable; also reserved, private, extremely opinionated, and unable really to reveal himself to anybody."[72] While to most people Fulton Sheen was gregarious, loveable, kind and generous beyond expectation, a few, generally priests and intellectuals, thought him rather odd, mysterious, even irritating.

There was a sense of otherness in Fulton's mental landscape that produced his loneliness. This feeling of distance from other people had at least three causes. The first was his intellectual prowess. Having a brilliant mind and an excellent education would set anyone apart, of course. However much Sheen went out of his way to empathize with the great majority of his fellow citizens, he was made constantly, and quite naturally, aware of the superiority of his intellect and knowledge. He could talk about issues and people, ancient and modern, and about the deepest questions of mankind, which to him meant everything, with only a handful of people. This was as true when he was thirty-four as eighty-four years of age. How many, after all, enjoyed reading Thomas Aquinas in Latin, studying Hegel in bed late at night, and delving deeply into science, psychology and history, as well as philosophy and theology?

Being in New York regularly was obviously easier for an intellectual of his caliber than being in, say, Oklahoma City, but the nature of his education and his interests sealed off many avenues of communication. How many of the leading Gotham intellectuals could share Sheen's enthusiasm toward medieval Catholicism, his convictions about loyalty to the Magisterium of the Church, his admiration for the Spanish Nationalists, and (perhaps above all) his stern views on personal morality? He could have found scholars with his interests at Catholic University, but, for reasons that defy complete explanation, he did not grow very close to any of them—not his old friend Charles Hart, not his fellow philosophers and theologians, not even the professors who lived in the same house. Sheen was always extraordinarily friendly and kind, but you were never permitted to be his pal, and almost never able to enter into his inner self. Part of that barrier was created by his extraordinary intellect and learning.

When talking with average men and women, as well as children, Sheen would try to seek in them some store of information he knew little or nothing about and would steer the conversation in that direction. Longtime friend Yolanda Holliger remarked that Sheen did not want to overwhelm people with his brilliance. People invariably came away with the impression that he cared about them, and he did.[73]

This was sometimes not the case with clergy, however, especially as Fulton grew older. A priest observed that he had great difficulty engaging in small talk. At lunch with seminary students, for example, he would sit quietly as though utterly detached, and when called upon, he would quickly begin to orate.[74] As D. P. Noonan put it, "He believed in monologue, not dialogue."[75] A great many popular topics bored him. Matthew R. Paratore, who knew Sheen in his later years, recalled how you could watch his eyes wander if he thought you were saying something you really didn't understand— "He could cut you off cold." But when you made a point that intrigued him, those penetrating eyes would seem to grasp you. "Yes," he would say, and the discussion could continue. In Paratore's view, Sheen was an introvert, an intuitive type who spent most of his time in private—praying, studying, writing, preparing for the next challenge—and was probably never truly close to another person. As with St. John of the Cross, Fulton's battles were waged within himself. And they were not on display.[76]

Part of the interior struggle also involved celibacy. As he admitted throughout his life, celibacy was a tremendous burden for him to bear. In *The Way of the Cross* (1932), he wrote of the temptation "to give way to the demands of my lower nature when the spirit should have been served." His prayer when faced with "the promptings of the flesh" was: "When my frame rocks beneath the power of Satan, and my flesh is buffeted by the tempter, seal my senses and keep me mindful that my body is a temple of the Holy Ghost, and that only the clean of heart shall see Thee, O God!"[77]

Twenty years later, in *Three to Get Married*, Sheen said that the Holy Eucharist, "which is the Body of Christ, when worthily received, does diminish the uprisings of concupiscence. There is not the hardship imposed on a celibate priest that the sex-world would imagine, for, given power over the Physical Body of Christ, he already has the cure for the rebellion of his own physical body."[78] Seventeen years after that, in a television interview with Mike Wallace, Sheen said, "Celibacy is not an easy thing. I can see why a man wants to marry. Celibacy is a gift.... And it's always hard, it's always a wrestling. And there will be some who stumble." People were divided into two classes: "there are pigs and there are sheep. Pigs fall into the mud, they stay there. Sheep fall into the mud, they get out. They wrestle with the problem."[79]

In his autobiography, written in his eighties, Sheen said that "The preservation of celibacy is a lifelong labor, partly because of the weakness of human nature." Celibates, he wrote, are the ones who best understand the weakness of fornicators. "We priests who have never broken our vow of celibacy are often attacked on the ground: 'It is very easy for you; you are not tempted.' It is just the contrary that is true. The celibate is tempted perhaps more than anyone else." And when the priest is famous, "the keeping up of a love affair with the invisible love of Christ is a real battle."[80]

Deprived of the intimate love of a woman, Fulton dove deeper into the faith, drawing closer to Jesus and the Blessed Virgin Mary ("Despite the unglutted beast that strains in the body of every priest, she held onto the leash to tame its madness"),[81] praying constantly for the grace to be faithful to his priestly calling, pouring the tremendous energy that might have been spent in part on wife and family into his work. That was, after all, the major point of clerical celibacy. Sheen wrote in *These Are the Sacraments,* "Our Lord wished to have a group of men who would have the freedom to give full time to His service; hence He ordained in order that they who served the altar were to live by the altar. Celibacy in the Latin Rite stresses this quality of total dedication." Still, he felt the loneliness that is often the price of celibacy.[82]

Of the seven women who were closest to Fulton during his lifetime, excluding his mother, two were his personal secretaries, one was a nun, one was his most treasured convert, and three were relatives: Margaret Yates, Edythe Brownett, Marlene Brownett, Clare

Boothe Luce, Mary Fulton Carr (Baker), Joan Sheen (Cunningham), and Eileen Sheen (Khouw). Joan Sheen was a welcome addition to Fulton's life; he enjoyed her company and she was a constant reminder of the happy family he left behind in central Illinois. In a way, too, she was the daughter he could never have.

In a chapter devoted to the subject of loneliness in *Footprints in a Darkened Forest*, Fulton wrote eloquently about the loneliness of Christ on the cross, and argued that it was inevitable for the serious Christian. "Loneliness is indigenous to our state of life here below, partly because we are pilgrims on a journey to a Promised Land, partly because complete happiness is impossible here below, partly because, like young people who do not come into an inheritance until they reach majority, we do not attain fortune until death has intervened. As Augustine said: 'Our hearts were made for Thee, O lord, and they are restless until they rest in Thee.'" The command of the gospel is clear: Be ye not of this world. That seems like folly and superstition to most—except to the serious Christian, who lives on "alien soil."[83]

Then too, Fulton Sheen was an exceptionally otherworldly person, and such people can often seem distant, for at times they are listening to Someone Else. Sheen believed that miracles graced his life, and that he possessed (as we shall see) extraordinary powers of spiritual discernment. His daily Holy Hour before the Blessed Sacrament, he said, "became like an oxygen tank to revive the breath of the Holy Spirit in the midst of the foul and fetid atmosphere of the world." It was "the Hour that makes Life."[84]

Sheen was a man of deep prayer, who believed that "Neither theological knowledge nor social action alone is enough to keep us in love with Christ unless both are preceded by a personal encounter with Him."[85] It was He who occupied much of that inner space in Fulton Sheen's life which others could not touch. The great Christian saints can often seem odd and distant, for they perceive the invisible warfare taking place in the world. They give themselves, in extraordinary ways, to the One who calls them, nourishes them daily, and sends them on their often lonely, often painful, seemingly unrewarding journeys through life.

From Sheen's writings, we learn that he was aware of the alienation and loneliness that a few others saw in him, but understood this condition to be inevitable, and something shared with his dying Savior, his fellow priests, and untold millions of devout Christians. He did not dwell at length on the subject, perhaps because it might lead to self-pity, which he abhorred. Besides, there was too much work to do, and there were many other thoughts that occupied his mind in the mid and late 1930s, including his career in the Church.

IN SEPTEMBER 1938, the media began mentioning Fulton Sheen as a possible successor to the recently deceased Patrick Cardinal Hayes as archbishop of New York. While Sheen was a nationally known figure and well connected in Rome, his elevation to such an exalted post was unrealistic. New York was the world's largest diocese; Fulton was a monsignor in his early forties. His vanity was such, however, that he took the reports seriously, and so was crushed the following April when Pius XII appointed Bishop Francis J. Spellman to the post. On the day of the announcement, Fulton had lunch with Fr. John Tracy Ellis, who recalled: "Leaning his arm on the table with his head in his hand, he exclaimed, 'It is incredible. It is incredible. He has nothing.' So deeply dejected was he that he took to his bed and remained there for several days."[86]

Later, Sheen and Spellman were to cross swords, becoming bitter rivals for the role of America's most influential Catholic. It is instructive to learn from a personal friend that Sheen's quiet scorn for Spellman preceded the struggle by almost two decades. While Fr. Ellis revealed no details of Sheen's negative evaluation, the reasons surely included the new archbishop's lack of any great academic distinction and his limited public speaking skills. Spellman was weak precisely where Sheen was strong. The reverse was also true, yet Spellman's outstanding administrative ability and political skills were not likely to impress "America's Chesterton." In academia and in the Church, Sheen had never stood in awe of bureaucrats.

Ellis, who later became a distinguished Catholic historian, thought highly of Sheen. "I admired his priestliness—I was a witness to his daily Mass and holy hour, to name only two features of his prayer life—and I was impressed as well by his steady work habits, his reading, his love and zeal for the Church and ... his genuine thoughtfulness for those around him of whatever station in life," wrote Ellis. He noticed that when a topic arose over which the two of them differed, Sheen would politely change the subject.[87]

Ellis also was a witness to Sheen's extraordinary generosity. In late 1938, Mrs. William J. Babington Macaulay died in Rome. Extremely wealthy, she was a papal duchess widely admired for her gifts to the Church. Sheen, who preached at her Requiem Mass at St. Patrick's Cathedral, was among those named in her will, receiving what was then the princely sum of $68,824.[88] (Spellman, who received the same amount, listed it in his diary as $100,000.)[89] Sheen and Mrs. Macaulay, also known as Duchess Brady (her late husband was Nicholas Brady, an American public utilities magnate), had met at Lourdes and become friends.[90] In 1936, Fulton had introduced her to Cardinal Pacelli, later Pius XII.[91] For the last seven years of her life, Mrs. Macaulay, at Fulton's prompting, had observed a daily Holy Hour.[92]

Sheen spent his inheritance within a week, sending most of it to the Diocese of Alabama to help the Sisters of Mercy build the Martin de Porres Hospital, a small maternity hospital for black mothers in racially segregated Mobile. It was, in the words of the local archbishop, T. J. Toolen, "the only hospital in the city for colored and is very much appreciated by them."[93] Sheen was inspired to make the gift by his African-American housekeeper and cook, Mrs. Fanny Washington, for whom he had great affection. (When she converted in 1950, Sheen sent a car to bring her from Washington to New York, and he proudly presided at the service in St. Patrick's Cathedral.)[94]

Sheen also sent money to the Immaculate Heart of Mary Mission church at Hillview, Alabama, which opened in 1941.[95] Sheen funds went to build chapels and trailer chapels in North Carolina and Texas.[96] In 1942, upon receiving an invitation from a black woman, Sheen traveled to a small town in North Carolina and offered a mission on the steps of the public school. He apparently also left a donation that resulted in a church being constructed on the main street. A year later, at the request of a non-Catholic in a small town near Birmingham, Fulton traveled with a priest in a trailer through the state of Alabama, "talking on road corners and in cornfields to anyone who would listen." The week-long tour concluded with a giant rally on the grounds of the Blessed Sacrament Church in Mobile.[97]

For many years thereafter, Sheen sent book royalties and speaker's fees to Alabama, and encouraged friends to do likewise. The small maternity hospital he founded blossomed into a much larger facility that opened in 1950 at a cost of $600,000, most of it donated or raised by Sheen. He and Archbishop Toolen were on hand for the dedication.[98]

Living in Sheen's home, John Tracy Ellis got to know and admire Fulton's secretary, Margaret May Yates. Born in 1913, the daughter of English immigrants, "May," as she was known, was raised in Massachusetts and graduated in 1933 from Regis College in Weston, Massachusetts. She was hired by Sheen later that year and stayed with him for twenty-one years until her marriage. Several times she accompanied him on his European journeys.[99] Described by a cousin, Anne Charnley, as "pretty, elegant and single," Yates was totally devoted to her employer.[100] Charnley herself enjoyed "hanging around" the office in Sheen's house and remembered him as relaxed, "lovely, friendly and very funny," as well as "a great mimic." Still, as May said, "he was always a priest," wearing his clerical apparel at virtually all times and exuding a dignity and a sanctity that were unmistakable. The Blessed Sacrament was reserved in his home, by special permission granted by the Vatican, and Mass was said daily.[101]

Mary Dunn had similar memories of her boss, saying that he could be extremely amusing, and he was "a brilliant actor." He would sometimes do an excellent Charlie Chaplain imitation for the secretaries, complete with the famous walk and gestures. The women, invited daily to join Sheen for a tea and candy break, delighted in his company.[102]

During the war, May Yates arranged for her cousin Dorothy Farmer to join the staff. She handled secretarial duties for a few years before leaving, at Fulton's suggestion, to work for Clare Boothe Luce. Farmer enjoyed Sheen as much as Yates, especially for his sense of humor. Anne Charnley more than once saw Farmer on the telephone with her employer, "screaming in laughter."[103]

John Tracy Ellis fully appreciated Sheen's virtues, but he grew impatient with his vanity. One feature of it was particularly irritating: He would read his next Sunday's sermon aloud at the table. Trying tactfully to stop this practice, Ellis brought a book of poetry to lunch one day and asked Fulton to tell him which selection he thought appropriate to end a sermon he was preparing. Fulton got the point, and the practice of mealtime sermonizing ended.

And then there was his passion for wearing purple. When Cardinal Mundelein of Chicago died in October 1939, Sheen's name again appeared in the press as a possible successor. This time, however, Fulton showed no interest. Ellis remarked, "Mention New York and the big expressive eyes gleamed; mention Chicago and they revealed something akin to boredom."[104] Fulton's ambition had outgrown his native Midwest.

In 1938, Sheen began planning a new home, to be constructed in fashionable Wesley Heights, near American University and the National Cathedral, and two blocks from the house he shared with Ellis. For $8,000 he purchased a large lot situated at the end of Hawthorne Lane, a dead-end street, along Foxhall Road, an upper-middle-class neighborhood featuring lovely homes. (The deed contained a clause explicitly excluding blacks, Jews, Armenians, Persians and Syrians—a common clause in land deeds for similar properties at the time.)[105] Plans for the home were designed by the head of the Catholic University School of Architecture, Frederick Vernon Murphy, who had a long list of distinguished buildings and homes on his resumé.[106] (Murphy's wife recalled that when her husband presented the bill to Sheen, the priest took offense, having assumed that the architectural plans were done for free.)[107] The 4,000-square-foot home cost $35,000 to build and another $30,000 to air condition—the latter being an unusual luxury at the time.[108]

While financial records are lacking, it appears that book royalties and speaking fees were the likely source of the funds required to build Sheen's home. He had published twenty books by 1940, and many of his speaking engagements—100 to 150 a year—undoubtedly involved stipends. In 1953, his lecture fees ran as high as $2,500, and were rumored on several occasions to have hit $5,000, but by then he was a television star.[109]

Catholic Hour listeners often sent gifts to Sheen. Some sent cash, as we have seen, but it would have been entirely out of character for him to use it selfishly. In 1951, he stated that "every cent I received while on the Catholic Hour was always turned over for the past twenty years to the National Council of Catholic Men."[110] That wasn't literally true, as much if not all of the cash that arrived at his home through the mail was sent to the needy; but that discrepancy seems unimportant. Other radio listeners, however, sent jewelry. Fulton had a Jewish friend, Herbert Trigger, who bought those goods from him and, according to Joan Sheen, always paid her uncle more than their worth. The proceeds went into the monsignor's pocket and were distributed to those who asked for help.[111] Donations often appeared when least expected: a nephew recalled seeing people stuff money into Sheen's coat pockets as he walked through a Chicago hotel.[112]

One wealthy Sheen convert, Mrs. Elisabeth Cobb Rogers, was scandalized by Fulton's cavalier attitude toward money, noting that he would give away anything he had and then sometimes find himself pressed for funds.[113] To the pleas of people who urged him to be more prudent he would respond, "God replaces whatever is given away in time or energy or money."[114] Sheen said in his autobiography that he "never liked money and gave it away as soon as I received it."[115] In an early book he wrote, "Our shrouds will have no pockets."[116] Elsewhere he described "the beautiful doctrine of detachment, by which men free themselves from the passion of wealth for the glory of God and the salvation of souls—even though that wealth is only their own will and a few fishing boats and tangled nets."[117]

On the other hand, the new two-story house at 4646 Hawthorne Lane, completed in 1941, did not exactly seem to represent apostolic poverty. (It sold for $1,150,000 in 1999.) The stunning house was ultramodern, standing clearly apart from the more traditional homes on the same block. Some thought it belonged in Beverly Hills rather than suburban Washington, and one wag called it Sheen's "Hollywood fantasy." Made of white brick, it had a spectacular white circling staircase, from the basement to the second floor, which could be seen through windows from the street. On the other side of the house, large windows looked out over the big, sloping, wooded back yard. The interior of the house was filled with mirrors, including one on the basement level of the staircase. The color scheme throughout was dark red and dark green. Sheen's private chapel, where he said Mass daily, was on the first floor, and the second floor had a recording studio. There was piped-in music all through the house. Sheen did his serious writing in a basement study piled high with books, working on a desk that consisted of a large plank balanced on two sawhorses. Later in the day, he would work in his study on the second floor.[118]

Two of the three bedrooms were occupied by fellow Catholic University professors who paid rent. (Ellis decided to avoid the six-mile commute and live on campus.) Father Patrick Skehan was an assistant professor of Semitic languages, and Father William J. McDonald was in the philosophy department. Three dogs soon rounded out the household: an English setter named Lord Cholomondeley (pronounced "Chumley"), a white Pyrenees who went by the name of Siotcain, which is Gaelic for Sheen (and pronounced "Seehawn"), and a St. Bernard called St. Bernard of Menthon.[119]

Fulton belonged to Washington's Columbia Country Club and played tennis twice a week with a professional. He always drove a new black Cadillac (donated by a Washington car dealer).[120] So did his secretary, May Yates. He had a cook and a gardener.[121] Later he would also have a houseboy who doubled as his driver and did odd jobs. Mary Dunn, who did secretarial work at the house, said that Sheen lived "in extravagance."[122]

The anomaly of the saint living in splendor escaped Fulton until his old age, when, looking back, he deeply regretted his many concessions to comfort. Others, of course, saw it at the time. Journalists described the new home in detail, sometimes with a whiff of disapproval. We can only imagine the jealousy that welled up within Sheen's colleagues at Catholic University. They, after all, were devoting their lives to the campus, and being paid very little for their efforts. Twenty years after Fulton's death, and nearly half a century after he moved from Hawthorne Lane, neighbors still clucked about the fancy cars and beautiful women (no doubt referring to Yates, celebrity guests, and an assortment of converts) they saw coming and going from the monsignor's home.[123]

Yet it was also true that at the time, cardinals, archbishops and bishops often lived in luxurious quarters and traveled by chauffeured limousine. In the depths of the Depression, for example, Philadelphia's Dennis Cardinal Dougherty paid $115,000 for an estate featuring sixteen rooms, five baths, a pool, a stable, a six-car garage, and magnificent grounds. The cardinal spent another $100,000 improving the structure and adding rooms.[124] So perhaps, in Fulton's eyes at least, it was fitting that one of the Church's major spokesmen in America should own an extraordinary home and drive a Cadillac.

Still, such a lifestyle did little to encourage the selflessness central to Christian teaching and to Fulton's own preaching, and it clashed sharply with the humble ways other priests and monsignors kept. The luxurious living of these years stands as a curious contradiction in Fulton's character, a surrender to pride and worldliness that later evoked personal shame and public confession. Perhaps his prodigal giving was an unconscious device allowing him to justify his equally prodigal self-indulgence.

Sheen's opulence was beyond even the hope of the millions of ordinary men and women who were emerging from the ravages of the Great Depression, only to find that the United States was rushing down a path that seemed certain to involve all Americans in the horrors of the Second World War.

FIVE

The Loss of God,
the Beginning of Tyranny

A keen student of Communist literature and history, Sheen was not deceived by the Popular Front of 1935. He spoke and wrote often about the Reds, then garbed in their liberal, pro-FDR costume, and not just in the context of the Spanish Civil War. In a Lenten sermon at St. Patrick's Cathedral in 1936, he asked, "Why can't the modern mind see there is nothing new in communism? It is a groan of despair, not the revolution that starts a new age. It is the logical development of civilization which for the last 400 years has been forgetting God." To Sheen, communism was the "new slavery" that "takes possession not only of the body, the labor and the private property of man but also of his soul."[1]

That same year, Fulton attacked Earl Browder, general secretary of the Communist Party USA (who soon sought to make a speech at Catholic University in reply). Calling attention to the 1935 and 1936 proceedings of the Communist Party in Moscow, Sheen charged that the Soviets were using the "disguised approach" to take over countries by working from within labor unions, peace societies, and antifascist organizations. "The tactics are the same whether it is called abroad the United Front or the Popular Front or in this country the Farmer-Labor party."[2] On another occasion, Sheen quoted from the official program of the Third International, calling attention to such terms as "revolution," "forcible" and "suppression of resistance," and characterizing the Communist effort to identify with the farmer, the laborer and the man in the bread line as "deceit" and "humbug."[3] He told one audience that Catholics "must go down to the poor and the unemployed and build up as

strong a Christian proletariat as they would a Communist proletariat.... Communism leaves nothing in the soul of man but hate.
The poor are our blessed heritage from Christ, who first championed their cause; and we must keep them."[4]

Sheen published five anticommunist pamphlets in 1936–37 and
spoke on the subject several times on the radio. The *Catholic Hour*
programs addressing the issue of communism were popular. The
executive secretary of the National Council of Catholic Men did a
mass mailing throughout the country, calling attention to a Sheen
series on "the fundamental philosophy that is common to Nazism,
Communism, and Fascism." The letters were used to expand station coverage of the *Catholic Hour*.[5]

In early 1938, a self-described "liberal-minded American" from
Massachusetts strongly objected to Sheen's negative description of
communism on the radio, and sent a copy of his complaint to the
Federal Communications Commission. The Communist Party was
a legal entity, he pointed out, and in his judgment was far more just
and more truly religious than its vilifiers, who included Hitler and
Mussolini. Sheen responded in a public letter, quoting chapter and
verse of the Soviet constitution to buttress his account of Communist teachings and practice. He added that he kept careful track
of Communist activity. "I am a subscriber and faithful reader of the
Daily Worker, the *Communist*, the *Communist International*, the
International Press Correspondence, and the *Moscow Daily News*,
besides hundreds of Marxist publications emanating from International Publishers of New York and Moscow." He chided his
attacker for relying on less authoritative sources. "I am not surprised that you believe in the achievements of Russia if your reading is limited to the *New York Times* and *The Nation*."[6]

A short time later, in a *Catholic Hour* broadcast, Sheen argued
that the best way to keep fascism out of American life was to keep
out communism. He spoke of "Americanism," a vaguely defined
staple of Catholic as well as Protestant patriotic rhetoric, tied to the
"sacred" rights and liberties of man as recognized by the Founding
Fathers in the Constitution. And who was doing the most to protect

Americanism? asked Sheen. "The schools that never mention His name? The universities and colleges that dissolve the Deity into the latest ultimate of physics or biology? The professors who adjust their ethics to suit unethical lives?"[7]

These and similar questions would soon be asked by members of Congress. In 1938, by a vote of 191 to 41, the House created the Special Committee on Un-American Activities, headed by right-wing Texas Democrat Martin Dies. The Dies Committee would soon be charging that 1,121 government workers were "sympathetic with totalitarian ideology" and alleging that the Roosevelt administration was "soft" on Russia. Headlines about Reds in high places were commonplace in the daily press. Millions were concerned about communism.

While there was nothing wrong in acknowledging communism for what it was, or for that matter objecting to Communist teachers (a defensible position on the ground that such teachers did not possess an open mind and were by definition subversives), Sheen's sweeping generalities about schools and professors were inadvertently lending credence to the cynical politicians, hucksters and fanatics who were setting the stage for a second Red Scare. Sheen continued this type of attack during and after the war.[8]

In March of 1939, Sheen was greatly encouraged when his friend Eugenio Cardinal Pacelli became Pope Pius XII. Speaking to a nationwide audience from the pulpit of St. Patrick's Cathedral, he called the Pope "the only unified moral voice left on earth."[9]

Bishop Francis Spellman of Boston was no doubt even more elated. The grandson of Irish immigrants and son of a grocer from Whitman, Massachusetts, he had taken a degree at Fordham and earned the S.T.D. at the North American College in Rome. In 1925, after several productive years in the Archdiocese of Boston (where he was disliked and ignored by his superior, William Henry Cardinal O'Connell), Spellman used Roman connections to return to the Eternal City as an attaché to the Secretariat of State at the Vatican— the first American to serve on the Secretariat. Here he began his own friendship with Pacelli, soon to be named a cardinal.

Spellman was ambitious and adroit, working his way up the ladder of Church politics through hard work and a network of friends. He became a papal chamberlain in 1926 and a domestic prelate (a top-ranked monsignor) three years later. By 1931, he was a trusted Vatican official, handling sensitive matters in the struggles with Mussolini. That same year, Pacelli asked Spellman to translate the Pope's first international radio address for the English-speaking press and to go on the radio himself to deliver a digest of the talk for Americans. For the first time, Spellman was well known in his own country.[10]

Spellman served Pacelli as his assistant, traveling companion, and translator. Pacelli admired the younger man's energy, efficiency, cleverness, and informality. Spellman had great regard for the secretary of state's aristocratic dignity, sophistication and learning. He was also attracted by Pacelli's power, and by the idea, in many minds, that Pacelli was headed for the papacy.[11]

In 1932, Pacelli consecrated Spellman the auxiliary bishop of Boston at a splendid ceremony in St. Peter's Basilica in Rome. Pacelli loaned Spellman his personal vestments for the service and presented him with an episcopal ring "containing a magnificent sapphire surrounded by diamonds with a fragment of the True Cross set in gold."[12] Spellman was the first American to receive episcopal consecration at St. Peter's.

Four years later, Spellman escorted the Vatican secretary of state on a month-long tour across the United States that included dinner with newly reelected President Roosevelt. A friendship soon blossomed between the bishop and the president, both adept politicians seeing something in each other worth cultivating. In 1939, being close to both the president and the Pope made the aspiring cleric almost giddy.[13]

Spellman's appointment as archbishop of New York and military vicar of the United States Armed Forces quickly followed. President Roosevelt said, in an unctuous handwritten letter, "Do I have to tell you that very rarely have I been made so happy as when the announcement of your elevation to the Archbishopric came? It was what I had so hoped for, yes, and prayed for—and now best of all you will be near me in New York when I retire from Washington."[14] The Catholic vote, after all, was an important ingredient in the New Deal coalition.

Spellman was involved in the president's decision, announced on Christmas Eve, 1939, to send a personal representative, Episcopalian businessman Myron Taylor, to the Vatican. The appointment was designed to provide the administration with an important European listening post, but it had political repercussions.[15] The Protestant response was overwhelmingly negative. Scores of editorials, articles, and official statements condemned the move as a mingling of church and state. A Lutheran leader labeled the appointment "un-American."[16] (In fact, as Spellman pointed out, this was the eighth time the United States had sent a representative to the Vatican.) Fulton Sheen, however, sent a telegram to Roosevelt calling the appointment "the first concrete recognition any great nation in modern times has given to the spiritual and moral foundations of peace," and he often and eloquently defended the president's action.[17]

The new Pope, Pius XII, had studied Marx, had seen Germany repel a Communist takeover during the Weimar Republic, and was fully aware of the violence that Bolsheviks had wreaked on both Catholic and Orthodox Christians. Having served ten years as nuncio to Germany, and being a devotee of the German culture and language, the Pope also understood the evil that Hitler represented. Pius XII was not sympathetic toward the Nazis, but he feared the Soviets more. Above all, he was concerned with preserving the Church. (Myron Taylor's assistant concluded that the Vatican regarded the militant atheism of communism as "more obnoxious than [Germany's] modern paganism.")[18] Perhaps, Pius XII thought, he could come to an agreement with Mussolini and Hitler about religious practice, and both were vital in stopping Communist expansion.

His predecessor, Pius XI, had issued an encyclical in 1937 that said: "Whoever exalts race, or the people, or the State . . . above their standard value and divinizes them to an idolatrous level, distorts and perverts an order of the world planned and created by God." Pius XII himself, in October 1939, declared that "Whoever considers the State to be the end toward which all is directed and all must bow is of necessity an enemy and an obstacle to all true and lasting progress among the nations." Both encyclicals were aimed at the Nazis, who were harassing clergy and closing Catholic schools and seminaries. Still, the thought of what Communists would do to Catholics if they swept through Europe kept Pius XII from issuing stronger encyclicals and excommunications against fascists.

When Pacelli was still the Vatican's secretary of state, Sheen had spent more than an hour with him in Rome discussing world affairs. Pacelli spoke "with considerable vehemence against Hitler and Nazism," Sheen later recalled. The two met again when Pacelli visited the United States, and then once more at a dinner party in Rome hosted by Duchess Brady.[19] As noted earlier, Fulton sent his publications to Pacelli, and warm letters were exchanged on several occasions. It was clear to a nephew of Sheen's, who saw the two men emerge from a private session in 1939, that they greatly enjoyed each other's company.[20]

Beginning in 1939, Sheen would have a private audience with the Pontiff annually. For the first dozen years, Fulton talked with Pius XII about the subjects he was to discuss on the following year's radio programs. During one audience, the Pope rose and began reading a paper in his own handwriting. Sheen later reported: "Humility forbids me to reveal all that he said about my being a 'prophet of the times' and that 'you will have a high place in Heaven.' Nothing that he said was infallible, of course, but his words gave me much consolation."[21]

Not surprisingly, Sheen's positions on world affairs in 1939 were almost identical to the Pope's. Foremost in his mind was the preservation of the Church, but he was also intensely interested in the preservation of American democracy and freedom. In March 1939, Sheen expressed his belief in the possibility of a union between Nazism and communism (although in 1937, Germany, Japan and Italy had signed the Anti-Comintern Pact, a pledge of mutual support against the Russians). They were united, he said from the pulpit of St. Patrick's Cathedral, in their common hatred of God.[22] That summer he again warned of a Soviet-Nazi peace pact. "There is not a vast difference between them. What class is to Russia, race is to Germany, what the bourgeois are to the Russians, the Jews are to the Germans."[23]

Another possibility was a marriage of convenience between the democracies and the Soviets against Nazi Germany, a prospect Sheen deplored in his Easter sermon: "When the democracies of the world summon to their aid an anti-God nation to help them combat an anti-religious nation, thoughtful men must ask themselves the question: 'If the democracies summon red devils to fight brown devils, how can we be sure that democracy is on the side of the angels and fighting the battle of God?' "[24]

Soon Fulton again fanned the fires of an anticommunist passion that seemed on the verge of breaking out across America. Citing primary Soviet sources, he called attention to the Popular Front and its tactics of "boring secretly from within." Communists, he said, "are urged to wheel their Trojan Horse into our labor unions, religious organizations, political parties, athletic associations under the guise of a peaceful United Front, until they can tear off their mask and throw this country into a barbarous Civil War such as they instigated in Spain, so that they may emerge victorious and thus honor their beloved Comrade Stalin."[25]

Speaking before a convention of 3,150 Catholic teachers of the Diocese of Brooklyn, Sheen proposed the creation of a "central clearing house" to which Catholic, Protestant, and Jewish teachers of New York could send the names of colleagues "who send out their children to a Communist parade, or who turn over their classrooms to some member of a Communist organization, or a Nazi or Fascist organization." He wanted all such public school teachers fired. "Just watch the parade and see if you can recognize any children from their classrooms. Find out who sent them there, who organized them, and if they are drawing their pay from American people, then they have the solemn obligation to keep our schools American."[26]

In May, Sheen was one of several Catholic leaders who called for a boycott of the New York World's Fair because the $4 million marble, granite, and steel Soviet Pavilion featured a tall shaft topped by a heroic Russian worker holding aloft a red star. Sheen declared that no American should attend the fair "until the American flag is placed above that of communism."[27] When the Nazis and Soviets signed a nonaggression pact on August 24, as Sheen had predicted, and then began carving up Poland, the Soviet Pavilion at the fair quickly canceled an anti-Nazi film it had been showing and substituted one about Lenin.[28] In December, now busily devouring Finland, Russia pulled out of the fair altogether.[29] The *New York Times* editorialized, "After their work is done in Finland the Soviets will find, among other things, that they have earned the lasting distrust and contempt of the American people."[30]

Much of the world was now at war, and the Soviets and the Nazis were allies. (Italy entered the war on June 10, 1940.) When Sheen visited Pius XII, the Pope asked him if he was surprised by the Communist-fascist pact. No, said Fulton, he was not. "I'm glad you are not surprised," Sheen quoted the Pope as saying. "Anyone who knows the philosophy of these movements knew they were bound to unite. I expected it for a long time, but it is a very grave danger to the world. But we shall have peace."[31] The Vatican remained officially neutral throughout the war, Pius XII working and pleading constantly for an end to the hostilities.

Congress had passed neutrality acts in 1935, 1936 and 1937, and while the last favored the British, the mood in the United States was overwhelmingly in favor of isolationism. President Roosevelt, who saw beyond this parochialism, could do little to defeat it. When Germans marched into Poland, and France and England declared war, he sighed, "God help us all."

American Catholics chose isolationism or interventionism in part according to ethnic origins. The Irish, with their anti-British prejudice, tended toward isolationism.[32] Most American bishops opposed intervention, and in general so did the Catholic press. This was Sheen's inclination.[33] But he spoke more often about the Red menace he saw looming at home and abroad. In April 1940, he said that the Soviet attack on Finland "revealed the true character of the Moscow Reds." Russia is dead, he declared, "like a falling man who has already passed the 17th floor of a skyscraper. Actually, he is still alive, but the principle of death is in him."[34]

In May, Sheen returned to the New York World's Fair, now without a Soviet exhibit. Speaking at the Temple of Religion before an audience of 2,500—including Governor Herbert Lehman and Mayor Fiorello La Guardia of New York—and over a major radio station, he expressed delight that "the forces of anti-God and slavery have been removed from our midst," and proceeded to lecture on freedom under God (the title of a book he was publishing later that year, based on his *Catholic Hour* addresses).[35] He repeated a familiar theme that expressed his contempt for both "isms" wreaking havoc in the world, and pointed to the source, in his judgment, of their malignancy:

> *The anti-God regime is always the anti-human regime. What more clearly proves it than the Red Fascism of Communism and the Brown Fascism of Nazism which, by denying the spirit of God as the source of human rights, make the State the source? But if the State is the giver of rights then the State can take them away. It is ever true that the loss of God is the beginning of all tyranny.*

The editor of *The Tablet* called the speech "truly great," adding that "The fine militant style of the Monsignor, combining heat with light, was interrupted time and again with tremendous applause."[36]

୶

EARLY IN 1940, Sheen told the congregation at St. Patrick's Cathedral that his personal correspondence had now reached an average of six thousand letters a day, many from people seeking information about the Catholic Church. He announced that he would give personal instruction to all who requested it.[37]

A short time later, Fulton was hospitalized with a severe case of the flu. (He preached a sermon at St. Patrick's Cathedral with a temperature of 102, and that evening, against the advice of his physician, did his *Catholic Hour* broadcast.)[38] In the following year, he was again hospitalized for overwork.[39] But in neither case was he down for long. There were sermons and books to be written, broadcasts to be prepared, students and converts to teach.

Henry Ford II was one of Sheen's most celebrated converts. He was twenty-three, fresh out of Yale University, and a Methodist who wanted to marry Anne McDonnell, a member of a prominent New York Irish family.[40] According to D. P. Noonan, Sheen later said that "The inspiration was certainly Anne McDonnell. But Henry was a religious man in his own way." When it became known that he was being instructed by Sheen, Ford received a lot of mail "telling him what a terrible thing he was doing."[41]

Sheen presided at the wedding service on July 13, 1940, before more than five hundred people described by the *New York Times* as "a distinguished gathering," crowded into a New York church. (Kathleen Kennedy, one of the daughters of then Ambassador Joseph P. Kennedy, was a bridesmaid.) A choir led by the musical director of St. Patrick's Cathedral performed classical selections. Seventy-nine-year-old auto magnate Henry Ford I, who had thought seriously about disinheriting his son for becoming a Catholic, danced with the bride during a lavish reception. The young couple received almost a million dollars' worth of wedding presents. The union had the blessing of Pius XII.[42]

On Good Friday of 1940, movie star Loretta Young and actor John Wayne's wife, Josephine, went to St. Patrick's Cathedral to see and hear Msgr. Sheen. Young, a cradle Catholic, had heard Fulton on the radio and had seen photographs of him, but the two had not met. The two women, thanks to the efforts of Young's husband, sat in the first row and were "absolutely mesmerized" by Sheen's performance in the three-hour service. "He had tremendous acting ability and a God-given sincerity," said Young. At the conclusion of a riveting sermon, Fulton theatrically raised his arms and cried out, "Father, into thy hands I commend my spirit . . ." and the huge cathedral bells began to toll. Sheen lowered his arms and silently left the pulpit, leaving the thousands in the cathedral stunned—and then, anticipating Easter, jubilant and thankful.

Back in the apartment, Young's telephone rang. It was Sheen's secretary inviting her and Mrs. Wayne to dinner that evening at The Colony Restaurant. Young learned that Fulton hosted such a dinner after each Good Friday service. She later remembered the "long, thin table" and the delightful repartee among the eleven people present. She thought Sheen "a superstar." Young and Sheen became friends, seeing each other at least twenty times in the coming decades and communicating by telephone. Taking a cue from the Good Friday sermon, Young began saying the Rosary daily.

Sheen often came to dinner with Loretta Young when he was in Beverly Hills. "Nothing ever got him down," she recalled, observing that he was fond of saying, "Everything is God's will." The actress found her conversations with Sheen "always positive," and she "never heard him criticize a single person." He struck her as being concerned about everyone. "He reminded me that Stalin had a soul and asked me to pray for him. I did until the day the dictator died." Young and actress Irene Dunne, two of Hollywood's most prominent Catholics, used Sheen as a confessor and personal adviser. Fulton tried unsuccessfully in the 1950s to save Young's marriage. "He was always helpful," she said. "He always prayed for me."

Young recalled that when you went to Sheen's apartment for dinner, you were asked to arrive at 5:45 or 6:00 P.M. and were expected to leave at 7:50. If you lingered, Fulton would say it was time to go. The guests understood that he would be up very early to start his nineteen-hour day.

Once when Loretta Young was in New York, she and Irene Dunne asked Sheen to lunch at the fashionable Twenty-One restaurant. When Sheen arrived at Young's apartment, he found both movie stars lavishly dressed and looking gorgeous. "We wanted to make a big impression," Young later recalled. Fulton was startled, and said it would be wiser for the three to have lunch in the apartment. Years later, he explained to Young that it would not have seemed appropriate for him to be seen at Twenty-One with two striking young actresses. This concern for appearances accompanied a genuine appreciation of the women's beauty. "Not all of God's people are ugly," Sheen remarked to Young. In fact, she thought Fulton knew perfectly well that he was physically attractive himself, always impeccably dressed and well groomed. "We dress for God," he would say. "We are his representatives."

At a later time, Sheen had to endure a rumor circulated through Beverly Hills (but kept from the press) by an angry husband that his actress wife, a convert, had been having an affair with the monsignor. A photograph had been taken of the actress in shorts, getting into a car with Sheen. The actress denied the accusation, and no one believed the story, Young recalled. But Sheen refused to enter the city again until the husband had died.[43]

☙

IN MID-OCTOBER of 1940, Sheen delivered the homily at a Pontifical Mass marking the hundredth anniversary of the establishment of the Catholic Church in Los Angeles. More than 110,000 persons jammed the Los Angeles Memorial Coliseum, and another 5,000 stood outside on a beautiful day. The celebrant was the Most Reverend Amleto Giovanni Cicognani, apostolic delegate to the United States, and Catholic officials from all parts of the United States, Mexico, and Hawaii were on hand, including twelve archbishops and thirty-six bishops. Some twelve hundred priests and nuns formed a gigantic cross on the green playing field, and a huge canopy shielded the dignitaries from the sun. The procession took an hour. The service was called "the greatest religious spectacle in the history of the west."

By now, Belgium, Holland and France had fallen to the German invaders, and the Battle of Britain was well under way. The U.S. Army was being modernized, the nation had its first peacetime draft, and President Roosevelt had agreed to give Britain fifty destroyers in exchange for leases on British bases in the Western Hemisphere. The 1940 election campaign was in full swing, with the incumbent promising never to send American boys into another foreign war, and calling America "the great arsenal of democracy." Most Americans continued to be isolationists, but a great many citizens were becoming seriously concerned, in foreign correspondent Edward R. Murrow's words, about the lights going out in Europe. One had only to watch the newsreels at the movies to see the death and destruction overwhelming Europe. Just before the Pontifical Mass began in Los Angeles, people stood and bowed their heads as a military band played the "Star-Spangled Banner."

In his address, Sheen covered a variety of topics, calling for peace between Jews, Protestants and Catholics; denouncing materialism and similar philosophies as the cause of war (a war he called "a veritable judgment of God"); and criticizing California for being the only state to tax parochial schools, which were "the bulwarks of true American democracy," teaching that "liberty is the doing of what we ought to within divine law" and not that "liberty is the liberty to do as we please." He also deplored the negativity and divisiveness that he saw on the political stage.

> *All around us are people who are ceaselessly hating someone or something, shouting "Down with capitalism! Down with labor unions! Down with religion! Down with government! Down with economic royalists! Down with property! Down with this class! Down with that class!" But I say "Up from class hate! Up from all hate! Let us stop downing things, and start looking up, up, up, up to God!"*

A reporter for the *Los Angeles News* exclaimed, "It was one of the two or three greatest addresses I have ever heard in my life."[44]

Sheen had correctly predicted the pact between fascists and Communists. Now, in January 1941, he told his radio audience: "Mark these words: The enemy of the world in the near future is going to be Russia, which is playing democracies against dictators and dictators against democracies, which is using peace when it can and war when it must, and is preparing, when Europe is exhausted from war, to sweep over it like a vulture to drink its blood and make away with the spoils." The Cold War, still some five years away, would come as no surprise to Sheen.[45]

In March, Congress passed the Lend-Lease Act, enabling the United States to give further aid to Great Britain. Isolationists such as Senator Robert Taft of Ohio were livid, contending that America was again being sucked into international conflict. Most Americans remained convinced that we should be no more than a source of supplies for those under siege. But it would not be long before American destroyers began to escort British ships as far as Iceland to protect them from German ships and submarines. Tension grew throughout the nation as the front pages, the radio, and the movie newsreels seemed to speak of nothing but war.

At the Easter service at St. Patrick's, Sheen said that the war might crack "the hard shell of materialism and apostasy from God that overlays our civilization." Our hope for America, he declared, "is grounded not in the major plans for defense, not in increased production of engines of war. It is grounded in a risen Christ and a revitalized spirituality." At the close of the service, Archbishop Spellman bestowed a special papal benediction upon the 7,500 worshippers crammed into the cathedral.[46]

Sheen told a thousand Catholic union members in May that "monopolistic capitalism" could not outlast the war, and that capital could be saved only by making "every laboring man a defender of capital, and the only way to do that is to give him some capital to defend." He predicted as well that world peace could only be achieved by the efforts of Pius XII. "In the world today that is organized on the basis of balance of power and that has increased its wars, it is about time that politicians ceased setting a limit to religion and that religion began setting a limit to politics." He repeated his description of the Pope as "the only moral authority that is left in the world"—a phrase that could hardly please a great many Protestant and secular Americans, let alone the many Catholic supporters of President Roosevelt.[47]

Soon the University of Notre Dame granted honorary doctorates to three men including Sheen and Joseph P. Kennedy. Sheen gave the baccalaureate sermon, a powerful indictment of what he saw as the moral decay of contemporary America, blended with a more subtle call for isolationism. Some things, he said, were not worth fighting for: monopolistic capitalism, corrupt and Red-infiltrated trade unions, a Godless system of public education, a legal system "which declares that the State is the source of all rights and liberties," a "social system which destroys the sacredness of treaties by permitting the break up of marriage through divorce," and a "system of tolerance" that produces "a national impotency to deal with fifth columnists" and "breeds atheism, anti-religion and anti-Semitism." It is not America as it is that should be saved, Sheen declared, it is America as it ought to be: A nation rededicated to God and to the basic principles of the Declaration of Independence.[48]

In a scholarly symposium in which he was said to represent the Catholic view of the postwar political and social scene, Sheen called for an international organization that would "respect the rights of God, assure mutual independence of peoples, impose fidelity to agreements and safeguard the true liberty and dignity of the human person." There would be a legislative and executive body in the organization and a judicial body "composed exclusively of representatives of religious groups.... [T]he point of having such a judicial body of this kind is to insure that in the future war be declared by ethical and moral groups and not by political groups, as they are at present." This theocratic proposal, especially by a prominent Catholic, drew heated replies.

One response came from Bishop G. Bromley Oxnam, a prominent liberal Methodist. Writing in the *Protestant Digest,* Oxnam asked, "Does the Roman Catholic Church really look forward to the day when it will choose judges for a World Court?" He wondered if the proposed judicial body would exclude Muslims, Hindus, Buddhists, and others. He also asked if there was implicit in this proposal "the repudiation of democracy, and the setting up of a new dictatorship." Behind Sheen's suggestion, he concluded, was the assumption that the Catholic Church was the one true Church of Christ, given by God the right to speak with final authority in the realm of religion. Oxnam found this idea "repugnant," and knew that others did as well.

Citing Sheen's proposal and Archbishop Spellman's assertion that the doctrine of the separation of church and state was but a "shibboleth," Oxnam warned of "clerical-Fascism" and "Coughlinism." He noted the union of church and state in predominantly Catholic countries and the difficulty that evangelical Christians had in preaching the gospel in those countries. "It makes little difference whether it be a brown shirt, a black shirt, a red shirt, or a shirt with the collar on backwards. Let the church remember that the political shirt-makers are sewing at once with a double thread, 'a shroud as well as a shirt.' If religionists march the road of dictatorship, it will become the march of death."[49]

A Jesuit letter writer soon accused the *Protestant Digest* of being violently anti-Catholic and pro-Communist.[50] But Oxnam had a point. Sheen's proposal did indeed assume that the Catholic Church contained the full truth of Christianity, and it omitted the non-Christian religions entirely. But Oxnam was wrong about the Catholic approach to church and state. In the 1940s, such a separation existed in Mexico, Portugal, the Irish Free State, and France. And in America, the Catholic hierarchy had always endorsed the fundamental principle of separation of church and state.[51] Sheen himself took it for granted. In a Memphis speech of 1940, he acknowledged this basic liberty and said that the complete overthrow of the Constitution would be necessary to overturn it.[52] But Oxnam was also off target in linking Catholics with Nazis. The Methodist leader's extremism would be magnified in a few years when he claimed that Protestantism was the true shield against totalitarianism and that Catholic countries were the most vulnerable. "The answer is found in soil and atmosphere. The soil is enriched by liberty and the atmosphere cleansed by truth wherever Protestantism prevails." Oxnam's sympathetic biographer, Robert Moats Miller, seriously questioned his geographical and historical knowledge, asking, among other things, "If 'freedom-loving Protestant lands' are immune to totalitarian rule, how explain the ease with which Protestant Norway and Protestant Denmark and Protestant Holland (though in fact with a large Catholic population) fell to the Nazis?"[53]

What emerged from Sheen's proposal for a postwar world judiciary and Oxnam's rejoinder was little more than a reassertion of the vast gap between the basic assumptions about religion and politics that divided orthodox Roman Catholics from liberal Protestants. Both Oxnam and the editors of the *Protestant Digest* were clearly anti-Catholic, and more than a little sympathetic toward the far Left. (Replying to the Jesuit letter writer, the editors deplored Catholicism's "authoritarianism" and "idolatry," defended their support of the Spanish Loyalists, and declared, "Insofar as 'the basic tenets of Socialism and Marxism' are consonant with the demands of justice we are indeed sympathetic with them.")[54] And Sheen, for all of his talk about amicability between Christians, was not about to deny that the Catholic Church was the sole depository of the fullness of Christian truth and the only hope for world peace.

Fulton said repeatedly that he did not identify with either the Left or the Right in their confrontations at home and in the world. He told his radio audience, "The terms reactionary and liberal are so relative they mean little to thinking men who have either a knowledge of history or a remnant of reason."[55] Nor did he see the Catholic Church as the defender of either position, but rather as occupying the middle of the political spectrum, crying out for immutable, God-given truths. "The ideas of the Church are like her vestments; always well dressed but never the slave of passing fashion."[56]

The real war that Sheen saw in the world was between "the forces of anti-God and slavery" on one side, and on the other, America and the Christian faith, embodied in the Catholic Church. Protestants, liberal or conservative, might dispute his understanding of the "real war"; they might speak of a "Protestant America" based on the numerical dominance of Protestants in the population. But to Sheen (more often than not) that represented moral and spiritual weakness—something to be overcome, not celebrated. And he had a standing offer to give personal instruction to all potential converts.[57]

But weren't Catholics subservient to an alien master in Rome? If so, how could they be truly patriotic? The questions were perennial in America, and had been raised at length against Al Smith in his bid for the presidency in 1928—even though Smith had taken an oath to uphold the Constitution nineteen times in his long public career and had served four terms as governor of the nation's largest state. Sheen flatly rejected the notion of a conflict between loyalty to the nation and to the Church. He said in 1938, "We Catholics love America—we love it more than Italy, more than Germany, more than Russia. We love its Constitution and its traditions and we want to see them preserved; we love the flag which is the symbol of our liberty and for that reason we reject a system which recognizes only one flag—namely, the red flag."[58] American democracy and Catholic Christianity were virtually one to Sheen; both were based on God's truth and both were struggling against the forces of darkness in both the far Right and the far Left.

At times, Sheen sounded like an American populist, revealing pride in his small-town and rural background. In a radio talk of March 16, 1941, he launched a full-scale attack on intellectuals such as H. G. Wells, George Bernard Shaw, John Dewey "and the new lawyers who teach that ideas are instruments of power." He said,

> *Communism has won more recruits in one single University in New York than it has won among all the farm hands of Illinois and Iowa put together.... It was the intelligentsia and the professional signers of Communist propaganda who told us three years ago that Russia was the hope of Europe against the Nazis; but who among the common people ever believed it? It is the intelligentsia who tell us that the invasion of Finland, Latvia, Estonia is not imperialism, but the act of a "friendly nation"— the common people call it barbarism.*

The hour of the common man was dawning, Sheen declared. The Messiah walked this earth teaching children and fishermen. "If I wanted a good moral judgment about the war, I should a thousand times prefer to get it from a garage man, a filling station attendant, a WPA worker, a grocer's clerk, or a delivery boy, than from twenty-three Ph.D. professors I know about in just one American University." The reason was easy to find. "The educated know how to rationalize evil; the masses do not. Evil to them is still evil. . . . Their judgments are better because their moral sense is higher, for virtue does not increase in direct ratio with learning." It was character, not learning, that made a nation great; and "character is in the *will*, not in the intellect."[59]

∽

IN THE SPRING of 1941, the Third Reich attained its peak. It held Denmark, Finland, Norway, Belgium, the Netherlands and France. In early April, Nazis attacked Yugoslavia and marched into Greece, hanging the swastika over the Acropolis. In North Africa, General Rommel captured two thousand British troops, including three generals.

In June, Hitler broke off his alliance with Stalin and sent his troops into Russia. The Soviet leader was flabbergasted, having deluded himself for months that the troops and equipment massing at the country's borders were simply a diversionary tactic by the Führer. Soviet military leaders pleaded with him at their peril. Since 1937, Stalin had purged his military high command, killing almost 37,000 officers.

American Communists, who had condemned Roosevelt as a warmonger, now rallied behind him and called for American intervention in the war. Roosevelt extended Lend-Lease to the Russians, a move that displeased both the Vatican and the American Catholic hierarchy. It was not that they opposed aid to the Russian people, who were heroically resisting the Nazi invasion, but rather that America was assisting a Communist government that stood for world revolution. Roosevelt persuaded Stalin to issue a statement of religious freedom to assuage Catholics, and he fatuously declared that the churches were open in Russia. (Eleanor Roosevelt said that the "only difficulty" about religion in the Soviet Union "was a lack of educational opportunity for priests and ministers.") The Vatican released a list of papal representatives in the Soviet Union who were either imprisoned or missing.

In October, Sheen told a large audience in Windsor, Ontario, that the Western democracies should extend aid to the Soviets only on condition that true religious liberty in Russia be restored, that the Communist Party in America be suppressed, and that all ideas of communist revolution be abandoned. He was especially intent on stamping out communism within the United States because, he said, if Russia fell, New York City would become world headquarters of the movement. If Hitler defeated Stalin, he predicted, there would be sabotage of American industry on a scale undreamed of, because the United States would be blamed for allowing Russia to be defeated.

Sheen warned of a propaganda drive to make Russia appear to be a land of religious freedom. He was critical of photographs scheduled to appear in *Life* magazine showing priests in their vestments holding services without interference. When he was shown the photographs in advance and asked for his opinion, he declared, "They are censored and all bear the stamp of Joseph Stalin." Then he asked, "Why didn't you take a couple of pictures of a concentration camp?"[60] (A similar presentation by *Life* in 1943, glorifying Russia and its leaders, would draw heated protest from many Catholics.)

On a whirlwind speaking tour, Sheen told an audience in Columbus, Ohio, that when Stalin and Hitler, "these two gangsters," got together, the size of their mustaches was the only difference between them. Nazism was more dangerous to the United States externally, he said, while communism was the greater evil internally. Sheen challenged President Roosevelt "to be something more than a politician, to be a moral leader of the world."[61]

In November, in a speech in Brooklyn, Sheen called for the destruction of Nazi paganism. "Hitler is attempting to crush Russia, not communism. He would destroy Christianity all over the world if he could." Sheen hoped that both forces would exhaust themselves on the Eastern Front. One of the worst possible consequences of the war would be a Russian victory, for "If that improbability ever occurred, America's problems would be just beginning."[62]

Sheen paid no attention to Japan in his speeches, although that summer the Japanese army had conquered the major cities and the coastline of China and was moving into Southeast Asia and the Dutch East Indies. When Pearl Harbor was attacked on December 7, 1941, the stunned American people rallied behind their weary chief executive to begin the war effort. Isolationism, which had been strong throughout the summer and fall (in September, eight out of ten opposed entering the war) died a sudden death. On December 10, Hitler declared war on the "half Judaized and the other half Negrified" citizens of the United States. Mussolini quickly followed suit. Russia and the United States were now officially on the same side of the war. Harold H. Tittman, assistant to Myron Taylor (Roosevelt's representative to the Vatican), moved into Vatican City, and the president agreed to extend quasi-diplomatic recognition to the Holy See.[63]

Throughout the war, Fulton continued to travel, lecture, preach, teach converts and students, appear on radio, and write. He reiterated his now familiar contention that the war was a judgment of God upon the world. "There are certain moral laws and their violation entails consequences," he said in Ottawa. "Sin brings adversity and this adversity is the judgment of God upon the world. Now judgment does not mean that God strikes us in an arbitrary fashion. No, these laws are imminent. History is the working out of the judgment of God." Before Pearl Harbor, Sheen often spoke of the nation's shortcomings, but in 1942 he said that American soldiers "are fighting because they believe in Christian ideals, in liberty and the survival of spiritual values. They are fighting with a purpose towards an end, and that end is not materialistic."[64] He wholeheartedly backed the Allies and the United Nations, seeing the struggle as one involving the highest ideals of mankind. In May 1942 he made a movie newsreel clip calling upon all Christians to support the war effort.[65] "We are not just fighting for freedom," he declared in Houston. "Freedom is only a shibboleth, an atmosphere—what are you going to do with it? What good is freedom of religion if there is no God to worship? This is a crusade to preserve the inalienable rights of all men, so that the hands raised in hatred may be folded in supplication—and embrace."[66]

The war was being waged against forces that opposed all religion and morality, Sheen told his national radio audience in January 1944:

> *Men of goodwill: unite! Unite because the new enemy is, as the Holy Father calls it, a "common danger." It is common to Jews, Protestants and Catholics. It makes no distinction among them. It does not even make a distinction between a Mussulman and a Christian when the former asserts the power of God is above the power of the state. We are all in the same boat because all men of goodwill are afloat on the sea of moral law.*[67]

As the war proceeded, Sheen grew deeply concerned about postwar agreements between the Allies. In October 1943, he asked, "Will there be another appeasement of Munich? Will the sop of the Baltic states, Latvia, Finland and half of Poland be given to Russia for such appeasement?"[68] William Randolph Hearst's *San Francisco Examiner* predicted that Stalin would "install in every country in Europe a Red Regime, which means more torture-chambers, concentration camps, massacres, atheism and continuous reign of terror."[69] By January 1944, Sheen was particularly concerned about the future of Catholic Poland: "Whatever happens to Poland will happen to the world." Should the Soviets keep it, he said, she will hold onto Latvia, Estonia and Lithuania, and move as far as the English Channel. And then, "We will have more Munichs, more appeasement and more conferences. The next war, if it comes, will be a war of the East and West." He charged that eight articles of the Atlantic Charter were rewritten in Moscow to conform to Soviet beliefs so that Stalin would sign the document.[70]

Sheen was by no means alone in pointing to the future of Poland as the supreme test of the success or failure of a postwar arrangement. In 1944, public opinion polls showed that Catholics were leaving the Democratic Party, fearing that it had become too pro-Soviet. Three out of ten voters believed that Roosevelt's reelection would help Communists in the federal government. Anticommunist Catholics organized the Polish-American Congress.[71] Buffalo's Bishop John Duffy declared, "If the Poles are forced to exist in misery and slavery then only a bitter, cruel world can be expected for all mankind." Catholics believed, correctly, that the massacre of the Polish officer corps in the Katyn forest was the work of the Red Army. They also denounced Stalin for allowing the Nazis to slaughter the Polish patriots who had counted on Soviet aid.[72]

When the Soviets attacked the Vatican as pro-fascist in early 1944, Sheen issued a strong statement defending the Church's actions in Spain, condemning both Nazism and communism, and again defending the Vatican as "the only moral force left standing between Europe and Barbarism." Sheen feared that this new aggression by the Reds against the Church spelled trouble for the future, possibly involving the signing of a separate treaty with Germany. "The time is now five minutes to twelve. America must be prepared for Russia's defection from the common cause and for the de-Christianization of Europe."[73]

Sheen's widely published assertion about a separate peace treaty between the Soviets and Nazis raised the eyebrows of certain top officials at the Federal Bureau of Investigation. An agent who had already interviewed Fulton was dispatched to see if the monsignor had a special source of information.[74] Within a few months, Sheen and FBI director J. Edgar Hoover had struck up a personal friendship.[75] (Sheen had publicly praised Hoover as early as 1938).[76] It was to prove fruitful in the years ahead.

∾

During the war, Sheen lost both of his parents. Delia died March 28, 1943, of cancer at the age of seventy-nine. Having been warned of her deteriorating physical condition, Fulton had been with her in Peoria only two weeks earlier.[77] She owned a complete, autographed set of her eldest son's books and was extremely proud of the author.[78] Newt, suffering from Altzheimer's disease, moved in with son Joe and his family, and died of a heart attack in 1944.[79] In their latter years, the Sheens had wintered in Florida, but often found excuses to return home as soon as possible. They never traveled to Washington or New York to see their sons. Joan Sheen later called them "simple folks" who enjoyed the rural life in central Illinois.[80] Fulton presided at both funerals, his suffering undoubtedly mitigated by his complete confidence in the love of God.

Newt's will divided his properties among his four sons. Fulton sold his inheritance to Joe, saying that he preferred the cash.[81]

∽

THROUGHOUT THE WAR years, Sheen feuded with National Council of Catholic Men officials over his radio talks on the *Catholic Hour*. He bristled when NBC pressured program directors to eliminate his anticommunist attacks on the ground that Stalin was now an ally of the United States. He became even angrier when a CUA theologian censured the religious content of his talks and lay officials corrected his grammar and demanded that he no longer denigrate Protestantism.

Sheen fought back by extemporizing on the program, by threatening to leave when his air time was cut slightly, by submitting his talks as close to air time as possible, and by telling others around the country of efforts to drive him off the air. At one point, he refused to read any more letters from Edward Hefferon, the executive secretary and his principal antagonist. Sheen largely ignored NCCM mandates to mend his ways, even after agreeing to abide by them.

When alerted to the fact that the March 4, 1945, broadcast would mark the *Catholic Hour's* fifteenth anniversary, Fulton ad libbed, "today is *my* fifteenth anniversary on the Catholic Hour."

On Easter Sundays, Sheen asked his radio listeners to write, promising to pray for him, and he would reply by letter, "remembering you in the light and not forgetting you under the stars." In fact, the thousands who wrote in received a form letter in return, promising to remember the addressee at Mass on a certain date. The form letter for 1945 contained the words, "In case I am not returned to the Catholic Hour next year." An NCCM official persuaded Sheen to delete the language, but only after many letters containing it were in the mail. The struggle continued into the post-war years. While both sides were to blame, Fulton's vanity was very much on display.[82]

෴

ARCHBISHOP FRANCIS SPELLMAN of New York, who would soon play a major role in Sheen's career, could easily match him in patriotic fervor and anticommunism. But he was far less skeptical of the president; indeed, he considered Roosevelt a God-given knight in shining armor who at all times deserved the full support of the American people. Roosevelt went out of his way to be cordial to the powerful archbishop, treating him as a personal friend and confidante. The master politician in the White House knew well the power of the Catholic vote. He knew, moreover, that no one in the United States was closer to the Pope than Spellman.

Others in the administration did not care for the archbishop, including the president's wife (a cousin thought she still harbored anti-Catholic sentiments learned in her childhood). Roosevelt aide James Rowe said later that "Nobody liked Spellman." And yet when the clergyman spoke about the Vatican, Spain, or Germany, "everyone listened very closely."[83]

Spellman was short, pudgy and bespectacled, walked with a bit of a stumble, and lacked any sort of charisma. He was not a good public speaker. He was not an intellectual. He was quick-tempered and strong-willed. But he had a keen mind, a phenomenal memory and a genius for administration. He was a tireless worker, excellent fund-raiser, and shrewd businessman. "Spellie," as insiders referred to him (but never to his face), had a sentimental streak that occasionally came to the surface, to the surprise of many who thought him a "cold fish." And he strove hard to be holy. Msgr. George A. Kelly, who knew him well, likened Spellman to baseball star Eddy Stanky of the Brooklyn Dodgers: The most valuable player among the all-stars was not the best hitter, pitcher or fielder; he was the leader.[84]

As the nation's military vicar, Spellman had large responsibilities. There were some 500 Catholic chaplains in the armed forces at the time of Pearl Harbor. That number escalated to 3,270 commissioned chaplains, plus an additional 2,018 civilian priests who served as auxiliary chaplains. A master administrator, Spellman chose his subordinates wisely.

In 1942, Spellman asked the Vatican to supply him with another bishop for the Military Ordinariate. He recommended three candidates, including Fulton Sheen. (Sheen's private expression of contempt for Spellman uttered in 1939 had obviously not reached the proud archbishop's ears.) He described Sheen as "America's most distinguished pulpit orator," who was "probably the best known of any Catholic priest in America, excluding the Cardinals and Archbishops, whose record for convert making is unequalled in American History, and who would add prestige to the office." On the other hand, Spellman pointed out, Sheen lacked administrative experience. The Vatican chose not to select Sheen, perhaps because he was the youngest candidate on Spellman's list and the least qualified in practical experience in a parish or diocese.[85]

Archbishop Spellman devoted much of his considerable energy to travel and personal relations with men and women in the field. In 1941 he traveled 18,000 miles, starting in Alaska and concluding in the Southwest, interviewing 300 Catholic chaplains in 92 Army posts and Navy stations. In 1943, he was gone 24 weeks on a world tour that covered 46,000 miles. The next year he made a western European tour that lasted three months.[86] Whether or not Spellman was Roosevelt's agent on these travels remains unclear.[87] But the record shows clearly that the president was entirely cooperative, placing all the necessary diplomatic and military services at the archbishop's disposal, and that Spellman sent Roosevelt personal reports.[88]

On his world tour, Spellman met with General Franco (to whom he explained American intentions in the war), Pius XII (who gave him his own pectoral cross and chain, saying that he feared the two would never meet again in this life), King George VI of England, Prime Minister Winston Churchill, General Charles De Gaulle, General Dwight D. Eisenhower, and an apostolic delegate in Istanbul named Archbishop Angelo Roncalli (the future Pope John XXIII). But he spent most of his time visiting troops in hospitals and battlefields, celebrating Mass, sharing his warm smile and optimism, and taking down the names of average Joes so that he could write a letter to their loved ones at home. Spellman's friendly biographer later estimated that "tens of thousands" of such letters were written. The archbishop also raised funds for world relief and left financial gifts, for example giving $5,000 to aid the children of Malta.[89]

Many GIs and others wrote letters home expressing deep appreciation for the archbishop's efforts. A sergeant in Germany recalled a Mass for two thousand near the battlefront in Germany.

> *He is a little man of considerable years, and the shelter afforded him little protection from the weather. When he gave Communion, he had to come out from under the shelter and I noticed that his vestments were drenched and just hung on his body and the water literally streamed down his bare head and over his face. Still he paid it not the slightest attention but went on with the service. . . . His words were plain but they were inspiring and had I been in a massive Cathedral, I could not have been more deeply touched than I was as I stood there in the woods midst all the misery of the weather. I'll long remember this Mass and I'll long remember Archbishop Spellman. He certainly lifted the hearts of many men this morning.*

A monk who traveled with Spellman through Syria, Galilee and Lebanon wrote to his bishop, "I might add that the memory of these days in the company of such a humble, devout and great man will remain a cherished one with me." President Roosevelt, after his conference in Tehran, wrote to the archbishop, "I ran across your trail on several occasions and all I can say is that everyone loved you everywhere you went."[90]

Many liberals and others greeted Spellman's travels with horror, portraying him as an official (and thus unconstitutional) representative of the president, the lackey of Franco and the Pope, pro-Hitler, and the like.[91] An eight-part series in the *Christian Century*, a major voice of liberal Protestantism, asked "Can Catholicism Win America?" The answer was a sad and at times angry "yes." Catholic leaders, editor Harold Fey warned, have "cast off the inferiority complex which naturally characterizes an alien minority and have begun boldly and aggressively to assert their power."[92]

Spellman joined others in pleading with the president to limit Allied bombing in and around Rome. He made the same plea publicly. Before an audience of 75,000 Holy Names men at New York's Polo Grounds, Spellman asked for prayers "that Rome, the city of the soul, eternal Rome, be spared destruction, and above all that Rome be not destroyed by us."[93] In March 1944, Spellman and Sheen appeared together at the unveiling of a painting to be presented to the Pope and stressed the need to spare Rome. Sheen warned that if the United States attacked the Eternal City, "we will suffer, if not through war then through pestilence."[94]

Roosevelt, however, resisted making any pledges that would interfere with the military effort. In July 1943, the Roman basilica of San Lorenzo was bombed, a move that deeply distressed Pius XII but may have led almost immediately to the overthrow of Italian Fascism.[95]

In the course of several private conversations with the president, Spellman grew deeply concerned about the future. In September 1943, Roosevelt shocked his guest by telling him that Austria, Hungary and Croatia would fall under some sort of postwar Russian protectorate. Stalin would also get control of Finland, the Baltic States, the eastern half of Poland, and Bessarabia. Spellman's typed notes of the conversation have the president saying, "There is no point to oppose these desires of Stalin, because he has the power to get them anyhow. So better give them gracefully." At times, FDR seemed pro-Russian, and was confident that he could deal with Stalin more effectively than could Churchill, who was "too idealistic."

A year later, Spellman was again shocked to learn that the president had agreed—temporarily, as it turned out—to the Morgenthau Plan, a proposal to destroy Germany's industrial base and turn the country into a rural area. He was concerned too by private statements of Roosevelt, such as "The Pope is too worried about communism" and "Russia has need of protection. She has been invaded twice, you know. That is why we shall give her part of Poland and recompense Poland with a part of Germany."

Spellman was astonished in 1945 when a seriously ailing Roosevelt traveled all the way to the Crimea (a 6,000-mile voyage to Malta, a 1,400-mile flight to the Crimea, and an eight-hour automobile ride over winding mountain roads) to meet Stalin at Yalta, because the Soviet dictator refused to leave his country. "Don't worry. I know how to talk to Stalin," the president told Spellman. "He is just another practical man who wants peace and prosperity."[96]

Roosevelt, however ill, was no fool. He understood how far west Stalin's army had gotten by February 1945, and how it would require a war with America, which was unthinkable, to drive them back to prewar borders. He knew how the Russians had suffered during the war, and how they were responsible for 94 percent of the German army's casualties. Since June 22, 1941, the Red Army had lost some eleven million dead. In accordance with the best military thinking of the time, Roosevelt believed that Russian troops would be needed to invade Japan. And there was the postwar world to ponder: If the United States and Russia could not get along, the world might be plunged into preparations for yet another world war.

Even before the fighting had ended, Spellman, like Sheen, had grave concerns about what lay ahead. Both men had reservations about their commander in chief. Both feared that the Soviet Union, the Church's most deadly enemy, might somehow emerge from the pain and bloodshed victorious.

ᕫ

THE BEST OF SHEEN's wartime books was *Whence Comes War,* which appeared in 1940. Here Fulton dealt with a wide range of issues including the question commonly asked of all clergy: Why doesn't God stop the war? His answer was that since man had started the war, it was his responsibility to end it, and that God could intervene only at the cost of destroying human freedom. Sheen's specific target was the British writer H. G. Wells, who said he would spit in the "empty face" of an omnipotent God who could look upon the current suffering and do nothing. Sheen responded,

> *The only time some men, like Wells, ever think of God is when they want to find someone to blame for their own sins. Without ever saying so, they assume that man is responsible for everything good and beautiful in the world, but God is responsible for its wickedness and its wars.... They ignore the fact that God is like a playwright who wrote a beautiful drama, gave it to men to act with all the directions for acting, and they made a botch of it.*[97]

In the same work, Fulton further explored the issue of whose side God was on. His answer was more complex than one might have expected from listening to his patriotic speeches. "God judges men not by their nationality but by their justice; not by their flags but by their hearts; not by the quantity of their pleas, but by the righteousness of their prayers." True, God can be more on the side of those who in general acknowledge, fear and worship Him. But God, he said, is also on the side of the just Russian and the just German, while he opposes Stalin and Hitler. "God is with the just English and French who seek to serve, know and love God, according to the light of their consciences, but He is not with those who would oppose Hitler and Stalin for reasons of imperialism."[98] In another wartime book, Fulton put it this way: "God is on the side of those who do His Will."[99]

Sheen blamed the religious breakup of the West for much of the violence and chaos plaguing the world. This was an attack on Protestantism as well as his more common targets of pragmatism and secularism. When true religion, the Catholic faith, was abandoned as the sole source of stability and justice in the world, Fulton wrote, it was every man for himself, feeling free to be his own authority in religious matters and abandoning his duties to the community by practicing laissez-faire capitalism. "Like human corpses which having lost their spiritual unity become the prey of vultures, so modern man having lost his faith became the prey of dictators who, seeing men serving no common purposes, devoured them into new unities of the race as in Germany, and the class as in Russia." Contrast the 320 million Catholics in the world, unified spiritually, he said, with the quarreling sects that have helped bring disaster on the world. Unity under Pius XII, the 252nd successor to St. Peter, was the only way to bring peace and to create a brotherhood of man with the Fatherhood of God.[100]

Sheen also devoted several pages in *Whence Comes War* to what he said was the vital relationship between religion, by which he meant Catholic Christianity, and democracy. "A religion can live without democracy; it can live under tyranny, persecution and dictatorship—not comfortably, it is true, but heroically and divinely. But democracy cannot live without religion, for without religion democracy will degenerate into demagogy by selling itself to the highest bidder," meaning that the sole source of right and wrong would be determined by public opinion polls. Religion alone teaches the true nature of man, Sheen argued, and democracy's survival "depends upon an electorate imbued with morality which God and religion alone can give."[101]

God and War appeared in 1942. Only 116 pages long and bearing evidence of haste, it contains some of Sheen's most stirring prose as well as superb insight into the problem of pain and the nature of evil. "It is not easy for us to explain why God permits evil," Sheen wrote, "but it is impossible for the unbeliever to explain why good exists; he cannot tell us why a material, soul-less, God-less, cross-less universe should be the center of self-sacrifice, purity, love, faith, a Cross, martyrdom, and a willingness to die rather than offend God." If the unbeliever asks, "Where is your God now?" Sheen wrote, "the believer may retort 'Where are your gods now? Where is your god Progress in the face of two world wars within 21 years? Where is your god Science, now that it consecrates its energies to destruction? Where is your god Evolution now that the world is turned backward into one vast slaughterhouse?' "

As to the perennial question of the nature of accident in a God-filled universe, Sheen cited Scripture in three places to show that "it must never be assumed that catastrophe is a special sign of sin." He added, "What we seem to forget is that death is not the greatest evil; sin is. . . . The best lives are not always saved in battle; otherwise the heroes who die in battle and whose names we inscribe on our war memorials would all be wicked men." The world is a "proving ground for character," and if this globe were the end of things, "if man had not an immortal soul, if the scales of justice were not balanced beyond the grave, if the loss of physical life were a greater evil than sin, then the Goodness of God could be identified with our good health, our fat bank deposits, and our freedom from wounds."[102]

In 1943, Sheen published a small prayer book of sorts intended for Catholics in wartime. *The Armor of God* contains a variety of religious services, Bible readings, quotations from great Catholic writers, and the complete text of one of Fulton's favorite poems (recited from memory to millions of listeners over his lengthy career), Mary Dixon Thayer's "To Our Lady," which begins, "Lovely Lady dressed in blue—teach me how to pray!"[103]

Seven Pillars of Peace (1944) is notable for Sheen's observations on what he perceived to be the breakdown of the family during the war. Working parents and the secularization of the schools, he feared, were doing irreparable damage to the nation's youth. Rosie the Riveter and the eighteen million other women employed in industry were neglecting their children, Sheen said, often just out of the desire to make more money. "And what kind of peace will we have if, during the war, these mothers turn out future mothers with a sordid background of disease and crime? Our soldiers at the front are entitled to better wives when they return, or else the fighting is all in vain. This war's greatest casualty so far is—*the American home.*"[104]

In April 1945, Sheen was in San Francisco, speaking before an audience of fifteen thousand and urging changes in the Dumbarton

Oaks proposals for the United Nations, specifically the major role the Soviet Union and its puppets were to play in the new world organization. Speaking as a private citizen, he wanted to see more about the sovereignty of God and His moral law, and an international bill of rights and liberties incorporated in the United Nations. "There will be no United Nations," he declared, "unless there is recognized a common Spirit, a common God, a common Justice to which all subscribe, which prompts each state to give to another that which is its due, and which prays, 'forgive us our trespasses as we forgive those who trespass against us.' " He suggested that the role of the Vatican in the new world body be indirect and concentrated on securing the moral foundation of peace.

Sheen expressed hope that delegates to the United Nations would include at least a sprinkling of representatives of the Red Cross, moral and religious leaders, and Catholic, Protestant and Jewish clergy to leaven the group of politicians. (A short time earlier, *The Protestant* magazine had displayed the signatures of 1,600 American ministers and religious leaders opposing religious representation in councils of state and alleging that the papacy had thrown its weight into the war on the side of the Axis powers.)[105] "The politicians MUST feel the weight of public opinion," Sheen said. "The old men must not waste on paper what the young men purchased with their blood."[106]

Earlier that same day in San Francisco, Sheen had sharply criticized the late President Roosevelt. "At Yalta," he said, "three men with a stroke of a pen delivered the eastern part of Europe up to a Godless nation."[107] Charges of a Yalta "sellout" by an ill and "soft" FDR, influenced by Communist and pro-Communist advisers, were already becoming a staple of right-wing, anticommunist rhetoric. Hearst's *New York Daily Mirror* called Yalta "a Red Munich." Hearst columnist George Sokolsky said that the wartime conference had ushered in "the Era of Stalin" and would allow the Soviet leader to unify "Europe under the rule of Moscow." The American Left fired back with charges that Hearst was "Hitler's helper," that Sokolsky was a fascist agent, and the like. The *New Republic* called for the use of sedition laws to quiet the conservative press.[108]

In fact, Roosevelt had done fairly well at Yalta, gaining the respect of most historians then and later. He agreed to Stalin's demand for three votes in the General Assembly of the United Nations, and a veto power by the major nations. In the delicate question of Poland, Stalin agreed to conduct "free and unfettered elections," which was the best Roosevelt could get from him. The Declaration of Liberated Europe committed all three leaders to help form democratic governments in eastern Europe. In a secret treaty, Stalin agreed to enter the Asian war within three months of the German surrender in return for several concessions and some real estate, including the Kurile Islands.

The only way the American president could have dislodged the Soviet army from eastern Europe, which it had wrested from the Nazis at a terrible price in blood, was by war with the Soviet Union. That was not thinkable in 1945, with Hitler still alive and the Japanese yet unconquered, or in the aftermath of the peace, with American troops clamoring to get home, the public howling for an end to wartime restrictions, and a world pinning its hopes on the United Nations.

Still, when Stalin failed to honor his pledge about free elections, and Poland remained behind what Churchill would call the Iron Curtain, Sheen's early reaction to the Yalta accords was widely shared, especially among Catholics. This angry judgment would grow in the postwar years. In 1952, when the liberal *New York Post* publisher Dorothy Schiff met with Cardinal Spellman, Sheen, and five other top New York clergymen for lunch, numerous topics were discussed, but Schiff remembered in particular the subject of Yalta coming up, and the vehemence with which the clergy denounced Roosevelt's concessions.[109]

Another point of postwar controversy was the Church's stance toward the Jewish Holocaust. Sheen knew that the Vatican had condemned anti-Semitism in 1928, and he did not countenance the stories of papal complacency. "All during my life," he wrote in his autobiography, "attacks against the Church have hurt me as much as attacks against my own mother."[110]

American Catholic leaders, concerned over German persecution of Jews, called on Roosevelt in 1937 to intervene in some way
without direct involvement in European affairs. In November 1942,
the Church hierarchy in the United States issued a proclamation
denouncing racial persecution of all kinds and citing specifically a
"deep sense of revulsion against the cruel indignities heaped on
Jews in conquered countries and upon defenseless people not of
our faith." Sheen himself had often spoken out against anti-Semitism,
and in 1939 he received an award from the New York B'nai B'rith as
one of several "outstanding protectors of human rights."[111] Later
he wrote that "Anti-Semitism is anti-Christianity."[112]

Sheen could not have believed charges of anti-Semitism against,
as he put it, the "Church built upon a Rock and governed by the
Man with Keys."[113] And he never lost his complete confidence in
Pius XII. In 1941 he declared to his radio audience, "I shall trust . . .
the Chief Shepherd and Vicar of Jesus Christ; and I shall trust in
that authority to the end of my life, for if God's Truth and Justice
which He gave to His Church cannot be trusted, then nothing can
be trusted."[114] Moreover, he knew Pius XII personally and could not
have dreamed that he was the cold and cruel monster later portrayed by Rolf Hochhuth, John Cornwell, and other critics of the
Pope. Sir Francis Osborne, a non-Catholic British diplomat who
was a minister to the Vatican from 1936 to 1947, wrote years after
the war, "Pius XII was the most warmly humane, kindly, generous,
sympathetic (and, incidentally, saintly) character that it has been
my privilege to meet in the course of a long life."[115] Sheen was always
in complete agreement with that view.[116]

◦∿◦

FOLLOWING THE COLLAPSE of Germany, while President Truman
met with Churchill and Stalin at Potsdam to decide what to do with
the remains of the fallen foe, the first atomic fireball appeared in
the desert in Almagordo, New Mexico. It was the test explosion of
the Manhattan Project, the super-secret project designed to develop
an atomic bomb. Truman did not hesitate to employ it to bring the

war to a rapid close and save the tens of thousands of American lives that would have been lost in a land invasion of Japan. (Just taking the small island of Okinawa cost 12,000 American lives.) On August 6, a bomb leveled four square miles of Hiroshima, killing nearly 80,000 people. Three days later, another 60,000 people were killed at Nagasaki. Within a few days, Japan had surrendered and World War II was over.

While all Americans were jubilant about the ending of hostilities, a few questioned the use of the atomic bombs. Most of these dissenters were on the left, and their reservations and objections would be heard through the rest of the century and beyond. The Federal Council of Churches issued a formal statement: "We believe we have committed an atrocity of a new magnitude.... We cannot believe it was even essential to the defeat of Japan. Its reckless and irresponsible employment against an already beaten foe will have to receive judgment before God and the conscience of mankind. It has our unmitigated condemnation."[117]

Fulton Sheen was among the first to pronounce the use of the bombs morally wrong. In a speech at the Aquinas Institute in Rochester, he asked, "Suppose Hitler had dropped this bomb on undefended cities. How barbaric that would have been!" Public opinion in the United States condemned Nazis for burning people in furnaces, he said, yet shrugged off the killing of many thousands with a single atomic bomb. He predicted that atomic bombs would not protect the world from war any more than the invention of the gun silencer or dynamite. "Religion alone can save us."[118]

Sheen's appeal to religion—at least to a religion, such as his own, that sought peace, justice and mercy—rang true. For the nation as well as the individual, a religion of love can be a powerful weapon in overcoming the cruel, irrational and dangerous forces that cause men to kill each other. The fact that Christians themselves have waged wars of aggression over the centuries has less to do with the religion of the warriors than with an unwillingness of the combatants to obey the teachings of its founder. The crucial point is not that they were Christians, but that they failed to be *good* Christians.

This was a concept that Sheen often applied to "bad" Catholics. The problem, he said, was that they were not Catholic enough.

The atomic bomb, the failure of diplomats to curtail the expansion of Soviet control, and the postwar concerns of the American people, involving economics far more than religion, left Sheen with a bitter taste in his mouth at the end of the Second World War. In 1948 he wrote that the First World War was fought "to make the world safe for a democracy without God" and the second "to make an imperialism without God."[119] Still, he was overjoyed that America had won, and saw the hand of God, and in particular the Blessed Virgin Mary, in almost every detail of the world struggle. As he wrote:

> *The Council of Baltimore on December 8, 1846, consecrated the United States to the Immaculate Conception of Our Blessed Mother. It was only 8 years later that the Church defined Her Immaculate Conception. It was on December 8, 1941, the Feast of the Immaculate Conception that the United States went to war with Japan. It was on May 13, 1945, Mother's Day, the day on which the entire Church celebrated Sodality Day of Our Lady, that the United States Government proclaimed a National Thanksgiving for V-E Day. It was on August 15, 1945, the Feast of the Assumption of Our Blessed Mother, that victory came to us in the war with Japan. It was the nineteenth of August, 1945, that the United States Government declared official V-J Day and this happened to be the anniversary of one of the appearances of Our Lady of Fatima. On September 1, 1945, the first Saturday of the month which Our Lady of Fatima asked should be consecrated to Her, General MacArthur accepted the surrender of Japan aboard the* Missouri. *It was on September 8, 1945, the Birthday of Our Lady, that the first American flag flew over Tokyo, and as it was unfurled General MacArthur said: "Let it wave in its full glory as a symbol of victory for the right."[120]*

SIX

Reaching Out

During the 1930s and 1940s, the Catholic Church in America blossomed. Traumatized by the blatant anti-Catholicism of the 1928 presidential election, Church members had responded by creating separate Catholic scholarly organizations, professional societies, book clubs, trade unions, even summer camps. But during the Depression and in the war years they began to return to mainstream American life. In part, this had to do with Roosevelt's courting of Catholic leaders and the unprecedented recognition given by the administration to Catholic interests and aspirations.[1] Participation in the war effort was also a factor; while representing 20 percent of the population, Catholics accounted for nearly 35 percent of America's soldiers. There were still vast theological and ethical differences between Catholics and Protestants, along with deep-seated suspicions on both sides, yet there were many examples of friendly dialogue and mutual understanding. And the hostility still evidenced by Protestants stemmed partly from the fact that the Catholic Church was thriving.

In 1940, there were nearly twenty-three million Catholic communicants in America, almost three times as many as the Methodist Church could claim, and the Methodists were by far the largest Protestant denomination in the country. Catholics outnumbered any single Protestant denomination in thirty-five of the forty-eight states. There were 145 bishops and archbishops in the country, and some Protestants believed that they spoke with one voice, often a voice that was heard, they implied, behind the scenes. A leading liberal Protestant stated, "There can be little doubt that the action of our government in helping to defeat democracy and to enthrone clerical fascism in Franco's Spain was decisively influenced by the desires of the American hierarchy."[2]

Mass attendance was in the 75 percent range or better (in contrast to flagging attendance in increasingly secular western Europe). In Philadelphia churches, for instance, especially those with second- and third-generation American families, attendance at Sunday Mass hovered around 90 percent. Charles R. Morris, an able historian of American Catholicism, described the appeal of the Mass: "The total experience—the dim lights, the glint of the vestments, the glow of the stained-glass windows, the mantralike murmur of the Latin—was mind-washing. It calmed the soul, opened the spirit to large, barely grasped Presences and Purposes. For a trembling moment every week, or every day if they chose, ordinary people reached out and touched the Divine."[3] Penitents frequently encountered long lines at the confessional. Morris explained, "Few religions could match the gratifying closure, the guilt-resolving certainty, of the Catholic Confession. Commit any sin, sink to any level of degradation, and but kneel nameless and enshadowed in the confessional, recite the sins truthfully, and walk out to skies bright with grace."[4]

Latin liturgy, Gregorian chant and Renaissance polyphony, meatless Fridays, fasting before Mass, the Rosary, the Baltimore Catechism, retreats, the novena (in 1938, seventy thousand people attended thirty-eight novena services at Our Lady of Sorrows in Chicago every week), kneelers, large families dressed in their "Sunday best," mantillas and chapel caps, religious in habits, statues, large Gothic or baroque churches with dark, quiet places and side altars, elaborate priestly vestments, the smell of incense, the sound of bells at the Consecration, the feeling of awe at the miracle of Transubstantiation—these were all common features of the American Catholic world in the time of the Church's fastest growth and greatest self-confidence.[5]

Parochial education was booming; in 1943 there were over two million pupils in almost 8,000 schools, and 16,838 men in Catholic seminaries. Some nine million people subscribed to 333 Catholic newspapers in 1942. More than a hundred publishing houses were linked with the Catholic Press Association. There were 726 Catholic hospitals.

Protestant paranoia was in some sense justified by the strong spirit of evangelism reflected in the "Make America Catholic" movement. Catholics reported about 86,000 converts annually in the United States. A serious attempt to reach African Americans was under way. Urban laborers were increasingly attracted to the pro-labor teachings of Leo XIII, the "Pope of the working man." More than half of working-class Catholics belonged to trade unions (in sharp contrast with Protestants, for whom organized labor had little appeal). A National Catholic Congress on Social Action, held in Milwaukee in 1938 and again in Cleveland in 1939, attracted scores of bishops, hundreds of priests, and tens of thousands of laity.

After an absence going back to the Teddy Roosevelt administration, Catholics reappeared in presidential cabinets. Franklin D. Roosevelt named three, and Truman appointed four. FDR nominated Frank Murphy to the United States Supreme Court, only the fifth Catholic in American history so honored. This was no accident. Catholics in America tended to be working class (55 percent by World War II), urban, and Democrat. Historian Kenneth J. Heineman has observed, "By 1940, the nation's twelve largest Catholic and Jewish cities provided nearly enough votes to elect the president.... Since Roosevelt never won the majority of middle and upper-class Protestant votes, working-class Catholics and Jews became the backbone of the New Deal."[6] Close to three-quarters of Catholic voters supported Roosevelt in 1936, about 70 percent in 1940, and two-thirds in 1944.[7]

The Supreme Court, on the other hand (despite Catholic appointments), was moving in a less sympathetic direction, propelled by liberal warnings against governmental aid to parochial schools. A 1930 decision had permitted Louisiana to purchase textbooks for parochial school students. Similar proposals at the federal level prompted the influential pragmatist John Dewey to caution

that assistance to Catholic schools amounted to "the encouragement of a powerful reactionary world organization in the most vital
realm of democratic life with the resulting promulgation of principles inimical to democracy." Such aid, said Dewey, would reverse
key victories over "centuries of systematic stultification of the human
mind and human personality."[8]

In 1940, the court ruled that on the basis of the Fourteenth
Amendment, passed just after the Civil War to protect freed slaves,
it had the authority to apply the standards of the First Amendment
to the states. This meant that the free exercise of religion and the
prohibition against the establishment of religion, found in the First
Amendment, could be applied to state and local situations as well
as to Congress.

In the case of *Everson v. Board of Education* in 1947, the court
defined "the separation of church and state" more clearly than ever,
setting the stage for future decisions limiting the rights that many
Christians, and Catholics in particular, had long taken for granted.
Government action, said the court, must neither advance nor inhibit
religion; the government must be neutral. Still, the 5–4 *Everson* decision upheld the constitutionality of a New Jersey statute authoriz-
ing free school bus transportation to both parochial and public
school students. This prompted a huge rally in Washington, sponsored by the American Unitarian Association and broadcast nationally on the radio, condemning aid to Catholics, and Catholics in
general. Four Supreme Court justices attended the rally.

A year later, in *McCullom v. Board of Education,* the court rejected
a program for releasing children from public school classes to receive
religious instruction on public school premises from representatives of their own faith. One month after the *McCollum* decision,
the United States Senate refused to grant a federal charter to the
Catholic War Veterans on the ground that it might violate the principle of the separation of church and state, now widely thought to
be the original intent of the Founding Fathers.[9]

In 1948, the administrative board of the National Catholic Welfare Conference, in the name of all American bishops, published a

document criticizing both Supreme Court decisions for adopting an "entirely novel ... interpretation" of the First Amendment, one that would endanger our "original American tradition" of "free cooperation between government and religious bodies—cooperation involving no special privileges to any group and no restriction on the religious liberty of any citizen." Catholic legal scholar Gerard V. Bradley later noted that because of the decisions "public authority could no longer aid religion, even where it would do so without discrimination or coercion, for fear of seeming to prefer religion over what the Court called 'non-religion.' The Justices subordinated, that is, the free exercise of religion to the appearance, or any evidence, of its establishment."[10] The struggles of Catholics to be fully accepted by all Americans, and by the liberal elite in particular, were obviously far from over.

Many liberal intellectuals were outraged by the Church's prosperity during this period. A wide assortment of publications attacked Catholicism by linking Protestants with capitalism, democracy and scientific truth, while identifying Catholics with intolerance, ignorance and totalitarianism. Some critics on the left associated Catholicism with communism, others with fascism. In 1940, pragmatist philosopher Sidney Hook called Catholicism "the oldest and greatest totalitarian movement in history." The highly respected Protestant theologian Reinhold Niebuhr lamented the chasm "between the presuppositions of a free society and the inflexible authoritarianism of the Catholic religion."[11]

These attacks reached their crescendo in 1949 in Paul Blanshard's best-selling book *American Freedom and Catholic Power*. Begun as a series of twelve articles in *The Nation,* Blanshard's book called the Catholic hierarchy rigid, medieval, fascist, totalitarian, tyrannical, bigoted, un-American, arrogant, dishonest, and the enemy of science and objective learning. One typical sentiment: "The Vatican's affinity with fascism is neither accidental nor incidental. Catholicism conditions its people to accept censorship, thought control, and, ultimately dictatorship."[12] Another: "There is no doubt that the parochial school, whatever may be its virtues, is the most important divisive instrument in the life of American children."[13] Blanshard called for "a resistance movement" to prevent the Church from taking over America and crushing "Western democracy and American culture." He criticized Sheen six times, twice for attacking religious liberalism on the radio.[14]

Liberal reviewers heaped praise upon the polemic. John Dewey cheered Blanshard's "exemplary scholarship, good judgment, and tact." McGeorge Bundy of Harvard University called the book "a very useful thing." Liberal Supreme Court Justice Hugo Black applauded it and marked his copy carefully. His son later recalled, "He suspected the Catholic Church. He used to read all of Paul Blanshard's books exposing power abuse in the Catholic Church." Invited to Harvard, Blanshard voiced pleasure that "the new movement against Catholic aggression is rising not on the fringes, the lunatic fringes of religion and fanaticism, but right in the hearts of American University leaders."[15]

But if elite culture was saturated with anti-Catholic bigotry, popular culture was more open. By the late 1930s, Catholics portrayed in movies tended to be highly sympathetic figures. Spencer Tracy, Pat O'Brien, and Ward Bond played heroic, tough-guy priests. The 1943 film *Song of Bernadette,* which depicted the miracle at Lourdes, received twelve academy award nominations and won four. Crooner-actor Bing Crosby was a popular sensation in *Going My Way,* which won seven Oscars in 1944, and in *The Bells of St. Mary's. The Fighting Sullivans,* a box office hit in 1944, told the true story of five Catholic brothers killed during a naval battle in World War II. That same year, in *Keys of the Kingdom,* Gregory Peck played a heroic Catholic missionary. Loretta Young and Celeste Holm were engaging nuns in the 1949 film *Come to the Stable.*

This acceptance of Catholicism did not seem imperiled by the Church's increasingly hard-line stance against what it regarded as the growing licentiousness of the film industry. At the behest of Catholic movie magazine mogul Martin Quigley, the Jesuit theologian Daniel Lord had authored the first film Production Code, a response to the public's demand for some kind of censorship. In

1930 the major studios agreed to the voluntary code, which contained specific restrictions on obscene language, sex, violence, ethnic insults, drug abuse, and religious ridicule. When the Depression prompted movie studios to increase the sex and violence levels to get people back into theaters, Catholic officials pressed for stricter enforcement of the code. In 1934, Catholic bishops created the Legion of Decency to promote high moral standards in movies. Hollywood officials, fearful of a box office boycott by Catholics, agreed to submit their scripts and films in advance to the legion office in New York. Legion ratings were published in Catholic, Protestant, Jewish, and secular newspapers. The sympathetic treatment of Catholics in movies was no doubt intentional.

Church officials were often under fire from the left over movie censorship, but they did not retreat. Archbishop Spellman, in the thick of the battle, declared in 1942:

> *The fifth column of the saboteurs of our factories and public utilities has its counterpart in the filth of those who piously shout censorship if they are not permitted freely to exercise their venal, venomous, diabolical debauching of the mind and body of our boys and girls. I am against harmful censorship but that does not mean that I must condone those who wish to include among America's freedoms the freedom to kill the bodies and souls of their fellow Americans, the freedom to be cruel, the freedom to be obscene, the freedom to steal and the freedom to spread disease.*[16]

After the war, the battle over film censorship intensified. When Spellman and the Legion of Decency worked to prevent the showing of *The Miracle,* the charge being that it mocked the Incarnation (which it did), the American Civil Liberties Union, the American Jewish Congress, and a group called Protestants and Other Americans United for the Separation of Church and State objected strenuously. The *Daily Worker* claimed that Spellman was trying to establish "a clerical political tyranny in violation of the United States Constitution." In the end, the United States Supreme Court agreed, and the decision was considered "a humiliating defeat for Cardinal Spellman."[17]

◯⁓

BY 1945, FULTON SHEEN'S prominence was such that critics of things Catholic often referred to him as though he were a top Church official. In May of that year, for instance, a leading Congregational minister, Harold Ockenga of Boston, told the third annual convention of the National Association of Evangelicals that the Roman Catholic hierarchy was "now reaching out for control of the government" of the United States. He called the assignment of diplomats to the Vatican "a sinister portent in America, the activity of an alien political philosophy in American affairs, which is a greater menace than Communism itself." He added, "The political activity of the Roman Catholic hierarchy is doubly dangerous because Americans are unaware that the philosophy of Msgr. Fulton J. Sheen may involve a change in American culture almost as fundamental as that of Josef Stalin."[18] Adding fuel to evangelical frustrations was the success that Sheen was having with converts. The list of prominent people he personally brought into the Church was growing long, and untold thousands of others were entering anonymously as a result of Sheen publications, media presentations, sermons and talks.

One of his most celebrated converts was Louis Budenz, an attorney and labor leader who had abandoned the Catholic faith of his youth and joined the Communist Party in 1935, eventually becoming managing editor of the *Daily Worker*. In the Christmas 1936 issue, Budenz wrote a lengthy article posing a series of questions to Sheen and challenging his attacks on communism. The monsignor responded with a pamphlet entitled *Communism Answers the Questions of a Communist*, which quickly sold 65,000 copies at a nickel apiece. Sheen's sources were almost exclusively Soviet decrees and publications. When asked how he could speak against people who were in the forefront of the battle for the downtrodden, for example, Sheen cited numerous Soviet newspapers and documents describing in detail the economic misery experienced by those living under communism. When challenged to cite evidence that Communists consistently called Catholic priests "fascists," Sheen produced a list of citations to prove the point, adding, "I am rather surprised that a Communist is not more familiar with Communistic literature and should have asked for texts. But there they are."[19]

In the spring of 1937, Sheen invited Budenz to dinner for a chat. "I'm having dinner with a leading Communist tonight," Sheen told a Boston reporter. "In fact, I'm looking forward to the encounter with a great deal of pleasure."[20] That evening, Sheen ended the verbal sparring by citing articles of the Soviet constitution that Budenz knew nothing about. He then said he wanted to talk about Budenz's soul, and the ensuing discussion included such topics as God, grace, and the Blessed Mother.

Budenz was shaken by the encounter. Later he wrote, "In the course of the years I have met many magnetic men and women, have conferred with governors and senators, have stood in court twenty-one times as a result of labor disputes—breathlessly awaited the verdict and each time experienced the triumph of acquittal—but never has my soul been swept by love and reverence as it was that April evening."[21]

Still, Budenz pondered Sheen's remarks for eight years before contacting the monsignor to say that he wanted to return to the Church and bring his family with him. Sheen visited the Budenz home secretly, at night, for several months. On October 10, 1945, Sheen removed Budenz's excommunication and baptized and confirmed his wife and three daughters at a special ceremony in St. Patrick's Cathedral baptistery.[22] After Sheen gave the news to the Associated Press, a shocked Communist official called him to confirm the story. Upon hearing it was true, the man used language, Sheen recalled, that "cannot be found in any manual of prayer." Budenz's name was still on the *Daily Worker* masthead. "We caught the Communists with their red flannels down," Sheen said gleefully.[23] Fifty-four-year-old Budenz told reporters, "Communism, I have found, aims to establish a tyranny over the human spirit; it is in unending conflict with religion and true freedom." With Sheen's assistance, Budenz was hired as an assistant professor of economics at Notre Dame.[24]

Budenz did a great deal of testifying about communism and Communists before the FBI and congressional investigating committees, and at court and administrative proceedings between 1946 and 1957, when he suffered a severe heart attack. His charges against foreign policy expert Owen Lattimore, in defense of "top Russian spy" allegations made by Senator Joe McCarthy, were highly controversial at the time and later.[25] There is no known link between Budenz's testimony and Sheen, but Sheen was probably supportive. He had a strong affection toward Budenz and his family for the rest of his life, saving three letters that documented the friendship. In 1978, Budenz's widow wrote, "The decision to leave the Communist Party and to become Catholics involved much more soul searching and cerebration than most people realize. You, who were such an important part of the whole process, have a better idea of what went into making us Christians. I shall always remember that you had the courage to take a chance on us, a chance that was a high-risk venture."[26]

"Turning" Communists became something of a Sheen franchise. Another case was that of Bella V. Dodd, a New York attorney who had been active in leftist circles since the early 1930s and had joined the Communist Party in 1943. In the spring of 1950, testifying before the Tydings Committee, which was investigating charges by Senator McCarthy, she revealed considerable sympathy toward the Communist Party of the United States.[27] One day, while Dodd was testifying before the House Committee on Un-American Activities in Washington, Senator Howard McGrath of Rhode Island challenged her to meet with Fulton Sheen. She accepted the challenge, and the two met in a small outer room at Sheen's home. After pleasantries were exchanged, Fulton said that she looked sad. "When the conversation came to a dead end, I suggested that she come into the chapel and say a prayer. While we knelt, silently, she began to cry. She was touched by grace." Later, Sheen gave her instructions, baptized her, and received her into the Church. (Dodd had been

born a Catholic, but her baptismal records could not be found.)
With communism behind her, she taught law in Texas and later at
St. John's University in Brooklyn.[28]

Gertrude Algase (pronounced "Algaze") was in her mid-forties
and recently widowed when she converted from Judaism under
Sheen's direction. She was fairly well known in New York as a highly
aggressive and effective literary agent.[29] In 1942, soon after becoming a Catholic, she signed Sheen to a contract. A year later, she
became Spellman's literary agent. The archbishop was deeply
impressed when Algase told him that she could have gotten him
$10,000 for a *Saturday Evening Post* article he had written for free.[30]
She was given an office near Spellman's, and priests on the staff,
admiring her physical appearance and brassy ways, called her "Mortal Sin." Algase soon edited a series of Spellman articles and a book
on his wartime travels, and she helped him write poetry. Spellman's
official biographer reported, "Thus began the Archbishop's second
creative period. It was to bear fruit in a shelf of slender volumes,
and a shower of royalties poured into the coffers of various charitable and educational organizations over a million dollars." Spellman's only novel, *The Foundling*, became a best-seller in 1951.[31]

Algase would later have such clients as historians Charles and
Mary Beard, journalist Arthur Krock, and John F. Kennedy. She was
also known locally for her charitable events, being the founder of
the Alfred E. Smith Memorial Dinner, which raised a quarter of a
million dollars a year for a diocesan hospital, and the New York
Foundling Hospital Christmas Party. Both events were conceived
in cooperation with Spellman, whose fund-raising abilities were
already becoming legendary.[32]

Ada Smith, born in 1894 in Alderson, West Virginia, and known
internationally as the black nightclub owner and entertainer Bricktop, began listening to Fulton Sheen on the *Catholic Hour* when she
was in her late forties. She had become interested in the Church
through a convert friend, and Sheen's radio addresses sealed her
desire to become a Catholic. Ada consulted with a New York priest
and was baptized on December 5, 1943.

A few years later, Bricktop eagerly seized the opportunity to meet Sheen, an encounter she would describe as "beautiful." Some time later, in Rome, the two met again. Bricktop said she was broke and needed money. "He went and got a checkbook. 'What do you need? Five hundred dollars, five thousand, what?' " She accepted five hundred. Fulton was astonished when Bricktop eventually appeared at his office to return the $500. It was the first time in his long lending career that anyone had repaid him. One of the entertainer's most cherished gifts was a Sheen book inscribed by the author to "My child in Christ, Bricktop, who proves every walk of life can be spiritualized."[33]

Grace Moore was a world-famous opera singer and actress who had starred in eight movies between 1930 and 1940. In 1946, she contacted Sheen and expressed her desire to enter the Church. Her schedule was such that Sheen gave her instruction in three days, but he refused to baptize her until she had taken several months more to consider the step she was taking. In early 1947, the forty-eight-year-old singer was killed in an airplane crash in Copenhagen. Sheen sadly noted that she was to have been inducted into the Church upon her return to the United States.[34]

For years Fulton enjoyed telling the story of how Grace Moore refused to believe him when he said that he could not sing. A speaking voice that beautiful, she asserted, must have its counterpart in song. After the two sang a duet, Moore concluded, "You are right. You have no voice."[35]

Sheen was not at all bashful about sounding out potential converts. D. P. Noonan recalled, "He always looked about for prospective candidates, such as a person alongside him on a plane ride. Many a stewardess has an autographed book of the Bishop's, or a treasured rosary given her by him. Sheen used to give TWA a plug by quipping, 'Travel With the Angels.' When he journeyed on a train, or met someone by chance on the street, Sheen was always on duty for the Church."[36] In his autobiography, Sheen told of being summoned to pay a call at a fashionable Manhattan apartment house along the East River to console a man whose wife had committed suicide. The man turned out not to be at home, so Sheen asked the elevator operator who lived in the other apartment on the same floor. Hearing it was the renowned violinist Fritz Kreisler, then seventy-two, Sheen rang the bell and introduced himself. After a brief conversation, he asked Kreisler and his wife if they would like to take instruction for the Church. They accepted the invitation, and after two months they received Communion.[37]

Sheen remained a personal friend of the Kreislers to the end of their days. "Fritz Kreisler was one of the finest and noblest men I ever met in my entire life," he wrote. Fulton especially enjoyed the musician's intellectual prowess. "When I would quote a text from the Old Testament, he would read it in Hebrew; when I would quote a text from the New Testament, Fritz would read it in Greek." An unpublished Kreisler piece, changed to waltz time to satisfy Fulton, became the theme song for his television show.[38] He spoke at Kreisler's seventy-fifth and eightieth birthday celebrations, and delivered the eulogy at the violinist's funeral in 1962.[39]

Another high-profile convert, Clare Boothe Luce, was a beautiful, brilliant and unprincipled woman of thirty-two when she married Henry Luce, publisher of *Time* and *Fortune,* in 1935. Having worked and schemed her way out of poverty with the aid of an ambitious mother, Clare was a successful journalist who would soon become a well-known playwright and screen writer. In her youth, Luce had married a millionaire twice her age, with whom she had her only child, a daughter named Ann, and after her first husband's death she had devoted herself to what she called a "rage to fame." She traveled the world during the war as a reporter for Henry Luce's *Life* magazine, and served two terms in Congress, where she became known as a brainy champion of minority groups and trade unions.

In the course of her rise to prominence and afterward, Luce was skilled at manipulating men, doing whatever was necessary, often through sex, to get what she wanted, and leaving the widespread impression that she was cold, calculating, and often cruel. Irwin Shaw called her "feminine as a meat axe."[40] Her conquests included married multimillionaires Bernard Baruch and Joseph P. Kennedy.

That Luce would have any interest in religion, let alone Roman Catholicism, was something no one would have guessed. She wrote later, "Broadly speaking, I was a liberal. And like a good pragmatist, I lived liberally."[41] Then one day in 1945, Sheen telephoned Congresswoman Luce and invited her to dinner. Sheen had been alerted by a Jesuit priest who had been in contact with Luce and knew of the deep depression she was suffering at the death, in an automobile accident, of her daughter a year earlier. When the dishes had been taken away, the monsignor turned the subject to religion. "Give me five minutes to talk to you about God, and then I will give you an hour to state your own views." When he got to the subject of the goodness of God, Luce exploded, "If God is good, why did he take my daughter?" Sheen replied calmly, "In order that through that sorrow, you might be here now starting instructions to know Christ and His Church."[42]

Clare took instruction for five months. She wrote later, "It took Father Sheen several months to clear away that thick fog of prejudices and superstition acquired through a lifetime."[43] Sheen recalled, "Never in my life have I been privileged to instruct anyone who was as brilliant and who was so scintillating in conversation as Mrs. Luce. She had a mind like a rapier."[44] Of Sheen, Luce wrote, "For this brilliant teacher, this good and gifted professor of Catholic philosophy, I thank God." She observed, "I never knew a teacher who could be at once so patient and so unyielding, so poetical, so practical, so inventive and so orthodox." And she denied, as some insinuated, that Sheen was a Svengali who tricked or charmed into joining the Church. There was nothing "particularly hypnotic" about Sheen, said Luce.

> What "hypnotizes" his converts is the sudden and unfamiliar
> sight of Truth and Love and Life eternal, which his instructions
> open up to them.... I have often been asked, "Would you have
> become a Catholic, if you had not had Sheen to give you instruc-
> tions?" My answer, "Of course." God intended me to be a Catholic
> or He would not have sent me to Father Sheen, the one best

*equipped to rid my mind of nonsense and fill it with the sense of
Our Lord Jesus.*[45]

In the first of three articles in *McCall's* magazine on the subject,
Luce wrote of her conversion, "Well, I suppose that the over-all reason, the one that includes all the others and, therefore, one might
say the real reason, is that upon careful examination, Catholic doctrine seemed to me the solid objective Truth."[46] The article prompted
a thousand letters to pour into the magazine. A Notre Dame priest
interested in converts wrote, "Perhaps not since Newman's time has
the publication of an Apologia created a greater stir."[47] In a letter
to her still shocked friends, Clare enclosed a slim compendium of
Jesus' words as recorded in the New Testament, saying *"Jesus Christ
Himself was the Real Reason!"*[48]

Sheen almost always asked converts to find another priest to
hear their first confession.[49] When he asked Clare what kind of confessor she wanted, she replied, "One who has seen the rise and fall
of kingdoms." Fulton selected his friend Auxiliary Bishop James
Francis McIntyre, Archbishop Spellman's right-hand man.[50] (Spellman had already been named a cardinal by this time and would
soon be given Pius XII's own ceremonial hat and the titular church
that had once been part of the Pope's cardinalate. McIntyre was
soon named coadjutor archbishop of New York.)[51] Sheen received
Luce into the Church in St. Patrick's Cathedral on February 16, 1946.
Only six people were present.

One sympathetic friend, a non-Catholic, wrote that "Clare always
had the capability of being great. There was her wonderful brain,
her beauty, and her real desire to serve her country and all the peoples of the world. But there was something lacking. Her conversion
to Catholicism had given her the humility, the gentleness, and the
warmth to love individual people, as opposed to a sense of duty to
humanity. These were the things she needed to make her the really
great woman she is."[52] Actress Loretta Young later recalled that Luce
changed completely. "She remained strong, but in a positive way. I
couldn't believe she was the same woman after her conversion."[53]

For the rest of her long life, much to Sheen's joy, Luce would be an articulate champion of the Catholic faith.[54]

Sheen and Luce remained very close personal friends for decades. Fulton wrote her scores of admiring and encouraging letters in his own hand, signed "me" and "himself." He dedicated each Wednesday Mass to her, along with his second Christmas Mass.[55] One letter to "Clare Dear" said that he was prouder of her than any other convert.[56] In another, he called her his "best friend."[57] During a private audience in Rome in 1949, Pius XII and Sheen both extolled the virtues of Mrs. Luce. Sheen wrote to her, "Clare, you must come to Rome before the Holy Year—before October! I cannot tell you in words the warmth of his Personal Affection for you. And it made *me* so happy because I love you too."[58] Fulton said a Mass every year for Luce's departed daughter, Ann, writing often of the sacrifice she made so that her brilliant mother would be led to Christ and bring light to generations of men and women.[59] At one point, Fulton wrote, "I had a dream about a wonderful friend whose name was Clare & whom I instructed and then in turn inspired me. When I woke up, I was as glad it was only a dream. For if it really happened, I never would have been able to thank God enough."[60]

Gretta Palmer was a prominent freelance journalist in 1947. A graduate of Vassar, she had grown up with virtually no religious instruction and considered herself an atheist. She dabbled in Freud and believed in little more than the inevitable progress of the human race. Palmer was first jolted from what she called the "atheist's cell" by the world war: this was mankind regressing, not progressing, and physical and social scientists seemed to have no clue how to solve the problem of human hostility. She was appalled to hear a priest, in answer to her questions about changing the hearts of men, refer to original sin. Wartime travels, however, added to her perplexity about human nature and ultimate values as she observed the pain and heroism of combat troops. After the war, Palmer fell into despair.

In 1947, *Look* magazine assigned Palmer to write an article on Fulton J. Sheen and his converts. Sheen refused her request for an interview, saying that he did not like publicity and that the conversions were not his doing but the result of God's grace. Palmer gained an interview by noting that she had been baptized a Catholic and had fallen away from the faith. Sheen agreed to talk with her about returning to the Church if she would not use anything he said for publication.

At their first meeting, Sheen spoke of many things, but not about Palmer herself, and said he was available if she ever wanted to see him. At a second meeting, Sheen urged her not to reject reason in her pursuit of truth. "That's the mistake the followers of Hitler made. That's the kind of thing that makes people believe that some man in Moscow, Idaho is God, because he claims to be. Let me tell you what we Catholics believe, and if your reason rejects it, go away with my blessing. But I beg you, as a friend, don't throw in the sponge on using your intellect."

Sheen's encouraging words drove Palmer to Chesterton, and then to a vast assortment of books both for and against Catholicism. The atheist's cell began to crumble, as she later wrote:

> *I found that there is no fact or hypothesis of modern physics or astronomy which cannot be comfortably accommodated inside the ample arms of the Church. I discovered that, historically speaking, people seem to* leave *the Church because they want forbidden things, never because they want a deeper truth. I found that people* enter *the Church because they want the fulfillment of either heart or brain or soul. Many men have abandoned Rome because they wished to worship at the altar of man's self-sufficient intellect; nobody ever left the Church because the best in him could not find fulfillment there.*

Palmer also took Sheen's advice to read the Gospels "very slowly," and was overwhelmed with the possibility that the story could be true. Jesus, she wrote,

> could *have been a madman when He claimed to be God, but it is a curiously catching madness in which the world has believed*

for two thousand years. He could have been a cruel liar making gulls of the disciples by promising redemption. If so, it is odd that such a lie told to a group of fishermen in an obscure village of a backward colony, a kind of ancient Puerto Rico, should have toppled empires and led generations of men to martyrdom and monasteries and scholarly concentration on this lie. The only possible alternative answer is the truth of what He said: that He was truly God, and truly come to save the world.

Sheen gave Gretta instruction and received her into the Church. She wrote and lectured about her conversion and sent the monsignor to at least one potential convert some time later. And she got her story on Sheen and his converts for *Look,* now written with an enthusiasm that would have been impossible while she inhabited, as she put it, "the cramped and narrow universe in which I lived my life until a year ago. The name of it is Hell."[61]

Palmer observed in the *Look* article that Sheen's conversions included average Americans as well as the rich and famous: "on a single day in Lent this year he baptized 43 men and women, whose number included a Jewish manicurist, a Baptist minister, half a dozen atheists and a practicer of Yoga. He is beginning an all-Negro instruction class in Washington and a New York group open to anyone at all." She asked Fulton why people were hungry for instruction. He replied, "Sin is the strongest incentive. People today are tired of having their sins explained away. They want their sins forgiven. They don't want to be told, any more, that it was all the fault of their parents or of their environment or that their glands made them behave that way. What they long to find is Mercy."

Palmer's piece also revealed Sheen's generosity toward his converts. Along with his time, knowledge and sympathy, he gave copies of G. K. Chesterton's *Everlasting Man* (a difficult and demanding book) and *All Things Considered,* as well as his own new book *Preface to Religion.* Fulton generally refused to accept money from converts. (At least once, he made an exception in the case of Luce, suggesting that the donation be used to pay his secretaries. "Through them I am able to reach more people for good.")[62] Palmer reported that "he gives away his earnings from lecturing and teaching with a reckless generosity that appalls his secretarial staff. The royalties he should receive from his books... are always consumed by the gift copies he mails out, in rivers, to those who write to him. His stamp bill alone runs to over $900 a year."[63]

The following year, Elizabeth Bentley quietly took instruction from Msgr. Sheen. Bentley had been a long-time Communist Party member and spy who went to the FBI, confessed, and was now being called upon frequently by congressional committees to testify about the extent of Red infiltration in the federal government. (Whittaker Chambers was summoned by HUAC to substantiate Miss Bentley's recollections, the start of the public allegations involving Alger Hiss.) Louis Budenz recommended Sheen to her. Emmanuel Sigmund Larsen, a former State Department employee suspected of spying, also contacted Sheen in 1948 about the possibility of receiving instruction into the Catholic Church.[64]

IN JULY 1948, *Time* magazine reported that the Catholic population in America had increased by 807,524 during the previous year, and now numbered more than 26 million. The priesthood had grown by 1,277, to a total of 41,747, and Catholic colleges had more than doubled their enrollment in two years. The number of converts was a record-breaking 115,214. The article featured Father Lester J. Fallon, the celebrated mail-order priest who during the war had signed up 38,000 servicemen. It also quoted Jesuit Father John E. Odou, director of Convert Makers of America (founded in 1944), saying, "Trains, hotels, depots, beauty parlors are all crowded with potential converts. That is why the slogan used by every C.M.O.A. is: 'Never let an opportunity slip.'" But the "most famed proselytizer of all," noted *Time,* was Fulton J. Sheen. Several of his maxims about converts were included, such as "Win an argument and you lose a soul," and "There are three rules of dealing with all those who come to us: KINDNESS, KINDNESS, KINDNESS."[65]

Sheen conducted his convert classes in different ways, depending on his schedule, the location, and the number of people involved. In 1945, converts came to the Roosevelt Hotel in New York, where Sheen usually stayed on *Catholic Hour* broadcast weekends. Two women from Sheen's staff would greet the people and play Sheen audio tapes; the monsignor would often appear at the end of the hour-long sessions to answer questions and talk individually to the aspirants. Joan Hartmann was one of these staff members, and would become Sheen's executive secretary for six years. She later called her former employer "fabulous," describing him as kind, outgoing, and concerned with people from all walks of life.[66]

In 1947, Fulton hosted convert classes in his home in Washington. Each convert received from forty to a hundred hours of instruction, depending on the level of need. A reporter observed, "A novice receives both instruction and prayer, and it is said among churchmen that [Sheen's] novices receive far more prayer than those of any other instructor."[67]

In 1950, Mary Downing, eager to leave the Episcopal Church and become a Catholic, drove from Philadelphia for several weekends to listen to tapes by herself in Sheen's home. Margaret Yates was her encouraging and helpful hostess. On Sunday evenings, in the Sheen living room, Downing listened to the monsignor on the *Catholic Hour*. After hearing all the tapes, she met with Sheen personally on the day he announced that she was to be brought into the Church.[68]

Fulton told an interviewer in 1946, "I can say that I prefer the instruction of souls to any other work I do." But as usual, he preferred to give the credit to God and not himself. "I never keep a record of converts lest I fall into the error of thinking I made them. The Good Lord would never let me have another. He would punish me for my pride. I say this in great sincerity. We must pay more attention to the unimportant for the sake of our own sanctification. It would be a terrible thing to die and hear that you had already had your reward in praise for what you had done." God's grace was responsible for conversion, he said. "I happen to be walking under

the trees where the apples are ripe. I sometimes get credit for growing them or even for plucking them, but I didn't grow the apples,
God did."[69]

Sheen wrote often about converts and conversions. He observed
that each conversion started with a crisis, accompanied "on the one
hand, by a profound sense of one's own helplessness and, on the
other hand, by an equally certain conviction that God alone can
supply what the individual lacks." One can plunge into despair, cynicism and even suicide, or reach out to the Creator for help. Sheen
wrote in *Peace of Soul*, "The grace of God comes to us in just the
degree that we open our souls to it; the only limit to our capacity
to receive Him is our willingness to do so.... The latch is on our
side and not on God's, for God breaks down no doors. We bar His
entrance." He added, "God is the most obvious fact of human experience. If we are not aware of Him, it is because we are too com-
plicated and because our noses are lifted high in the air in pride,
for lo! He is at our very feet." The whole meaning of Christianity,
wrote Sheen, "is contained in the simple phrase of the creed, 'He
descended from Heaven.' "[70]

Preface to Religion, given to converts, is one of Sheen's most
impressive books. Clearly and powerfully written, the 228-page publication is a guide to both Christianity and the Church. Its contents
include:

> *If you want to know about God, there is only one way to do it:
> get down on your knees.*

> *Atheism, nine times out of ten, is born from the womb of a bad
> conscience. Disbelief is born of sin, not of reason.*

> *If you do not worship God, you worship something, and nine
> times out of ten it will be yourself.*

> *Much of modern education is merely a rationalization of evil. It
> makes clever devils instead of stupid devils. The world is not in
> a muddle because of stupidity of the intellect, but because of per-
> versity of the will. We know enough: it is our choices that are
> wrong.*

You can love the lovable without being religious; you can respect those who respect you without religion; you can pay debts without being religious, but you cannot love those who hate you without being religious; you cannot atone for your guilty conscience without being religious.

Press a rose petal between your fingers, and you can never restore its tint. Lift a dew drop from a leaf, and you can never replace it. Evil, in like manner, is too deep-seated in the world to be righted by a little kindness or reason and tolerance.

The modern man who is not living according to his conscience wants a religion without a Cross, a Christ without a Calvary, a Kingdom without Justice, and in his church a "soft dean who never mentions hell to ears polite."

Have you noticed that as men lose faith in God, they become selfish, immoral and cruel? On a cosmic scale, as religion decreases, tyranny increases; as men lose faith in Divinity, they lose faith in humanity. Where God is outlawed, there man is subjugated.

Most of what Sheen had to say in *Preface to Religion* he had said before—in some cases, many times. But his handling of such topics as Faith, Hope, Charity, Is Religion Purely Individual, and How You Are Remade was seldom so skillful and compassionate.[71] Not surprisingly, the book was an effective tool for winning converts.

Sheen did not mention Protestant churches in the course of his convert instruction unless someone made an inquiry, and he advised other Catholics to follow the same policy. "If one presents the Church as the prolongation of the Incarnation, as the Mystical Christ living through the centuries, as Christ speaking His Truth through His Body, as He once spoke it through His human nature; forgiving sins through His new Body as He forgave them through His human nature, then there is no need of refuting a sect that came into existence 1,600 years after the death of Christ." In the postwar world, he wrote, people were suffering from confusion and a heightened awareness of guilt and sin, and those were the primary issues the convert maker should address.[72]

Many Protestants, especially among Catholic-hating fundamentalists, resented what they saw as Sheen's condescension as well as his success in causing converts to "swim the Tiber." One such critic was William Ward Ayer, a successful New York Baptist minister and radio preacher. The fundamentalist leader, converted in 1916 at a Billy Sunday revival, was a trustee of Bob Jones University and Eastern Baptist Seminary. His Calvary Baptist Church had grown from 400 to 1,600 members during his thirteen years in the pulpit. In 1947, Ayer came in third in a radio poll seeking to discover "New York's Number One Citizen," running behind Cardinal Spellman and Eleanor Roosevelt.[73]

In August 1948, Ayer wrote a two-part attack on Sheen in the *United Evangelical Action,* a monthly publication of the National Association of Evangelicals, a conservative Protestant organization founded five years earlier and representing scores of denominations. Ayer had a solid working knowledge of Sheen and began his attack by expressing admiration for Sheen's learning, wit and publication record. But he soon referred to "Romanism's peculiarities and those doctrines and paganistic procedures which are always offensive to liberty-loving and Bible-believing Protestants." And he followed this with a complaint about the "un-American attitude of the daily newspapers—engendered apparently by fear of the stern Roman hierarchy," as shown in the refusal to report that more Catholics were converting to Protestantism than the other way around. He was particularly angry at the press for ignoring his own successes.

Ayer examined each of the major Sheen converts and concluded that not one could be said to have been a true Protestant before entering the Catholic Church. He thought Clare Boothe Luce predisposed to Roman Catholicism by having had a Catholic mother and by being "unstable," as proven by her dalliance with Freudianism, Marxism, and liberalism before meeting Sheen. Heywood Broun, Ayer noted, had been a religious "nothing" before converting.

Louis Budenz had been a Catholic before accepting communism; and during their crucial conversation, moreover, Sheen had discussed Mary. Ayer remarked, "An enlightened Protestant is forced to ask, 'To what was Budenz converted?' There is no mention of the Savior here, no thought of atonement for sin—only an exaltation, in true Romanist fashion, of Mary, whom they paganistically call the mother of God. This is not Christian salvation but a satanic system of religion based upon the false premise of Mary's priority. This is not the faith of the New Testament!" As for Henry Ford II, "Apparently he was religiously 'nothing' and joined his fiancée's church as a convenience." Moreover, the press reported that Ford took his first Communion the morning of his wedding. "The whole procedure gives the appearance of 'spiritual shot-gunnery,' making religion a convenient prerequisite to conjugal love and marital experience."

Ayer then attacked Sheen's character. "It is reported that the wife of a millionaire supplied him with generous amounts of money while she was alive and left him an outright personal legacy of $160,000 in her will. As a secular priest he is entitled to spend and keep as much money as he can get." He concluded his articles by warning that Catholics, led by the likes of Sheen, were "planning complete religious totalitarianism that will destroy our religious liberty, bring about collusion between church and state, and turn America into the chaos which has blighted Europe for hundreds of years."[74]

Sheen, who almost never responded to critics, had no official comment about the Ayer articles. When they appeared, he had just returned from an exhausting world tour with Cardinal Spellman and other Church leaders.

∽

CARDINAL SPELLMAN HAD accepted an invitation from the archbishop of Melbourne, Australia, the Most Reverend Daniel Mannix, to help him celebrate the centenary of his archdiocese. Since Spellman was also national president of the Society for the Propagation of the Faith, he chose to use the occasion to visit some of the missionary and military centers throughout the Orient. The original travel plans were expanded when the cardinal, still inspired by his wartime travels as military vicar, accepted several invitations from military and civil authorities in the Far East.[75]

Having suppressed his initial misgivings about Spellman (expressed privately to Fr. John Tracy Ellis in 1939), Sheen was on excellent terms with the prelate. It was a wise policy, for the cardinal was known to demand absolute loyalty and obedience from the priests who sought his favor. Sheen and Spellman had seen much of each other over the years at St. Patrick's Cathedral and elsewhere. Both were Irish, personal friends of the Pope, unshakably loyal to Church teaching. Spellman could not help but admire Sheen's intellectual and oratorical gifts, as well as his sense of humor. In 1948, according to his official biographer, the cardinal was grooming the monsignor "for higher things."[76] So Sheen was invited on the worldwide journey as a friend and protégé who would deliver speeches and sermons.[77]

Spellman and his party landed at Honolulu on April 24. In a diary he kept for the journey (internal evidence strongly suggests it was intended to be read by others and perhaps published), Sheen noted that "A great crowd was at [the] airport awaiting the Cardinal and the first passenger off the plane was a huge blonde wearing a big red hat."[78] For his part, Spellman noted in his own diary that Sheen "had three fat wreaths hung around his neck … while mine was adorned with only one delicate one. But I am still ahead of him in Indian tribal headdresses and I think, too, in moccasins."[79]

The *Honolulu Star-Bulletin* treated Sheen almost as Spellman's equal, running a photograph of the two with the local bishop and carrying an interview with Sheen about international affairs. While Sheen gladly commented on the recent electoral victory of the Vatican-backed Christian Democratic Party over the Communists in Italy, saying that "the skies are brighter now," Spellman refused to comment.[80] Was Sheen trying deliberately to upstage the cardinal? Not at all; such a move would have been self-destructive. Sheen, famous and outspoken, was simply being himself. Spellman, much less eloquent, more politically astute, and ever mindful of his vast influence in the Church and the world, chose to stand aside and let his protégé do the talking. Indeed, that is why Fulton was brought along on the trip. Evidence suggests, moreover, that Spellman was amused by all of the attention the monsignor attracted.

Sheen had not flown over the Pacific Ocean before and was delighted by the new experience. He heard confessions in the Fiji Islands, and entered in his diary a quantity of data about the people of the islands, especially the Catholic minority. "About 200 Fijians are converted a year by the 30 Catholic priests and a small number of nuns," he noted. Fulton's sense of humor was much in evidence (as it would be throughout the diary). He observed that the Fijians "use a very narrow wooden comb and apply some vegetable roots to make their hair stand up straight as if they were frightened by a Wall St. depression. They also rub a black deposit from the swamps into their hair to kill the lice. Sometimes the hair is dyed to pinkish orange with coral lime without the aid of Elizabeth Arden." On the largest island, Viti Levu—about the size of Connecticut, he observed—some of the missionaries had been using Sheen sermons on the natives; *"Now* I know why their hair stands on end."[81]

In Sydney, Australia, Sheen spoke to a crowd of 25,000 people: 10,000 inside the tightly packed cathedral and 15,000 outside listening to loudspeakers. Sheen wrote in his diary, "I am amazed how well-known my name is in Australia. There seems to be little difference from the States. . . . Cardinal Gilroy said that last night's sermon was the greatest he had ever heard. He is a saintly, good man—despite any exaggeration." Sheen was on the radio four times during his first day in the city.[82]

Sheen again made local headlines by his comments at a press conference on world affairs. He criticized the United Nations, declaring it incapable of dealing with "any problem because it is grounded upon power, not upon law." The United Nations, he said, "would be more effective if we stood it on its head. Power should not be vested in the big nations." Sheen added that in his judgment the United Nations had signed its death warrant at San Francisco when it decided that prayers at the proceedings might be offensive to some of the delegates. Spellman once more refused comment on political questions—"My job is the Ten Commandments."[83]

Following a civic reception for the cardinal in the Sydney Town Hall, Sheen was mobbed in the street by adoring local citizens, including a number of children. Photographs of the joyous encounter were splashed all over the front pages of local newspapers, and also appeared in at least one New York newspaper. To many, it must have seemed that Sheen was the star of the tour and that Cardinal Spellman was tagging along with him.[84]

In Melbourne, fifty thousand people turned out at the show grounds to greet the visiting clerics. Spellman, who had just preached a sermon at the cathedral, turned to Sheen and, without any warning, asked him to speak to the crowd. (Fulton confided to Clare Boothe Luce, "I know now why the Cardinal invited me. He tosses out the first ball and then asks me to pitch the rest of the game.")[85] Sheen reported, "I told Irish stories for a few minutes and then gave a talk." A dinner followed, and then he left immediately to do an hour-long radio broadcast on the subject of communism. The next day, Spellman said privately to Sheen, "We are very proud of what you are doing both for America and Australia." Sheen wrote in his diary, "There is absolutely no jealousy in that man." The following day, at the Grand Centenary Ball held at the Melbourne Town Hall, Spellman introduced Sheen to the crowd of 2,100 by saying, "This will be his 99th talk today."[86]

The clerics followed a whirlwind schedule with teas, dinners, talks, official gatherings, religious services and rallies filling almost every hour of the very long days. Fulton, physically healthy and thoroughly enjoying the adulation of huge crowds and dignitaries, enjoyed himself immensely. At one point in Melbourne he gave a Holy Hour at 3:00 P.M. in a downtown church. The local cardinal presided, and 40 bishops and 250 priests were on hand. Thousands of people were in the streets listening to Sheen by loudspeaker. "It surpassed anything I ever saw in America, even the Three Hours at the Cathedral," he wrote in his diary. "After the Hour it took me an hour and a half to get through the crowds even with cops and motor-cycle policemen. I never heard so many 'God bless yous' in my life."[87]

Some Australian Protestant ministers branded Sheen "the great-est menace that has yet visited Australia." In his diary he mused, "Menace to what? they did not say."[88]

On May 7, Fulton addressed some 20 bishops and 3,000 priests ("I talked on the *Corpus Physicum* and the *Corpus Mysticum* for an hour"), followed by what a local newspaper called "a stirring denun-ciation of Communism" before a crowd of 20,000 in the huge Exhi-bition Hall, with another 15,000 outside standing in the rain to hear the talk over loudspeakers.[89]

May 8 was Fulton's birthday, and Cardinal Spellman offered a toast at a luncheon for clergy who had studied in Rome. This was followed by much singing and gaiety. Sheen had to leave the party early to address 2,000 trade union men and women. "I spoke to them an hour and honestly the reception they gave me made me ashamed. They lined the streets and cheered as my car left. It was really touching.... I never met such enthusiastic people."[90]

That evening, Sheen spoke at a banquet for 700 Catholic laity. The next morning he attended at Mass in Exhibition Hall, with 15,000 present. "After the Mass I was besieged for autographs. I stood for an hour autographing with at least 10 plainclothes men trying to protect me. But the people pressed so much that I lost the top half of my fountain pen and had my toes stepped on many times and my purple ripped from my back. Then the police made a fly-ing wedge for a door near the auditorium and with the greatest of difficulty got me into the police car and back to the Cathedral for dinner." There he gave a talk to 700 men, and after a visit to a local college, he dictated letters for an hour. After dinner, he attended a pageant at the Melbourne race track with 100,000 people present. "Such cheering as my car passed a line of people about 2 blocks long. They seemed to have enjoyed my talks and broadcasts. I sneaked out of the pageant to come home and write."[91]

Sheen estimated that in a single week he had talked eight hours and forty minutes, twice to audiences over 30,000. "I never realized that in the short space of a week such an impression could be made."[92] By another account, Spellman gave thirty-two talks and Sheen fifty in the course of those seven days.[93]

Fulton was never too busy, however, to pay attention to personal requests. In Tasmania, he received a letter "from a wife whose husband had lost the faith. She wanted me to get her husband back to confession. I phoned him and when he came [to Sheen's room,] in 30 seconds I had him on his knees."[94]

Back in Sydney, at a luncheon attended by two cardinals and an assortment of other clerics, Spellman paid tribute to Sheen. He said, as Sheen recalled,

> *I want to say a word about Msgr. Sheen who in America is doing more than any Cardinal, any Archbishop, or any Bishop to make the faith known and loved. He is one of the truly apostolic souls of our time. He has the ear of Catholics and he has the ear of non-Catholics and I rejoice to know that the Australians love him as much as we do. I brought him on this trip to give him some recognition and to pay a debt, but I find that I have only increased the debt, if there be such a thing.[95]*

En route to New Zealand, Sheen poured praise for Spellman into his diary, lauding his humility, charity, generosity and good humor. "He is a wonderful man[,] God bless him." He again noted that Spellman did not reveal "a spark of jealousy" toward him.[96] Later, however, at a dinner for missionaries in Bangkok, Spellman quietly bristled when Sheen tried to outdo him with superlatives about the Maryknoll Fathers in his speech. "Not wishing to engage in any debates with the redoubtable Monsignor," the cardinal recorded in a private letter, "I decided not to continue the discussion."[97] Clearly Spellman somewhat resented the attention paid to Sheen.

Yet the two men remained on good terms as they continued in their frantic pace through Asia, each stop filled with the now well-established pattern of duties and enjoyments experienced in Australia and New Zealand. In Java, Fulton was appalled by the mosquitoes and the unsanitary conditions of life, but nothing could dampen his high spirits. He wrote, punning, in his diary: "After dinner we visited a fish market on a street corner, pretty fish in the sense that they smelled pretty bad[,] I think they were smelt—I am sure they did." On a serious note, he reflected, "A visit like ours to Batavia gives one an entirely different impression of the world, enlarges a point of view, develops sympathy for others and makes one mission minded." Sheen's eloquence was also on display in his diary: "Once over the waters we looked down on tiny little atolls which once were volcanoes which after vomiting and belching in sheer exhaustion sunk into a deep sleep in the sea. Only caps remain as if to salute the sky whose fires they once challenged."[98]

In Singapore, Sheen spoke over a nine-state radio network, extolling, among other things, large families.[99] (The cardinal was thrilled to discover a family with twenty-four children.)[100] In Bangkok, he visited Buddhist temples and learned that Catholic missionaries had a difficult time winning converts in the area. He was shocked by the poverty, dirt and extreme heat.[101]

In Saigon, Fulton noted the civil war then raging, "the French fighting some nationalists under Communist officers supplied with Russian guns." He preached a sermon in French and observed that there were 100,000 Catholics in Saigon.[102] In Hong Kong, which he thought "beautiful, beautiful, beautiful," he got dysentery, his first close encounter with illness on the trip. It did not prevent him, however, from giving speeches and radio broadcasts, one of which was heard in Scandinavia.[103]

In Manila, the clerics visited a hospital filled with wounded soldiers. Sheen noted how Spellman visited each of the 1,340 patients over a period of three hours. "His devotion to soldiers is manifested at every stop. Only a good man would so exhaust himself in bringing joy to his fellow men." Fulton soon made a radio broadcast in which he suggested that all United Nations delegates be obliged to lay their hands on the wounded and pledge that they shall not have suffered in vain.

After an almost two-hour drive in blazing heat, Sheen and his travel companions then visited a leper colony. Fulton was deeply moved by the 833 patients. "I was so impressed that I probably gave the best talk of my life." He called the visit to the leprosarium a highlight of the trip.[104]

Actress Loretta Young recalled that Sheen had a special concern for lepers. He told her that he was repelled by a disease-ravaged hand when it was extended to him, but he soon reached out, and all the fear left him. That hand was like the hand of Jesus.[105] In the early 1960s, Sheen would befriend a young leper named Paul Scott who came to him in misery and desperation at St. Patrick's Cathedral. Fulton did everything he could, including finding and furnishing an apartment for him. "He invited Paul once a week to dinner," D. P. Noonan later recalled. "Because it was difficult for Paul to use his hands, the Bishop cut the meat for him." Scott became one of Sheen's many unheralded converts.[106]

On the way to Shanghai, the plane flew over Corregidor and Bataan, and Fulton recorded a summary of the bitter wartime struggles that had occurred in both areas. On arrival in China, a missionary soon introduced him to a young Chinese woman who wanted to enter a convent but lacked the necessary funds. Sheen gave her "a small dowry" and the rosary that Archbishop Mannix of Australia, a Sheen favorite, had given him. In Shanghai, Spellman told Sheen that he was too exhausted from speech making and should not undertake any more assignments without his approval; but a radio broadcast and a university lecture were already scheduled.[107]

At a luncheon in Shanghai, a former American ambassador to the Soviet Union, William Bullitt, told Sheen that Communists in the U.S. State Department were undermining Chinese stability by requesting a union of the Communist north with the Nationalists, and by blocking American military assistance to the Nationalist army.[108] At dinner with Mme. Chiang Kai-shek, a Methodist, in her lavishly decorated home, Sheen boldly tried to convert her, promising that she would find a superior form of Christianity in the Mass. When he invited her to church, she pleaded a previous engagement. Sheen later recalled Mme. Chiang saying, "There will never be any peace in China until China becomes Christian." In his diary, Fulton wrote, "She is not far from the kingdom of God.[109]

In Nanking, Sheen gave more talks and joined his associates for dinner with Generalissimo Chiang Kai-shek. Through an interpreter, Chiang expressed his deep gratitude for American aid and told how much he trusted in God's will. Spellman responded with expressions of deep affection. The next day, Sheen made a radio broadcast carried all over China, boldly proclaiming the Catholic faith.[110]

In Txingtae, Fulton had a private conversation during dinner with Admiral Oscar C. Badger "about the Chinese and Russian situation." In his autobiography, Sheen recalled that the admiral told him, "I asked the State Department for a thousand Marines to be sent to northern China to stop the Communist advance. The State Department refused."[111]

On their way to Tokyo, the clergymen looked out of the airplane window and marveled at both the destruction at Hiroshima and the natural beauty of Mount Fuji. Tokyo was 60 percent rubble from Allied bombings, but the Imperial Hotel, which had survived a massive earthquake years earlier, was still intact, and the party stayed in the famed building designed by Frank Lloyd Wright.[112]

The new arrivals lunched with General Douglas MacArthur the next day. "He looks you straight in the eye when he talks," Sheen wrote in his diary, "and gives the impression of authority and power." Sheen kept a record of MacArthur's table talk:

> *I wished I had 800 Catholic missionaries for every one I have now.*
>
> *The world struggle is not economic nor political but religious and Theological. It is either for God or atheism.*
>
> *If the intellectual age of European culture is to be compared with a man of 45 years of age, Japan is 9, a bad boy, a barbarian at heart, ruthless, and cruel, who could be made good if he were adopted by good foster parents....*
>
> *The basic effect of the East is want of leadership. The West*

throws up great leaders in moments of need but I cannot find a single good leader in the East.

MacArthur predicted that Russia would try to make a peace treaty with Japan within a year in order to "get us out of here. It cannot do anything so long as I am here sitting on its flank."[113]

After a speech at Sophia University, attended by the premier and other top Japanese officials, and a radio broadcast "to the intellectuals of Japan," Sheen retired to his room. He was soon visited by a friend, General Charles Willoughby, who "spoke of the great danger facing the world because of Russia and the great importance of the Spanish victory in Spain before the World War."[114]

The party traveled to the Imperial Palace the following day, their cars crossing the moat where two thousand Japanese soldiers had committed suicide on the day of the Japanese defeat. Fulton thought the buildings and grounds unimpressive, and the Emperor himself no less so. "The Emperor sat on no throne, but on a chair and said he tried to prevent the war, but could not and was glad when it was over. He rejoiced in the work of the missionaries and the work of the U.S. Gov't in rehabilitating. He is a little man with buck teeth, looked frightened and in general gave the impression of being a puppet who doubted even his 'divinity.' If he is a god, I am an atheist."[115]

Sheen soon preached at a Solemn Pontifical Mass in Hibya Hall, the largest hall in Tokyo, which was packed with four thousand people. The sermon, broadcast over the Far East Network, was bold, as he himself reported in his diary. "It was the first time in the history of Japan that anyone spoke publicly of the Emperor (not mentioning his name) and suggested the transcendence of the false religion which centered around him. The conclusion was: Japan is the land of the Rising sun but the sun is the Son of God Who is the Light of the World."[116]

As Fulton prepared to leave Tokyo following two more speeches that day, one eleven miles away in Yokahama, he reflected on the Japanese people in his diary, their industrious ways, cleanliness, courtesy and general physical attractiveness. He longed for their conversion, and wrote, "I love the Japs."[117]

Their journey concluded, the Spellman party flew to Wake Island, where they observed the albatrosses or "gooney birds," looking awkward when taking flight from land. The travelers then returned to Honolulu. It was soon on to Los Angeles and then to New York on June 13. "Thank God," wrote Fulton on the last page of his diary.[118] The fifty-two-day journey had covered 43,000 miles. Sheen had given more than two hundred speeches, lectures and sermons.[119]

Sheen wrote in his autobiography that it struck him during this trip that it might be "shortsightedness" by Catholics to "impose the Aristotelian philosophy on the Eastern mind; that it would have been better to have gathered up the good religious aspiration of the Eastern people in the natural religions to bring them to revelation." Catholic missionaries, he thought, "should start with what is good in the religions they find in their countries as Our Lord started with a drink of cold water in converting a Samaritan, as Claudia began with a dream in understanding Christ far better than a rational husband, and as Paul began with an inscription to a pagan deity to convert two souls in Athens."[120] It was an interesting, sophisticated, and unusual reflection by a man famous for his conversions.

SEVEN

Global Thinking

F rom his earliest books and sermons, Sheen declared his antagonism toward the claims of some scientists and social scientists. He acknowledged that such disciplines as physics, psychology and sociology were valuable and important, but when their experts went beyond the legitimate borders of their academic fields and pretended to be philosophers, curtly dismissing the supernatural, he objected strongly. Fulton was particularly critical of behavioral and Freudian psychology. He wrote in 1929, "Psychology is talked of as if it were a new science. Now it is degenerated into a study of the subconscious mind—that unthinking unconscious cellar part of our mental lives—in an attempt to make us believe that we are better men when we glorify the irrational and have not our wits about us."[1]

Sheen was often given to such sweeping generalities. While dismissing "the nonsense of Behavioralism," he declared in 1931 that "Psychology first lost its soul, then it lost its mind, finally it lost its consciousness."[2] This failure to distinguish the specific from the general, often seen in his Thomistic writings, sometimes weakened the young priest's credibility and generated critics. Perhaps it was the failing of a professional public speaker, eager to arouse an audience with stirring rhetoric and fearful of boring them with facts and details—the stuff effective arguments are made of.

No doubt this penchant for the general stemmed also from a lack of intellectual dialogue. Sheen was rarely challenged about anything he said and wrote. He did not have regular personal dialogue with, say, individual physicists or sociologists or even philosophers who could test his theories and argue about his conclusions. He read great writers in these fields, to be sure, but in the privacy of his study and without anyone to suggest that his interpretations might be mistaken. Indeed, as we have seen, Fulton was not one to listen very carefully to the views of others.

Freudianism, still fashionable in the postwar era, was a special concern of Sheen's, as it was an enemy of the Church every bit as much as Marxism. It offered not only a manual for everyday conduct but also a competing cosmology, and it vied for the souls of those who, in Sheen's view, desperately needed higher truth. As ever, the monsignor was not shy about expressing his opposition.

Preaching at St. Patrick's Cathedral in March 1947, Sheen attacked Freudian psychoanalysis in sweeping terms, contrasting it with the Catholic Sacrament of Confession. According to a *New York Times* story, Sheen said that psychoanalysis was "a form of escapism" that failed to relieve "the unresolved sense of guilt of sin" from which "most people who consult psychoanalysts are suffering." Far better, Sheen declared, to go to Confession, which "is the key to happiness of the modern world." In the sacrament, "You don't look so much on your sins as you look upon your Savior, who restores you to relationship with the Heavenly Father." Psychoanalysis lacked any norms or standards, he said, and thus, "There are no more disintegrated people in the world than the victims of Freudian psychoanalysis. Confession gives you the standard of Christ, the perfect personality."

Freudianism, Sheen charged, was based on "materialism, hedonism, infantilism and eroticism." A method he described as "transfer of the affection to the analyst" was used "when the patient is a young and very beautiful woman. It is never found to work among the ugly or the poor." Sheen contended that "most psychoanalysts cater only to the rich."[3] A *New York Herald Tribune* story interpreted the sermon as an attack on psychiatry in general.

Two weeks later, Dr. Frank J. Curran, chief psychiatrist of St. Vincent's Hospital in New York, resigned his post at the hospital and as psychiatric consultant in the Chancery Office, following refusal by archdiocesan officials to clarify or repudiate Sheen's attack. Many of his Catholic patients, he said, were now afraid to receive treatment, fearing that they were committing a sin. Sheen's importance was such, Curran stated, that many took his statements as the official Catholic position on psychiatry.[4]

Four Catholic psychiatrists, including Curran, publicly denounced Sheen's attack in July. Psychiatry was a recognized medical specialty, they asserted. "It occupies the same position in the field of medicine as does surgery or any other specialty concerned with the relief and care of human suffering." The four were especially incensed that the monsignor had called their practice irreligious. "It is a fundamental tenet of the Catholic Church that there can be no conflict between true science and religion."[5]

A few days later, prominent psychoanalyst A. A. Brill, the translator of Sigmund Freud, spoke harshly of Sheen before a meeting of rabbis in New York City. He called the statements as reported in the *New York Times* "false views" and "foolishly untrue." He thought Sheen might be jealous of the success of Joshua Loth Liebman's book *Peace of Mind*, which was sympathetic toward psychoanalysis. "In brief," Brill said, "Msgr. Sheen is entirely governed by the 'omnipotence of thought' which is characteristic of primitive thinking."[6]

Sheen then wrote a stinging letter to the *New York Times*, contending that he had been misquoted in the newspaper and that a *New York Herald Tribune* reporter, who had taken his story from the *Times* reporter, had further misconstrued what he said as an attack on psychiatry in general. Sheen said he had indeed attacked Freudian psychoanalysis, but not psychoanalysis in general, and in the first paragraph of the sermon he had called psychiatry "a perfectly valid science." In fact, he had referred several people to psychiatrists within the past two months. He spoke for the Catholic Church, Sheen said, only when he condemned Freudian psychoanalysis for its denial of sin and for its inability to deal effectively with the "problems which affect the whole man." He quoted other prominent critics of Freudianism, adding that psychoanalysts "ought to be generous enough to believe that a man who prefers Jung, Allers or Adler to Freud is not an enemy of psychiatry." He concluded the letter with a series of highly sarcastic analogies.

Dr. Lawrence S. Kuble, chairman of the public education committee of the New York Psychoanalytic Institute, found Sheen's explanation far from satisfactory. In a letter to the *New York Times*, Kuble stated that two days after the sermon, he had requested a copy. Sheen had replied that his sermons were never written and that no copy existed. But in his recent letter, Kuble noted, Sheen had quoted a sentence from the first paragraph of the sermon, four months after its delivery. Moreover, in early June Sheen had claimed not to have seen a newspaper report of his sermon, yet in his recent letter he claimed to have sent a letter of protest to the *New York Times* on April 9. "Against what then did he write his letter of protest?"

Kuble wrote that he had tried through friends and associates, and in a personal letter to Sheen that went unanswered, to find out exactly what the monsignor had said and what his views were. All to no avail. Sheen seemed to approve of Jung, Allers and Adler, but all three employed Freud's methods to some extent, said Kuble. He added, "We cannot help feeling that all serious, thoughtful people have a right to expect greater honesty and greater humility from anyone who pretends to represent the search for the good life."[7] The matter ended at that point. Sheen came away from the fracas appearing, at least to some, unduly petulant, confused and even untruthful.

Given the powers of his memory and his penchant for repeating and publishing his talks and sermons, Fulton could indeed have quoted from a sentence delivered in a sermon four months earlier. It is also possible that he was misquoted and misunderstood by the newspaper reporters. The *New York Times* quotations, however, sound very much like Sheen, and most of what he was alleged to have said later appeared in Sheen publications. In any case, Fulton could surely have handled the press and the professionals with the courtesy and consideration he almost unfailingly showed to others, avoiding the rancor that spilled over into the newspapers. He was being challenged by people qualified to raise objections to his generalities, and his harsh and sarcastic response revealed his distaste for the experience. Liberal writer Fanny Sedgwick Colby commented in the *American Scholar* that the incident raised serious questions about the Catholic Church's ability to meet the moral challenges of contemporary society.[8]

In November, Sheen gave a speech in Houston condemning Freudian psychoanalysis and listing it with Marxism as the two most influential and destructive intellectual systems of the century. He said that both Marx and Freud believed in conflict and revolution, and both were anticultural because they dismissed religion, morality, art, philosophy, literature and law as products either of economic or of biological determination. Freud, he charged, "has created very often greater mental diseases than he has cured."

Half of the speech sounded very much like the sermon at St. Patrick's in March. Knowing this, Sheen added, "note that I have not used the word psychiatry. I'm not talking about psychiatrists. I'm not talking about psychoanalysts in general. I'm only talking about Freudian psychoanalysis."[9]

Sheen's best-seller of 1949, *Peace of Soul*, contains an extended and well-documented presentation of his objections to Freudian psychoanalysis and its challenge to the Christian understanding of human existence. One chapter is titled "Psychoanalysis and Confession," the same as Sheen's March sermon. There is a reference in it to the patients of psychoanalysts returning repeatedly to have "the whole life analyzed (*if they have the money*)." And the "process of transference" is discussed at length and in the same critical spirit that was reported in the *New York Times*.[10]

In *Peace of Soul* Sheen defined his terms, belatedly, in chapter six, making certain that his readers understood he was not against psychiatric treatment per se. "Psychiatry as a branch of medicine is not only a perfectly valid science—it is a real necessity today. . . . Most of the psychiatrists doing such necessary work today are *not* psychoanalysts." He also pointed out that he was not condemning all psychoanalytic treatment. He further refined his target to include

Freudian psychoanalysis, "at least that of the 'orthodox' brand."[11] Still, Fulton's penchant for generalities remained clear, as in: "Psychoanalysts all agree ..."[12] And readers could be forgiven if psychology, psychiatry, and psychoanalysis seemed at times to be synonyms, equally deserving of the author's scorn, their adherents being "those unscientific charlatans who see in human nature no difference or transcendence over that of a cockroach."[13]

It must be added, however, that *Peace of Soul* is one of Sheen's best books and deserved the widespread applause that it received. The writing is consistently inspired, expressing the timeless Christian message that "nothing *really* matters except the salvation of a soul." The book surely ranks among the most powerful Catholic polemics of the postwar years.

The theme of patriotism also appears in this best-seller. Monks and nuns, Sheen wrote, living in the "shades and shadows of the Cross where saints are made," were "hidden dynamos of prayer ... doing more for our country than all its politicians, its labor leaders, its army and navy put together; they are atoning for sins of us all." As he had for many years, Sheen continued to be deeply concerned about what he perceived to be America's religious and moral failings, failings that he believed could be overcome by the prayers of the righteous. Those in monasteries and convents, he asserted,

> are averting the just wrath of God, repairing the broken fences of those who sin and pray not, rebel and atone not. As ten just men would have saved Sodom and Gomorrah, so ten just saints can save a nation now. But so long as a citizenry is more impressed by what its cabinet does than by its chosen souls who are doing penance, the rebirth of the nation has not yet begun. The cloistered are the purest of patriots. They have not become less interested in the world since leaving it; indeed, they have become more interested in the world than ever before. But they are not concerned with whether it will buy and sell more; they care—and desperately care—whether it will be more virtuous and love God more.[14]

The fate of the United States ranked near the top of Sheen's concerns in these years. He believed that his country was engaged in a clash with a deadly enemy that had long challenged the Church throughout the world and was now threatening the nation's survival, and thus it was up to Americans to be prayerful and diligent, especially when the enemy was within as well as without.

∽

POSTWAR SOVIET DESIGNS on Turkey and Greece and Stalin's blockade of the western sector of Berlin in mid-1948 intensified anticommunism throughout the West and particularly in the United States. The Truman Doctrine and the Marshall Plan, announced in 1947, and the North Atlantic Treaty Organization, constructed in 1949, were designed to halt the spread of communism. President Truman declared, "I believe that it must be the policy of the United States to support free peoples who are resisting attempted subjugation by armed minorities or by outside pressures." Those who opposed this policy and in any way spoke favorably of Stalin or his agents were increasingly under suspicion of being either Communist or pro-Communist, a charge that could have dire consequences for the accused. There was extremely little sympathy across the nation for members of the Communist Party itself, for although the party was legal, few knowledgeable observers doubted that it was a tool of the Soviet Union. FBI director J. Edgar Hoover declared it a "fifth column."

In 1947, the president announced a new loyalty security program, designed to weed out Communists and their sympathizers from the executive branch. One could be dismissed or denied employment even for "sympathetic association with" a totalitarian, fascist, Communist, or subversive organization or group. Within four years, more than 2,000 government employees had resigned, and 212 were dismissed. Politicians began tripping over each other to denounce Reds and to prove their toughness toward the "Communist menace." The House Committee on Un-American Activities (HUAC) held sensational hearings on the movie industry. Labor unions began purging their leadership of Communists and fellow travelers.

Following Truman's dramatic upset of Thomas Dewey in the 1948 election, the "Communists in high places" issue burst into a full-scale Red Scare. In large part, this involved Republican frustrations and a determination to win the next presidential contest at any cost. But additional developments at home and abroad contributed to what would be called "The Great Fear." Charges by Whittaker Chambers against Alger Hiss created a national uproar. To many on the right, Hiss was a symbol of the Ivy League, New Deal bureaucrat, and if he was guilty of treason, then perhaps the entire Washington Establishment might be full of Reds and their sympathizers. In 1949, Department of Justice employee Judith Coplon was formally charged with being a Soviet spy. Russia exploded its first atomic bomb. Eleven leaders of the Communist Party were convicted of violating the Smith Act, the first peacetime sedition law since the eighteenth century. And when China, the world's most populous nation, whose leader Chiang Kai-shek had received more than $2 billion in American aid since the war, fell to the Communists, many on the right claimed that China had been sold out by Reds and pro-Reds in the American State Department.

In early 1950, Hiss was convicted of perjury (everyone understanding that his real crime was espionage). President Truman announced work on the hydrogen bomb, which escalated fears about the future of the globe. Dr. Klaus Fuchs, a British scientist, was arrested for leaking information to the Soviets about the Manhattan Project, an arrest that soon led to charges against Julius and Ethel Rosenberg. In February, Senator Joe McCarthy of Wisconsin charged that the State Department had 205 Reds among its employees and that he and Secretary of State Dean Acheson, a Hiss defender, knew their names. The Korean War broke out in June, a "police action" that soon bogged down into what seemed to be a war of attrition.

Millions of Americans were now required to take loyalty oaths. Libraries were eager to purge their shelves of "subversive" volumes. Several actors and screenwriters, accused of communist sympathies or activities, were branded by "blacklisters" and could not find work. Some leftist professors and teachers were hounded and fired. Several states set up their own "un-American" activities committees. Liberals in Congress, eager to assert their patriotism, sponsored an addition to the rigorously anticommunist McCarran Act that permitted the attorney general of the United States, during a presidentially declared "internal security emergency," to arrest and detain anyone "he had reason to believe" might engage in subversive activities. Newspaper headlines screamed almost daily about the latest charges and findings of Reds in all walks of American life. J. Edgar Hoover claimed that the United States contained 540,000 Communists and fellow travelers.

American Catholics were in the vanguard of the anticommunist movement. During the first five years after the war, they had watched Stalin's forces crush the Church in the Iron Curtain countries. Rallies and parades were held to express sympathy with Joseph Cardinal Mindszenty, arrested and imprisoned for life for criticizing Soviet aggression in Hungary. Cardinal Spellman, speaking from the pulpit of St. Patrick's Cathedral, called on the leaders of the United States to "raise their voices as one and cry out against" the "Satan-inspired Communist crimes." The Catholic War Veterans and Knights of Columbus (which had 600,000 active members) spoke out vigorously against Communists and those thought to have the same methods and goals.[15]

One of the nation's most militant and outspoken anticommunists, Spellman was as worried about internal subversion as he was about the onslaught overseas. In October 1946, he warned that the Reds "are today digging deep inroads into our own nation" and are "tirelessly trying to grind into dust the blessed freedoms for which our sons have fought, sacrificed and died." A year later, unimpressed with the Truman administration's efforts to rid the government of Communists, he declared, "once again while Rome burns ... the world continues to fiddle. The strings of the fiddle are committees, conferences, conversations, appeasements—to the tune of no action today."[16]

The majority of American Catholics, however, stuck with the Democratic Party. They voted for Truman two to one in 1948 and would favor Stevenson over Eisenhower by a small margin in 1952. A careful student of the subject, Donald F. Crosby, concluded that American Catholics were only slightly more anxious than the majority of Americans about the Communist issue, and on the whole did not support a massive Red hunt. Most of that activity took place on the elite level of Catholics, among writers, editors, political leaders, directors of fraternal organizations, and leading clergy.[17]

No one in the Catholic Church in America spoke out more often about the threat of communism than Fulton J. Sheen. His radio programs, speeches, sermons, articles, pamphlets and books reached many more Americans than Spellman's pronouncements. On communism, as on so many other topics, Sheen was widely thought to be the premier spokesman of the Church in the United States. His knowledge of the subject was probably unrivaled by any other member of the Church hierarchy, and no one, certainly not Cardinal Spellman, could match his eloquence in explaining to the American people the danger that faced them. Sheen's concern about the issue was such that he went beyond advocacy into activism.

The Federal Bureau of Investigation first became interested in Sheen in 1943, when a Michigan businessman who had heard a Sheen speech condemning Nazism wrote to Hoover suggesting that an agent contact the monsignor. The writer thought that Sheen might identify people who opposed his speech, bringing to light a number of Nazi sympathizers. Hoover thanked the informant for his letter, and the bureau began collecting newspaper accounts of Sheen's speeches.[18]

In early 1944, the FBI sent an agent to Sheen to inquire about the source of his prescient allegation that the Soviet Union was preparing to make a separate peace with Germany.[19] Hoover soon made a personal contact with Sheen, sending him a copy of a speech he delivered before the Daughters of the American Revolution. Sheen responded with an invitation to dinner. A friendship began to develop.[20]

On March 25, 1946, newspapers reported that in a speech before the Catholic Institute of the Press in New York, Sheen had charged that a "full fledged Soviet agent" had been "picked up" in a closed congressional hearing on Capitol Hill within the past week. He declined to name the individual but said he believed the person was from Chicago and was a committee employee. When asked if the employee was in custody, Sheen replied, "I think he should be, don't you? He's an enemy of his country."

When J. Edgar Hoover saw the story, he wrote to an aide, "What is there to this?" Secretary of State James Byrnes also inquired of the FBI about Sheen's statement. An FBI spokesman told the press that the bureau would not comment on the charge. In fact, the FBI knew nothing of the matter.[21]

It seems that Sheen was referring to Harold Buckles, an employee of the House Rules Committee, who had been questioned in secret session the previous week by a House Military Affairs subcommittee. Nothing had come of the inquiry, and committee chairman Harold Sabath had dismissed any doubts about Buckles' loyalty. "I don't think Sheen would have said anything if he had known the facts."[22]

In the same speech before Catholic newspaper representatives, Sheen implied that the State Department was covering up information about subversives. He noted that a naval attaché named Wylie had disappeared mysteriously in Poland and that there had been no mention of the incident in an American newspaper. The State Department replied that Wylie had drowned the previous January when he accidentally fell off a bridge in Warsaw.

In both cases, Sheen was apparently making unsubstantiated allegations—but we cannot be certain. In 1974, Sheen told doctoral student Mary Jude Yablonsky that there were three major sources of his information during that period. In the first place, he had an informer inside the upper echelons of the American Communist Party, and was close to him for two years. "Secondly, I had a secretary who was Russian and who would read Pravda and the other Communist publications every day and would give me the information. Then thirdly, there was a tremendous amount of material that was circulating as Communist documentation done by scholars which I used." The only information he used from newspapers, he said, was in speeches published in the *New York Times*.[23]

Giving a speech in Harrisburg, Pennsylvania, later in 1946, Sheen claimed that a Communist, "probably linked" with Soviet espionage in this country, had tried to become his traveling companion. The story was true; Sheen called the FBI to check out the applicant, and was told that he had been visited by a Soviet agent.[24] The relationship between the priest and the bureau grew closer. Throughout 1947 and 1948, and perhaps longer, the FBI checked the loyalty background of prospective converts for Sheen.[25]

Sheen spoke at a communion breakfast in New York for more than four hundred FBI personnel and their spouses in May 1947. After praising the FBI fulsomely, he unexpectedly stayed for the entire proceeding. When Hoover was informed by an agent about the breakfast talk, he wrote a warm letter of appreciation to Sheen.[26]

In the spring of 1948, Sheen published *Communism and the Conscience of the West,* one of his best books. (Hoover personally ordered a copy for the FBI library).[27] Two of Sheen's most often repeated historical allusions appear in the early pages. Historian Arnold Toynbee, he noted, had declared that "sixteen out of the nineteen civilizations which have decayed from the beginning of history until now, decayed from within." The West, and America in particular, Sheen believed, was rotting from within and would pay the inevitable price of destruction unless it reformed. "As Western civilization loses its Christianity it loses its superiority. The ideology of communism rose out of the secularized remnants of a Western civilization whose soul was once Christian."

A few pages later, Sheen criticized perhaps the most sacred concept of the liberal secularist: the idea of progress. He observed, "The interval between the Napoleonic and Franco-Prussian wars was 53 years, the interval between the Franco-Prussian War and World War I was 43 years, and the interval between World War I and World War II was 21 years—and this at a time when man has all the *material* conditions necessary for his happiness." In recent times, Sheen declared, people in the West had abandoned a sense of the supreme purpose of life and had devoted themselves to creating a perfect city of man to displace the City of God. They called this delusive striving "progress," and shortly discovered that it left them in despair, facing a challenge from hell that they knew not how to counter.[28]

Nothing in Sheen's book even suggested the reckless conduct associated with the Second Red Scare. It was also completely devoid of political partisanship. (Although many thought Cardinal Spellman a conservative Republican, he too remained largely nonpartisan.)[29] The true struggle going on, in Sheen's view, was not between political parties but was "moral and spiritual and involves above all else whether man shall exist for the state, or the state for man, and whether freedom is of the spirit or a concession of a materialized society."[30]

The book received a glowing review in the *New York Times* by Bernard Iddings Bell, who said that Sheen had acquired "something of the stature of a prophet."[31] A newspaper book review by Robert K. Walsh, passed around among top FBI officials, predicted that "Neither the extreme left nor the far right will like his book. It reveals more weaknesses than they dream exist in their ideologies. But, with clear thinking and strong writing, Msgr. Sheen points to a straight road and a means of staying on it. He has charity for Communists and hope for the people of Russia. He has faith that the conscience of the west can be moved from cowardice and confusion."[32]

On May 1, 1949, Cardinal Spellman, Vice-President Alben W. Barkley, and Sheen spoke before thirty thousand people gathered on a rainy day in New York's Polo Grounds at an anti-Soviet rally organized by the archdiocese. Sheen's talk received the most attention in the *New York Times*. He said that the meeting had a triple purpose: to pledge the loyalty of all Catholics, to pray for the persecutors of Christians in the Soviet-ruled countries, and to identify with their victims. On the first point, with Paul Blanshard undoubtedly in mind, Fulton declared, "There is not one intelligent man in the world today who believes that the state has anything to fear from the Church. Communism cannot be judged by its foreign policy. We have been on the record on this from the beginning, and we say that Communism is intrinsically evil."[33]

The rally, and Sheen's remarks, were wholly in conformity with Vatican policy. That same year, struggling against Reds throughout Europe, Pius XII declared that anyone joining the Communist Party or supporting communism in any way would be excommunicated.

In late June, Fulton published an article in the *New York Times* criticizing the Voice of America broadcasts to the Soviet Union and the satellite countries for emphasizing the material glories of the free world and ignoring the spiritual and moral needs of its listeners. Claiming to know "the psychology of the Russian people," Sheen asserted, "There is not a single mother in Russia who would be willing to give up her son in another war in order to enjoy some American prosperity, but many a mother would be willing to give up her son to gain freedom of the soul." The captive peoples "are not sighing for a day when they will have our business men selling them our tractors, but rather they are sighing for the churches and monasteries which can be rebuilt when Russia once again becomes holy."[34]

Sheen was not the original critic of the Voice of America. As early as 1945, Republicans had claimed that the Office of War Information, the network's parent organization until 1948, had been infiltrated by Communists. Republican Congressman John Taber of New York had carried on an annual campaign against Voice funding. The South Korean government banned Voice broadcasts during the Korean War. In the early 1950s, former President Herbert Hoover and Senator Joe McCarthy would contend that Reds and their sympathizers needed to be rooted out of the Voice of America. It was part of the long-range right-wing attack on the loyalty of the State Department. The reign of terror that followed can in no way be attributed to Sheen. He had pled for a spiritual emphasis and was not implying by his criticism that Communists were behind the broadcasts.[35]

Sheen joined Texas oil man George Strake and Rev. Lucian L. Lauerman, a Catholic University of American colleague, in a month-long tour of Europe beginning in July 1949. On departure from New

York to Lisbon, Sheen told newsmen that Stalin was "possibly the most stupid politician in the history of the world" for having so alienated the United States since the close of the war. He declined to comment on the current public squabble over federal aid to parochial schools between Eleanor Roosevelt and Cardinal Spellman, a struggle in which Spellman wrote angrily to the First Lady (who had initiated the encounter), "your record of anti-Catholicism stands for all to see ... documents of discrimination unworthy of an American mother!"[36]

༄

FULTON LEARNED IN the late summer of 1950 that Cardinal Spellman had succeeded in getting the Vatican to name him national director of the Pontifical Mission Aid Societies in the United States.[37] He was also to be one of Spellman's auxiliary bishops in the Archdiocese of New York. Sheen sent his letter accepting the episcopal honor to Spellman with his nephew Fulton J. Sheen II, who was headed for New York on his way overseas.[38] At long last, Fulton was to have his miter.

The Vatican soon made the announcement of the directorship; Fulton would resign from Catholic University and assume his new office on the first of November.[39] The popular title for his position was Director of the Society for the Propagation of the Faith. (Spellman himself was chairman of the Society's Episcopal Committee.) Sheen now had much of the authority he had long sought. The American branch of the Society for the Propagation of the Faith raised the bulk of the millions sent annually to Rome to support the Church's worldwide missionary activities. Fulton's presence in Rome would be formidable, his proximity to the Holy Father closer than ever. He would also reside in New York, a city he dearly loved, and continue the *Catholic Hour* broadcasts. "My entire energies," he said publicly, "will be dedicated to this work, which has the unique value of contributing to the peace of the world through peace of soul."[40] In his autobiography he reflected, "It was very consoling to have a universal mission and to consider the world as my parish."[41]

The episcopacy would be announced later. Cardinal Spellman prided himself on his ability to persuade the Vatican to name his associates bishops. He had seen to it, for example, that his chief administrator, Monsignor Francis A. McIntire, was made archbishop of Los Angeles in 1948. (Sheen gave the consecration sermon, crediting McIntire, his confessor, with being "the greatest spiritual inspiration of my life, not because of what he has told me about the priesthood but because of the way he has lived it.") Spellman would later preen and crow, according to an aide, when McIntire was named a cardinal on his recommendation.[42] During the whole of Spellman's career as head of the Archdiocese of New York, twenty-four bishops would be anointed at St. Patrick's, nearly all after the imposition of his own hands.[43] To make room for Sheen at the Society, Spellman had its current director, Monsignor Thomas J. McDonnell, elevated as coadjutor of Wheeling, West Virginia.[44]

D. P. Noonan, a former Sheen assistant, reported having once heard Fulton say that he deemed his nearly quarter of a century at Catholic University wasted.[45] If in fact he made the statement (no one else has quoted Sheen similarly), it was a reflection merely upon his long-standing ambition to be elevated within the Church. Teaching classes two days a week had not inordinately restricted his activities across the country during the year or overseas in the summers. But at fifty-five, he wished to be recognized officially for the talents he possessed and for the energy he was expending on behalf of the faith. Now that his promotion was at hand, he might well have looked upon the long years of teaching as time that could have been spent more productively. Still, he had no animosity toward Catholic University and would return many times in the years ahead to give talks, conduct services, and visit with friends. The campus itself would remain extremely proud of its one-time student and professor.[46]

That fall, Sheen sold his impressive Washington home and moved to New York. He took an apartment on the fourth floor of an old brownstone building at 109 East 38th Street that housed the Society offices; two priest assistants also had apartments nearby. A basement area in the building contained a kitchen and a dining room. There was a living room on the first floor, and a baroque chapel on the second. One entered Sheen's large, book-lined study through two office doors at the rear of the chapel. Thirty employees came in and out of the building each day. Although Sheen had many repairs made to the worn but elegant brownstone, its condition was a far cry from the comfort and style of his Washington home. Still, he seemed happy, and would live there for the next sixteen years.[47] The climb to the fourth floor was his only complaint.[48]

In time, as Sheen generated more activity in the building and drew more personnel, New York Fire Department officials became seriously concerned about overcrowding. This prompted the director to move the Society headquarters to fashionable 366 Fifth Avenue, near the Empire State Building (where it remains to this day).[49]

Soon after settling in New York, Sheen quietly purchased a large house in Yonkers with a view of the Hudson River, listed in his brother Tom's name to protect his privacy. The urban house had a large porch that Fulton enjoyed walking back and forth on when the weather was inclement. A woman served as housekeeper and cook, and Fulton visited on weekends, eager to get away from the tensions of his job. A few years later, when the house began to show considerable deterioration, Sheen moved his weekend visits to a modest three-bedroom house in suburban Mt. Pleasant. This time the house was listed in the name of his favorite niece, Joan Sheen Cunningham.[50] Fulton had the house carpeted in red, installed a chapel, and purchased a dining room table that would seat twelve. Another niece, Marie Sheen, later recalled, "We kids would be at one end" of the table and the bishop at the other, "drinking his cup of hot water and eating a biscuit." The existence of these retreats was known by few but family members and friends.[51]

Fulton brought his long-time secretary, Margaret Yates, with him to New York. She soon married and resigned, but she and her former employer remained good friends over the years ahead.[52] Gloria Dixon, a vivacious, attractive redhead in her mid-thirties, was hired largely to assist with converts. Working one-on-one, she played tapes for the aspirants and arranged for them to discuss matters with Sheen personally. She was totally devoted to the director, remained unmarried, and worked for Sheen until her death in 1965.[53]

Edythe Brownett became Sheen's personal secretary in 1950, and would serve him faithfully and efficiently for the rest of his life. At twenty-four, Edythe was a quiet, serene, tall, tactful, highly intelligent, and extremely attractive woman who wore her blond hair in a chignon. She was a graduate of Chestnut Hill College, a Catholic school for women in Philadelphia, and had worked in a publishing house and a foundling home before accepting Sheen's job offer.[54] Tom and Yolanda Holliger, who knew her well, thought that Edythe resembled actress Grace Kelly.[55] Fulton's niece Eileen Sheen later recalled, "She made me think of a Madonna statue come to life.... There was something nun-like about Edythe. I could never imagine her at an amusement park, jazz bar, [or] country fair picnic."[56]

Sheen had gotten to know Joseph and Kathryn Brownett, and their daughters Edythe and Marlene, years earlier when the family regularly attended his *Catholic Hour* broadcasts. (Thirteen-year-old Marlene first attracted Fulton's attention, sitting alone in the front row at a lecture for the Knights of Columbus in Bayonne. For the rest of his life, he spoke and wrote fondly of Marlene as his "front row rooter.")[57] A personal and long-lasting friendship developed.

In Fulton's employ, Edythe shared her New York apartment with her mother, never married, and was totally devoted to the man she and Gloria called "the Boss." Marlene Brownett later said of her sister, "She worked twenty-four hours a day" during the almost thirty years of her association with Sheen. Among other duties, Edythe took care of Sheen's scheduling and travel details ("That was more than a full-time job," she said), handled his personal appointments, supervised his correspondence, and made arrangements for the many visitors to the Society, especially missionaries. Almost the only typing she did was confidential correspondence between Sheen and the Vatican.[58] D. P. Noonan thought that Edythe's influence on Sheen was excessive.[59] Mary Baker, who knew Edythe for many years, remembered her as strong-willed and "very independent."[60] Fulton thought her indispensable.

The director of the Society for the Propagation of the Faith was largely a public relations figure who traveled, preached, wrote, stayed in the news, and raised funds. Cardinal Spellman knew that those qualifications fit Sheen exactly. In November 1950, Spellman told the thirty-second annual meeting of the bishops of the United States about his complete confidence that Sheen would "give a good account as he has done in everything with which he has been connected."[61] The Society bureaucracy took care of administrative matters. That was fortunate, for Sheen had practically no administrative experience and found the day-to-day operations and details of the organization of little or no interest. Still, he gave personal attention to those working for him, always greeting them with encouragement and a smile. He also led the staff in daily prayer, the Rosary, and, later, scriptural meditations.[62] Reporter James C. G. Conniff wrote, "Morale among his staff can challenge any in New York."[63]

Soon after arriving in New York, Sheen plunged into the work of raising funds. D. P. Noonan, who saw him in action, gave Fulton great credit for his energy and zeal. "Sheen in his day accomplished ten times as much work as any businessman on Madison Avenue."[64] Father Charles McBride, Sheen's assistant at the Society, would exclaim: "He never sleeps at all. Well, maybe five or six hours. At breakfast he's likely to regale Father Tennant and me with some odd bit of information he's picked up in the encyclopedia in the middle of the night."[65] Soon, donations began to soar, and Americans were contributing almost two-thirds of the collections made by the Society across the world.[66]

Whenever Sheen would ask for a specific amount in his call for donations on radio or television—say, a dime—thousands of letters would pour into the Society office daily. Every Catholic school-child in the country, Edythe Brownett recalled, would send in a dime or one of those offering folders with several coins. At times, ten thousand letters would arrive in a single day, about one-third of them from non-Catholics. One day, thirty thousand letters arrived, and the staff coped as best they could.[67]

Sheen immediately changed the Society's magazine, calling it

Mission, cutting it to pocket-size dimensions, and adding lively photos and brisk articles. The magazine had been losing about $200,000
a year, but with Sheen's alterations and promotion it turned a profit
of $200,000 in a single year.[68] He designed a World Mission Rosary,
with different-colored beads for each of the five continents that
Catholics prayed for and worked in. Within a couple of years, more
than a quarter-million of these rosaries had been mailed.[69]

Sheen also originated the "God Love You Medal," designed by
renowned jeweler Harry Winston. It featured an image of the Virgin, with the seal of the Society on the reverse side. The ten letters
in the words "God Love You" were raised to frame the entire medal,
thus forming a decade on which prayers could be said. A silver medal
went to those who sent in five dollars, and a gold-filled medal was
mailed to ten-dollar contributors. "The medal of Our Lady can be
blessed and indulgenced," said an accompanying brochure.[70]

Sheen's writing also stimulated giving. He soon began editing
a second Society magazine, *Worldmission,* which contained articles,
book reviews by leading missionaries, and Sheen editorials, often
pleading for donations. (A collection of these editorials would appear
in 1963 as the book *Missions and the World Crisis.*) Fulton was also
writing a syndicated newspaper column, soon labeled "Bishop Sheen
Writes." Begun in 1949, it would appear in the secular press for the
next thirty years, often calling attention to missionary activity. A
second syndicated column, "God Love You," was designed for
Catholic newspapers and frequently contained appeals for funds.[71]

Sheen's intense personal commitment to world missionary activities made an impression on many. Monsignor Clarence Schlachter,
an Indiana diocesan director of the Society (which had 130 offices
throughout the United States), said later, "He just sold you, and you
were convinced that what you were doing was the most important
job, the only job, really in the world."[72]

In mid-1952, Sheen told a reporter, "Last year our missionaries
cared for over fifty-four million young, aged, sick, orphans, and victims of leprosy—and only ten percent of these peoples were Christian. Fifty-four million! We tended more souls than did the Red

Cross, and worked without what might be called an overhead." Still, Fulton wasn't satisfied. "Our money was sent to the six hundred and fourteen areas—each as large as New England—covered by the society. We must do better.... The world has suddenly become missionary-minded. The two great missionary movements that campaign for mankind are Communism and Christianity. We must not falter."[73]

Fulton's zeal, however, irritated top officials at the National Council of Catholic Men, sponsor of the *Catholic Hour*. On April 4, 1951, Archbishop Robert E. Lucey, episcopal chairman of the council, wrote to Cardinal Spellman describing "an outline of the current problems we have been having with Monsignor Sheen." There had been earlier problems. In the mid and late 1940s, *Catholic Hour* officials had criticized Sheen privately for speaking about politics, and there were other complaints about his alleged hauteur. In 1950, Sheen had angrily boycotted rehearsals for the twentieth anniversary show of the *Catholic Hour* because of his unhappiness with the script, which, perhaps coincidentally, sharply limited his time on the air.[74]

Now, the archbishop complained, Sheen was not submitting his talks a month in advance, as required. Moreover, in February he had publicly announced the World Mission Rosary and implied that listeners should enclose donations when requesting one, which was a violation of *Catholic Hour* policy. NCCM officers didn't want the money sent directly to Sheen and insisted that the rosaries be offered free of charge. Still, on subsequent broadcasts Sheen urged listeners "to write to the National Council of Catholic Men or to me" for the World Mission Rosary.[75] NCCM income dropped as people began sending donations to the Society for the Propagation of the Faith and as additional administrative costs were incurred to handle the flood of mail arriving at the *Catholic Hour*.

In March, NCCM officials wrote to Sheen seeking reimbursement for the funds it had lost. Sheen replied with an angry letter blasting the NCCM for charging him with misappropriating funds and threatening not to appear on the next program as scheduled.

The NCCM leaders backed off, sending all the monies it had received from the rosary appeal to Sheen at the Society. On his last two broadcasts of the season, Sheen again appealed to listeners to write to him for the rosaries. Archbishop Lucey told Cardinal Spellman that the program had suffered a loss of at least $3,000 and complained, "Our listeners are not able to distinguish between Monsignor Sheen, the Missions and the Catholic Hour." Sheen exacerbated the issue by talking about it publicly on at least two occasions, accusing NCCM officials, Archbishop Lucey said, of embezzling funds.[76]

We do not know if Spellman confronted Sheen about the matter, but it seems likely; the cardinal was not one to countenance insubordination of any kind. In a similar incident, Spellman, in response to a newspaper story saying that Sheen was going to open a religious articles store, ordered him to desist. Fulton complied.[77]

∾

SHEEN WAS INFORMED in mid-May 1951 that the Vatican had officially named him a bishop. In a private letter of acceptance, he stressed his unworthiness and declared, "The Bishopric shall be to me, not an honor, but a responsibility, not a reward, but as a summons to sacrifice."[78] He was soon on his way to Belgium, where he spent a few days with the royal family; he had known King Baudouin for many years.[79] He then went to Germany and delivered four talks to American soldiers, including a vigorously anticommunist speech in Berlin.[80]

On May 22, 1951, the Most Reverend Amleto Giovanni Cicognani, apostolic delegate to the United States, announced that Sheen had been appointed titular bishop of Caesariana and auxiliary to Cardinal Spellman. (J. Edgar Hoover sent Sheen a glowing personal letter of congratulations. Sheen's reply began, "My dear Friend.")[81] The cardinal had four other auxiliary bishops, three in New York and one to assist him in his duties as military vicar of the armed forces of the United States.[82]

The consecration was scheduled for June 11 in Rome at the Church of Sts. John and Paul, of which Spellman was titular head.

This was a great honor, bestowed upon Spellman himself many years earlier, and arranged personally, Sheen told a nephew, by Pius XII.[83] Insiders knew that the Pope always called Sheen by his first name.[84] (One of the few documents Fulton kept during the rest of his life was the Pope's personal Christmas greeting and apostolic blessing, received in December 1949.)[85] Sheen would be the only Spellman nominee to be consecrated outside the United States. An internal biography of Sheen, prepared by the FBI in mid-1953, said this was the first consecration in a century of an American priest who had not lived or been a seminarian in Rome.[86]

Several rumors have swirled over the appointment and the consecration ever since. One story has it that Sheen somehow "went around" Spellman to secure his miter.[87] Many years later, Fulton was alleged to have told a priest that Spellman had not wanted him to be his auxiliary bishop and that he deliberately placed the service in Rome, where it would take place "under cover of darkness."[88] The stories are without foundation, and probably stem from memories involving the later deterioration of relations between Sheen and Spellman.

Bishop Edwin Broderick, a long-time member of Spellman's staff and the cardinal's personal secretary from 1954 to 1964, later denied that there was anything extraordinary about Sheen's consecration other than it was an honor to be made a bishop in Rome.[89] Monsignor Hilary Franco, who worked for Sheen from 1959 to 1966, agreed emphatically.[90] In his autobiography, fudging slightly about the sequence of events, Fulton wrote, "I afterward learned that this was done through the good graces of Cardinal Spellman."[91] In fact, Spellman sent Sheen a telegram, shortly *before* the consecration, stating: "RENEWED CONGRATULATIONS AND PRAYERS ON CONSECRATION."[92] The Cardinal did not attend the service in Rome, probably because of a schedule conflict.[93]

D. P. Noonan later asserted that Sheen told him he chose to be consecrated in Rome, as he did not want Spellman to be present.[94] Even if Fulton said this, it is probably untrue. There is no evidence of serious tension between Spellman and Sheen during the early

1950s. Hilary Franco said that in 1951, Spellman was "still crazy about Sheen."[95] The cardinal, as Spellman later reminded Sheen and others, was personally responsible for Sheen's new position and his miter. He was, and had long been, Fulton's patron.[96]

On June 11, Fulton J. Sheen became a bishop. The three-hour service was viewed by 300 to 400 people, including James G. Dunn, the United States ambassador to Italy, and about eight members of Sheen's New York staff. Fulton Sheen II, a student at Louvain, was the only family member in attendance. Also there, at Monsignor Sheen's invitation, was the entire crew of the military airplane that brought him from Berlin to Rome.[97] The consecrator was Adeodato Giovanni Cardinal Piazza, a good friend of Spellman's, assisted by two other co-consecrants.[98]

Immediately after the service, the new bishop, his nephew, and several others met privately with the Pope. Fulton J. Sheen II said later that the close friendship between Pius XII and his uncle was obvious to all present.[99] In the course of the papal audience, the Holy Father gave Bishop Sheen a pectoral cross. Sheen reportedly turned down an invitation from Pius XII to stay for a few weeks of vacation; he wanted to get back to work. "I thought Your Holiness had me made a bishop because there was a job to be done," he was quoted as saying. From Rome, Sheen flew to Lourdes—his twenty-third visit to the shrine—to give thanks and to pray for guidance. He returned to the United States on an unscheduled flight to protect his privacy and was back at his desk on Monday morning, resuming his nineteen-hour-a-day work schedule.[100]

In his autobiography, Sheen recalled with some embarrassment and regret his delight in reaching his life-long goal. "The ring on the finger, the zucchetto on the head and the title 'Bishop'—all these things have a ring about them and all contribute to a sense of false euphoria, which I confess having had." He also enjoyed the privileges awarded a bishop: "his place at table, the extra-soft prie-dieu and the reverence born of faith." Still, the glow eventually faded. "In a very short time I discovered that I was no different than before, that the clay was just as weak as ever, that the esteem people paid me was not necessarily the way the Lord looked on me. It took me some time to discover that the jewel in the ring does not necessarily become a jewel in a crown of Heaven."[101]

Back at his office, he and Spellman coordinated their efforts, both of them keenly concerned about raising funds for the world's poor. In early 1952, Spellman wrote a letter to Sheen thanking him for personally adding $42,980 to the Society's coffers over the past year. The bishop had made a personal donation of more than $17,000, his "God Love You" column brought in more than $11,000, *Mission* magazine added more than $5,000, the sale of rosaries amounted to more than $1,200, and an annuity in the name of a priest-friend accounted for the balance.[102] Sheen soon reported that the Society's Gross Special Fund contained more than $818,000 and the Gross General Fund amounted to more than half a million dollars. Sheen praised Spellman highly for his generosity and kindness toward the Society: "you have made New York foremost among all the cities of the world in that charity which Pius XI called 'the greatest of all charities.'"[103]

The relationship between the cardinal and the bishop was proving productive, but Spellman was anxious that Sheen know from the beginning who was boss. In 1951, Bishop Sheen needed an assistant at the Society, and Spellman recommended Msgr. Edwin Broderick, who was on Spellman's staff of five priests at St. Patrick's Cathedral. The cardinal admired Broderick and had paid all his expenses at Fordham University, where he earned a doctorate in English. After a private conference in Sheen's apartment, the offer was made and accepted. Sheen began introducing Broderick to others as his assistant. In a short time, however, Spellman changed his mind and named Broderick to another position in the archdiocese. Sheen would have to find another assistant.[104]

Ironically, Broderick's new position as assistant director of the Confraternity of Christian Doctrine would greatly involve Bishop Sheen. Broderick was to be in charge of media activities. He soon changed the name of the organization to the Catholic Apostolate for Radio, Television, and Advertising (CARTA) and began hunting for a television outlet for Catholic evangelization.[105]

In the summer of 1951, Sheen returned to Illinois to visit his family and friends. He celebrated Mass for the first time in his home town as a bishop and drew huge crowds of well-wishers. For the first time in many years, he went to El Paso to see his birthplace and a drugstore where he used to buy sodas. At one point during his visit he quoted Aristotle: "The really perfect movement is the circle because it always goes back to its beginnings. I have come back to my starting point—the city, the people, the clergy, the streets...."[106]

Yes, but Sheen had long since outgrown his origins. He was now a citizen of the world.

EIGHT

The Television Man of the Year

In late 1951, Monsignor Edwin Broderick wrote to the major networks and to all archdiocesan priests in New York, attempting to create some sort of Catholic presence on television. At the time, both on radio and on television, religious broadcasting tended to be relegated to the wee hours of the morning and other times when few were listening.

The popularity of television was booming in the early 1950s. By the middle of the decade, two-thirds of all American homes would own at least one TV set. Television was altering the nation's culture as people chose to stay home and sit in front of the small screen for hours on end, watching the likes of *Kukla, Fran and Ollie* or *I Love Lucy,* professional wrestling, the news, or even serious theater and classical music. The introduction of TV dinners in 1954 meant that people would rarely have to interrupt their viewing. Roller rinks, movie theaters, night clubs and dance halls suffered as a consequence.

The power inherent in reaching millions of people in their front rooms nightly was immediately recognized. To avoid controversy, network executives sternly censored sex, violence, profanity and bad taste. Advertising, at first limited, began to swell appreciably as business leaders saw the awesome prospects for increasing sales. Politicians quickly learned how to present themselves in an appealing way.

Books and articles poured forth on the subject of television in the late 1940s and early 1950s. Some authors feared that the nation would become a collection of mindless robots and zombies; others realized that the television screen had potential for great good. Perhaps the cultural level could be elevated, practical knowledge disseminated, and principles of social justice popularized. To Christians, the TV boom also opened avenues for saving souls. Small wonder that the nation's largest church would be among the first seeking to establish a major presence on television.

Monsignor Broderick had attended numerous *Catholic Hour* broadcasts and went to Sheen to see if he might be interested in doing a television program. The bishop welcomed the idea, saying he would like the format to resemble his instruction classes for converts. He proposed giving a twenty-minute talk followed by ten minutes of questions and answers. He thought the programs could be televised from various New York churches.

Broderick took the idea to the Du Mont Network, a minor player in the industry. Most of its executives were Catholics, and two of them in particular liked the proposal but objected to filming the programs around town, for reasons of expense. (The budget was minimal; Sheen would not receive any money.) They proposed using the Adelphi Theater, just off Broadway on Forty-fourth Street, which seated 1,100. Broderick could be the producer and Frank Bunetta, the network's senior director for television, could serve as director. Sheen accepted this plan. As the first broadcast neared, Broderick began passing out free tickets to friends and fellow priests, hoping to fill the theater.[1]

Initially, the half-hour program was to be carried by only two stations, one in New York and the other in Washington, D.C. It was placed on Tuesday evenings at 8:00 P.M., a slot dominated nationally by NBC's *Texaco Star Theater*, featuring "Mr. Television," the comedian Milton Berle. At the same time, the CBS network was offering a show headed by singer-actor Frank Sinatra. Few expected Sheen to have much if any impact on ratings. In fact, the industry called his program placement "an obituary spot."[2] The bishop, said one agent, was "a dead duck."[3] Du Mont considered the Catholic program a public service broadcast. There would be no dancing, singing, action or romance—just a Catholic bishop on a stage, a talking head, followed around by three (later two) cameras.

The simple set, designed by Sheen convert Jo Mielziner, looked like a rector's study, complete with rows of books, a desk and several chairs. A four-foot Renaissance statue of Madonna and Child, on a pedestal, was clearly visible. A blackboard, which Fulton used on occasion to emphasize a point and make rough drawings, was the only prop. (He always wrote "J.M.J." at the top of the blackboard, and much of the public, at first puzzled, eventually learned what it stood for.) Sheen changed the original title of the program, *Is Life Worth Living?*, to the more positive *Life Is Worth Living.*[4]

Director Bunetta told Sheen that he would be given several notices of time remaining during his talks; the bishop said he wanted only one: "fifteen seconds." (This later became two minutes.) Bunetta was astonished, saying he had never encountered a performer with such self-assurance.[5] From the start, Sheen was popular with the show's forty or so crew members, being conscientious, professional and courteous. (At the conclusion of the first series, he had to be talked out of giving each person involved a handsome tip.) He wore a slight amount of makeup, solely for lighting out his beard.[6]

Five minutes before going on the air, the bishop would step to the wings of the set, stand alone, bow his head and pray. (He could become somewhat irritable if interrupted at this point.) On receiving the director's signal, up came the head, and those piercing eyes appeared to glow. His whole figure seemed to grow larger as he stepped before the cameras, heard the thunderous applause, and flashed that appealing smile. It was showtime for Fulton J. Sheen.[7]

Life Is Worth Living made its debut on February 12, 1952. From the first to the last program, Sheen appeared in full episcopal regalia, including a black cassock with purple piping, a purple ferraiolo (cape), purple zucchetto (skull cap), and on his chest the large gold pectoral cross given to him by Pius XII at his consecration. He was accustomed to dressing that way when giving public lectures, he explained to his producer and director.[8] On the initial program, three guests shared the spotlight: journalist and convert Gretta

Palmer; Herbert Trigger, a Jewish friend; and Marlene Brownett, the eighteen-year-old sister of Sheen's secretary. The guests asked Sheen what Brownett later called "canned questions."[9] Soon the program featured only Bishop Sheen. Each week he spoke for about twenty-seven minutes and twenty seconds, without notes or a Teleprompter. He always concluded exactly on time.[10]

Sheen worked long hours on his television talks; he said later that he spent as much as thirty hours in preparation for each.[11] "Being a good speaker," he would tell an interviewer, "is ten per cent delivery and ninety per cent thinking, study, sweat, and hard work." He also claimed, "I have never written out a speech and I have never memorized a speech in my life." (In fact, all of his *Catholic Hour* speeches were written out and approved by censors before delivery.) A talk began with an outline, Sheen explained. "In the course of a week's preparation, I make possibly eight or ten outlines and destroy all of them. The night of the telecast, I may still have the last one but I wouldn't bring it to the studio. By that time, it's in my head."[12]

Sheen delivered each of his talks to a local professor in Italian, and then in French before Marie-Jose Ravaud, a young graduate of Rosemont College. He wrote in his autobiography that this practice helped him to "clarify the subject in my mind."[13] Ravaud said that Sheen's French accent was not quite as perfected as hers, but his vocabulary was superior. She recalled how the bishop would put notes for his next talk on a yellow pad, and he always had a memorized ending, to be used once the signal was given that time was running out.[14]

At one point, Sheen told Broderick that he had been called to Rome for two weeks. To cover his absence, he went into a television studio and filmed two complete broadcasts in one session, again displaying his total preparation and flawless delivery.[15]

Sheen spoke on general themes such as alienation in modern civilization, character building, freedom, war and peace, and suffering, plus a wide assortment of practical topics including what to do about fatigue, how to handle teenagers, and dealing with boring work. He spoke of God, of course, but in a way that would rarely offend Protestants or Jews. This was a new approach for Fulton Sheen, one he thought necessary to maximize his effectiveness.

A Jewish observer who admitted having a strong anti-Catholic bias, Marvin Epstein, was nevertheless drawn to Sheen. "I found myself wondering 'How could he be making pronouncements which no person could reject, regardless of faith—because they simply made such maximal common sense?' "[16] The manager of the Adelphi Theater, Saul Abraham, said, "Most Tuesday nights I just stand backstage and let the guy hypnotize me. He's got everything. In more than 50 years of show business I've never seen such respectful, intelligent audiences as this man draws."[17]

Sheen told a journalist that he was not deliberately talking down to his audience. "I try to establish a common denominator. The theory that the average person has an IQ equivalent to a 12-year-old child has to go. I am on television for the same reason I enter a pulpit or a classroom. Namely, to communicate and diffuse Divine Truth. I am not the Author, but only an heir and trustee."[18] On television, he wrote, he was employing a technique used by Jesus with the woman at the well and by St. Paul at Athens.

> *Starting with something that was common to the audience and to me, I would gradually proceed from the known to the unknown or to the moral and Christian philosophy.... Never once was there an attempt at what might be called proselytizing. It was for the audience to decide that I stood for something which they needed as a complement in their lives. The illumination that fell on any soul was more of the Spirit and less of Sheen.*[19]

As always, Sheen brought humor into his talks—jokes, puns and stories collected over the decades of writing and speech making, along with new material submitted by friends such as joke writer Harry Hershfield and entertainer George Jessel.[20] A writer in *Theater Arts* observed, "All of Bishop Sheen's TV sermons open in a light vein, then move on to more serious matters, closing with a benediction and his most frequently uttered phrase, 'God love you.'

Like an actor who has trod the board for years, Sheen knows when to move upstage, when to modulate his voice, when to 'throw away' a line, when to ease tension with one of his studiously corny jokes."[21]

How corny? The blackboard on stage was on a swivel, and when the camera wasn't fixed on it, a stage hand would turn it over and it would appear to have been mysteriously cleaned. Fulton would say, with a smile, that the chore was performed by "my angel, Skippy." Explaining that television workers were union men, the bishop once told viewers that Skippy belonged to Local 20 of the Cherubim. On another occasion he asked, "Did you hear about the nice lady who went into Brentano's and asked for Rabbi Sheen's *A Piece of My Mind?*"[22] He told of Adam walking with Cain and Abel outside the Garden of Eden and saying, "Boys, that's where your ma ate us out of house and home."[23] More than once, he said, "Long time, no Sheen." Then there was: "I see you're back to have your faith lifted." Comedian Jackie Gleason, often in the control booth with Broderick, marveled at Sheen's way with humor. "What a pause," he would say.[24]

The messages and the humor were part of the Sheen magic, but there was more. The resonant tones of his voice, his majestic appearance, and his performing skills, formed by thousands of speeches and sermons over more than three decades, left many in awe. One writer exclaimed, "His language is vivid, his gestures eloquent. His naturally hypnotic eyes look even deeper under TV lights."[25] A television director said, "His whole technique was the magnetic effect of the way he looked into the camera. I hate to use a cliché, but the word is 'telegenic.' He was made for the medium."[26] A journalist observed, "Hollywood friends say he has more true acting genius in one of those fingertips than most full-time professionals."[27]

Academy Award winner Loretta Young thought her old friend's performance outstanding. When negotiating a contract for a television program bearing her name, she stated specifically that she would not agree to a time or day that would conflict with *Life Is Worth Living*. She not only did not want to compete with Sheen, she wanted to watch him.[28]

A series of twenty-two Sheen talks, published as *Science, Psychiatry and Religion,* illustrate the breadth and depth of the television presentations. The talks included topics Sheen had spoken and written about for years, such as "The Atomic Bomb," "The Glory of Science," "Psychology and Psychiatry," and "Why Do the Innocent Suffer." The intellectual pitch was often quite sophisticated, on a level unimaginable on prime-time television in subsequent generations. The talk on the atomic bomb, for example, began with a brief history of atoms and contained quotations by and allusions to: Democritus, Sir James Jeans, Hermann J. Muller, Sir Robert Robertson, the Goncourt brothers, Albert Einstein, Winston Churchill, Leo Szilard, and Alexander the Great. Sheen also raised and answered the question "How much energy is released by either the fission or the fusion of an atom?"—demonstrating his meticulous preparation for the program. The impressive data displayed in "The Glory of Science" make the same point. To the millions who watched him, Sheen offered far more than the gospel clichés common to sermons.[29] He muted his Catholicism (although in "Do We Talk Too Much?" he mentioned the happiness and holiness found in a Trappist monastery), but he was not at all diffident about his Christianity, devoting an entire talk to the life of Christ.[30]

Life Is Worth Living went on the air at the right time, for the 1950s marked a golden age for American churches. In 1952, 75 percent of Americans told pollsters that religion was "very important" in their lives. Five years later, 69 percent believed that religion was increasing its influence on national life, and 81 percent said they thought religion could answer all or most of life's problems. In the mid-1950s, a record 49 percent of Americans reported having attended a church or synagogue in the past week. The song "I Believe" was a popular hit, even inspiring President Eisenhower, he said. The words "under God" were added to the Pledge of Allegiance. "In God We Trust" became the nation's official motto. The National Council of Churches called for "a Christian America in a Christian world."[31]

The Sheen program expressed and intensified the religious mood of the American people. Du Mont offices soon began to be overwhelmed with mail—8,500 letters a week at first. There were four times as many requests for tickets to see the show as could be filled. The program was soon carried by seventeen stations. With more than two million viewers a week, it had a television rating higher than any other religious or intellectual show. The Milton Berle show fell ten points.[32] (Berle and Sheen became good friends, however. The comedian called the Bishop "Uncle Fultie," a play on his own nickname "Uncle Miltie." Sheen once opened his own program with, "Good evening, this is Uncle Fultie.")[33] Frank Sinatra's competing CBS program soon went off the air. Bishop Sheen had quickly become a national sensation. On April 14 he was on the cover of *Time* magazine.

The Reverend Carl McIntire, a fiery New Jersey fundamentalist and radio preacher, was one of no doubt many hard-core Protestants enraged by Sheen's sudden fame. In his magazine the *Christian Beacon*, he condemned the Du Mont network and *Time*, arguing that Sheen was part of a "very real threat" to the United States from aggressive papists. His broadcasts were slanted and missionary-oriented, McIntire charged, and should not be presented without equal time being given to a representative of the evangelical position. Sheen's programs were "coming at a time when there is a strong consciousness in regard to these things, and it is going to have a reverse effect, with increasing objection and protest."[34]

Critics of the Church focused on its rapid growth. Indeed, between 1940 and 1960, even cautious estimates had the membership doubling, from 21 to 42 million. (There may have been nearly 40 million Catholics in America as early as 1956.)[35] In 1954, there were 158,069 religious sisters running hospitals and parochial schools. There were 46,970 priests and 32,344 seminarians. Two-thirds of Catholic laymen and three-fourths of the laywomen reportedly attended Mass regularly. Between 1949 and 1959, Catholic school enrollments leaped from 2,607,879 to 5,600,000. By mid-century there were some 580 Catholic publications with more than 24 million subscribers. Catholics were moving swiftly into the middle class and into suburbia.[36] They did not seem subversive and "un-American" to most people; in fact, the odds were good that the average American would know someone who had converted to Catholicism. In the decade preceding 1954, there had been more than a million converts.[37]

Bishop Sheen's phenomenal success on television was a sign that millions of Americans had gone beyond the crude caricatures so familiar in the nation's history, and were willing to accept Catholics as Christians and friends. A bishop in full regalia who was charming, funny, learned and sensible could win allies, as well as converts, for the Church. It was exceedingly difficult for reasonable people to think of Fulton Sheen as a dangerous and malevolent subversive.

～

SHEEN TRAVELED TO Ireland, to the little village of Croghan in north Roscommon where his grandmother was born, in late April of 1952. He was there to dedicate the rebuilt, 150-year-old parish Church of St. Michael's. The village and the farmsteads out in the country were decorated for the occasion. Irish, American, and papal flags were everywhere. The church was filled to its capacity of six hundred for the dedicatory service and a Pontifical High Mass, and a large crowd gathered outside. Afterward, on a platform outside the church, people applauded as a nine-year-old local girl presented the bishop with a silver-mounted and inscribed blackthorn walking cane. Thousands gathered that evening to hear Sheen preach, some in the church, the rest outside listening to loudspeakers.

In a message to the press, Sheen declared, "Peace will come to the world when two things happen: when Poland is free and when Ireland is admitted to the United Nations. Until then we shall have the cold war; after that, a heart-warming peace."[38]

In Rome a few days later to make an annual report for the Society for the Propagation of the Faith, Sheen spoke before an overflow crowd at the American Catholic Church of Santa Susanna. The sermon was filled with warnings about Communist infiltration, and included the story, already made public in the United States, of how one subversive attempted unsuccessfully to join his own

office staff. Sheen warned Romans that in the forthcoming munic-
ipal elections they were "face to face with tyrannical danger," as the
Reds were making an earnest effort to win.[39]

And yet back home, Sheen made no direct effort to influence
American elections in 1952. The Second Red Scare was in full force,
and Republicans, eager to win, were accusing Democrats on all levels of Communist and fellow-traveling activities. Senator Joe
McCarthy was cheered wildly during his speech at the Republican
National Convention. The Republican nominee, famed war hero
Dwight Eisenhower, joined the struggle, assuring Americans that
he would cleanse the government of all subversives. Richard Nixon,
an anticommunist with credentials to rival McCarthy's, was selected
to be his running mate.

Although Sheen was forthright about his anticommunism on
his television shows, he remained outside the partisan frenzy. He
said nothing publicly about McCarthy, later explaining to an interviewer that he was totally uninterested in politics, including the
politician McCarthy, who was no authority on communism in any
case.[40]

Cardinal Spellman, on the other hand, was widely thought to
be a McCarthy supporter, having declared in 1953, "The anguished
cries and protests against 'McCarthyism' are not going to dissuade
Americans from their desire to see Communists exposed and
removed from positions where they can carry out their nefarious
plans."[41] The cardinal appeared publicly with McCarthy in April
1954, when the senator was under widespread attack for his reckless charges. A personal representative of the cardinal's defended
McCarthy as late as November of that year, when he was nearing
censure by the United States Senate.[42] With McCarthy soon in the
grip of despair and alcohol, Spellman responded to the plea of the
senator's anxious wife by arranging for the adoption of a five-week-
old orphan from the New York Foundling Home—an unsuccess-
ful attempt to shake McCarthy out of his suicidal doldrums.[43] Spellman also befriended Roy Cohn, McCarthy's most obnoxious and
controversial assistant.[44]

The long years of experience with Soviet imperialism and treachery abroad, and the reality of Soviet spying at home, led many Catholics into the error of believing rough-and-ready Irishman, Marine, and super-patriot Joe McCarthy to be an authentic and effective enemy of communism. The Catholic press was especially susceptible to this error. Donald F. Crosby concluded that McCarthy's popularity with Catholics was "slightly stronger than with the rest of the population." Still, Chicago's Bishop Bernard J. Sheil was militantly anti-McCarthy, as were an assortment of intellectuals, writers and clerics. Efforts by Paul Blanshard, editors of *The Nation*, and others on the left to make a Catholic issue out of McCarthyism are unpersuasive.[45]

Party was more important than religion in determining one's reaction to the Second Red Scare. And a great many political leaders who should have known better, from both major political parties, including John F. Kennedy, were pro-McCarthy. To Republicans especially, the senator from Wisconsin apparently served a valuable political purpose: He helped win the White House in 1952 for the G.O.P. Had he been sufficiently cynical to stop his reckless crusade after Eisenhower took over, McCarthy would have been embraced by people across the political and religious spectrum. Instead, his fantasies and lies, mixed with abundant quantities of liquor, drove him over the brink and into an early grave.

The Second Red Scare did not threaten the United States Constitution, as its most hysterical opponents repeatedly claimed. Joe McCarthy did not hold Catholics, let alone the American people, under his spell. In fact, as Professor Crosby has concluded, most Catholics "turned a deaf ear to the political arguments arising over McCarthyism."[46] Indeed, one public opinion poll taken in the summer of 1954 found: "The number of people who said that they were worried either about the threat of Communists in the United States or about civil liberties was, even by the most generous interpretation of occasionally ambiguous responses, *less than 1 percent!*"[47]

Still, McCarthyism divided the country, froze American foreign policy disastrously, persecuted untold hundreds, and left deep scars on several of the nation's institutions. As this became more apparent, many of those who had supported the witch hunt increasingly recognized their serious error—Cardinal Spellman among them. In his authorized biography, published in 1962, there is a single reference to McCarthy in the index. "All I know about him," Spellman said in an audacious act of revisionism, "is what I read in newspapers."[48]

If Fulton Sheen did not directly participate in the Second Red Scare, he was instrumental in laying the foundations for it. Anticommunism had been a staple of his books, articles, speeches and sermons for decades, and he was often careless about the targets of his zeal. Sweeping generalities about teachers, professors and intellectuals, for example, played into the hands of those who wished to destroy academic freedom and condemn all instructors and thinkers on the left as subversives.

In early 1950, a few days before Joe McCarthy made his initial appearance in the nation's headlines with his speech in Wheeling, West Virginia, Sheen spoke at an anticommunist conference sponsored by fifty-seven organizations. Most of the featured speakers were active in the Second Red Scare. General Walter Bedell Smith warned that Moscow-controlled fifth columnists were at work to overthrow the American government. Hearst newspaper columnist George Sokolsky said that Reds had successfully smeared "business, banking, the Catholic Church and the Republican party." California state senator Jack B. Tenny asserted that Communists were active in both houses of his state legislature. U.S. senator Karl Mundt of South Dakota, a McCarthyite, added his weight to the attack. Voices of responsible anticommunism were also on hand, including James B. Carey of the C.I.O. and Rev. Daniel A. Poling, editor of the *Christian Herald*. But Sheen's presence at the conference and his speech describing the anticommunist activities of the Church gave credence to liberal critics who charged that the Catholic Church was in league with the far Right.[49] It might have been guilt by association, but that was fashionable at the time, and something Sheen ought to have guarded against.

In 1952, Sheen published a 64-page booklet titled *Crisis in History*. Consisting largely of recycled material, it might have been, and perhaps was, used by McCarthyites to document the authenticity of their election-year charges. Intellectuals were linked with treason: "The educated people who should have been the protectors and guardians of the nation's heritage have been to the greatest extent its traitors." Sheen attacked the Tydings Committee, which had investigated and exposed the lies of Senator McCarthy, and also the Voice of America. He derided politicians as being morally obtuse and interested only in "bread and circuses." He condemned the State Department and the Truman administration, though not by name: "Decent American citizens have known for years, for example, that there was a pampering of Communism in high circles, but a powerful group setting their party politics above the good of the country succeeded in suppressing the wishes of the people." He derided peace talks with the Soviets, supported the Korean War, and lauded General MacArthur.

Sheen failed to submit any names of Reds in high places or in universities, content once again to rely on generalities. "America! Be Warned!" he wrote; the nation was rotting from within, and the Reds were responsible for much of the disaster. "The conquest has been effected through boring from within, or through the tactics of the Trojan Horse."[50]

If this was really the case, then why not ruthlessly root out all the Reds, and all the pinks with them? That was the question asked by McCarthy and his followers, as they cast their net for traitors widely, irresponsibly, and dangerously. Even though he did not support McCarthy or even mention him, Sheen indirectly buttressed some of the senator's most cherished claims. One can readily understand how many Catholics, trusting the good judgment and personal holiness of Cardinal Spellman and Bishop Sheen, could have found McCarthy's wild and irresponsible charges persuasive.

Sheen would never acknowledge any culpability in the McCarthy hysteria. He neither implicated nor defended himself. Yet if his public life occasionally revealed a measure of irresponsibility and arrogance, his private works consistently redeemed him.

◡

IN AUGUST 1952 Sheen received a letter from Marian Cahill, the grief-stricken wife of FBI agent Vincent Cahill, telling him that their five-year-old daughter, Suzanne, had been suffering from acute leukemia and had only six months to live. Mrs. Cahill, pregnant and soon expecting her next child, got the idea of writing to Sheen after watching him on television. The bishop replied ten days later, inviting the couple and their daughter to call on him at the Society headquarters. In an internal FBI document, the agent recorded:

> *He greeted us with great warmth, and was extremely cordial and gracious and went to great lengths to make our visit a happy and memorable one. The Bishop gave Suzanne several lovely gifts to delight a child, including a gold ring and an ivory rosary, both of which were subsequently buried with her. In addition he gave her his biretta which he autographed as well as a statue of the Blessed Mother and an ivory crucifix. He presented my wife with a beautiful World Mission rosary and gave me a heavy St. Christopher medal for my car.*

The visit lasted forty-five minutes, with Sheen giving a special blessing to Suzanne and also blessing her parents. "We cherish this visit deeply," wrote Cahill, "since it gave us a considerable amount of strength and consolation to stand behind us for what we were to face."

Sheen stayed in touch with the couple throughout the crisis. He was in Washington at a bishops' meeting when Suzanne passed away, and immediately wrote to her parents offering condolences and spiritual advice. He wrote again when a new child, Marian Theresa, was born a few days later. In all he wrote six letters, stayed in contact with the agent's wife when she was later hospitalized, and left a standing invitation to visit if there was anything he could do to assist them.[51]

Sheen soon invited the Cahills to his television programs, where they often went backstage, once meeting violinist Fritz Kreisler there. He also invited them to his apartment for dinner (they once danced in his front room while the bishop played "April in Paris" on his electric organ) and visited them several times at their apartment in the Bronx and later at their home in Yonkers.[52] Fulton lavished gifts, cash and attention on the ten children the Cahills would ultimately have. He baptized five, confirmed seven, and officiated at the marriage of three. Vincent and Marian named a son, born in 1959, Fulton John Cahill.

One year, just before Christmas, Fulton bought the two oldest Cahill boys new Schwinn bicycles. They were delivered at the apartment of Marian's mother, and the delighted youngsters promptly went out to ride their bikes around the neighborhood. When the family and the bishop returned to the Cahill apartment, Fulton noticed that one of the bicycle wheels was out of adjustment. He sent Vincent for a wrench and, in fine overcoat and homburg hat, he wrestled with the bicycle wheel in the hallway to get it straight. A neighbor, who had had a few beers, came out of the elevator, saw what was going on, said little and entered his own apartment. The next morning, he told Vincent that he truly must have drunk too much the night before: He thought he had seen Bishop Sheen fixing a bicycle in the hallway.

Jeanne Claire Cahill received Bishop Sheen's four-year scholarship to Rosemont College, and the bishop attended her graduation. Marian Cahill wrote later,

> *Looking back over a span of 27 years of a close and loving friendship with our entire family, I think of the countless blessings bestowed on us, and how very much the Bishop strengthened our faith and that of our children by his example. To each of us he was a vivid picture of a true living Christ. He emulated all God's teachings and put them into practice with a cheerfulness and never-failing trust in God's boundless mercy and love for all people.*[53]

On occasion, Vincent Cahill would go walking with the bishop on the streets of New York. Sheen was widely recognized, and sometimes a worshipful crowd, gathering in part to kiss his ring, would tie up traffic. Cahill noticed the special attention Sheen paid to the charwomen and the news boys, often giving them money. Fulton joked privately that he had given away the same $100 bill forty times and it kept reappearing. He meant that for every $100 he distributed to the needy, his funds were replenished in like measure by someone else's generosity. "He'd get it and give it," Cahill said later. The word he emphasized most strongly when later describing Sheen was "kind."[54]

For Sheen, charity was a long-term investment in people. Following one Good Friday service at St. Patrick's, for instance, a disheveled woman with what Fulton thought was a haunted look returned to the main altar and began cursing him violently. When he calmed her down, she admitted that she had come to the service intending to steal purses, but instead had been greatly moved by the sermon's commentary on the good thief. She further stated that she was wanted by the FBI, and showed clippings of accomplices who were in prison. When Fulton asked her if she was a Catholic, she said yes, and she had practiced her faith until she was fourteen. After no doubt many consoling and encouraging words from Sheen, the woman made her confession and began attending Mass daily.

In time, it dawned on Fulton that he was harboring a criminal. He went to FBI officials and told them about the woman. When he said that she was now a daily communicant at St. Patrick's, the charges against her were dropped. The woman was unable to work, so Fulton personally supported her for about twenty years until her death.[55]

❧

IN EARLY SEPTEMBER of 1952, Sheen's office announced that the bishop (then on a visit to Puerto Rico) would, after twenty-four years, discontinue his talks on the *Catholic Hour*. The explanation given was that Sheen did not have time to do both radio and television, and wished to devote all of his attention to the latter.[56] The bland announcement masked the often bitter squabbling between *Catholic Hour* officials and their star speaker. Sheen, however, praised NBC publicly for the many years it had carried the program, saying that "No industry in modern history has contributed as much to religion, good-will and inspirational living."[57]

The Admiral Corporation, manufacturer of radio and television sets, announced on October 21 that it would sponsor *Life Is Worth Living* for a period of twenty-six weeks over a coast-to-coast Du Mont network. The cost would be about a million dollars, and would include a donation to the Society for the Propagation of the Faith. (A *New York Times* reporter thought the Society was a United Nations agency.) Sheen would donate his fee, which he later recalled was $26,000 per show, to the organization.[58]

Sheen stated in his autobiography that the Society "made the contract and merely used me as their spokesman."[59] In fact, Cardinal Spellman made the initial contact with the corporation, and the deal, as the *New York Times* reported at the time, was worked out by Sheen's literary agent, Gertrude Algase.[60] When Algase requested her commission, she and Sheen had a "violent" quarrel, the bishop claiming that she was trying to take money away from the missions. Algase bitterly accepted the rebuke, and continued to represent Sheen.[61]

This marked the first time that a religious program was financed by a corporation that would advertise its products on the air time; commercials were to appear at the opening and closing of the program. Noting how extremely unusual it was for religion to be presented nationally in prime time, Jack Gould of the *New York Times* declared that Sheen "undoubtedly is going to have the largest regular audience of any prelate in history."[62] Seventy-five stations carried the program the first year, and the Admiral Corporation hiked the number to 132 in the next.[63]

The Admiral programs proved to be extremely popular; there was a wild rush for tickets. Sheen's office reportedly received some 25,000 letters a day. (Edwin Broderick said that Sheen was often guilty of "blarney" when it came to numbers. Almost all of the letters came to his office, he said, and Sheen had no idea how many arrived.)[64] Cash and gifts of all sorts poured out of letters and packages to help the missions. "We opened a yellow envelope and $10,000 in cash fell out," Sheen later reported. He asked viewers to send him a dime for the world's poor, and "We were deluged from then on with coins taped to letters." An actor, Ramon Estevez, changed his name to Martin Sheen with the bishop's permission. President Eisenhower wrote Fulton a letter regretting having missed the opportunity to stop for a chat while driving down a New York street.[65]

Awards poured in upon the bishop. He won the 1952 Emmy Award for "Most Outstanding Television Personality," beating out such show business giants as Jimmy Durante, Edward R. Murrow, Lucille Ball and Arthur Godfrey. In his acceptance remarks, which he claimed were impromptu, he said, "I wish to thank my four writers, Matthew, Mark, Luke and John."[66] (Tom Holliger, a cousin who was staying with Sheen, noticed the next morning that the statuette had been casually placed on a steam radiator. When he mentioned it, Sheen merely shrugged.)[67]

The *Radio and Television Daily* nationwide poll of radio and television editors named Sheen "Man of the Year" on television.[68] The Freedoms Foundation of Valley Forge, Pennsylvania, gave Sheen and his program an award, presented by Vice-President Nixon, for "outstanding contributions to a better understanding of the American way of life during 1952."[69] The Advertising Club of New York named him "Our Television Man of the Year."[70] The Catholic University Alumni Association awarded him the Cardinal Gibbons Medal for "distinguished and meritorious service to Our Blessed Lord, our beloved America and our Alma Mater," an award personally presented by Cardinal Spellman.[71] *Look* magazine listed "Life Is Worth Living" as "Best Religious Program" for three different years. President Eisenhower invited Sheen to dinner at the White House.[72]

One of the most newsworthy of Sheen's programs occurred on February 24, 1953. The bishop read the burial scene from *Julius Caesar,* inserting the name of Russian leaders and speaking of Stalin's death as if it were actually occurring. Then the Soviet dictator died on March 5. When Milton Berle heard the news, one of his writers said, "Why can't you do something like that?" Another writer, familiar with Berle's propensity to lift material used by others, replied, "What for? They'll say Milton stole the bit!"[73] Sheen later met a woman who said she converted after hearing the broadcast. He sighed, "There was absolutely nothing in that telecast that would draw a soul to the Church. God just used it as an instrument. 'Paul plants, Apollo waters, but God gives the increase.' "[74]

In 1952, Sheen published *The World's First Love,* an eloquent and exhaustive tribute to the Blessed Virgin Mary. Dedicated to "The Woman I Love," the book deals with such topics as the Immaculate Conception, the relationship between early Church tradition and Scripture, Jesus' "brethren" mentioned in the Bible, St. Paul's use of language when discussing the Incarnation, virginity and love, and the Rosary.[75]

There was little new in *The World's First Love.* Much of it had appeared a year earlier in a radio broadcast publication entitled *The Woman.* An exposition on man's freedom was very familiar to Sheen fans. There are more shots at communism and at pink as well as Red professors. Some huge generalizations appear, such as: "No normal mind yet has ever been overcome by worries or fears who was faithful to the Rosary." But on the whole, the book was one of Sheen's best. It was highly acclaimed by reviewers, adopted by five book clubs, and translated into German, Italian and Portuguese.[76]

Sheen was eager to cash in on his popularity, furiously recycling his previously published materials in a blitz of books that undoubtedly brought a great deal of money to the mission field. In 1953, a collection of newspaper columns called *Way to Happiness,* perhaps designed by Gertrude Algase to tap into the self-improvement fashion of the period, sold extremely well. The first book of Sheen's printed television talks also appeared that year under the title *Life Is Worth Living, First Series,* and it sold well. This was followed in 1954 by three similar volumes.

Other works were also spreading Sheen's fame. *The Divine Romance,* first published in 1930, was now in its tenth edition of

5,000 copies. *Love on Pilgrimage,* a set of radio talks delivered in 1946, was in its third edition of 25,000 copies. *The Woman* collection of radio talks was in its fifth edition of 30,000. The *Life of Christ,* consisting of fifteen talks delivered on the *Catholic Hour* in the spring of 1952, went into its second edition of 20,000 within four months. In addition, a phonograph album of *Catholic Hour* broadcasts that Sheen recorded in 1946 had sold almost 50,000 copies by 1953.[77]

Three new books, a booklet and a fifth volume of *Life Is Worth Living* transcriptions made their debut in 1955. *Way to Inner Peace, Way to Happy Living, God Love You,* and the thirty-page *The True Meaning of Christmas* were aimed at mass sales. *Way to Happy Living* sold for fifty cents in paper and was available in grocery and drug stores. *Thoughts for Daily Living* made its debut in 1956, and two more volumes of *Life Is Worth Living* transcripts appeared in 1957.

A master's thesis could be written on the sources used in Sheen books, especially during this period. *Way to Inner Peace,* for example, appears to be a collection of the bishop's syndicated newspaper columns. *God Love You* cites material coming from twenty-five Sheen books and an unnamed quantity of newspaper columns, and might well be an anthology. The same is true of *Go to Heaven* (1961). Later books such as *Walk with God* (1965) and *Guide to Contentment* (1967), both initially priced at under a dollar, are unidentified collections of brief reflections on a wide variety of topics that may have stemmed from any number of Sheen writings.

Although these publications were plentiful, unoriginal and inexpensive, they contain the usual Sheen wit and wisdom, and in intellectual content at least, they stand considerably above the Christian optimism books by Norman Vincent Peale and an assortment of "feel good" fundamentalists to which they have been compared. Brief essays such as "Love and Ecstasy," "Blood, Sweat, and Tears," and "Inscape," in *Way to Happiness;* "Forgiveness Not Enough" and "Inner Nakedness" in *Way to Happy Living;* and "Memory" and "Pleasures" in *Way to Inner Peace* undoubtedly helped many literate

Americans in their quest to lead happy and healthy Christian lives. The fine writing revealed in "Crutch or Cross" and "'Me,' 'I,' 'Thou,'" in *Way to Happy Living*, for example, is rarely found in the popular works of Sheen's Protestant peers in the 1950s. The fact that the bishop did not emphasize Catholicism in these publications not only increased sales but no doubt helped reduce anti-Catholicism in the United States.

∾

COMMUNISM WAS STILL very much on Sheen's mind in 1953. It was receiving national attention as well. The new administration was busily firing "communist sympathizers" in the executive branch. The Korean War ended in an angry deadlock, but the Soviets and the Chinese seemed as aggressive and hostile as ever. Secretary of State John Foster Dulles, while failing to honor a campaign pledge to "roll back" the Soviets in Eastern Europe, was hawkish and busy. Joe McCarthy was attracting headlines daily by announcing the discovery of Reds in an ever-growing list of areas of American life, including the CIA.

The FBI was not on the list. No one, not even McCarthy, was daring and foolish enough to question the patriotism of J. Edgar Hoover. Yet without Hoover, there would have been no Second Red Scare, for through him came the leaks, tips, and subtle statements of approval that kept the scare going. (He and McCarthy appeared together at a championship boxing match and at the racetrack. Former bureau agents served on McCarthy's staff. The far Right often had access to FBI information.) In 1953, virtually everyone, outside the far Left, respected Hoover, even if they disliked him. A long-running radio program, several sympathetic movies, and an assortment of other carefully designed public relations efforts made the FBI one of the nation's most honored institutions. Hoover's authority was such that a word from him could have stopped the Red hunters cold. He knew who most of the authentic Communists and fellow travelers were. That he chose to aid and abet the fanatics, politicos and shysters who led the Second Red Scare—up to the point, during the Army-McCarthy hearings, when McCarthy embarrassed him publicly with a document he should not have divulged—is a permanent blot on his reputation.[78]

Fulton admired Hoover's fervent anticommunism, his dislike of liberalism, and his often declared commitment to traditional American values. Like almost all of his fellow citizens, Sheen was unaware of the dark side of the director—the zealous hater, racist, and tyrant whose hunger for power was insatiable and whose methods were often illegal. That part of the Hoover portrait would become public only after his death. Sheen would have been shocked, for example, to learn that the Socialist Workers Party endured sixteen years of illegal FBI surveillance. In the course of that endeavor, the bureau planted 1,300 informants in the party, paying them a total of $1.7 million, and committed 193 burglaries, photographing or removing 9,864 party documents.[79] The bishop would have been astounded to learn that from the 1930s to the 1960s, dozens of America's most prominent authors were kept under surveillance by the FBI because their writings were considered subversive. The list included Ernest Hemingway, Pearl Buck, Carl Sandburg, Thorton Wilder, John Steinbeck, Sinclair Lewis, and William F. Buckley Jr.[80]

In early May, Sheen received a personal invitation from J. Edgar Hoover to speak at the graduation exercises of the FBI National Academy in June. The letter was delivered by agent William M. Whelen of the New York FBI office, described in a confidential internal memo as a personal acquaintance of Sheen's.[81] In a warm reply to the director, Sheen accepted.[82]

The bishop gave a rousing patriotic address on June 12, before an audience of 1,400. He praised the FBI and law enforcement officers in general, and discussed the nature of freedom ("the right to do whatever you ought"), the purpose of man's existence ("to serve his God and country"), the balance between rights and duties (if people taking the Fifth Amendment before congressional committees "do not recognize their Constitutional duties, they surrender their Constitutional rights"), the relationship between democracy and divinity ("if we wish to keep our rights, we must keep our

God"), and politics in general ("Whether we are right or left does not really make very much difference. The biggest problem is whether we are going *up* or *down*"). The conclusion was designed to bring people to their feet:

> *This great Republic of ours chose, not the serpent that crawls in the dust, not the lion that goes about seeking its prey that it might devour it, not the fox who overcomes its enemy by stealth[. America], in full consciousness of its own dignity and the full promise of what it was destined to be in the nations of the world, chose as its symbol, the Eagle, flying onwards and upwards on to God.*

Immediately after the ceremony, Hoover wrote to Sheen, lauding him for "one of the finest and most inspirational talks I have ever heard," adding that it was "a distinct honor to have had you with us."[83] He soon sent photographs of the event and expressed his desire to have an edited version of the talk published in a bureau magazine. He also said that he intended to turn over a copy of the talk to conservative newspaper columnist David Lawrence.[84] Sheen thanked the director for the photographs, noting, "I am very happy to have a record and a memento of my association with a department which is so truly American both in its tradition and in its outlook."[85]

When Hoover sent a letter to Sheen congratulating him on receiving the Cardinal Gibbons prize at Catholic University, the bishop replied, "I accept your words of praise as the window pane receives rays of light, not to store them, but to let them pass through me, back again to God, the Giver of all gifts. Your good wishes are an assurance of a friendship that I cherish, and your gracious message is a delight to my heart."[86] Sheen was placed on the bureau's private mailing list, remaining on it at least through the 1960s, an honor bestowed by Hoover on those worthy of his highest praise and trust.[87]

In 1956, Sheen delivered a speech to a thousand FBI personnel and their families at a Communion breakfast.[88] The following year, top FBI official Lou Nichols mentioned in an internal memo "Bishop

Sheen's friendliness and close cooperation with the Director and the FBI." In 1958, Sheen wrote to Hoover, "You have built up a tradition toward Divine justice in this country which has been incomparable to the life of free peoples. The quality of the men who surround you, their excellent philosophy of life have combined to personalize justice in what is called a Department. May the Lord bless you and yours."[89]

At some point, Hoover made Sheen a "Special Service Contact." As defined in an internal FBI document of 1954, "Special Service Contacts are prominent individuals who have volunteered their assistance to the Bureau. Bureau approval must be obtained to designate an individual as a Special Service Contact and an annual report concerning each Special Service Contact, relating the services rendered, must be furnished to the Bureau." The program was created in 1941, discontinued in 1945, and recommenced in mid-1950 after the outbreak of the Korean War.[90]

With the passions aroused by the Korean War arrested and the Eisenhower administration reassuringly rooting out Reds, Hoover again discontinued the Special Service Contact program in 1954.[91] Some individuals so named, however, were kept on as contacts for their local FBI offices. Sheen remained on the New York list. His services, whatever they may have been, were terminated in 1967, when Sheen moved to Rochester. We only know from an internal FBI document that Sheen "over the years has maintained an active interest in the bureau, has been of assistance whenever called upon, and has met a number of bureau officials who have had occasion to visit the New York office."[92]

In 1967, Sheen told members of the FBI National Academy Association that law enforcement officers "are defenders of God's justice, His sense of right"—earning a warm letter of thanks from Director Hoover.[93] Two years later, an agent reported privately to Hoover, "Bishop Sheen expressed most sincerely his admiration for you and the work of the Bureau. He informed me that you are one of the greatest men in our country today, and hopes that you will continue in your present capacity."[94] Just as Richard Nixon hornswoggled Billy Graham, presenting himself to the evangelist as a pious man of prayer, so J. Edgar Hoover, appearing to be the honest and selfless patriot, deceived Fulton J. Sheen. It is by no means unusual for the crafty and unprincipled to use those striving to be holy; the cynicism often necessary for fame and prosperity is, as Sheen said, off limits to the serious Christian.[95]

∾

IN 1955, FULTON wrote an article for *Look* magazine that was a warm and memorable tribute to his friend and patron Pope Pius XII, then nearing eighty years of age. Sheen told the story of the former Archbishop Eugenio Pacelli being confronted by Communist thugs in Munich in 1919, nearly adding his own name to the list of 325 people they had killed that day. The experience, Fulton wrote, left the future Pius XII fearless. He called the Pope a "dry" martyr, one who suffers persecution for his faith without the personal shedding of blood.

> *Perhaps no Pope in history has seen so many martyred for the faith as has Pius XII. The first 32 Popes, including St. Peter, were martyrs for the faith. They were the wet martyrs. The present Holy Father has seen millions tortured, persecuted, exiled and martyred under the beatings of the hammer and the cuttings of the sickle of communism; he has agonized under the double cross of nazism and borne in his body the marks of the sticks of fascism; he has seen the slow attrition of the world, as the shores of Western civilization gave way to the floods of Communist aggression—all this and other sorrows, he felt as his own. As the nerves send the message of every torture of the body to the brain until it becomes dizzy with the concentration of it all, so too the sorrows of the world come to a head in him.*

The Pope had granted Sheen a private audience on a recent trip to Rome, and Fulton again swore allegiance to his Holiness. Pius XII answered, "It is true that Divine Providence has invested me, although unworthily, in this position as head of the Church, but as a man I am nothing ... nothing ... nothing." Fulton thought that expression of humility a sign of true greatness. "There is something mysteriously divine about a great human life 'emptying himself' after the fashion of the Son of God—becoming the Son of Man."[96]

Meanwhile, honors and requests for personal appearances continued to pour into Sheen's office. The senior class of the University of Notre Dame named the bishop "Patriot of the Year" for 1955. (J. Edgar Hoover had been the winner the year before.)[97] In May, he delivered the commencement address at Dumbarton College of Holy Cross University, appearing before a large audience on the campus hockey field with Archbishop Patrick O'Boyle of Washington.[98] The next day he helped pass out the diplomas at Rosemont College in Philadelphia, where he had appeared frequently since 1929. (He interrupted the ceremony by announcing the marriage, the next day, of a graduate, calling the young man to the stage and giving an impromptu sermon on Christian marriage.)[99]

In September, Sheen offered a Byzantine Rite Mass at Mount St. Macrina near Uniontown, Pennsylvania, before some 120,000 pilgrims. It was the climax of a week-long gathering of Eastern Rite Catholics. Sheen's performance marked the first Pontifical Mass ever sung in English, and the first in the Byzantine Rite to be celebrated, with special Vatican permission, by a Latin Rite bishop.[100] He soon participated in a similar service at the Cathedral of the Holy Cross in Boston. As Bishop Nicholas T. Elko of Pittsburgh, head of the Byzantine Rite of the Church in America, celebrated a Low Mass, Sheen translated from the Slavonic and led responses in English. An estimated eight thousand people were on hand to hear Richard Cardinal Cushing introduce Sheen as a man who combined the qualities of St. Francis of Assisi and St. Thomas Aquinas.[101]

Sheen gave two lectures at a missionary congress in Rochester, New York, in October. Some twenty thousand were on hand in the brand-new War Memorial Auditorium for the Mission Scenerama, which featured exhibits of missionary orders and talks by prelates from around the globe.[102]

That fall, *Life Is Worth Living* moved from Du Mont to ABC television and radio. With 117 television stations, the audiences would

Top: Fulton at ordination, 1919. (Courtesy of Mary Baker Carr.) Bottom: Sheen brothers—Al, Joe, Tom and Fulton—1929. (Courtesy of Connie Sheen.)

Top: Newt (left) and Delia (next to him) with relatives, 1941. (Courtesy of Eileen Sheen Khouw.)
Bottom: Fulton preaching Good Friday sermon at St. Patrick's Cathedral, 1937. (Broadcast over NBC.) (Courtesy of University of Maryland.)

Top: Fulton and actress Loretta Young, 1940. (Courtesy of Loretta Young.) Bottom: Fulton and Joseph P. Kennedy (second and third from left) at Notre Dame University graduation, 1941. (Courtesy of Notre Dame University.)

Top: Sheen and Sister Marlene Brownett, 1952. (Courtesy of Sr. Marlene Brownett.) Bottom: Sheen and Msgr. Klaus Mund, head of Germany's Society for the Propagation of the Faith, 1952. (Courtesy of Ursula Faymonville.)

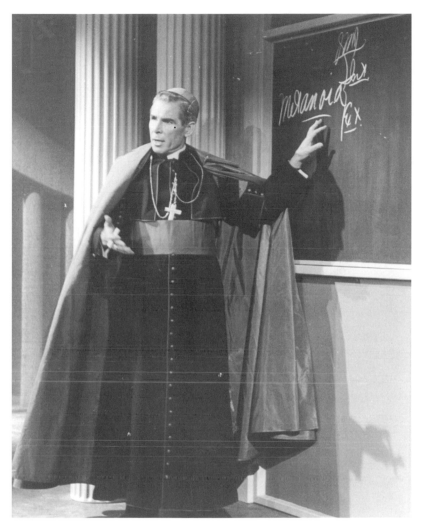

Sheen at blackboard during "Life Is Worth Living" television show. (Courtesy of University of Maryland.)

Top: Al, Fulton and Tom at Al's wedding, 1961. (Courtesy of Joseph Sheen Jr.) Bottom: Sheen and Cardinal Spellman, 1966. This photo was taken during the news conference that announced Sheen's removal from the Archdiocese of New York to Rochester. (Bettmann Archive, Corbis, October 26, 1966.)

Top: Fulton, Edythe Brownett and unnamed nun, 1975. (Courtesy of Sr. Marlene Brownett.)
Bottom: Fulton leaving Lennox Hospital in 1977. (Courtesy of Sr. Marlene Brownett.)

Fulton hugged by Pope John Paul II, 1978. (Courtesy of Sheen Archives.)

now be far larger and the contributions for the Society that much greater. The new schedule was Thursdays at 8:00 P.M., opposite comedian Grouch Marx's *You Bet Your Life*. Sheen quipped, "Viewers will now have a choice of two Marxes—Groucho or Karl."[103]

The year 1955, however, also contained tragedy and turmoil. In July, Fulton's brother Joe died at fifty-six of a heart attack. A very private and personable man, Joe had earned a law degree at Kent College of Law in Chicago, married, fathered eight adoring children, and become the president of the city of La Grange, Illinois, a Chicago suburb, where he and his family lived for many years. His daughter Joan said later that Joe was of all the Sheen boys closest to Fulton. She added that he was "very religious and did a lot of free work for people." Fulton presided at the funeral.[104] During the service, while kneeling at the altar with Joe's oldest son, he gave Joe Jr. his episcopal ring—the large, bejeweled, 300-year-old ring he had received when consecrated.[105]

Earlier that year, Gertrude Algase, Fulton's literary agent, broke completely with the bishop, hired an attorney, and appealed to Cardinal Spellman. She asserted that she was entitled to 10 percent of the television and radio payments made to the Society for the Propagation of the Faith for the bishop's ABC contract, which she claimed to have helped negotiate. In the course of her threat to sue, she wrote a confidential memorandum to her attorney stating that since 1942, when she went to work for Sheen, the bishop had made a total of $800,000 in royalties, and that more than half a million of this sum went to Sheen, the balance to the missions. This was exclusive of the Admiral Corporation contract made with Du Mont.[106]

Sheen left no financial records of any kind, and these figures, if true, are extremely interesting. If Fulton actually kept, say, $500,000 of his royalties over a dozen years, his claim to care nothing for money could appear to be rank hypocrisy. Of course, he might have given away most or all of it. That seems entirely plausible. In 1956, he told John Tracy Ellis that in 1955 he personally donated a million dollars to the Society for the Propagation of the Faith.[107] At the end of his life he would claim to have donated $10 million. Still, the entire issue of Sheen's personal finances remains uncertain for lack of evidence. A direct appeal by the author to Edythe Brownett shed no light on the subject; she spoke only of her beloved employer's expansive generosity.[108]

The one thing that would put Algase at ease and keep a scandal out of the newspapers was money. In November, the diocesan director of the Society, Vincent W. Jeffers, suggested quietly to Spellman that the woman be given 5 percent instead of 10.[109] According to Edwin Broderick, Sheen took the embarrassing issue directly to Pius XII, and Spellman also traveled to Rome for talks on the matter. Algase was quietly paid off, and the conflict remained private.[110]

Worse trouble appeared in 1955, as Sheen and Spellman began an epic feud that was to cloud the rest of Fulton's life. The immediate issue was money for the missions; but pride, on the part of both the bishop and the cardinal, also played a major role in the struggle. It was a story Fulton chose not to tell in his autobiography.

NINE

Backed up Against the Cross

Francis Cardinal Spellman—long-time personal friend of the Pope, ally of major political and governmental figures in the United States, a potent force in the mass media, and head of the richest diocese in the world—was a man accustomed to getting his way. Those who crossed him often paid the price. But even his vengeance was unpredictable. George A. Kelly, an archdiocesan administrator, feuded often with Spellman. Kelly recalled that the cardinal "could beat hell out of you" in the morning and in the afternoon make you a bishop. Once, on the way to Spellman's residence, the two got into a bitter argument. Spellman slammed the door in the younger man's face. Fifteen seconds later, he reopened it and said, "By the way, the Pope has named you a monsignor." Kelly knew that in fact Spellman had bestowed the honor.[1]

Edwin Broderick, who worked for Spellman from 1947 to 1964, serving as his secretary for a decade, noted that the cardinal was good to his priests when they got into trouble, showing kindness and concern. He stressed Spellman's talent as a builder, a brick-and-mortar priest who had a keen eye for real estate. Spellman's most glaring fault, in Broderick's eyes, was his temper. He could fly off the handle easily when confronted with something he found offensive, such as movies like *The Miracle, The Moon Is Blue,* and *Baby Doll,* all of which he condemned publicly and tried to keep out of theaters. The staff would have to calm him down and urge him to act with more deliberation. And often he would.

To Broderick, that was a major difference between Spellman and Sheen: the cardinal could be talked out of a rash and erroneous decision, but when the bishop made up his mind, that was the end of it. Both men, Broderick recalled, had extremely strong egos and iron wills; they were "very human."[2] Perhaps the clash between the two—the most powerful Catholic in the country versus the most popular—was inevitable.

It may be that Sheen had not entirely suppressed the derogatory view of Spellman he expressed in 1939 to John Tracy Ellis, and that once he had a considerable amount of authority of his own, he refused any longer to be bullied and ordered about by a man he considered his intellectual inferior. Both the cardinal and the bishop, to be sure, burned with pride. As John Cooney put it, "There was no room in New York for two prima donnas."[3]

There were two major incidents that provided a flashpoint in the relationship, the first in 1955. At this time, the United States government provided surplus food, free of charge, to the Catholic Relief Services branch of the National Catholic Welfare Conference, for distribution to peoples of all faiths in Europe. The commodities, aimed especially at war-torn countries, were distributed by Catholic missionaries. In the six months prior to May of that year, 256,540,754 pounds of foods, valued at more than $68 million, were dispersed. Expenses for delivering the free goods were shared by the federal government and the governments of receiving nations. Spellman and several others quietly admired the program as a tool for proselytizing, and feared that Protestant missionaries might get a share of the goods if they did not accelerate the distribution.[4]

Spellman wanted Sheen to provide additional funds for this effort from the Society for the Propagation of the Faith. He was used to having his way with Society funds, and had personally distributed them on his travels around the world.[5] The cardinal made his proposal to Sheen in a meeting of May 25, 1955. The bishop, for reasons that are not spelled out in the documents of the incident, rejected it.[6]

Spellman then arranged a meeting between Sheen and several priests to make the case. In addition, the cardinal spent an hour with Sheen urging him to provide the funds. Again, he refused.

Spellman wrote a friend, "I admit I fail to see the logic of the position of Bishop Sheen and Bishop Sheen gives no reason for his position. . . . He simply says that he will do what his Superiors in Rome tell him to do." Spellman vowed to go around Sheen, through Society officials in Rome, to obtain the money. He then threatened to use archdiocesan funds in this regard if he failed to obtain what he wanted from Sheen and his superiors.[7]

In a July 1 letter to Joseph P. Kennedy, recently returned from a papal audience in Rome, Spellman expressed mild dissatisfaction with Sheen. Multimillionaire Kennedy was planning a national organization to assist university students, and he had considered and apparently rejected Sheen as its head. Spellman agreed with Kennedy that Sheen was not the man for the job.[8] That same day, Spellman wrote to a Society official in Rome criticizing Sheen for his obduracy. "I am aware that Bishop Sheen has not taken a positive position in recommending this contribution of the Sacred Congregation of the Propaganda which would multiply benefits otherwise unobtainable, and whether this is because of humility or diffidence I am unable to determine."[9]

A few days later, the General Council of the Society sided with Sheen, rejecting Spellman's request. A Society official explained to the cardinal, "This refusal is motivated solely by the intention to use the limited financial resources at hand to the greatest possible advantage in the spreading of Christ's kingdom on earth."[10] Spellman was furious. Before leaving on a trip to Trinidad, he had a private meeting with Sheen and called him "a very foolish man." The cardinal confided to a friend in the Vatican, "I told him that there was absolutely no possible logical reason for him not to endorse this proposal which had the unanimous approval of all those intimately connected with the disposal of surplus foods. I pressed him to give me one reason for his opposition to the proposal, and he was absolutely unable to give anything except that he felt there was too much pressure." To Spellman, that spelled defiance of his authority—which it clearly was. He wrote that "the matter of the surplus foods is the first direct act of non-compliance with a suggestion that I have made, and incidentally it's the first act during the seventeen years I have been privileged to be the Archbishop. Some day perhaps I shall congratulate him on this distinction."[11]

In August, Spellman sent a blistering letter to a Society official in Rome, threatening to go to the Pope about the issue. (A leading Vatican official noted that Pius XII, ailing at the time, was consulted in a general way about the fracas.)[12] The following spring, Spellman attempted to persuade the Pope to replace Sheen as head of the Society and name himself as the successor. After five months of deliberation, Pius XII refused.[13] In July, Sheen spoke about his woes with Spellman for three hours over dinner with John Tracy Ellis. "The details were colorful and in certain respects rather grim," Ellis wrote later.[14] Regrettably, historian Ellis chose to keep those details confidential.

At some point, probably early, in 1957, the two prelates clashed again. For years, the federal government had been giving the Church surplus goods, largely powdered milk. Spellman turned these goods over to the Society for distribution to the world's poor, claiming that he had purchased the supplies and demanding millions of dollars from Sheen in repayment. Sheen refused to turn any money over to the cardinal, pointing out correctly that the surplus goods had been donated free of charge.

Spellman was again furious. Sheen appealed to Rome, but found difficulty in reaching the ailing Pope. Spellman offered his antagonist a wealthy New York parish in exchange for his resignation from the Society, but Sheen declined.[15] The cardinal also initiated three investigations into Sheen's life, hoping, without success, to find something incriminating to use against him. Eventually both men appeared before Pius XII, each presenting his case. Fulton's claim was documented: Spellman had not been charged for the surplus food. That meant, of course, that Spellman had lied to Pius XII and to Sheen. The Pope sided with Fulton, who remained in charge of the local Society funds.

One can imagine the cardinal's rage. He reportedly said to Sheen, "I will get even with you. It may take six months or ten years, but everyone will know what you're like."[16]

Outwardly, Sheen remained courteous and respectful toward Spellman. He was assigned to write flowery invitations for the celebration of the twenty-fifth anniversary of Spellman's consecration as a bishop. His form letter stressed the cardinal's resistance to such a celebration and the love and gratitude Sheen and other planners had for their leader. On the Silver Jubilee Committee's stationery, Fulton was listed as being in charge of the Papal Military Orders.[17]

The gala affair that Spellman allegedly tried to prevent out of embarrassment was held in Yankee Stadium on August 30. The apostolic delegate, four cardinals, eighteen archbishops, eighty-three bishops, and two abbots were on hand, along with thousands of cheering well-wishers. A large procession of uniformed police and firemen, members of the Holy Names societies, opened the ceremonies by marching from the left-field bullpen onto the baseball field, which featured a huge raised platform dominated by an immense cross. Then Spellman made a grand entrance from right field, escorted by twenty West Point cadets in full-dress uniform. He was clad in gold robes trimmed in scarlet; even his miter was gold with scarlet trim. The St. Joseph's Seminary choir, stationed behind home plate, sang "Behold the Great Priest."[18] Whatever Sheen may have thought about the pompous ceremony, he kept it to himself. He was in enough trouble.

According to D. P. Noonan, Spellman told students at St. Joseph's Seminary in New York that Sheen was the most disobedient priest in the country. "I want none of you to turn out like him."[19] The cardinal discouraged priests from inviting Sheen to preach. His annual appearance at St. Patrick's Good Friday service was dropped, and he now spoke in Jersey City. (Amid protests, Spellman claimed to know nothing of this, and ordered Sheen reinstated on the schedule.)[20]

In October 1957, Sheen "retired" from television. He said publicly that his departure was "dictated by spiritual considerations" and the desire to spend more time raising funds for the world's poor. Insiders heard rumors that Cardinal Spellman had forced Fulton off the air, which seems certain.[21] Still, the bishop held open the possibility of his return. Even though the show's ratings had dropped, ABC television had offered him network time to continue the *Life Is Worth Living* series on a sponsored or unsponsored basis.[22] There had been 127 shows, averaging 26 each season, from February 1952 to April 1957. In 1956 the program had been carried on 113 television stations and 300 radio stations, reaching an audience estimated at 30 million. The mass media would never experience its equal again. An authoritative book on television has declared that *"Life Is Worth Living* was probably the most widely viewed religious series in TV history."[23]

Spellman's vendetta against Sheen did not appear in the newspapers, and most laity in New York were no doubt unaware of it, but the news traveled fast in clerical circles. Fulton spoke with a few priests about his troubles, but refused to discuss the matter with laity, even those closest to him.[24]

Sheen had now lost his major platform for raising funds and enjoying his celebrity status. He lived daily with Spellman's wrath hovering over him. No doubt his speaking invitations declined and fund-raising efforts became more difficult. Personal opportunities for advancement in the Church were minimal at best. (As late as 1956, Sheen had taken seriously rumors that he was to be made a cardinal.)[25] Angry letters (now missing and discussed in the Author's Note) went back and forth between the cardinal and the bishop. And how galling must have been the taunts of Spellman's staff members who privately referred to him as "Full-Tone Jay" Sheen.[26] Few clergy risked Spellman's fury by open friendliness toward Sheen. One can well imagine the extent to which colleagues deliberately avoided him. In 1966, Fulton would tell a Byzantine Rite bishop that he was indebted to him, "for you are the one friend who stood by me in the dark, dark days of the not too distant past."[27]

Fulton's side of the struggle is not known in detail. In both confrontations with Spellman, apparently, he was simply unwilling to let money he had donated and raised be spent for purposes he deemed unworthy. It was largely a matter of principle, and he was prepared to pay the price. A few years earlier, his brothers had told

an interviewer of Fulton's cool courage as a young man, his determination not to give ground in the face of any person or situation
he considered unjust.[28] Of course, it was also a matter of pride.
Sheen reportedly said of his battles with Spellman, "Jealousy is the
tribute mediocrity pays to genius."[29]

❧

SHEEN WAS BY NO MEANS entirely out of the spotlight during his
years of disfavor with Spellman. The newspaper columns attracted
attention, as did Society literature. In 1957, the fifth of the *Life Is
Worth Living* transcriptions appeared, as did *Science, Psychiatry and
Religion*, a volume containing more *Life Is Worth Living* perform-
ances. A year later, Sheen brought out *Life of Christ*, which garnered
widespread critical acclaim and large sales.

His *Life of Christ* is largely a commentary on the scriptural
accounts, organized under sixty-one brief essays in roughly chrono-
logical order. Sheen fans found, as usual, much that was familiar.
While fully aware of modern biblical scholarship, he chose, as did
the Church, to reject almost all of it. Fulton wrote simply, "He will
not allow us to pick and choose among His words, discarding the
old ones, and accepting the ones that please our fancy."[30]

Sheen's gloss on the life and times of Jesus Christ is exceptionally well written, thoughtful and often poignant. Chapter One, titled
"The Only Person Ever Pre-Announced," sets the tone.

> *A third fact separating Him from all the others is this:* every
> other person who ever came into this world came into it to
> live. He came into it to die. *Death was a stumbling block to
> Socrates—it interrupted his teaching. But to Christ, death was
> the goal and fulfillment of His life, the gold that He was seeking.
> Few of His words or actions are intelligible without reference to
> His Cross. He presented Himself as a Savior rather than merely
> as a Teacher. It meant nothing to teach men to be good unless he
> also gave them the power to be good, after rescuing them from
> the frustration of guilt....*

A fourth distinguishing fact is that He does not fit, as the other world teachers do, into the established category of a good man. Good men do not lie. But if Christ was not all that He said He was, namely, the Son of the living God, the Word of God in the flesh, then He was not "just a good man"; then He was a knave, a liar, a charlatan and the greatest deceiver who ever lived. If He was not what He said He was, the Christ, the Son of God, He was the anti-Christ! If He was only a man, then He was not even a "good" man.[31]

The book is a hymn of praise, a product of decades of thoughtful prayer, worship and thought. The account of the crucifixion is extremely moving. Brief chapters on the words from and to the Cross (Fulton had published many such commentaries) are powerful. The "Trial Before Pilate" is a brilliant reconstruction. The concluding chapter, "Christ Takes on a New Body," contains the full force of Sheen's venerable polemics on behalf of the Church.[32]

After a lifetime of saying and writing much the same things about the Lord and His Church, why did Sheen decide to take the time out of his frantic schedule to pen yet another, lengthy account?

When *Life of Christ* appeared, Sheen told a couple of priests, during a breakfast after Mass, about his warfare with Spellman. Fr. Robert Paul Mohan, a former Sheen student at Catholic University, said later that Sheen was not whining, and he even salted the account with some humor, yet it was obvious that the difficulties between the bishop and the cardinal were severe.[33] A few years later, Sheen told Michael C. Hogan, a priest who served as his secretary, that Cardinal Spellman had harassed him about money at the Society for the Propagation of the Faith. The incident, he said, was "one of his crucifixions." Sheen told Hogan that *Life of Christ* was written because he wanted to go through the Lord's life, pondering the suffering and crucifixion to help his own situation.[34]

A preface to a 1977 reissue of the book makes it explicit that *Life of Christ* stemmed directly from Fulton's pain at the hands of Cardinal Spellman. Without naming the cardinal or the dates, Sheen wrote of suffering for about ten years of his life (from 1957 to Spellman's death in 1967), and of his need to find solace in the Cross of Christ. His "great trial" had driven him deeper into the Scripture and the mysteries of Christ's death and resurrection. He wrote, "Unless there is a Good Friday in our lives there will never be an Easter Sunday.... Christianity begins not with sunshine but with defeat. Sunshine religions that begin with psychic elation, end often in disillusionment and despair. So essential is dying to self the prelude to the true life of self." In Christ's sufferings, Fulton was able to bear his own. "During those days when my life was backed up against the cross, I began to know and to love it more."[35]

Fulton's friend Marlene Brownett, a postulant of the Sisters of the Holy Child Jesus, asked the bishop in 1959 to recommend spiritual readings. His response focused on the life of Christ. He wrote, "there is one idea that remains true: *nothing* better prepares the soul to love God as the Life of Christ. St. Thomas says that through the visible love we rise to the Invisible."[36]

That same year, the first of three books under Sheen's name but largely written by others appeared. *This Is the Mass, This Is Rome* (1960), and *This Is the Holy Land* (1961) feature often stunning photographs by Yousuf Karsh, some basic Catholic instruction, and an ample quantity of travelogue material. The volume on Rome shows Fulton and his grandnephew Jerry Cunningham examining, among other things, the Colosseum, the Appian Way, the Catacomb of St. Sebastian, and the Fountain of Trevi.[37] Sheen would write at length in his autobiography about his eleven-day trip to the Holy Land in 1959, being especially proud of a photograph Karsh took showing him holding a lamb at the Sea of Galilee—the spot where Jesus said, "Simon, feed my lambs."[38] These popular books were designed to make money for the Society for the Propagation of the Faith. The bishop himself wrote the narrative for a similar volume, *These Are the Sacraments* (1962).

❧

ALTHOUGH THE RED SCARE had ended, the Cold War remained hot, and Sheen stayed active in the anticommunist movement. In September 1957, he won the American Legion's Distinguished Service Medal, and gave a hard-line anticommunist, law-and-order speech that flattered his listeners and soon earned him another warm letter of congratulation from J. Edgar Hoover.[39] In November, the House Committee on Un-American Activities released a pamphlet, co-authored by Sheen, titled *The Ideological Fallacies of Communism.* In it, Sheen predicted that "all of us will live to see the end of communism" in the Soviet Union because that nation would eventually "receive the gift of faith."[40]

While Sheen was not quoted in the New York newspapers as often as he had been while in Cardinal Spellman's good graces, there were occasions when a major speech drew attention. In February 1958, he spoke at a bipartisan conference in Washington designed to promote the administration's $3.9 billion foreign aid program. Among those who participated were President Eisenhower, former President Truman, Secretary of State John Foster Dulles, Secretary of Defense Neil H. McElroy, Adlai E. Stevenson, Richard M. Nixon, Thomas E. Dewey, and Dean Acheson. Sheen declared, "Our moral duty to aid others is because the earth and the fullness thereof were made by God for all the peoples of the earth, and not for the privileged advantage of a few." The president of the National Council of Churches and the president of the Synagogue Council of America also gave their support to the foreign aid proposal. Cardinal Spellman must have seethed to read that Sheen represented the Catholic Church in America at the high-level conclave.[41]

When Sheen went to Rome in early June, 1958, he was granted a half-hour interview with Pius XII, an extraordinary honor. By this time the Pope had named Samuel Cardinal Stritch of Chicago to head the international Congregation for the Propagation of the Faith, the first American named to the post. Journalist Robert Neville thought the appointment clearly indicated a shift of power away from Cardinal Spellman and the Archdiocese of New York. Stritch's subsequent death did not alter the pattern, wrote Neville. He also noted that the Pope's friendliness toward Sheen was no doubt influenced by the fact that the American brought contributions with him totaling some $10 million, which was 70 percent of the Society's worldwide budget. Sheen's personal contribution for the year was reportedly $1 million.[42]

That summer, Sheen also traveled to Great Britain, Belgium and France. In August he was in Belgium to give first Communion to former King Leopold's daughter.[43] The following summer, King Baudouin made the bishop a commander of the Order of the Crown of Belgium.[44] Sheen and the king had become close friends, and the bishop made a trip to Lourdes that summer to ask the Blessed Mother to help Baudouin find a bride. On his own journey to Lourdes in 1960, the king found the right young woman; Fulton sent his blessings and some advice on marriage.[45]

Sheen took Marlene Brownett, his secretary Edythe's younger sister, with him to Lourdes in the summer of 1959, the first of three such trips they would make together. Marlene, who was about to enter a convent in 1959, recalled that Fulton thoroughly loved Lourdes. He would look at the crowds and say, "Here is the Church of the poor," by which he meant the poor in spirit. Marlene often discovered herself alone, as Fulton would wander off to say his prayers and greet the many people who recognized him. She remembers him as always kind and generous to these fellow pilgrims. Sheen said Mass at both the grotto and the Pius X underground basilica.[46]

Fulton had good reason to say prayers for the Church while at Lourdes, for there were hints of massive change in the air. Pius XII died in October 1958, and his successor, John XXIII, announced in the following January his intention to summon a Church council. Sheen knew that a Second Vatican Council had been considered since 1922, that Pius XII had endorsed the idea, and that plans had been drawn up before his death. And Fulton was not averse to all change; in mid-1956, he had expressed his hope that the Mass could one day be said in the language of the people.[47]

In mid-1959, Fulton's friend and spiritual adviser Archbishop James McIntyre submitted a number of proposals for change, including the mitigation of the rules for the Eucharistic fast, in order that "more and more faithful can approach Holy Communion." He would soon be a member of the committee established to study results of more than nine thousand questionnaires sent to the world's hierarchy requesting proposals for discussion. McIntyre was excited about what lay ahead, and so, no doubt, was Sheen.[48]

Vatican II came at a time when the American Church was facing numerous calls for reform. Catholic intellectuals led the way, wanting Catholic colleges and universities to be less Thomist and insular and more like the great research institutions such as Harvard. Sheen's old friend John Tracy Ellis was a major proponent of this view, publishing the essay "American Catholics and the Intellectual Life" in 1955 and setting off a chain reaction of "self-criticism" among scholars. Moreover, rank and file Catholics were becoming assimilated into the mainstream of American life, enjoying high educational and income levels and growing increasingly secular and less inclined to follow every dictate that came from Rome. Some thought that "being Catholic" would be redefined under John XXIII. Historian Philip Gleason remembers hearing the president of a women's college say that the past was irrelevant because the future would be entirely different.[49]

In his fund-raising capacity, Fulton visited John XXIII officially each year. The two men quickly became friends, enjoying each other's sense of humor and appreciating each other's struggle for humility. John XXIII had been the patriarch of Venice, and often, to Fulton's delight, told humorous stories about the experience. Once when a high tide flooded the Piazza di San Marco, he went into a small wine shop to escape the rising waters. The man behind the counter recognized the cardinal and stammered out, "Dry throat, Eminence?" The patriarch replied, "No, wet feet."[50] Short and portly with a large nose, John XXIII once told Sheen, "God knew from all eternity that I was destined to be Pope. He also knew that I would live for over eighty years. Having all eternity to work on, and also eighty years, wouldn't you think He would have made me better looking?"[51]

On their first meeting, the Pope gave Sheen a small silver gondola as a memento of his years in Venice. On another occasion, he invited the bishop to his home in northern Italy to meet his brothers and relatives; the whole town turned out to greet Fulton. The Pope gave Sheen a late-evening, personally guided tour of his private quarters, presenting him with a topaz episcopal ring and a pectoral cross, and saying, "Now put them in your pocket and hide them for the moment. I do not want to make other bishops envious." The Pope twice invited Sheen to co-consecrate missionary bishops. John XXIII told Fulton the inside story of his selection as Pope and swore him to secrecy. He also told him about his decision to summon the Second Vatican Council. Following the latter conversation, the Pope called in a photographer and said, "Come, let us have our picture taken. It may make some in the Church jealous, but that will be fun."[52]

John XXIII was aware of the struggle between Sheen and Spellman. He said to Fulton, "You have suffered much, which will bring you to a high place in Heaven. Is there anything that I can do for you?" Sheen told him there was nothing he wanted except to do the will of God. The Pope replied, "That makes it very easy for me."[53]

⁓

FULTON TURNED SIXTY-FIVE on May 8, 1960, but he continued his writing, traveling, and speech making at breakneck speed. His mind was clear and his health was good. He had suffered from a lingering case of hiccups in the late 1950s, but his personal physician, Dr. Elaine P. Ralli (one of his converts), had seen him through the illness. A nurse friend, the saintly and popular Cathy Yetman, looked after him.[54]

In October 1960, Sheen traveled to Argentina to assist the greatest Catholic crusade ever undertaken in Latin America. For decades, the faith had been slipping away in Argentina; with a population of more than 20 million, the nation had only 4,708 priests, compared with 50,000 in France with a population of 45 million. Missionaries from several countries were on hand to help. Sheen made twelve television appearances, said Mass in several humble parishes and in the cathedral in Buenos Aires, and lectured at the University of Buenos Aires law school and at the Holy Cross Institute. He spoke also in Rio de Janeiro during the two-week crusade, and was shocked at the poverty he saw about a mile inland from the beautiful beaches the tourists enjoyed.[55] The overall effort was judged a great success. At its close, some three million Argentines had attended services at the cathedral, and baptisms and marriages numbered in the thousands.[56]

Sheen played no role in the United States presidential election of 1960. Indirectly, though, he had helped pave the way for Democratic candidate John F. Kennedy by showing the American people, in his writings and in the media, that an Irish Catholic could be charming, intelligent and patriotic. Kennedy, the second Catholic candidate of a major party in the nation's history, fought an intense battle throughout the campaign against charges that his religious faith would hinder his objectivity and loyalty. (Ironically, JFK had lost his faith as a young man.)[57] Indeed, he went so far in pledging the complete separation of church and state, that many in the Catholic hierarchy, including Cardinal Spellman, opposed his election. But Richard Cardinal Cushing of Boston, an old friend of the Kennedy family, was supportive, and the great majority of Catholic voters went for JFK in November.[58]

In mid-November, Sheen flew to Africa for two weeks. He spent one of the weeks in Kenya, visiting East African mission stations and consecrating a local bishop. (In 1950, there were only two native Catholic bishops in all of Africa.)[59] Missionaries took the bishop several hundred miles through the vast deserts of the Suk country to a mission with a hospital staffed by two men without medical degrees. He saw patients with a variety of problems, including tuberculosis and gashes from lions.[60] Sheen later recalled a Mass he said in a church with a floor made of cow manure and clay, which made his eyes water constantly. While making his Holy Hour in that same church, he met a woman with ten children whose husband had deserted her. Her only consolation, she said, was in the Lord.[61]

During a week in Johannesburg, South Africa, Sheen encountered racial apartheid, which he abhorred. Against the wishes of the government, he visited a black woman who was an active catechist in a segregated area.[62]

On returning home, Sheen told Clare Boothe Luce that he had gone to Africa to try to identify himself "with the sacrificing missionaries, the simple faith of the people and outstretched hands of the lepers."[63] He later reflected on this and other journeys to the world's poor:

> *I began to think less of the problem of poverty and more of the poor; less of the problem of crime and more of the criminal; less about age and more about service to a Stranger Who lives with all the slum dwellers who have no place to lay their heads. All the little children separated from parents are as one child to that Stranger; all the delinquents, all those who are crying, weeping and complaining against God are really looking for that Stranger.... This Stranger will rise out of the slums, the dumps, the hovels, the emptiness of stomachs, the parched tongues, the burning fevers and the white sores of leprosy. He will stand before all who helped, saying: "I was hungry and you gave me to eat." Travel merely confirms the teaching of theology that humanity is one. The accidental differences of color and race and what jingles in the pocket are of little concern. The longer I live the more I become convinced that in the face of injustices we must begin to say I love. Kind deeds are not enough. We must learn to say I forgive.[64]*

In April 1961, Sheen and Spellman again clashed. Sheen wanted to employ Fr. Robert S. Toulman of Buffalo as assistant national director and general secretary of the Society. As he had with numerous employees over the years, Fulton no doubt "sensed" that Toulman was the right man for the job. (He had hired Edward O'Meara in 1956 and Hilary Franco in 1959 as personal assistants almost on sight, believing that God had sent them to him. "Trust your first impressions," Matthew Paratore heard Sheen say often.)[65] Instead of seeking Spellman's permission for the appointment, Sheen sent the request to the Rome offices of the Society, giving copies to Spellman and the other members of the Episcopal Committee.

Spellman was furious about the ruse, calling it "not correct" and "offensive to the Holy See." Bishop John A. Burke of Buffalo, who had also not been consulted, soon told Spellman that Toulman could not be spared. G. P. Cardinal Agagianian, of the Sacred Congregation for the Propagation of the Faith, wrote to Spellman, expressing dismay over the conflict. The appointment was not made.[66]

In the summer of 1961, Sheen and a favorite niece, nineteen-year-old college sophomore Eileen Sheen (Tom's oldest daughter), traveled to London, Ireland, Belgium, Lourdes, Rome and Barcelona. In London, Fulton was in meetings most of the time, while Eileen enjoyed herself as a tourist. She later remembered her uncle's love of bookstores and desserts, and his hard work even on vacation. "He'd write all the time. In the [early] mornings, he would be in meditation." In Ireland, they visited the family home in the little village of Croghan, where all the inhabitants turned out to cheer the famous bishop. "He was treated like a movie star." They visited a Carmelite convent. "The whole town was thrilled."[67]

Ireland was celebrating the 1500th anniversary of the death of St. Patrick, the great missionary to the Irish. Papal legate Cardinal Agagianian and many other dignitaries were on hand, and on the last day of the week-long celebration Sheen delivered a speech that, as D. P. Noonan put it, "stole the hearts of the Irish . . . and made them feel taller." Sheen expressed delight in his Irish heritage, noting especially the Irish people's great sense of humor, which had made the world a better and happier place. He said that God would manifest Himself in various ways to different nationalities on Judgment Day; to the Irish he would show his smile.[68]

In Rome, Fulton attended meetings in connection with the Second Vatican Council, then in the making. He and Eileen visited the catacombs, where they saw a poor African missionary preaching. "That is a very great man," Sheen said; he had sensed the greatness.

The bishop was a great believer in first impressions, Eileen said. The two travelers had an audience with John XXIII, and Eileen remembered that her uncle genuinely liked the Pope. "He had a lot of respect for people who were simple and straight."[69]

Sheen's presence in Rome was the result of being named by John XXIII to the pre-conciliar Catholic Action Commission, one of several such commissions assigned the task of presenting major subjects to be discussed. He was one of forty-three Americans who served as members and consultants to these commissions.[70] The proceedings were in Latin, as all the meetings of the council would be. Fulton later recalled dismantling a silly proposal by bishops on the commission to introduce a chapter on tourism into the council. He also tried, in vain, to persuade colleagues to propose a change of name for the Society for the Propagation of the Faith, because the word "propaganda" in the Latin form of the name had a negative connotation.[71]

Sheen felt more at home when the Pope named him to the Commission on the Missions soon after the council proceedings began. He was one of twenty-six members of the American hierarchy elected or appointed to the ten conciliar commissions, a number that exceeded the number of representatives from all other countries except Italy and France.[72] Fulton attended every commission meeting, which required him to make three and sometimes four trips a year to Rome.[73]

During the polling of bishops from around the world on topics proposed for the council, Sheen submitted several recommendations including a chapter on women. He wrote later, "I had a strong conviction that the feminine principle in religion had been neglected. Many world religions were without the feminine principle and we were beginning to live in an age when women were coming into their own." He always thought it a mistake that the council chose not to accept his proposal.[74]

The Second Vatican Council opened on October 11, 1962. On hand were some 2,500 bishops, 60 percent of them from Asia, Africa, and North and South America. By contrast, the Council of Trent four hundred years earlier had been a Mediterranean meeting, and at the First Vatican Council in 1870, there was not a single bishop from Africa or Asia.[75] Several hundred *periti*, theologians and other experts, were also present at Vatican II, but were not allowed to mingle with council members. Cardinal Spellman, widely recognized as the titular leader of the American hierarchy, invited Father John Courtney Murray, S.J., a foremost defender of religious freedom, who was to have a major impact on council proceedings. (Although often associated with John F. Kennedy's call for the absolute separation of church and state, Murray had actually voted for Eisenhower twice and thought Kennedy a "lightweight" who was an extremist on separatism.)[76]

The bishops sat in two great tiers, banks of chairs ten rows high, on both sides of the nave of St. Peter's Basilica. Sheen later recalled, "Since they were dressed in their choir robes, an onlooker would have seen a cascade of color stretching 360 feet from the inner doors of the basilica to the Tomb of St. Peter under the dome."[77] He noted the presence of forty-nine bishops and a single cardinal from the Iron Curtain countries. One Yugoslav bishop, who had had gasoline poured over him and ignited, looked almost like "a walking ghost."[78]

Fulton wholeheartedly agreed with the Pope that the council was needed. He was one of many who thought the time had come to open the Church more fully to the needs of the world, but without abandoning its historical and vital role of saving souls. There was clearly room, in his judgment, for change in many areas of Church life, including greater efforts toward Christian unity, a cause espoused by John XXIII when announcing his decision to convoke the council. Sheen wrote later,

> *The answer was not to be found either in an isolation from the world by erecting a red "STOP" light outside of St. Peter's Square; neither could the Church answer the same challenge the world hurled at its Head on the Cross: "Come down and we will believe." "Come down from your belief in the sanctity of marriage." "Come*

*down from your belief in the sacredness of life." "Come down
from your belief; the truth is merely what is pleasing." "Come
down from the Cross of sacrifice and we will believe."*[79]

Sheen saw himself as a centrist who wanted both fidelity to historic
and biblical teaching, and at the same time a commitment to rec-
tifying social injustice, "for example, paying shamefully low wages
to a farm laborer or a maid or an employee."[80] He sought to open
the Church to the world and the world to the Church, an aim shared
by the vast majority of bishops attending the Second Vatican
Council.

The first major pronouncement of the council came on October 20, a "message to humanity" proclaiming that "all men are brothers, irrespective of the race or nation to which they belong."[81] The
next day, Sheen preached a sermon at a special Mass for English-
speaking journalists, sharply criticizing press coverage of the council for its emphasis on dissension and disagreement. He urged the
congregation to examine the account in the Book of Acts of the first
ecumenical council at Jerusalem, and declared that no journalist
could understand a Church council "unless he has the spirit of
Christ."[82]

Thirteen major subjects were discussed at the council, and the
assembled bishops could make their views known by either written or oral "interventions." The Americans proved reluctant to speak;
of the 2,205 spoken interventions, only 118 were delivered by American bishops. Cardinal Spellman was the most active, contributing
131 oral and written interventions on the various topics. Fifty-six
American bishops submitted observations orally or in writing.[83]
Three American prelates served on the presidency of the council:
Spellman, Albert Cardinal Meyer of Chicago, and Archbishop
Lawrence Shehan of Baltimore. A keen student of council proceedings, Monsignor Vince A. Yzermans, thought that Cardinal
Meyer and Archbishop John J. Krol of Philadelphia were the most
effective Americans at the council.[84] (Meyer would become a car-
dinal in 1965 and Krol in 1967.)

Vatican II lasted from October 11, 1962, to December 8, 1965. There were 4 sessions, 168 general meetings, and 10 plenary meetings. A total of 147 reports were made and 2,212 speeches given. Sheen attended faithfully, and was the only American on the Commission on the Missions for the duration of the council. He enjoyed himself immensely, writing later, "To be a part of that Council, to mingle with more than two thousand bishops from different nationalities and cultures, and to sing the Creed together with them each morning is a Council of Nations which would make the United Nations blush for want of a common commitment."[85]

Sheen did not speak out during the first council session. In early November, 1962, he reported to Marlene Brownett in a handwritten letter: "We open at 9 A.M. & close at 12:30 noon. The Mass to the Holy Synod is offered daily—a dialogue Mass answered by the Bishops. The devotion is heavenly.... Everyone is allowed to talk if he wishes. Too many want to talk. If one speaks over 10 minutes one hears ... 'the ringing of the bells.' He is told to *sit down*. A Cardinal was told the other day, his time was up." After remarking on the curious ways Latin was pronounced at the council, Fulton wrote, "It is marvelous to be a part of the infallible Church teaching. I thank God I live in these times.... It will be a different world at the end of the Council. The Spirit is everywhere over us, as at Pentecost."[86]

In his autobiography, Sheen reproduced numerous jingles that bishops wrote and distributed among themselves to keep the mood from becoming overly solemn. "The amount of humor that anyone gets out of the world is the size of the world in which he lives," Fulton wrote. Noting, for example, that Richard Cardinal Cushing of Boston (another veteran of Spellman warfare) spoke loudly to all assembled, one wag penned:

Cardinal Cushing of Boston avows
Though he's not a Latin scholar
He can certainly holler,
At the Council he brought down the house.[87]

Sheen was greatly saddened to learn that John XXIII had died on June 3, 1963. In his less than five years in the Vatican, the Pope had issued eight encyclicals, advanced liturgical reforms (including making the liturgy the first major topic of consideration at the council), canonized ten saints and beatified Mother Elizabeth Ann Seton (the first native-born American so honored), expanded and increased the international representation of the College of Cardinals, reached out to other Christians in the world, and ushered in a new era for the Catholic Church by summoning the council. More than anyone had expected, John XXIII was a strong and enlightened leader.

Two of the Pope's encyclicals received special attention throughout the world: *Pacem in Terris* ("Peace on Earth"), a path-breaking call to world peace based on natural law, and *Mater et Magistra* ("Christianity and Social Progress"), an expansion of social doctrine stated earlier by Leo XIII and Pius XI. Fulton was especially taken by the latter encyclical, quoting liberally from it in a book and noting its call for public authorities to concern themselves more intensely in such areas as public health, education, and the care and rehabilitation of the handicapped. Fulton called the encyclical an illustration of John XXIII's "love of humanity."[88]

Shortly after the Pope's losing battle with stomach cancer, Fulton told reporters that the Pope, although elected in his late seventies, "in four years undid 400 years."[89]

Sheen quickly became friends with the new Pope, Paul VI, who addressed the second session of the council when it opened on September 29, 1963. In one of their annual private audiences, Fulton observed that the Pope was aptly named "Paul" because he had been crucified with Christ. "Yes," Paul VI replied, "every night about midnight I open my mail of the day. Almost every letter has a thorn in it. When I put my head on my pillow at night, I really lay it on a crown of thorns. But I cannot tell you what an ineffable joy it is to suffer all this for the sake of the Church."[90] Upon this Paul would fall the continuation of the council and the supervision of the unprecedented impact it would make on Catholicism.

꙰

WITH THE REST OF the world, Sheen was shocked at the assassination of John F. Kennedy on November 22, 1963. Fulton had met Joseph P. Kennedy and must surely have heard some of the many stories of his ruthlessness and lechery. Cardinal Spellman knew him better. According to an aide, he said after a telephone call from the Founding Father in 1960, "That is a truly evil man."[91] It appears certain that Fulton was not privy to similar accounts of the son's reckless behavior. His grief at the president's death, in which he compared Kennedy favorably with Lincoln and spoke of his "heroic image," along with later commentary, strongly suggest that Sheen venerated the young chief executive throughout the remainder of his life. In the book *Footprints in a Darkened Forest* (1967), Kennedy was included in a chapter on "Modern Saints," along with John XXIII, Ghandi, and Dag Hammarskjöld. Following a very brief and simplistic account of Kennedy's life, Sheen wrote, "But what he left behind was the truth that politics may be a sublime vocation, for 'here on earth God's work must truly be our own.' "[92]

Early rumblings against the Camelot Myth—JFK as a saint, the administration as an assembly of gods—appeared in the early 1970s. In the fall of 1974, on a television series he was beginning, Sheen deplored charges against both Kennedy and Thomas Jefferson, branding such allegations (apparently regardless of the evidence) as unpatriotic. "As soon as we find a great man, we impugn his motives."[93] This was a predictable response: Kennedy, after all, was Irish, Catholic, and handsome. Like most people, Eileen Sheen recalled, her uncle was attracted to beautiful people, associating good looks with moral goodness.[94] Moreover, the behavior of scoundrels, even when they are politicians, is often beyond the imagination of holy people. Thus could cynical politicos use Billy Graham for their own advantage for many years. The fiery preacher was stunned to discover the real Richard Nixon on the tapes recorded in the Oval Office.

The more complete Kennedy story did not begin to tumble out into the press until 1975, when a leak from a congressional hearing triggered an avalanche of sordid revelations about the slain president. Whatever Fulton thought about the new information, he said nothing for the record. Perhaps he simply refused to read the books and articles, thinking them, by definition, scandalous and irreverent. Polls show that most Americans responded likewise.

∽

THE FIRST OF THE Vatican II documents, the "Constitution of the Sacred Liturgy," was promulgated by Paul VI on December 4, 1963.[95] This provided guidelines for changes in liturgy that were to stun Catholics all over the world, highlighting the importance of Scripture, the active role of the laity, a "noble simplicity" in rites, use of the vernacular language, the revision of hymns, and the scaling back of the number of sacred images and statues in churches. This was all to be done "to meet the circumstances and needs of modern times."

In November 1964, only a month after the Vatican issued the "Instruction on the Liturgy" stressing gradual and informed change, the vernacular Mass was introduced all across America, with the traditional altar relocated or disregarded in favor of a movable altar or table, and the priest now facing the people. Further changes, some even more radical, were to come within the next two years. The Church that could not change, did.

The same month also saw the issuance of *Lumen Gentium*, the "Dogmatic Constitution on the Church," arguably the most impressive work of the council. While declaring the Catholic Church to be the true Church of Christ, reaffirming the supremacy of the papacy and the importance of apostolic succession, and clarifying the vital but subordinate role of the Blessed Virgin Mary, the document stated that elements of truth were to be found outside of the Church's visible structure. This was a striking declaration of tolerance and amicability toward Protestants and the Orthodox. As for Jews, Muslims and others, "Those also can attain to salvation who through no fault of their own do not know the Gospel of Christ or His Church, yet sincerely seek God and moved by grace strive by their deeds to do His will as it is known to them through the dictates of conscience." The document also admitted the importance of constant change, for the Church, "in need of being purified, always follows the way of penance and renewal."

One of the changes announced in this document was the restoration of the permanent diaconate "as a proper and permanent rank of the hierarchy." The order was to be open to older, married men as well as younger men who were expected to be celibate. Sheen openly supported the restoration of the permanent diaconate, while Spellman vehemently opposed it. Sheen also submitted observations concerning the importance of missionary activity.[96]

Between sessions of the council, Sheen made another television series. In 1962, he had done a brief series on the life of Christ. Two years later, his *Quo Vadis America?* failed to interest a network, was syndicated, and received little attention. By 1964 the winds of radical change were beginning to sweep America, and Sheen no doubt seemed to many like a relic of decades past.

Sheen made headlines once again in April 1964 by blasting the United States Supreme Court. In an appearance before the House Judiciary Committee, he said that the court had exceeded its competence in ruling against prayers and Bible reading in public schools. "While I fear for a country which outlaws prayer in schools," Sheen said, "I fear still more for a people who surrender control over their lawmaking bodies." He told reporters that Congress might reverse the decision, supported by mainline Protestant church officials, through a law reaffirming the First Amendment. This amendment was designed to preserve the rights of both the religious and the irreligious, he said, but the court had ignored the obligations to the religious.[97] Unhappiness with this and similar decisions by the nine unelected lawyers sitting on the Supreme Court eventually helped fuel the new Religious Right, a potent force in the Republican Party.[98]

After the fourth session of the Second Vatican Council opened in the fall of 1965, Sheen left the proceedings briefly for New York to serve as special narrator for the CBS network's coverage of Paul VI's visit to the United Nations. It was the first visit of a Pope to the

United States. That same year, Paul VI reappointed Sheen to the post-conciliar Commission on the Missions.[99]

In October 1965, Vatican II addressed the Church's "vocations crisis" in *Optatum Totius,* the "Decree on Priestly Formation." Shortly before the council opened, Giuseppe Cardinal Pizzardo, prefect of the Sacred Congregation of Seminaries and Universities, revealed that in the 1,100 dioceses associated with the congregation, there were 228,653 priests serving 418,000,000 Catholics. To reach a ratio of one priest for every thousand Catholics, 190,000 more priests would be needed.

In a written intervention on the subject, Sheen called for modernization of seminary training. He wanted to see the following paragraph incorporated into the council declaration:

> *The time for vacations seems to us to be too long, therefore: the theological course should be prolonged to ten months; during the scholastic year, once or twice a week, the seminary directors should see to it that the students visit and aid the sick, the poor, non-Catholics, fallen-away Catholics, young people, those in jail, laborers, etc. During the summer vacation, seminarians, with the consent of the ordinary of the place, should be sent to give spiritual aid in those places where there is a great need of priests, so that they learn from the time of their formation to bear "the burden of the day and the heat."[100]*

When the document was published, it included a recommendation for "opportune practical projects" during summer vacations, and a plea for seminarians to be taught to minister especially to "the poor, the children, the sick, and sinners and the unbelievers."[101]

Apostolicam Actuositatem, the "Decree on the Apostolate of the Laity," appeared in mid-November. The document was the first by a council to treat specifically the role of the laity in the Church. This issue was paramount to the Pope and to many bishops. Paul VI had named eleven laymen to be official observers of the Second Vatican Council proceedings, a first in Church history. By the third session, there were twenty-eight lay auditors, including seven women—the first time women were so recognized. (Sheen shared with Clare Boothe Luce a limerick that emerged after Leo Cardinal Suenens first suggested that there be women observers. Two lines went: "The Bishops are churls, / Let's call in the girls.")[102] By the fourth session, the number of official lay auditors rose to forty-one, and included Americans Mark Work, executive director of the National Council of Catholic Men, and Mrs. Catherine McCarthy, president of the National Council of Catholic Women. Six members of the group addressed the council fathers. Many others were named consultants to one or another commission. The lay auditors contributed significantly to the formation of the "Decree on the Apostolate of the Laity."

Apostolicam Actuositatem assigned to laity certain functions usually connected with pastoral duties, "such as the teaching of Christian doctrine, certain liturgical actions, and the care of souls." It stressed the need for holy lives, and acknowledged that "there are many persons who can hear the Gospel and recognize Christ only through the laity who live near them." Both Sheen and Spellman, in written interventions, warmly endorsed the decree. It passed the council by 2,340 to 2.[103]

On December 7, the council issued *Ad Gentes,* the "Decree on the Church's Missionary Activity." This decree had a long and interesting history. For one thing, it was the only council document introduced by the Pope himself. On November 6, 1964, Paul VI had shattered tradition by appearing before the council and stressing the need for the draft document then in the hands of the bishops. One of the proposals in the document was to establish a central missionary commission under the Congregation for the Propagation of the Faith.

Twenty-eight council fathers spoke on the document soon after Paul VI's appearance, many of them highly critically. The last to speak was Bishop Sheen, who had served on the commission that had written the proposed document and who had submitted five written interventions on missions in the course of the council proceedings. He endorsed the proposal for a central missionary commission, calling it "the true Catholic solution to this problem

of the diversity of mission." He also called for the Church to identify more closely with the poor.

> *As chastity was the fruit of the Council of Trent, and obedi-*
> *ence the fruit of the First Vatican Council, so may the spirit of*
> *poverty be the fruit of this Second Vatican Council.*
>
> *We live in a world in which 200 million people would will-*
> *ingly take the vow of poverty tomorrow, if they could live as well,*
> *eat as well, be clothed as well, and be housed as well as I am—*
> *or even some who take the vow of poverty.*
>
> *The greater number of bishops in this Council are living in*
> *want or in persecution, and they come from all peoples and*
> *nations.*
>
> *As only a wounded Christ could convert a doubting Thomas,*
> *so only a Church wounded by poverty can convert a doubting*
> *world.*

The council nevertheless voted by a wide margin to send the document back to the Commission on the Missions for revision.

After a revised statement was produced, Sheen presented a written intervention that was the longest submitted by any American
on any topic: sixty-one double-spaced typewritten pages. In it, the
bishop proposed a World Council of Missions that would, among
other things, "elaborate a single strategy for the evangelization of
the world which will be concretized through the union of persons
and material and distinguished leaders to serve the entire Church."
That portion of the proposal failed in a subsequent vote. But the
final document, the first any council had created on the topic of
missionary activity in the Church, was approved overwhelmingly.
It contained virtually everything Sheen had wanted: statements on
the Church and the poor, world missionary work directed and coordinated by the Propagation of the Faith, and the statement that all
bishops "are consecrated not just for some one diocese, but for the
salvation of the entire world."[104]

Sheen later told a priest who was a civil rights activist about the
wealth of information he had collected during the Second Vatican

Council from Third World bishops. These prelates, short of funds and living in very modest accommodations in Rome, often depended on Sheen for financial assistance during the council. In turn, they shared accounts with him of life in missionary areas, greatly stirring Fulton and increasing his desire to help the poor overseas. The experience also reinforced his commitment to civil rights at home.[105]

On December 7, 1965, the Second Vatican Council also issued *Gaudium et Spes*, the "Pastoral Constitution on the Church in the Modern World." It marked the first time that the Church in council had specifically addressed the most pressing issues of the modern world. *Gaudium et Spes* spoke magnificently of man's dignity, natural rights, individual conscience, and the social order. It declared that

> *whatever is opposed to life itself, such as any type of murder, genocide, abortion, euthanasia, or wilful self-destruction, whatever violates the integrity of the human person, such as mutilation, torments inflicted on body or mind, attempts to coerce the will itself; whatever insults human dignity, such as subhuman living conditions, arbitrary imprisonment, deportation, slavery, prostitution, the selling of women and children; as well as disgraceful working conditions, where men are treated as mere tools for profit, rather than as free and responsible persons; all these things and others of their like are infamies indeed. They poison human society, but they do more harm to those who practice them than those who suffer from the injury. Moreover, they are a supreme dishonor to the Creator.*

The council stated unequivocally that "every type of discrimination, whether social or cultural, whether based on sex, race, color, social condition, language or religion, is to be overcome and eradicated as contrary to God's intent."

On science, which many moderns considered the sole source of truth, the council declared, "if methodical investigation within every branch of learning is carried out in a genuinely scientific manner and in accord with moral norms, it never truly conflicts with faith, for earthly matters and the concerns of faith derive from the same God. Indeed whoever labors to penetrate the secrets of reality with a humble and steady mind, even though he is unaware of the fact, is nevertheless being led by the hand of God, who holds all things in existence, and gives them their identity."

As for politics, the document stated: "in virtue of her mission and nature she [the Church] is bound to no particular form of human culture, nor to any political, economic or social system.... She has no fiercer desire than that in pursuit of the welfare of all she may be able to develop herself freely under any kind of government which grants recognition to the basic rights of person and family, to the demands of the common good and to the free exercise of her own mission."

Regarding the common man: "Among the basic rights of the human person is to be numbered the right of freely founding unions for working people. These should be able truly to represent them and to contribute to the organizing of economic life in the right way." Aid to the poor was emphasized, even to the point of stating, "If one is in extreme necessity, he has the right to procure for himself what he needs out of the riches of others."

On war and peace, the council decreed that "the arms race is an utterly treacherous trap for humanity, and one which ensnares the poor to an intolerable degree.... Divine Providence urgently demands of us that we free ourselves from the age-old slavery of war."

At the same time, the council warned against falling in love with the world to the point that revealed and historic truths were compromised. The centrality of Jesus Christ was reaffirmed. "The Lord is the goal of human history, the focal point of the longings of history and of civilization, the center of the human race, the joy of every heart and the answer to all its yearnings." The document also reaffirmed the Church's traditional position on birth control: "Marriage and conjugal love are by their nature ordained toward the begetting and education of children." It labeled abortion and infanticide "unspeakable crimes." Still, there was a frank acknowledgement of the worldwide population explosion, and a statement that "Men should discreetly be informed, furthermore, of scientific advances in exploring methods whereby spouses can be helped in regulating the number of their children and whose safeness has been well proven and whose harmony with the moral order has been ascertained."[106]

Fulton Sheen could find little if anything to disagree with in this historic document. He had taken similar or identical positions on these issues all of his clerical life. Still, there were items he wanted to be included that were not. In the deliberations on *Gaudium et Spes*, Sheen urged the council in a written intervention to make a bold statement on women, and in his remarks he defended the professional woman and the necessity of equality. But Sheen was by no means a feminist. Instead, he highlighted the distinct qualities which only women could give to modern civilization, including "purity, protection of the weak, sacrifice, procreation, the sustaining and care of human life."[107]

In another intervention, Sheen called for more cooperation between Catholics and Protestants in social justice activities. He also called for greater application of Christian principles to the economic order, calling for chaplains in industry, and in the Third World countries for "mobile schools" that would move from diocese to diocese instructing both clergy and laity in the social and economic doctrines of the Church. Sheen thought too that affluent Catholics should be encouraged to surrender voluntarily some of their land and wealth to the underprivileged.[108]

During the course of the Second Vatican Council, Sheen submitted interventions on other topics as well. When Catholic education was being discussed, he urged Catholic universities not to neglect "the spiritual goal to which they are ordained." He also backed trade schools, stating that not all young people were "fit for higher education."[109]

When the "Declaration on the Relationship of the Church to Non-Christian Religions" was debated, Sheen joined Cardinal Spellman in speaking out against anti-Semitism. The final document spoke glowingly of the Jews, rejected all persecution and discrimination, and declared of all faiths: "The Catholic Church rejects nothing in these religions. She regards with sincere reverence those ways of conduct and of life, those precepts and teachings which, though differing in many aspects from the ones she holds and sets forth, nonetheless often reflect a ray of that Truth which enlightens all men."[110]

Sheen contributed as well to the passage of the "Declaration on Religious Freedom," a document that council scholar Vincent A. Yzermans has called "beyond a shadow of a doubt, the specific American contribution to the Second Vatican Council." It was a significant break with tradition. For centuries, the Catholic Church had asserted that civil governments had an obligation to recognize and support it. In 1846, Pope Pius IX declared, "The state must recognize [the Catholic Church] as supreme and submit to its influence.... The power of the state must be at its disposal and all who do not conform to its requirements must be compelled or punished.... Freedom of conscience and cult is madness."[111]

In 1928, however, Father Francis P. Duffy, famous for his World War I exploits, helped Al Smith write a fairly sophisticated statement declaring the presidential candidate's commitment to "absolute freedom of conscience for all men" and "the absolute separation of Church and State." The widely published campaign document won applause from both Catholics and Protestants all across the country.[112] During the 1950s, Jesuit theologian John Courtney Murray, S.J.—much to the irritation of the Vatican—argued that the doctrine enunciated by Pius IX was not an absolute, and that religious freedom was a human right. John XXIII opened the doors for Murray, and Cardinal Spellman became a Murray champion. In 1960, Spellman called for a statement on religious freedom, and soon invited Murray to the council.

Sentiment for such a statement emerged at the council in late 1963 and stemmed from a widespread concern for ecumenism. Some council fathers had great qualms about this cause and tried to delay matters; but the great majority of bishops, especially the Americans, wanted a declaration on religious liberty and were determined to pass one. Sheen was one of many American bishops to express support in 1964, and Cardinal Spellman was active throughout the struggle. The American press followed the issue carefully.

With the support of the Pope, a text on religious freedom was passed overwhelmingly on September 21, 1965. Murray was a major drafter of the document. The final vote, taken in December, was 2,308 to 70.[113]

Dignitatis Humanae, promulgated by Paul VI on December 7, 1965, declared that "the human person has a right to religious freedom." That right was based on "the very dignity of the human person as this dignity is known through the revealed word of God and by reason itself." The exercise of religion, "of its very nature, consists before all else in those internal, voluntary and free acts whereby man sets the course of his life directly toward God. No merely human power can either command or prohibit acts of this kind." Government "ought indeed to take account of the religious life of the citizenry and show it favor, since the function of government is to make provision for the common welfare. However, it would clearly transgress the limits set to its power, were it to presume to command or inhibit acts that are religious." The document also demanded that government "acknowledge the right of parents to make a genuinely free choice in schools.... [T]he rights of parents are violated, if their children are forced to attend lessons or instructions which are not in agreement with their religious beliefs, or if a single system of education, from which all religious formation is excluded, is imposed upon all."[114]

Sheen returned from the final council session greatly pleased by the proceedings. He was especially happy about *Gaudium et Spes,* as it stressed "the truth that the dignity and freedom of the human person is inseparable from salvation." Still, like others, he quickly sensed the emerging extremes among Catholics: on one side were conservatives who wanted to be in the world but not of it, clergy and laity unconcerned with the social dimension of Catholicism; and on the other were the worldlings who wanted to see the Church guided by the world, the flesh and the devil, and who were intent on casting aside or drastically altering Church teaching. Sheen thought the council declaration struck the right balance for the personal and the social. He quoted paragraph 30:

> *... no one ignoring the trend of events or drugged by laziness contents himself with merely individualistic morality. It grows increasingly true that the obligations of justice and love are fulfilled only if each person, contributing to the common good, according to his own abilities and the needs of others, also promotes the public and private institutions dedicated to bettering the conditions of human life.... Let everyone consider it his sacred obligation to esteem and observe social necessities as belonging to the primary duties of modern man.*[115]

BY THE TIME THE Second Vatican Council finished its work at the end of 1965, America was in an advanced stage of upheaval. Despite the Civil Rights Acts of 1964 and 1965 outlawing racial discrimination in America, civil rights remained a serious concern. In the summer of 1964, blacks rioted in Harlem and Rochester, New York. The Watts riot of 1965 left 34 people dead, 1,100 injured and $40 million in property damage.

Betty Friedan's *The Feminine Mystique* was helping to create a core of feminists that would soon demand and get radical changes in American life. The Beatles were popular, prompting John Lennon to boast a year later, "We're more popular than Jesus now." Many young women wore their skirts at mid-thigh, used the pill, and rejected traditional ideas of femininity. Congress was busily passing a torrent of bills to implement the Great Society, spending billions and strengthening federal authority and responsibility to an unprecedented degree. (When Lyndon Johnson left office, there were 435 federal domestic social programs, 390 more than when Eisenhower departed.) Demonstrations and riots on American campuses were becoming routine.

The campus disruptions often reflected American activity in the Vietnam War. American bombing raids began in February of 1965. That spring, Congress voted $400 million for the war effort, and American troops became engaged in a ground offensive for the first time. In July, President Johnson agreed to use saturation bombing and send ten thousand troops. Antiwar protesters were on television news every night, and public opinion was beginning to shift away from the administration. The far Left was lined up behind Hanoi. The far Right, on the other hand, was just as solidly behind the troops.

Cardinal Spellman strongly favored the war effort. In his view, the United States was fighting communism, much as it had for decades, and that made the war effort a crusade. Moreover, many South Vietnamese were Catholics. In Vietnam during Christmas week, 1965, Spellman repeated Stephen Decatur's toast of 1815: "Our country! In her intercourse with foreign nations may she always be in the right; but our country, right or wrong." Spellman's hawkish stance was a serious obstacle in his effort to be friendly with Paul VI, who worked for peace.[116]

By the close of 1965, Sheen had not publicly commented on the war. It is likely that he supported it for the very reasons Spellman did. He had never rejected any effort to fight communism. He must have noticed, however, that numerous Catholics were among the outspoken opponents of the war. Daniel and Philip Berrigan, one a Jesuit and the other a Josephite priest, earned Spellman's wrath for their antiwar activism.[117] Sheen must also have winced at media reports of escalating violence and bloodshed, for like Paul VI, he prayed fervently for an end to the curse of war.

In 1966, Sheen's schedule was as busy as ever. He led an eight-day retreat in January for the Trappists of Our Lady of Gethsemane, in Kentucky, enjoying himself thoroughly.[118] (He had been there before, telling Clare Boothe Luce in 1949, "They were the eight happiest days of my life. I never asked myself when the retreats would end for I did not care." In another letter to Luce, he wrote, "I am actually receiving all the inspiration. They are all saints.")[119] In May, he was in Poland and in Rome.[120] In July, he was in Ireland, preaching retreats in Belfast and Cork.[121] At one point he was elected to the administrative board of the newly created National Conference of Catholic Bishops (which replaced the National Catholic Welfare Conference).[122]

That summer he taped a television series in color; but these programs failed miserably to recreate the excitement of their counterparts in the 1950s. (They are on sale today as *Life Is Worth Living* videotapes, and unsuspecting purchasers may think they are getting the earlier series.) Taped before a live audience, Fulton's timing was off; there were long pauses, and the physical posing often seemed artificial. Moreover, the self-deprecation was repetitive, and the jokes were feeble, evoking little audience response. The continual reappearance of a clean blackboard, prompting him to rewrite "J.M.J." at the top, seemed pointless. Worst of all, Sheen's presentations were often somewhat confused; they had not been rehearsed in Italian and French beforehand, and it showed.

Two programs illustrate the series' problems. In "The Psychology of the Rat Race," Sheen confused his definitions, leaving the outline of the talk a jumble. His attack on the "now moment" contained sweeping generalities—"Nobody can be happy who is interested only in the now"—and was less than clear. (In fact, it was a tangled version of a radio talk he gave in 1949.) He failed to add a short column of double-digit numbers correctly, and in embarrassment tried to make light of it by referring more than once to his audience as a collection of mathematicians. He raised his hands to signal the end of the talk. The audience might not otherwise have known.

In "The Psychology of Temptation," Fulton failed to talk much about psychology, or temptation. Again, the outline was muddled. He claimed to have healed a seriously alcoholic woman by lecturing to her for ninety minutes on the love of God. He told a childhood story about stealing a geranium from a local market. A story about Fritz Kreisler and his television theme song ended with the cliché, "Never underestimate the power of a woman," evoking mild laughter from the audience.

In both programs, Sheen came across as nice, positive, and humorous. But the magic was nearly gone. The series died quickly in syndication.[123]

∾

ON OCTOBER 26, 1966, Pope Paul VI officially named Fulton Sheen bishop of Rochester, New York. It was shocking, front-page news. Sheen was seventy-one and lacked parish and administrative experience. He was now to leave the Society for the Propagation of the Faith, where he had been a striking success. The *New York Times* reported that he raised more than $100 million during his sixteen years as director. A later examination showed the total sum to have approached $200 million. (In 1950, donations amounted to $3.5 million; in 1965, the figure had skyrocketed to nearly $16 million.)[124] Sheen would leave New York, where he was widely known and loved, for what its citizens regarded as the boondocks.

Fulton had been anticipating this day for months. He and a handful of others knew that Cardinal Spellman had ended the more than ten years of intense personal struggle by finally banishing his famous adversary from the Archdiocese of New York. Rochester was the revenge that Spellman had promised all those years ago.

To many the move was a shock because they expected that Sheen, despite his age and lack of experience in a parish or diocese, would be Spellman's successor as archbishop and cardinal. It would be a natural step up from the Society for the Propagation of the Faith, and it was said that Spellman had that in mind when he initially recommended Sheen to his post.[125] But the hostility between the men made that succession impossible. Sheen had headed the Society for the Propagation of the Faith for sixteen years, and for more than a decade of that time he had kept Spellman's hands out of the till, demanding and receiving total control of the funds he raised and donated. The cardinal thought this a direct affront to his authority and integrity. Moreover, Sheen had embarrassed Spellman in front of the Pope. Spellman might have borne these insults if Bishop Sheen had begged forgiveness. But Fulton firmly believed himself to be in the right and was not about to grovel before Spellman. As early as 1964, Sheen said later, he was told that he must give up his position as director of the Society.[126]

During the Vatican II years, the enmity between the cardinal and the bishop, far from abating, may actually have increased. Sheen's renewed television ventures in 1964 and 1966 might well have been undertaken in defiance of Spellman's wishes.[127] Once the proceedings in Rome were completed, Spellman began to think seriously about evening the score.

The cardinal had no choice. He was seventy-seven years old in 1966, and Paul VI, following a recommendation made by Vatican II, had requested the voluntary resignation of bishops when they reached their seventy-fifth birthdays. The implication was that the Holy Father was at liberty to accept or reject it. The decree *Ecclesiae Sanctae* was designed to get rid of old obstructionists, and some thought it aimed especially at Spellman. The cardinal's militant pro–Vietnam War stance had clashed with the Pope's, and he was losing his political clout in New York, now run by the young liberal John Lindsay. Many Catholics thought Spellman had already outlived his usefulness to the Church and in an era of rapid change was a definite liability.[128]

But Spellman was far from ready to retire, and he made his case to the Pope, no doubt forcefully. Paul VI, sometimes eager to avoid controversy, agreed to let Spellman stay. The cardinal gleefully announced the decision at St. Patrick's on October 11, 1966.[129]

The papal decision was made earlier that year, perhaps in March, and perhaps at the very same time Spellman advised the Pope that he did not desire Sheen to be his successor and that he wanted to be rid of him. Joan Sheen said later that Spellman wanted her uncle "out of New York entirely. There was great jealousy."[130] The cardinal knew that removing his antagonist from the archdiocese would not be easy. Fulton was highly popular with Vatican Propagation officials due to his fund-raising abilities, and he was known to be on excellent terms with the Holy Father. He was still the most widely known and popular Catholic priest in America. Spellman must have known exactly how to get his way with Paul VI, however. A perceptive student of the cardinal has called him "perhaps the closest equivalent of a twentieth-century American Richelieu that our secular republic has produced."[131]

Fulton was summoned to Rome on April 13, told of the papal decision to transfer him from the Archdiocese of New York, and given his choice of several positions. He later told a priest he had ordained that he was offered two archdioceses and five dioceses.[132] He selected Rochester, no doubt because of its close proximity to New York City. One can well imagine Fulton's bitterness at being deprived of his leadership at the Society and driven from the city he had loved for decades. In 1974, he bluntly told a friend, Fr. Patrick Collins, that Spellman had gotten rid of him.[133]

Rochester was a good choice, not only because of its location but because it was ripe for change. Bishop Edward Kearney was nearly eighty-two years old and had led the diocese since 1937.[134] To pave the way for Sheen, Spellman quietly had the Vatican, on March 9 (a month before Fulton was summoned to Rome), transfer the auxiliary bishop of Rochester, Lawrence Casey, to Paterson, New Jersey. Bishop John Joseph Boardman, who had accepted the position in Paterson three days earlier, found the offer retracted. Spellman had a long acquaintance with both Kearney and Casey, and knew that the bishop was highly dependent upon his young auxiliary. Once Casey was gone, Kearney would retire willingly.[135]

Just over two weeks after Spellman announced his own continuation in office, he called a press conference at his residence to announce that Paul VI had appointed Sheen bishop of Rochester. For thirty minutes he and Fulton stood together, smiling for photographers ("both were beaming" said one story) and lying to reporters. Spellman declared, "Just as every priest looks forward to the day when he can be a pastor, so I am sure, every bishop dreams of having a diocese of his own—not because of worldly ambition, but simply because a bishop by calling is a shepherd, and a shepherd seeks a flock." Fulton claimed he had first learned of the appointment two days earlier, saying, "I am a soldier in the army of the church. The general has told me to go to Rochester and I love it." He added, "I am a lover of souls, and in Rochester I will be even closer to priests and people."[136]

Two weeks later, Sheen told a *New York Times* reporter that he was going to recommend to the nation's Catholic bishops, soon to meet in Washington for their annual conference, that the Church in America devote no less than 5 percent of its revenues to aiding the world's poor. "There should never be a new church built here that costs more than, say, $1 million. If a diocese insists on spending more for a church, it ought to pay something like a 20 per cent tax for missions." The article noted that in 1965 the Catholic Church in the United States had contributed about 60 percent of the Church's global missionary support.

Fulton fed the media more blarney about his new position, claiming that Cardinal Spellman told him he had not known of the appointment beforehand. He again expressed joy about going to Rochester. On a more earnest note, he promised to implement the reforms of Vatican II quickly. "It will be a pastoral administration," Fulton said, prompting the reporter to add that the bishop was "apparently all set to remold Rochester into a demonstration diocese of his church in America."[137]

There was at least one truth in Fulton's expressions of delight at going to Rochester: He would be out from under Spellman's direct authority. He confided to a bishop friend, "I will be going to Rochester on December 15th. 'The snare is broken and the bird is free.' "[138]

Spellman, the auxiliary bishops of the archdiocese, and nearly three thousand worshipers were at St. Patrick's Cathedral on December 11 to hear Sheen give his farewell sermon. Memories of decades of Masses, sermons, crowds, celebrations, and sorrows must have been heavy on his mind and soul as he mounted the stairs leading to the most prestigious Catholic pulpit in the country. Whatever bitterness he felt was thoroughly disguised. Fulton began his twenty-minute sermon with words of gratitude to Cardinal Spellman for "those priestly intimacies that have drawn us ever closer together."

The cardinal sat in his throne to the left of the altar. After the Mass, the two men embraced, drawing vigorous applause.[139]

It was a good show. Nothing of the rancor between the two men surfaced in the media. But Msgr. George A. Kelly, who worked closely with Spellman for many years, said later that it was common knowledge among insiders that the cardinal had pulled the strings to get Sheen sent to Rochester in order to prevent the bishop from becoming his successor. When reminded by the author that the press at the time carried reports that Spellman knew nothing of the appointment in advance, Kelly laughed loudly.[140]

TEN

Exile

In 1960, Rochester was a city of 318,611. Monroe County, in which it was situated, had a population of 586,387. The Roman Catholic Diocese of Rochester contained twelve counties, encompassing 7,455 miles. The boundaries extended from Lake Ontario on the north to the Pennsylvania border on the south; from Livingston County on the west, bordering the Diocese of Buffalo, to Tioga County on the southeast, bordering the Diocese of Syracuse.[1] A door-to-door diocesan census taken in the spring of 1965 indicated that Catholics numbered 449,198, about 36 percent of the total population of the twelve diocesan counties. The Diocese of Rochester compared in size to those of Seattle, Scranton, and Oakland, California. There were nearly six hundred clergy, ten times the number of staff members working for Sheen at the Society.[2]

Rochester was a conservative and wealthy city. It was often referred to as "Smugtown," a title bestowed by writer Curt Gerling in the first of a two-volume history of Rochester published in 1957. Eastman Kodak, the largest employer in the region, had 41,000 employees, and there were more than 800 manufacturing plants in the city. The local chamber of commerce could boast of, among other things, the University of Rochester, the Rochester Institute of Technology, the Eastman School of Music, a famous hospital and medical school, and the Rochester Philharmonic Orchestra. Catholics in the city were proud of St. Bernard's Seminary, which trained clergy for the diocese and elsewhere; Nazareth College for women; and St. John Fisher College for men. In 1965, Becket Hall, a house of studies to prepare those going on to St. Bernard's for theology, was attached to St. John Fisher College.[3]

Bishop Kearney, who had guided the diocese through the Depression, World War II, the peak of the Cold War, and now into the revolutionary 1960s, was much beloved. He was a good speaker with a lively Irish wit, a genial civic leader, a spiritual guide intensely devoted to Mary, and a skilled brick-and-mortar man. Between 1950 and 1965 he established twenty-two new parishes. A drive for educational expansion that concluded in 1965 brought in pledges totaling $10.5 million dollars. By the end of 1966, the diocese had thirteen diocesan or private high schools within its boundaries, with 10,350 students.[4]

There were never enough clergy and religious to teach religion to all the children of the diocese. As early as 1953, thoroughly trained lay catechists were at work. Nuns were teaching catechetical methods at St. Bernard's Seminary in 1964, the first time nuns were admitted to the faculty. More than two thousand trained lay teachers were active in the diocese by the end of 1966.[5]

Bishop Kearney had long been interested in Church reform. When Pius XII gave permission for evening Masses in 1953, the practice was promptly adopted. In 1958, the Holy See requested active participation by the laity in worship, and within a year, one-third of the diocese's parishes had adopted the dialogue Mass with responses in Latin. The vernacular Mass was introduced in late 1964, as it was throughout the United States. Additional reforms introduced the following year were quickly put into practice. New architectural designs for churches, based on Vatican II decrees, were implemented even before they were mandated. All over the diocese, priests were devising makeshift altars allowing them to face the people. Singing during the Mass was an obstacle to many, inspiring one priest to write:

> *Latin's gone,*
> *Peace is, too:*
> *Singin' and shoutin'*
> *From every Pew.*

Polls taken by the diocesan newspaper, however, showed a generally favorable response to all the reforms.[6]

By the time Sheen arrived, numerous ecumenical efforts had been made in response to Vatican II. Several Catholic and Protestant parishes were inviting each other's members to "Open House" get-togethers, clergy and seminary professors were in dialogue, and an interfaith school for young people was launched in August 1966. In March of that year, the first Ecumenical Day of Prayer for Christian Unity was held at the large Eastman Theater. Diocesan historian Fr. Robert F. McNamara observed, "The new ecumenical friendliness by no means melted all the icy walls that had stood so long between Catholics and non-Catholics; but the extent of the thaw was indeed marvelous and hopeful."[7]

Another change affecting the diocese was a shift in the area's ethnic composition. Blacks and Puerto Ricans had been moving into the area in sizable numbers since the 1950s. In April 1964, a Special Census showed 33,492 non-whites in Monroe County, almost all of them living in the city of Rochester.[8]

Through the end of 1966, St. Bernard's had no blacks in the student body or faculty, and the same was true of Rochester sisterhoods. The number of black Catholics in the diocese was small, and no qualified applicants had presented themselves. Sensitive to the civil rights movement, a Catholic Interracial Council (CIC) of Rochester, a lay organization, was created in 1960, one of many such associations across the nation designed to uphold the condemnation of racial discrimination issued by the American bishops in 1958. In August 1963, a new statement on racial equality by the American bishops was read in all Catholic pulpits in the United States.

The race riots that were shattering the nation's confidence came to Rochester, in two black ghetto sections, during three steamy July nights in 1964. The governor was forced to send 1,500 National Guard troops to quell the violence and patrol the streets with fixed bayonets. A thousand state, city, and county police were also on the scene. When it was over, 4 people had been killed, 350 injured, 750 arrested, and millions of dollars of property damage inflicted by rioters and looters.[9]

The trigger for the riot was an incident of alleged police brutality, but many observers pondered deeper causes of the disturbances. One of them was high unemployment in black areas, for which many blacks blamed Eastman Kodak, charging it with racism.[10] The same newspaper issue that reported the arrival of the National Guard also announced that the company had enjoyed record sales and earnings in the first half of 1964. It cited a company spokesman noting that most blacks in the area lacked the skills Eastman Kodak sought.[11]

A year later, the Catholic Interracial Council was growing restive toward Bishop Kearney, urging him to display more leadership in civil rights. He responded by again pledging his full support of the organization. That June, the Board for Urban Ministry of the Rochester Council of Churches funded the Chicago radical Saul Alinsky (the initial fee was $100,000) to come to the city and set up FIGHT, which stood for Freedom, Integration, God, Honor, Today.[12] Bishop Kearney had reservations about this militant approach to civil rights, yet CIC, St. Bridget's (an inner-city parish), and Loreto House (a privately funded preschool for blacks) became affiliated with FIGHT. In 1965 the diocese allotted $21,500 to help implement "Operation Head Start" in the inner city, and the Sisters of Mercy opened a social service center for black children.[13]

The majority of the Puerto Ricans were Catholic, and as early as 1954 the diocese had begun taking steps to assist them. In 1963, a Catholic family opened the St. Martin de Porres Center to do settlement work among Puerto Ricans, in cooperation with Rochester Catholic Charities. Two Rochester parishes hired Spanish-speaking priests, and several diocesan priests and seminarians learned Spanish. By 1966, there were also more than five hundred Cuban refugees in and around Rochester.[14]

Still, the diocese as a whole was known widely to be conservative and self-satisfied, reflecting the outlook of the people of Rochester as a whole. It had responded to the Sixties in several

meaningful ways, but it was never in the forefront. Matthew Paratore, who grew up in Rochester, recalled the community as provincial and the diocese, like Bishop Kearney, as "old school." St. Bernard's
Seminary was known as "the Rock," one of the strictest, most intellectually demanding, and most conservative seminaries anywhere.[15]
William Ferris, who played the organ and directed the choir at the
cathedral, said Rochester was "a very, very closed town" that did not
readily welcome outsiders, especially if they were famous.[16] Robert
Vogt, a longtime businessman in Rochester, described the city as a
sleepy, conservative place before the arrival of Bishop Sheen.[17]

Fulton Sheen had been to Rochester on numerous occasions to
give speeches and sermons, the first time in 1929. In 1955, his two
lectures at the National Mission Scenerama, a missionary congress
held in the brand-new Rochester War Memorial Auditorium, drew
twenty thousand.[18] His books and his radio and television programs
had made him well known to the people of Rochester by the time
he was appointed.

Three Rochester priests later remarked, in a booklet on Sheen
and the diocese, "People were puzzled. They wondered, 'Why? Why?
Why Rochester—a microscopic diocese? Why for so renowned a figure?' " One of the priests remembered exclaiming, "Wow, what an
honor for our diocese!"[19] Fr. William Graf, a veteran priest in the
diocese, soon heard the story, spreading rapidly within an inner circle of clergy and laity, that Spellman had sent Sheen into exile. What
other reason could there be, Graf asked himself, for someone as
world famous as Sheen to become bishop of a place like Rochester?[20]

Fr. Joseph P. Brennan, rector at St. Bernard's in 1966, recalled
that there were many tensions in the diocese when Sheen arrived.
The Vietnam War and the race issue were tearing at the fabric of
the broad ideological consensus that Americans had long enjoyed.
The reforms of Vatican II had angered many, some thinking the
Church had gone too far, and others, not far enough. Brennan soon
heard the story of Sheen's exile. The bishop did not discuss it directly
with him, but in many subtle ways he let it be known that his
relations with Spellman were "less than cordial."[21]

Others received the same message. Monsignor John F. Duffy remembered that after a luncheon with the bishop at his apartment, their eyes fell on a photograph of Spellman and Sheen looking at each other. Fulton quoted from the fourth station of St. Alphonsus Liguori's Stations of the Cross: "and their looks became as so many arrows to wound those hearts which loved each other so tenderly."[22]

A cheering crowd of about three thousand met Bishop Sheen at the Rochester airport for his formal arrival on December 14, 1966. (Some twelve thousand people had greeted Bishop Kearney in 1937.)[23] Sheen signed autographs and gave a religious medal to the youngest daughter of a man who had come to the airport with his wife and six children. In an airport ceremony, Sheen told the throng that since 1950 he had been "helping 800 dioceses in the world" and was now happy to be responsible for only one. "I have an ardent desire to spend myself and to be spent, to get my arms around Rochester." He said that he chose Rochester because the diocese was "the best of all" that were vacant. The mayor gave the bishop the key to the city, and Bishop Kearney boasted of the good weather on that festive day. In a reference to his television show, Sheen said, "Now you've seen me live, and I'm sure you are disappointed."

Sheen, Kearney and diocesan officials then drove to the downtown chancery, where the new bishop formally presented his credentials. A reporter noted that Sheen was letting Bishop Kearney remain in the bishop's mansion, while he lived elsewhere. "I would be a criminal if I drove him out," Sheen said.[24]

The bishop spent his first evening in the diocese at St. Bernard's Seminary. He wanted to spend his first night with the students, he told them, because the roots of the diocese were in its seminary. He assisted and preached at Mass the next morning and had a family breakfast with the staff and students. One student, Joe Hart, later remembered how Sheen paused and stared "for perhaps four seconds, that seemed like forever" when you were being introduced. It was as though he were looking through you, Hart said later. As was long his practice, Fulton was "sensing" the potential of every seminarian he met.[25]

The next day, Cardinal Spellman, more than forty visiting bishops (including seven of Spellman's auxiliaries), the lieutenant governor of New York, the mayor, Clare Boothe Luce, area clergy of all denominations, and a thousand other special ticket holders packed the neo-Gothic cathedral for the ninety-minute installation service.[26] Half of the audience were laity, as Sheen requested. Laypeople also took part in the offertory procession.[27] Sheen was described by a *New York Times* reporter as 71 but looking "at least 15 years younger today." The reporter also noted that Sheen "has had no previous experience in diocesan work except a few months as a newly ordained curate in his native Illinois."[28]

Kearney had wanted a gala ceremony, and the new cathedral choir director and organist, William Ferris, wrote special music that included brass instruments. At the service, he played the organ and directed the boys' and men's choirs. (After the consecration, Sheen told Ferris that he wanted a classical repertoire at the cathedral, including Gregorian chant. "This was unusual," Ferris said later, "for all sorts of freaky things were being done in churches at this time." Sheen had "a tremendous knowledge of music and liturgy," Ferris recalled, and he promoted the development of a seminary choir at St. Bernard's.)[29]

An apostolic letter from Paul VI was read, declaring, "Everything that you have so tirelessly accomplished in the past, by deed and by the spoken and written word to feed the sheep of Christ's flock has won for you universal acclaim. We now nourish the fond hope that in the future you will vigorously undertake even greater things."[30]

In his address, Sheen asked that all installation gifts be given to the missions. To donors and well-wishers, he said, "Your words and your kindness are like oxygen to my lungs and blood to my heart."[31] He asked two favors: "Write to me; pray for me."[32]

At the installation luncheon at the Manger Hotel, the 225 tables contained many people from Fulton's past. Both Tom and Al Sheen were on hand, as were Clare Boothe Luce, Mr. and Mrs. Jerry Cunningham (Joan Sheen), Mr. and Mrs. Thomas Holliger (cousin

Reeda's son), Edythe and Marlene Brownett and their mother, Msgr. Edward T. O'Meara, set designer and convert Jo Mielziner, long-time Jewish friend Herbert Trigger, convert Mary Downing, and Mr. and Mrs. Chester Baker (Mary Fulton Baker). Fulton went from table to table, welcoming his old and new friends. When a five-piece combo struck up "Hello Dolly," he took the baton and "directed" the number, much to the audience's delight. His formal remarks stressed the unity of Left and Right in a common cause.[33]

Four thousand people attended a civic welcome that evening in the ten-thousand-seat War Memorial, Rochester's largest hall.[34] Sheen may have been disconcerted; he was not used to seeing empty seats at one of his appearances. Something else undoubtedly caught his attention: Twenty-four bishops had been on hand for the luncheon, and more than forty were present at the public reception in the evening, but Cardinal Spellman attended neither; he had returned home immediately after the installation service.

～

SOON THE NEW BISHOP was traveling throughout the diocese, visiting landmarks, institutions and parishes. On December 21, he offered the annual Christmas Mass at the state hospital in Rochester. On Christmas day he said three Masses, one at the cathedral, a second in a parish, and a third at the city jail.[35]

At St. Francis de Sales Church in Geneva in December, Sheen had a pleasant conversation with the assistant pastor, Fr. Michael C. Hogan. When Hogan asked the bishop how he wanted things to be run, Sheen replied by asking his host what *he* wanted. Hogan found this "most unusual," as bishops usually made their intentions known from the start. The bishop returned a few weeks later to get a second look at Hogan. He and the pastor of the parish were ill, and Sheen quietly entered a confessional to help them with the day's work. Hogan recalled, "When some people found out later that they had gone to Bishop Sheen to confession, they nearly died."[36] Sheen soon summoned Hogan to Rochester and named him his secretary. (Edythe Brownett had remained in New York.)

Hogan never knew why he had been chosen. Surely one reason was his sense of humor. Fulton put two of the priest's gags in his autobiography, and called his secretary "a joy and an inspiration."[37] Sheen often had Hogan drive him to Macedon, where Fr. Eugene K. McFarland, a close friend of writer Erma Bombeck, regaled him with jokes. "The Bishop always enjoyed a good laugh," Hogan said later.[38]

Neither was Hogan ever quite sure what his specific duties were. Sheen's personal secretary, Jean Prochenko, did the typing and other office work. Hogan handled a variety of administrative chores and managed appointments, but he acted principally as the bishop's chauffeur. (A local Dodge-Plymouth dealer offered the bishop a new car every year.) They drove together all over the diocese, at times going as far as New York City, where Sheen kept his apartment in the old Society building on Thirty-eighth Street. While in the city, Hogan sometimes relayed messages of a critical nature to Sheen's successor at the Society for the Propagation of the Faith. Sheen, in Hogan's opinion, was too gentlemanly to reprimand his good friend Edward O'Meara directly.[39]

Hogan often visited Sheen's modest, second-floor apartment below his diocesan headquarters at 50 Chestnut Street. His quarters included a chapel where he meditated and prayed daily. Hogan noted that during his Holy Hour, Sheen would dictate thoughts into a recording device, usually filling two recording discs a day. A secretary would then type them up, and the bishop would use the contents for later sermons, articles and books.

Sheen brought his personal cook with him from New York. Hogan recalls that the bishop was "very selective" in his food. He kept in good physical condition by playing tennis twice a week with a professional, and he rode a stationary bicycle in his apartment. Hogan once asked him if he wanted to play golf; Sheen replied that he would when he got old.

Wherever Sheen traveled, he invited people to write to him. They did, and Hogan was overwhelmed with mail, so he and another priest devised form letters to handle the deluge. People in the diocese soon caught on when they compared their identical letters from the bishop.[40]

On the very first day of Hogan's employment, a fire destroyed a parish, killing the seventy-seven-year-old priest, who had tried to rescue the Blessed Sacrament, and a twenty-six-year-old nun who attempted to help him. Some students had committed arson. Hogan drove Sheen to the scene. The bishop was aghast to learn that the priest had left $7 million in stocks he had forgotten about and had not made out a will. The state took most of the money.[41]

On the second day of Hogan's new job, he and the bishop went to a college retreat in downtown Rochester. They discovered that the event had been scheduled for vacation break, and only a single row of students were on hand. Sheen, said Hogan, "was humbled in the beginning."[42]

About this same time, Sheen conducted a Requiem Mass and hosted a dinner for priests afterward. To illustrate his love for the people of Rochester, the bishop went out in the street and invited people to join the clergy for dinner. Almost no one accepted the invitation.[43]

Sheen offered a series of retreat talks to the people of the diocese, and requested the largest auditorium in Rochester, the downtown Masonic Auditorium. Very few people showed up, and Fulton was furious. "The whole world comes to hear Fulton Sheen," he said privately, "except his own diocese." He had overlooked the fact that the auditorium was located in an unsafe area.[44] Still, fear might have been overcome if the people of the diocese were sufficiently eager to hear their new bishop.

The rector of St. Bernard's Seminary said later that Sheen always thought Rochester was hostile toward him.[45] The local newspaper was unfriendly from the beginning to the end of Sheen's tenure in Rochester, often misquoting and attacking him.[46]

As part of his determination to implement the teachings of Vatican II, Sheen sought to create a *curia*, a board of counselors to advise him, and he chose to be as democratic about the process as he could. All diocesan priests received a letter asking them to nominate three priests whom he might "appoint as your leaders." He promised to count the ballots personally. The appointments were duly made in January 1967. Msgr. Dennis W. Hickey was selected the new vicar general.

Again in the spirit of Vatican II directives, the bishop appointed several priests to serve as vicars in certain fields of diocesan administration or in geographical districts. The first priest named would prove to be the most controversial: Fr. David Finks as vicar of urban ministry. Finks, thirty-six and newly ordained, was assistant pastor of the inner-city parish of Immaculate Conception. He was deeply concerned about civil rights and had joined both FIGHT and the Friends of FIGHT. The selection of Finks, made after he and a colleague had given a private presentation on the racial situation in Rochester, was an example of Sheen's "feeling" that someone was the right man for the job. The appointment also showed the bishop's firm commitment to taking action on behalf of the area's African Americans. Sheen had spoken with FIGHT officials even before meeting Finks, who later wrote, "As I accepted my letter of appointment that cold January day, I could see a FIGHT lapel button at the foot of the ornate crucifix which dominated his office desk."[47]

In a January speech to the chamber of commerce (screened in advance by Finks), Sheen likened Rochester to a beautiful woman with a pimple on her nose—a clear reference to Eastman Kodak, under attack by FIGHT, which was demanding that the corporation employ hundreds of blacks. Many, especially Eastman Kodak officials, resented Sheen's statement.[48] The citizens of Rochester were deeply divided over the issue of race, but Catholic and most mainline Protestant leaders were now united behind black demands.[49]

As Finks got deeper into the struggle of FIGHT against Eastman Kodak, he thanked the bishop for continuing to support him despite a lot of angry mail arriving at Sheen's office. Fulton responded, "Oh, I never read it. I make it a practice to read only positive letters. My secretary screens out all the unpleasantness."[50]

Time magazine, perhaps reflecting the influence of Clare Boothe Luce, reported in February 1967 that Sheen was doing "spectacularly well" in Rochester.[51] The bishop said he was "introducing democracy in administration," and the article noted the election of the vicar general and the formation of a new clerical advisory council of priests, also elected by the clergy. A lay administrative committee had been named to handle financial affairs of the diocese. The Finks appointment also received attention.[52]

Sheen somehow found time to travel outside the diocese. In January he was in Phoenix, Arizona, to give a speech at the request of Clare Boothe Luce.[53] In June, he spoke in Dallas to celebrate the fiftieth anniversary of the ordination to the priesthood of Bishop Thomas K. Gorman, a classmate at Louvain.[54] That same month, he addressed the New York State chapter of the FBI National Academy Associates in Buffalo, saying that law enforcement officers "are defenders of God's justice, His sense of right." J. Edgar Hoover, who had already congratulated Sheen on his appointment in Rochester, sent another warm letter of thanks. Sheen was apparently once again an FBI special contact, now reporting to the special agent in charge (SAC) at Buffalo. He remained on the special correspondents list, receiving mailings from the bureau. The bishop was also being considered for an appointment of some sort by the White House (which did not materialize), and was cleared by the FBI.[55]

While Sheen administered his diocese and gave talks elsewhere, he continued to write his two newspaper columns and publish books. In 1967, four new volumes appeared, three of them largely collections of previously published material. These books, like others before, were aimed at the mass market and maximum sales. *Lenten and Easter Inspirations* contained brief reflections on the Gospel accounts, tied to famous works of art and several contemporary photographs. Sheen speculated at one point that Simon of Cyrene, who helped Christ carry the cross, was black. "In the ACTS, there is a Simon, the Black Man, mentioned. In any case, Africa was the first country [*sic*] to share the Cross of Christ." A poem by black American poet Countee Cullen followed.[56]

By the spring of 1967, Sheen had the full machinery of the Diocese of Rochester in place. Beside Finks, four other diocesan vicars were appointed. Father Joseph W. Dailey was designated vicar of pastoral planning. His duties included the acquisition of property, the supervision of buildings, the study of rural and urban conditions, and the whole issue of diocesan administration. Father Albert J. Shamon was vicar of religious education. (Sheen went to St. Bernard's to see who was the top scholar in the class of 1940, apparently looking for a mature priest, and this led to Shamon's selection. When the priest protested by saying, "Bishop, appoint someone with more brains and know-how," Sheen replied, "I've got the brains and the know-how. I want men of faith around me.")[57] Father Bartholomew J. O'Brien and Father Raymond J. Wahl were given territorial jurisdiction, one in the western part of the diocese, the other in the south; they each managed a vicariate to replace the defunct deaneries of the diocese.[58]

The Priests' Council was elected by clergy divided into twelve age groups. Sheen reserved the right to name other priests to this senate, though his nominations would never exceed eight. The eleven elected members of the council, plus two members named by the bishop, had their first meeting on March 15. They established committees on inner-city programs, adult education programs, and priestly renewal programs. A fourth committee was created to draw up a constitution.

Sheen appointed a number of laity to his official family, including the diocesan attorney and an important banker. Throughout the diocese, with Sheen's approval, parishes began founding lay boards of education and lay advisory councils. Sheen changed the name of the Rochester Chancery, which he thought bureaucratic and impersonal, to the "Pastoral Office." The new bishop meant what he said about democracy in the diocese. Or so it seemed.[59]

Without consulting anyone, Sheen announced the closing of the Most Precious Blood School in Rochester, attended largely by Italians. When he appeared at new Becket Hall to bless it, a crowd of Italians was waiting for him. Angry people pounded on his car and waved signs. Some shouted "You son of a bitch" and worse. Sheen locked his car doors and would not emerge until the vehicle was safely inside the institution's garage. The bishop was greatly shaken. He ordered the school reopened the following day.[60]

Sheen had bold plans for St. Bernard's Seminary. He engaged a lay philosopher, Dr. Eulalio R. Baltazar, to teach a course on the philosophical background of dogma. In time, a number of non-Catholic professors would be hired by the seminary. At one point, the bishop wrote a letter to eighty of the world's leading theologians, inviting them to come to teach at the seminary. A few responded positively, and faculty were hired from Italy, England and Belgium. This caused quite a stir among the regular faculty, who wondered where the funds were coming from to hire these distinguished scholars. Fr. Joseph P. Brennan, the rector, was himself puzzled about the financial side of this push for distinction. He also wondered how his faculty, engaged exclusively in the training of priests, would get along with the theologians. Some faculty members were worried about retaining their jobs.[61]

Later that year, Protestants were hired to teach pastoral and preaching skills. Psychological testing was employed in order to weed out seminarians who might be emotionally or otherwise unfit. A board of seven laypersons—four men and three women—was created to "assist the seminary authorities in the selection of fit candidates for the altar." Headed by a former policeman, it had the responsibility of setting the disciplinary rules governing seminarians. This lay board, Sheen said proudly, was the first of its kind in a Catholic seminary in the United States.[62] His vicar for education, Fr. Albert Shamon, later remembered Sheen saying on several occasions, "Mind my words, Vicar, the laity will save the Church in the United States."[63]

The rector and the faculty were not consulted in advance about the lay board. Fr. Brennan first heard of the appointments through word of mouth. He invited the bishop and the board members, who had never been on the campus, to dinner at the seminary so that everyone might get acquainted. After dinner, Sheen made a few suggestions and then heard a polite rebuttal from faculty members eager to maintain their prerogatives.

Sheen was disenchanted by the women during the first meeting of the committee, so he invited only the men to the next meeting. He never called the board together again. Some clergy in the diocese began grumbling about the new bishop's lack of administrative skills.[64]

Two new spiritual advisers were assigned to St. Bernard's Seminary. To illustrate Sheen's vision of the seminary as a source of popular religious education as well as a source of continuing education for priests, a series of popular lectures on Holy Scripture was held in late June.[65]

Sheen changed the name of faltering St. Andrew's Minor Seminary to King's Preparatory Seminary and made it a co-educational high school. The institution, he said, would operate on "an entirely new concept in religious vocational education." Its aim would be the education of leaders, a "spiritual elite." The phrase "spiritual elite" caused some raised eyebrows throughout the diocese.[66] Things did not work out, and King's Prep closed in 1970.[67]

Sheen was vitally interested in the spiritual welfare of his people. He advised priests and seminarians to adopt his Holy Hour practice. He welcomed the Cursillo movement, a program designed to foster lay spiritual development, into the diocese. He urged families to undertake scriptural reading and acts of self-denial. He initiated Home Masses, giving priests permission to celebrate Mass in private homes during evening hours on weekdays. (Bishop Kearney would never have done that, Michael Hogan said later.)[68]

The Home Mass, which had roots in very early Christianity, was new in the United States and was based on a directive issued by the American Bishops' Committee on the Liturgy. In a pastoral letter, Sheen stated, "May God grant that the house church will turn the church life of this diocese not into a segregation but into a congregation; may it inspire a coming to Christ for the sake of going into the world, so that the church will not be a camp, but a march."[69] Sheen took the lead himself, saying Mass in the homes of both blacks and Hispanics and afterward visiting with attendees. Sister Mary Regis, R.S.M., known as "the Mother Teresa of inner-city Rochester," later recalled the bishop's efforts in her area with affection.[70]

Sheen's interest in missionary activity within the diocese was revealed when he imported nuns with experience in social work and created a "secular mission" whose three priests went into trailer camps, villages and farms, "wherever there is a door to knock on and a soul to save." He discussed plans to take out advertisements in secular newspapers to express Catholic news and views, but the idea fizzled when Sheen learned that the diocesan newspaper had a three-year contract with the company that printed it. He made changes in the Catholic newspaper staff and promised to write a weekly editorial for the publication.[71]

As always, Sheen found time to help bring individuals into the Church. One day, as the bishop and Hogan were visiting small-town parishes, they stopped in Wayland. Sheen was buying ice cream cones for about twenty or thirty children when a little girl came up to him and asked him to visit her sister. "Yes, where is she?" asked Sheen. "She's dead; she is in the undertaker's parlor." Sheen and Hogan went to the funeral home and saw the little seven-year-old girl who had been hit by a car. Sheen wrote later, "She looked alive and appeared like an angel." Fulton consoled the grieving family, telling them, as he had told Clare Boothe Luce on the death of her daughter, that great good would come from the accident. In time, two conversions resulted from Sheen's compassion. Fulton later made a special trip from New York to Rochester to baptize one of the converts.[72]

The bishop won a large story in the *New York Times* by announcing that children in the diocese would be confirmed at about the time they graduated from high school instead of at the traditional age of nine to twelve. "Confirmation must become a very serious crown of study when youth is ready to serve Christianity," he said. The issue was currently being debated in Rome, and diocesan bishops were free to make their own decisions. Priests from the United States Catholic Conference and the Archdiocese of New York told reporters that they thought the Diocese of Rochester would have the oldest Catholic Confirmation age in the world.[73]

Again in keeping with Vatican II pronouncements, Sheen was

highly active in the area of ecumenical relations. On January 30, 1967, he addressed a crowd of 2,300 in a Jewish synagogue. Introducing the bishop, Rabbi Herbert Bronstein said that one would have to go back to the fifth century to find a parallel to that evening's event.[74]

On February 22, Sheen addressed an audience of nine hundred Jewish and Christian leaders, sharing the platform with Rabbi Marc H. Tanenbaum, director of interreligious affairs of the American Jewish Committee. Because both faiths sought to bring religious values to bear on a secular world, said the bishop, "I believe we will draw closer and closer together as we realize that we are both called by God to this task." Christians, he continued, had begun to "recognize Jews as a living people. . . . At Mass I call Abraham my father, and I do it every day. We have the same God, and we are His people."

In his half-hour talk, Sheen spoke about God's promise of the Holy Land to the Jewish people. He also noted the suffering of Jews and Christians at the hands of Nazis and Soviet Communists. "Maybe these days of blackness and persecution through which we have all passed will draw us closer and closer together." When Sheen concluded, the audience rose to its feet with a roaring ovation. Fulton walked over to Rabbi Tanenbaum and embraced him. Tanenbaum later called it "an embrace that seemed to close an alienation gap of 1,900 years." The rabbi was off for Rome the next day to confer with Vatican officials on the status of Jewish-Christian talks.[75]

As the Church saw non-Christians in a brighter light after Vatican II, so also did it express charity and friendship toward Protestants. In April, Sheen attended an ecumenical weekend at Geneseo State University, lending his support for the creation of a university interfaith center. In mid-May, on Pentecost Sunday, the bishop spoke at the second annual Ecumenical Day of Prayer for Christian Unity, held at the Eastman Theater.[76] When Billy Graham came to Rochester to preach, Sheen urged all of his staff to attend as a gesture of good will.[77]

Sheen owned some three thousand books on Scripture by Protestant scholars, and was surprised that his vicar of education had not read any of them. "But, Bishop," Fr. Shamon sputtered, "we were taught in the seminary not to read Protestant Scripture commentators." Sheen guffawed, "Vicar, you've got to remember that the Holy Spirit works through them too."[78]

Later that year, Sheen and the president of the Rochester Area Council of Churches announced the establishment of a Roman Catholic–Protestant Office of Urban Ministry "to help solve the basic problems of the first citizen of the church—the poor man." Fr. David Finks and Rev. Herbert E. White, a Presbyterian minister, were appointed to run the office. While Catholics and Protestants would have separate boards, they were joining together in an office "hoping that this will be a symbol for further uniting of a common urban strategy."[79]

❧

BY THE SUMMER OF 1967, antiwar demonstrations and photographs and stories about mass destruction and slaughter in Southeast Asia were deeply troubling millions of Americans. The number of troops in Vietnam was escalating, from 385,000 at the end of 1966 to 486,000 by the end of the following year. Some 5,000 Americans lost their lives in the undeclared war in 1966, and about 9,000 would die in 1967. In May 1966, 10,000 protesters had marched in front of the White House. Senator William Fulbright, chairman of the Foreign Relations Committee, had held televised hearings on the war and was openly critical of American involvement. The following year, 50,000 would demonstrate near the Lincoln Memorial. Demonstrations were often led by Vietnam veterans, many in wheelchairs.

American college campuses were in a continuous uproar. Students burned draft cards, harassed military recruiters, and shut down campuses. A common student complaint (although untrue) was that the Americans fighting in Vietnam were mostly draftees and predominantly black. A favorite chant of the day was, "Hey, hey, LBJ, how many kids have you killed today?"

Closely linked to the war in Vietnam were the racial disturbances at home. That summer there were almost four dozen riots and over a hundred lesser incidents. In Newark, New Jersey, 26 people were killed and 1,200 injured. A major riot in Detroit lasted five days, cost 43 lives, injured 2,000, and destroyed 1,300 buildings. Federal troops had to be sent in to restore order.

On July 30, Sheen startled many in Rochester and elsewhere by requesting, from the pulpit of Sacred Heart Cathedral, the immediate withdrawal of American troops from Vietnam. His was the first unequivocal antiwar statement by an American bishop. Sheen saw the obvious link between the violence overseas and at home, and he spoke out—only, he said, as a Christian. He asked the president, who had called for a national day of prayer and reconciliation, to announce:

> *In the name of God who bade us love our neighbor . . . for the sake of reconciliation, I shall withdraw all our forces immediately from southern Vietnam, so that, in the words of Abraham Lincoln, we "may unite in most humbly offering our prayers and supplications to the Great Lord and ruler of nations, and beseech Him to pardon our national and other sins." . . . is this reconciliation to be limited only to our citizens? Could we not also be reconciled with our brothers in Vietnam? May we plead only for a reconciliation between blacks and whites, and not between blacks and whites and yellows? . . . to paraphrase the gospel . . . go and be reconciled to your northern Vietnam brother, then come back and offer your prayers.[80]*

The statement was wholly consistent with Sheen's views on war and peace and race, written and preached all of his life. It was also in harmony with the declarations of Paul VI, who had stated before the United Nations in 1965, "No more war, war never again!" On the other hand, it stood in sharp contrast to the pro-war statements made repeatedly by Cardinal Spellman. In December 1966, the cardinal had told American troops in Vietnam that they were "holy crusaders" engaged in "Christ's war against the Vietcong and the people of North Vietnam." He told three thousand soldiers in Da Nang that "less than total victory is inconceivable." The Vatican was reportedly embarrassed by Spellman's defiance of the Pope's call for peace. In January 1967, antiwar demonstrators disrupted the High Mass at St. Patrick's Cathedral and invaded the sanctuary. Columnist Drew Pearson said the conflict in Vietnam had become known as "Spellman's War."[81]

Was Sheen trying to humiliate the cardinal by his call for unilateral withdrawal from Vietnam? Perhaps. But his position was based as well on strong personal conviction. While always firmly anticommunist, Sheen had also long been concerned with issues of peace and justice, and was deeply saddened to see the country being torn apart over an undeclared war. Later that year, Sheen said that the money being spent on armaments for the war would be better invested in alleviating the suffering of the poor.[82]

While the press did not give major coverage to Sheen's sermon at Sacred Heart, several observers recognized its importance. The liberal *Christian Century,* for example, praised the bishop highly for his wisdom.[83] And many on the right, normally sympathetic toward Sheen for his religious and moral positions, were greatly displeased.

Seeing things from the ground level of the diocese, Sheen became more committed to social activism. From the first, he was vitally concerned about the plight of blacks in Rochester's inner city. He said New Year's Masses in the three principal inner-city parishes— St. Bridget's, Immaculate Conception and Mount Carmel—and soon presented their pastors with a questionnaire offering suggestions while seeking input about future planning. Sheen's questions included: Should priests live among the people in order to be more easily available? and, Should there be interracial visits and dialogue? The questionnaire was published, and several Protestant clergymen engaged in inner-city work praised the general approach.[84]

In May 1967, Sheen made public a tax he imposed on future construction in the diocese. The rate was to begin at 1.25 percent on buildings costing from $50,000 to $100,000, and go up to 3 percent on projects costing a half-million or more. The proceeds would go to Catholic missionary work and to the needs of the inner city.[85]

In fact, Sheen did not favor future construction; he once refused to enter a new rectory because he thought it too ornate.[86]

Sheen held a news conference in June in a park outside Immaculate Conception Church in the inner city, discussing his vision of housing for the poor. Afterward, a black woman holding a baby came up to the bishop and said, "You ought to see where I live." Sheen and his secretary, Michael Hogan, went with the woman to her home, where he met her husband and two other children. Fulton was deeply moved by the family's poverty. Vowing to do something about it, he took the mother and a real estate agent on a tour of the residential neighborhoods. When a suitable house was found, Sheen purchased it for the family out of his own pocket.[87]

The bishop charged Fr. Shamon to find ways to finance Rochester's seven inner-city parish schools. He devised a plan that divided the diocese into regions and resulted in prosperous parishes donating funds to the poorer ones. The bishop approved the plan, under which not a single inner-city school was closed. Sheen also named Fr. Roger F. Baglin, assistant pastor of St. Bridget's parish, to organize efforts on behalf of the area's Hispanics. The Guadalupan Missionaries of the Holy Spirit, based in Mexico City, soon opened a small house in Rochester and helped Hispanics in many ways.[88]

To help people in the more rural areas of the diocese, the bishop named Fr. John J. Hempel to head an apostolate called the Secular Mission. It sought out isolated Catholics, including migrant workers, who were unknown or uncared for. Sheen later summoned Hempel to Rochester to lead the new Office of Human Concern, which took charge of both the urban ministry and the rural apostolate.[89]

Sheen made financial reforms aimed at helping both parochial teachers and priests. Teachers in the parochial schools were paid between $2,000 and $3,000 a year in early 1967. The bishop ordered school superintendent Bill Roche to raise all salaries. This move was popular with teachers, of course, but raised financial difficulties for the system.

When Sheen came to Rochester, a pastor (the term came out of Vatican II) earned about $150 a month, and an associate made about $100. As was common across the country, the pastor kept the Christmas offering, which meant that having a large congregation was preferable. The bishop cancelled the Christmas offering to the priests and raised clerical salaries across the board.[90] Fr. Andrew Apostoli, ordained by Sheen, recalled that the Christmas offering decree earned the bishop much clerical resentment.[91] In addition, Sheen established a new diocesan pension plan for priests and set up a priests' personnel board.[92]

In August 1967, the *New York Times* published a lengthy and glowing account of Sheen's innovations and accomplishments in Rochester. David Finks declared, "The thing I like about Bishop Sheen is that he has great instincts.... He loves people; he has a real feeling for the poor." And Sheen told of his desire to make the diocese "a microcosm" of Vatican II reforms. But the article also revealed deep rumblings of discontent within the diocese. A priest said, "Bishop Sheen sure is shaking us up. Many of us still wonder whether he's our Bishop. Maybe his assignment here is a Vatican ploy to groom him for the Archdiocese of New York or for a cardinalate." Another priest declared, "He has too many plates in the air. Often, he doesn't follow through." An influential layman noted the bishop's friendliness toward FIGHT and his barb against Eastman Kodak, saying, "There is still the concept of Rochester as a benevolent company town, and many people resented the Bishop taking on Kodak." Many Catholics were protesting, he said, by dropping buttons in collection plates.[93] Sheen had inherited a large diocesan debt, and his stand on civil rights was making the task of raising funds extremely difficult.[94]

∾

SHEEN WAS IN ROME in early October, chosen by Paul VI as one of 188 prelates to attend a month-long synod of bishops, summoned to advise the Pope on doctrinal and organizational issues. Newspaper accounts of synod activities revealed a definite split between traditional and "progressive" bishops. Alfredo Cardinal Ottaviani, the seventy-six-year-old head of the Congregation for the Doctrine of the Faith, was by all accounts a traditionalist. But the historical winds were blowing against him. Even before the synod assembled, the Congregation had abandoned the practice of banning books it considered dangerous or heretical, and was in dialogue with certain bishops and theologians, choosing to work out doctrinal problems rather than simply condemn those advancing them.[95]

Sheen was clearly in the progressive wing, in the sense that he wholly endorsed the reforms of Vatican II and was eager to see them implemented. As Robert F. McNamara has put it, "His one constant fear was that Catholicism would be judged by other Americans as behind the times or irrelevant."[96] In what was reported in the *New York Times* as a "fervent" speech before the synod, he recommended his own experiment of enlisting laity to help select candidates for the priesthood. "It would be important to bring competent laymen into the running of our seminaries because some of them have a deeper spirit of faith than we find in some priests." He also advocated postponing ordination for two years, as young people were still immature in will and intellect and were "subjected to stimuli that bring about instability of character."[97] Such sentiments could not be expected to win friends for the bishop among his clergy and seminarians.

At the conclusion of the synod, Sheen wrote to Marlene Brownett, calling the sessions "marvelous" and warning her not to believe anything she read in the press. "The faith of the Church is strong, the Bishops love the Vicar of Christ, and there is a desire to 'pull in' souls closer to the Cross." He gave three talks, he said, and they were very well received. At a private audience with Paul VI, the Holy Father said to Fulton, "I am your friend. Do not kneel[;] let me embrace you as one I trust."[98] Perhaps this was in part to make amends for having sent Sheen to Rochester.

On December 2, Cardinal Spellman died of a stroke. Nine cardinals and over a hundred bishops concelebrated the Mass at St. Patrick's Cathedral. (It was the first Mass for a deceased cardinal celebrated entirely in English, which was ironic, as Spellman had resisted the full use of the vernacular liturgy.) President Johnson, United Nations secretary general U Thant, Governor Nelson Rockefeller, Mayor John Lindsay, Senator Robert F. Kennedy, Richard Cardinal Cushing and many others issued extravagant statements of commendation. There was indeed much to praise. At Spellman's silver jubilee in 1964, for example, the unprecedented expansion of diocesan facilities achieved under his leadership had required a press release of twenty-four pages.[99] The *New York Times* obituary, however, was more frank, describing the late prelate as out of touch with post-Vatican II developments and considered by many a relic of the brick-and-mortar days when authoritarianism and isolation were the style for Catholics.

The *Times,* perhaps proving that it was not privy to inside knowledge about the cardinal and the bishop of Rochester, reported that Sheen was among those mentioned as a successor. Fulton summoned all of his powers of charity and courtesy when writing his eulogistic statement: "The battlefields and soldiers will mourn, for they lost their chief of chaplains. The missions will grieve, for they lost their open-handed friend. . . . The death of a great man like Cardinal Spellman gathers up all humanity into one heart shedding one common tear. In life, he claimed our attention, our respect and our love. That does not deny him in death the more beautiful tribute of our prayers."[100]

At year's end, Fulton wrote to Clare Boothe Luce thanking her for a financial gift (she often sent money to Sheen, Spellman and the Pope) and describing his holiday activities: "I spent Christmas at the Cathedral here, then visited two jails and one penitentiary, saying Masses and preaching. The work is very hard, but I love it. I feel that I am sharing in the contemporary crucifixion and it gives me much joy."[101] A short time later, he wrote to Luce, "My work still continues to pile up. Another unmarried mother, a most pathetic case, coupled with several marriages that needed reconciliation, along with countless little charities have kept me so busy that I have done little instructing of converts. I do not know whether the Good Lord shares my estimate, but somehow or other I feel that nothing is more important. Anyhow to be at peace I must find more sheep for His green pastures."[102]

On January 5, 1968, Paul VI named two auxiliary bishops for the Diocese of Rochester: Dennis Walter Hickey, the vicar general, and John Edgar McCafferty, a member of the Priests' Council and a former chairman of the Diocesan Ecumenical Commission. They were welcomed by the diocesan clergy, for many were growing cold toward Bishop Sheen.

Michael Kelly thought Sheen extremely kind to his priests. He knew all of their names and ministered to those who were ailing. But some clergy thought him aloof, and they smarted at his domination of dinnertime discussions. Some resented the fact that he would not permit any of them to be laicized.[103] Some clergy considered the bishop's policies radical and perhaps designed to keep his name in the headlines. (It was noticed that his press releases went initially to the major newspapers rather than the local press.) Others, like Finks, thought him too conservative. Moreover, Sheen did not like to attend meetings, and clergy learned quickly that if a committee disagreed with him, he would call no further meetings.

Priests discovered that for all his talk of democracy, Sheen had an iron will and was given to doing what he wanted no matter what others thought or said. Robert McNamara has written of Sheen, "This reluctance to dialogue did not spring from any ill will, but from his total background. His churchmanship was basically 'old-fashioned'; he was too mercurial to seek advice readily; and his prime gift was as a monologist, not a dialogist. One does not easily unlearn lifelong or innate ways."[104]

An idea Sheen had in the spring of 1967 would bring all of these frustrations to a head: He would give to the federal government the property of an inner-city parish on which to erect housing for the poor. The Great Society was experimenting with a variety of programs to improve the lives of the disadvantaged, housing in particular, and Fulton thought the Diocese of Rochester could be a model of what the postconciliar Church could do to join the effort. Perhaps bishops all over the country would follow his lead.

Sheen informed the Vatican and the apostolic delegate of his plan in its early stages. But he spoke to Father Finks in only general terms, and he did not confer with city officials or the Rochester Housing Authority, which supervised all local public housing. On November 8, 1967, Sheen wrote directly to Robert W. Weaver, secretary of the Department of Housing and Urban Development (HUD), offering the property of an inner-city parish in Rochester with the stipulation that public housing be constructed on the site "within the shortest possible time." Weaver accepted the offer on January 29 and federal officials selected St. Bridget's, a 114-year-old parish with only a little more than a hundred members, mostly African Americans and Hispanics.[105] Local clergy had been talking of closing St. Bridget's since the late 1950s due to its low membership.[106]

On the advice of his chancellor, Fr. James M. Moynihan, Sheen convened the Board of Consultors, a body of priests appointed by the bishop and required by Canon Law.[107] The board approved the offer to HUD. Sheen also talked with St. Bridget's pastor, Fr. Francis H. Vogt, who was unhappy about the proposed gift. Sheen rejected Moynihan's suggestion that he consult with the people of the parish, on the ground that it would take too long.[108]

Sheen flew to Peoria in mid-February 1968 to celebrate Mass and preach at St. Patrick's Church, observing its hundredth anniversary. Fr. Thomas Henseler, who sent the invitation to Sheen and served as his driver during the visit, later recalled that on the Saturday before the main service, Sheen heard confessions for up to two hours and paid a visit to the local bishop. On Sunday the parish was packed; requests for tickets had come from all over the country. Newspaper reporters and television cameras were present in abundance.

A reception at the rectory followed. Sheen, still in complete bishop's apparel including gloves and miter, stood on the steps with several clergy, calling out to old friends and remembering aloud that as a young curate more than forty years earlier he had married one and baptized the child of another. "He had a phenomenal memory," Henseler recalled. Suddenly, Sheen turned to his host and said, "Tom, get me that woman." Puzzled, Henseler asked which one; there were some 250 people present. "The one in the yellow dress," he said, looking at a young woman perhaps 75 or 80 feet away. "I see trouble in her eyes." Sheen told Henseler to bring her into a room at the rectory, saying that the bishop wanted to speak with her, and to stand guard at the door to keep the meeting private. Henseler did as told, knowing that the woman in question was having serious marital problems. (He learned later that she was present only because someone offered her a ticket when she dropped off her daughter at the church to sing in the children's choir. She had not attended Mass in some five years.) After about twenty minutes, the two emerged from the room, Fulton with his arm around the woman. "This is one of God's children. She will be at Communion on Sundays," he told Henseler. "Now," he continued, "where's the press?"

After handling this delicate problem in private, he was willing to step back into the spotlight. He told no one of his meeting with the troubled lady. When Fr. Henseler recounted the story thirty-two years later, he choked up slightly as he recalled Sheen's supernatural kindness.[109]

∾

WHILE SHEEN WAS AWAY, rumors of the St. Bridget's offer began to leak out, largely through Finks, and there was talk of possible protests. Local urban renewal officials were unhappy, charging that HUD had gone over their heads in striking a deal with the bishop. Their own plans called for the retention of St. Bridget's.[110] Fr. Vogt's unhappiness was spreading through the congregation. Around the diocese, priests were up in arms over the bishop's exercise of his authority. Bishop Hickey suggested delay, but Sheen said that the matter had gone too far to turn back. Refusing to be deterred by "a few negative persons," Sheen issued a press release on February 28, 1968, Ash Wednesday, describing the deal he had made with the federal government.[111]

The *New York Times,* which first received the press release, noted that the property was worth $680,000 and included an acre and a half of land, a church, a rectory and a school. The parish was in an area targeted for urban renewal; demolition had begun in 1967. Weaver was quoted as saying that the offer was "excellent, feasible and most desirable." Sheen made his announcement on Ash Wednesday, he said, because the gift exemplified the Church's new concept of penance: that an act of charity is more meaningful than giving up meat on Fridays. A spokesman for the Archdiocese of New York told the *Times* that he was sure no comparable donation had ever been made by a Church prelate. A Catholic bishop, he added, has the right to dispose of any diocesan property as he chooses.[112]

The next morning, six pickets, students at Monroe Community College who had been working in the parish as volunteers, appeared outside the bishop's headquarters protesting the deal. They carried signs that read "Save St. Bridget's" and "God's House Belongs to His People." Fr. Vogt publicly called the bishop's gift a "mistake," adding, "there is enough property around without taking down the church and the school." He said that staff members of the church were "just sick" about the loss of the parish. A priest who declined to give his name told a reporter, "If the Bishop wants to make some grand gesture, he could move down here and live and then maybe he would be selling his books instead of giving away church property." The assistant pastor of St. Bridget's said that the telephone "hasn't stopped ringing and without exception the calls were adverse."

Sheen's initial comment to the press was harsh: "It is the need of the parish, of the diocese and all forces of the community to de-egotize their own interests."[113] Privately, however, he was agonizing. His usefulness in Rochester was over, he believed, and he decided to resign. "St. Bridget's was the last straw," Michael Hogan said later.[114]

That evening, while he visited a school, Sheen's car was surrounded by several hundred people gathered to protest "the destruction of our parish." Many threw pebbles at his car as the bishop passed.[115] Bitter telephone calls and letters poured in to his office.

Officers of the Priests' Association of Rochester (PAR), created in November 1966 and patterned after the outspoken Association of Chicago Priests, met with Fathers Finks and Vogt and drafted a letter urging Sheen to rescind the gift of property. Initially, there were twenty-two signers. The letter was delivered privately, with a request that the bishop receive at once an ad hoc committee of three priests to discuss the issue. As the hours passed and Sheen did not reply, over a hundred more priests added their signatures to the letter. Three of the signatories were members of the Board of Consultors who had earlier approved the gift.[116] Finks was now an outspoken critic, going to the local newspaper with his complaints. The *Rochester Democrat and Chronicle* condemned the bishop's action and backed the protestors. Sheen had a full-blown mutiny on his hands.[117]

Nothing in his life had prepared Fulton for this. He had almost always been popular, admired, favored, obeyed. Indeed, the entire structure of the Church, during his lifetime and for many centuries before, had been based on authority and obedience. That vital tradition was now crumbling around him in Rochester. Suddenly he was a tyrant, roasted in the press, denounced by priests and people of his own diocese. And all, he thought, because of his desire to help the poor. (A few months earlier, Sheen's friend and one-time confessor James Francis Cardinal McIntyre was similarly stunned and angered when a community of nuns, eager to carry out Vatican II reforms and more than a little influenced by feminism, challenged his authority. He too would face pickets before he retired.)[118] Several priests quietly visited the bishop, telling him that he would have to reverse the proposal or risk tearing the fabric of the diocese.[119]

On March 3, Fulton rescinded the offer to the federal government and made himself unavailable for public comment.[120] The local newspaper ran the headline "ST. BRIDGET'S SPARED; JOY REIGNS."[121] The parish had a "victory breakfast."[122]

Press accounts failed to give Sheen credit for his consultative efforts. The Priests' Association of Rochester objected to the deal on the ground that the bishop had not conferred with anyone in advance, which was untrue. Still, Sheen had clearly acted in undue haste, no doubt wanting to capture large headlines on Ash Wednesday. Perhaps if he had waited, gone out of his way to reach out to his clergy and laity, expressed his humility and good will, as he often had throughout his life, the incident could have been settled amicably. Pastor Vogt said later that if the bishop had first asked the people of his parish, they would probably have given him permission to give away the church and its property.[123] But Sheen's pride had been deeply wounded and his confidence in the protesting diocesan clergy shattered. Believing himself betrayed and rejected, he thought it time to heed the Lord's command to the Apostles when confronting a hostile town—to shake the dust off his feet.

In 1974, Sheen told a priest, Fr. Patrick Collins, about the St. Bridget's incident. Collins later wrote, "The pain was still palpable as he related the incidents to me that night. When he looked out his window and saw the pickets, said Sheen, 'That night, that very night, I resigned as Bishop of Rochester. It took Pope Paul VI some time to accept it. But that night, as far as I was concerned, I left Rochester.'" Collins added, "My sense was that he was still badly bruised by the experience and felt deeply the rejection and hurt. It seemed clear to me also that he failed to understand that he had brought the trouble on himself by failing to be a consultative bishop."[124]

Sheen revealed in his autobiography that he was at last sensitive to this charge. He stressed the daily meetings all officials of the Pastoral Office had, "to review common problems, personnel, requests and petitions. This was done in order to avoid individual and arbitrary action on the part of the bishop, and to receive benefit of the corporate judgment of those who were closely associated." He also noted that he had nominated the auxiliary bishops following a vote of the clergy naming the two men in question as outstanding priests in the diocese.

Fulton's account of the St. Bridget's incident emphasized his contacts with Rome early in the project. Opposition, he charged, was "artificially stimulated," but he failed to say by whom. He bitterly remarked that the St. Bridget's church, rectory and school were still standing, empty and abandoned in the inner city, "a monument to my failure to do anything about housing." He attributed his own resignation simply to old age.[125]

When the disaster of St. Bridget's occurred, Sheen had been the bishop of Rochester for only fifteen months. An immediate departure would probably not have been sanctioned by the Vatican. Fulton did not literally send in his resignation after he saw the pickets, but he knew that when the time was right, he would go to Paul VI and state his case.

After St. Bridget's, Sheen was not as buoyant or as optimistic or as venturesome as he had been. Finks observed, "He began to draw back into deepening seclusion, writing rambling jeremiads in the weekly *Catholic Courier-Journal,* sallying forth only for ceremonial occasions."[126] Sheen memorized the names of the 125 priests who had signed the petition against him, and when one of them would come up, he would say (no doubt resentfully), "He signed the list."[127] But the bishop continued to carry out his duties, and he made several further efforts to leave a positive legacy in the diocese.

Sheen remained interested in low-income housing. On April 16, 1968, the Bishop Sheen Housing Foundation was created. It was based on an earlier idea of having seventy "disciples" donate $10 a week for twenty-four weeks to build a housing fund. The initial achievements were modest but noteworthy: by the time Sheen left the diocese, eighteen low-income families had become homeowners. In 1980, a Sheen successor, Bishop Matthew H. Clark, united the Housing Foundation with a housing commission operated by the Episcopal Diocese of Rochester to create the Bishop Sheen Ecumenical Housing Foundation. It continues operating to this day.[128]

Sheen began a campaign against the construction of multimillion-dollar churches in July. Postwar church construction had skyrocketed from $26 million in 1945 to over $1 billion in 1960, and was still climbing.[129] In speeches, radio addresses and public statements, Sheen contended that funds being spent on lavish structures could be better spent on the poor. Moreover, existing churches should be devoted to more than worship, he said; they should be seen "as a place for service, mission, and caring." In a written statement titled "The Shape of the Church to Come," Sheen declared, "Because of its enlarged mission, the church will be a center for those who care spiritually for God, but also it will be a center for educational, physical, psychological and medical care for all who come to Christ." New church buildings, he said, "will fulfill the double commandment of serving God and neighbor; they will unite liturgy and service of neighbor as they were united by our Lord the night He instituted the eucharist."

In a talk in the small village of Prattsburg, Sheen suggested that some churches could be converted into motion-picture theaters for educational films, and into cafeterias for feeding the poor and the aged when not in use for religious services. He also proposed that affluent churchgoers in suburban parishes stock inner-city parishes with food and clothing, and that local hospitals contribute free medicine and personnel to church-housed dispensaries.

Fulton had now gone considerably beyond his attempt to donate church property to the federal government. But that failed effort was still very much on his mind. During a television interview, he said that the attempt fell through when parishioners complained. In short, the people of St. Bridget's, not their bishop, were to blame for rejecting a vision of charity and mercy based on the commands of Jesus Christ.[130]

$\sim$

THE SUMMER OF 1968 was the apex of the most revolutionary year of the century. The assassinations of Martin Luther King Jr. and Robert Kennedy, riots in 125 cities, and much-publicized battles waged between police and demonstrators at the Democratic National Convention convinced many that the country, if not the world, was coming apart. Polls showed that Americans were losing their trust in the nation's institutions, and the churches, often sympathetic to the cultural rebellion under way, were not immune from the growing cynicism. A Gallup poll taken that year showed that 67 percent of the public thought religion was losing its impact on society, five times the number who thought so a decade earlier.

In the middle of this firestorm, Paul VI issued *Humanae Vitae*, condemning artificial contraception as a form of birth control for Catholics. This hit American Catholics hard. Not only were most in favor of birth control, but they had read many predictions that the traditional teaching would be abandoned in the Church's quest to be more in harmony with the modern world. (It was revealed later that the Pope had overturned a decision of his top advisory committee.) Catholic scholar Ralph M. McInerny later contended that *Humanae Vitae*, not Vatican II, caused revolt in the Church, led by dissenting theologians.[131]

Many in the Diocese of Rochester were surprised and angered by their bishop's defense of both Paul VI and *Humanae Vitae*.[132] Perhaps they expected Sheen, heralded by radical *Ramparts* magazine as a left-wing Catholic, "the social butterfly of the Renewal Movement," to join the outcry.[133] If they did, they failed to understand him. Not only did he champion Paul VI personally, but he believed, as he always had, that the Holy Father expressed the mind of Christ. In April 1968, in an article published in the English edition of *L'Osservatore Romano* (the daily newspaper that since 1861 had been the voice of the Holy See), he repeated his belief in an essential Church teaching: "We reaffirm our allegiance to the Voice of Peter in Paul VI, for we know that we share in Christ's prayer for His Church only to the extent that we are united with Peter."[134] In so believing, Sheen was endorsing current as well as ancient teaching. The same point was clearly made in chapters two and three of *Lumen Gentium*, the "Dogmatic Constitution on the Church," written during Vatican II and promulgated by Paul VI. In his autobiography, Fulton prefaced a chapter on papal audiences with a brief sentence: "Where Peter is, there is the Church."[135]

Sheen had always opposed contraception and abortion and favored large families.[136] He continued to do so, likening birth control to violence. D. P. Noonan recalled, "Sheen always referred to birth control as birth patrol, for those who practice it, according to him, believe neither in birth nor control."[137]

Sheen's unhappiness in Rochester was intensified by an accident. On January 15, 1969, while at the Sisters of St. Joseph Convent in suburban Pitsford, he slipped on a patch of ice and broke his left arm.[138]

In May, Fulton quietly went to Rome, obtained a private audience with Paul VI, and submitted his resignation. The Pope reluctantly agreed to the request, promising to accept the resignation later that year.[139]

But Sheen still had much to do in Rochester before his departure. On June 1, he ordained Michael Cole, a former Anglican priest who was married and the father of four, to the permanent diaconate. Cole became the first permanent deacon in the United States. Sheen also named him head of the Family Life Organization in the diocese. The bishop had met Cole in 1968 while on a fruitless trip to Ireland and England seeking priests and vocations for the Diocese of Rochester. An English Catholic bishop introduced Cole to Sheen, and Fulton's impetuous "reading" of the young man prompted an invitation to Rochester and a promise to take care of the entire Cole family. The move proved unsatisfactory to all concerned. The Family Life assignment was especially difficult because the young convert had to defend *Humanae Vitae* without sufficient training. After Sheen retired, Cole returned to England and to Anglicanism.[140]

Sheen also had to deal with the future of St. Bernard's Seminary, which was running short of funds and students. In early June, the bishop suspended discussions of closer ties to the Rochester Center for Theological Studies, a corporation chartered a year earlier uniting St. Bernard's in certain ways with Bexley Hall, a small Episcopal seminary in Ohio, and Colgate Rochester Divinity School, a nondenominational institution. Sheen had supported the interdenominational concept, especially as it preserved "integration with identity." But racial disturbances at Colgate Rochester in March, magnified by a spineless response from seminary officials, prompted

Sheen to delay matters for a year. "Perhaps by that time," he wrote, "through the grace of God, calmness and sound judgment will prevail again in our nation and among our people."[141]

Sheen and Fr. Finks were now at loggerheads, engaging in several fist-pounding conversations that produced nothing but antipathy. Finks was a man of the Sixties, eager for "power to the people," and eager for personal authority as well. He was interested in organization and bureaucracy. Fulton had a more traditional approach to helping the poor, preferring to give the hungry food and the thirsty drink; he was bored by endless meetings, puzzled by images of black gloved fists shooting into the air, and angered by threats to burn down cities. However hard Fulton tried to be current and modern, it was almost inevitable that Finks and others would dismiss him as an old man who just didn't understand.[142]

On September 20, 1969, Fulton marked his fiftieth anniversary as a priest. He produced a twenty-page booklet for the occasion, distributed to friends, but asked that there be no celebration. The booklet, containing a photograph of Paul VI and Sheen, presented a series of brief observations stressing faithfulness to the Church, obedience to the Holy Father, and love for all the peoples of the world. There was also an oblique reference to his experience in Rochester:

> *Fourth, as bishop, I might, as head*
> *Feel the pain of every member of the Body.*
> *And as a weak cell of that Body,*
> *Sense unity with brother priests*
> *Who love that head whose name is Peter.*[143]

The Vatican announced Sheen's retirement in mid-October. At seventy-four, he was said to be retiring due to age. He was made the titular archbishop of Newport, on the Isle of Wight. Fulton was soon fond of saying that being the archbishop of an ancient Christian seat "is very much like being made a Knight of the Garter. It is an honor to have the Garter, but it does not hold up anything." He was later made assistant at the Pontifical Throne. In his autobiography,

Fulton called this an honor, "because my heart was always at the Throne of Peter."[144]

Sheen held a news conference in Rochester to discuss his resignation and introduce his successor, Msgr. Joseph L. Hogan, fifty-three, the brother of his private secretary. Simultaneous announcements of resignations and appointments had become a regular policy within the Church over the past nine months, angering many reform-minded priests in America who sought a voice in the selection process. What they did not know was that Paul VI had allowed his old friend the right to name his successor. Early in his tenure, Fulton had personally chosen Hogan, "sensing" that he should be the next bishop. Hogan, tall, good-looking, highly educated and popular, never knew why Sheen selected him.[145]

Fulton did not endorse the Vatican's claim that he was retiring due to age. When asked about his physical condition, he said he felt fit. "I just canceled my tennis in order to see you," he told reporters. "I am resigning the diocese. I am not resigning work. I am not retiring. I am regenerating." He said he expected to return to New York "to teach any place I can, do TV and enter into dialogue with unbelievers."

The press dwelt on the often controversial decisions made by the bishop in Rochester, and he addressed several of them. He said he could recite a long litany of his failures but was proud of several achievements, including the certified auditing of the diocese's finances, consultation with his priests on new appointments, and the purchase of homes for indigent slum families. "I move too fast," he said. "I'm a little too progressive."

In the front-page *New York Times* story, Rochester priests were said to have become disenchanted with the bishop because he failed to follow through on his own ideas or respond to the ideas of others. One young priest said, "He urged people to write him about their problems, but when they did they got form letters in response." Other troubles were recalled, including the St. Bridget's affair, and Sheen was said to have become disenchanted with Fr. Finks. The priests of the diocese were reported to be "overjoyed" by the choice of Hogan.[146]

When Fr. Shamon drove Sheen to the airport to leave Rochester, Fulton said, "Vicar, it used to be a glory to be a Bishop. But today, I would not wish it for my best friend."[147]

Two weeks later, Sheen appeared on the popular television program *60 Minutes*, hosted by CBS newsman Mike Wallace. In the course of the brief interview, Fulton said he continued to believe that the United States should pull out of Vietnam immediately. He spoke of his strong commitment to civil rights. Without mentioning Cardinal Spellman, he said also that he might have gone farther in the Church, "But I refused to pay the price." Wallace asked him what the price was. Fulton evaded the question, saying simply, "Well, I felt it would be disloyalty to my own principles and I think to Christian practice." There were simply things he would not do to become a cardinal. Wallace did not pursue the issue.

The thirty-four months in Rochester were discussed briefly. When asked why he became an innovator, Fulton replied that he was trying to carry out the teachings of Vatican II and thought he had made a difference. He said, "I was never given a chance to administer a diocese before. I am a man of ideas. I have been thinking these problems through for many years; this was the first opportunity that I had to implement them."[148]

ELEVEN

Frail Defender

*S*heen returned to Rochester on November 28, 1969, to serve as co-consecrator for his successor, Joseph Hogan.[1] He was undoubtedly relieved to be rid of his diocesan duties and responsibilities. And yet, as his autobiography makes clear, he grieved over his defeat in Rochester. His sorrow focused not so much on the actions that led him to resign, as on his own failure to achieve more during his time in the diocese. He had wanted, for example, to persuade a hospital to provide an ambulance, two nurses and an intern, a few days a week, to give medical assistance to the poor, particularly in the inner city. He had hoped to rent areas in large supermarkets where priests could reach out to the people. He had wanted to help the poor through public housing, which is why he offered St. Bridget's church to the federal government. All of these proposals came to nothing, and Sheen, in large part, blamed himself.[2] He had also failed to win the loyalty and love of his priests, his fellow shepherds. When one hundred of them turned against him, at the height of the St. Bridget's controversy, the pain was excruciating. Sheen felt that he had failed in his opportunity to move closer to the image of the Church prescribed by the Second Vatican Council. As he would soon write to Clare Boothe Luce, "the more you love, the more you suffer."[3]

Toward the end of his tenure in Rochester, Fulton asked his niece Joan (now Mrs. Jerry Cunningham) to find him a small apartment in New York. When she balked at the request, citing the extreme difficulty of securing housing in the city, Fulton repeated an axiom he had used for many years: "You can always do whatever you want to." Joan and her husband soon found a suitable apartment at 500 East Seventy-seventh Street.[4]

Before leaving Rochester, Fulton began giving away portions of his huge personal library. He offered Fr. Alfred Shamon his complete Scripture collection, explaining that he would have only three rooms in New York.[5] He gave a large number of his own books to St. Bernard's Seminary in Rochester.[6] He also deposited a number of tapes of his television shows in the seminary library.[7] The Cunninghams helped Sheen select furnishings for his new home, and friends moved him in.[8]

The apartment was upscale, with a fine view of the East River. David and Julie Eisenhower were neighbors. Fulton converted a second bedroom into a chapel, carpeted in blue. Matthew Paratore, a friend from Rochester who visited several times, thought it "an old lady's apartment," having frilly curtains and a glass bowl full of cheap little medals the archbishop would give to guests.[9] In early December, Sheen wrote to Vincent and Marian Cahill, "I am still unpacking and arranging the apartment, as well as developing 'dishpan hands' as I learn to cook. I never thought I would end up washing dishes and making my own bed. It is not an unhappy adventure."[10]

Most men in their seventy-fifth year would be ready to retire, yet Fulton was as eager as ever to travel, write, teach, preach and administer the sacraments. As he later put it, "If we live intensely, I believe that somehow or other we can work up until the day God draws the line and says: 'Now it is finished.' "[11] He quickly began accepting invitations. Edythe Brownett was again handling the bishop's mail, appointments and travel arrangements.

But the world Fulton encountered in 1969 and 1970 was very different from the old one, in which families sang around the piano, enjoyed church socials, and laughed at the antics of Red Skelton and Ozzie and Harriet. The war in Vietnam continued to rage, stirring demonstrations, violence and disillusionment within the United States. The Woodstock festival brought together some four hundred thousand young people to display their lack of inhibitions and their "flower child" conformity. Homosexuals, now calling themselves "gay," were rebelling against the "straight" norm. Feminists were pushing the Equal Rights Amendment. National Guard troops killed four students and wounded nine during demonstrations at Kent State University. Radical students blew up an entire building at the University of Wisconsin-Madison, killing a graduate student. New Left scholars were reinterpreting the past and viewing the present in the light of Marxism. The economy was slumping. Pornography, rock music, drugs, free sex, long hair, and informal and outlandish dress became mainstays of the national culture, embraced and amplified by the major media. The era over which Eisenhower had presided and in which *Life Is Worth Living* flourished was frequently ridiculed, sometimes as the "Ike Age."

The Catholic Church in the United States, along with the mainline Protestant denominations, reflected all this social turmoil. In both cases, the upheaval could be traced in large part to the intellectual elites who controlled major seminaries, religious periodicals and denominational machinery. More rapidly than the society at large, they were moving to the left, challenging tradition and authority and often the very basics of the Christian faith itself.

The Mass that Catholics had known, the fasting they had endured, several saints they had venerated, the liturgy they had memorized, the church music they had long been accustomed to—all were vanishing. Many old churches were stripped of their statues, tabernacles and kneelers. Many new churches looked like gymnasiums. Then too, there were the angry priests, nuns and monks who either left the Church, often to get married, or remained to doff their habits and work tirelessly to mold the Church into a vessel of the far Left, as they claimed—without convincing evidence—was intended by the Second Vatican Council.

Much of the rebellion within the Catholic Church began in the late 1960s, while Sheen was in Rochester. Twenty-six Catholic educators, representing ten institutions of higher education, met in Land o' Lakes, Wisconsin, and declared their independence of Church authority. Fr. Charles Curran at Catholic University led a bold assault on *Humanae Vitae*. (It took nineteen years, at Rome's insistence, to fire the dissident theologian.) The School Sisters of St. Francis in Milwaukee radically reorganized their order, invited Fr. Daniel Berrigan to speak on "The World in Revolution," and defied Roman instructions to resist secularization. Fr. James Groppi of Milwaukee made headlines as a fiery civil rights activist. The Immaculate Heart of Mary Community in California rose up against James Cardinal McIntyre and the Holy See, virtually abolishing their own order. Fr. Raymond Brown's *Priest and Bishop* challenged the authenticity of the priesthood and Apostolic Succession. Sociologist and best-selling novelist Fr. Andrew Greeley was becoming a major spokesman of the Left, specializing in disdain for hierarchical authority (once calling John Cardinal Cody "a madcap tyrant") and objection to *Humanae Vitae*. The National Conference of Catholic Bishops, created in 1966 as the successor to the National Catholic Welfare Conference, fell under liberal control, sanctioning and encouraging an assortment of liturgical novelties and in general pushing the American Church to the left. Fr. Theodore Hesburgh, the president of Notre Dame, became a highly popular liberal leader, inside and outside the Church. The Jesuits, once the soul of orthodoxy, became models of contemporary liberal activism.[12] By 1972, ex-Father T. Joseph O'Donoghue boasted in the pages of the liberal *National Catholic Reporter*:

> *Liberal Catholics have a locktight grip on the publication of catechisms and religious formation texts, and a similarly tight grip on university religious education departments, which train religious teachers at all levels. Liberal Catholics have mastered the techniques of designing structures and liaison patterns to multiply total impact. Pity the poor establishment, which sees the once docile Catholic populace of its area now constantly infused by liberal itinerants whose words endure in small but solid local liberal movements.[13]*

Numerous scholars and journalists have attempted to describe the causes of the rebellion that swept the American Church after

Vatican II. In large part, of course, it was a reflection of the times. No institution in America, with the possible exception of the armed services, was left unaffected by the storms of the Sixties. A prominent feature of the era, in all walks of life, was a growing passion to spurn the past and reject traditional authority, leaving all rules to the individual. This was true for the Church as well. Conservative historian James Hitchcock argued in 1979 that "it was finally the denial of the Absolute, or more accurately the flight from it, which was the essence of the Catholic crisis.... Unless the fact is recognized that ego-assertion—against institutions, superiors, laws, creeds—has now become more than a right, in fact a duty, much of what is happening in the contemporary Church will remain unintelligible."[14]

It was one thing for, say, the United Church of Christ to absorb and emulate the culture of the period; this liberal Protestant denomination had long accommodated itself to its cultural surroundings and had proudly given the individual responsibility for answering a great many of life's deepest problems. (The essence of Reformation theology, enhanced by the American experience, centers on the autonomy of the individual and the primacy of individual conscience.) But it was another thing for Catholics. Church authority was at the heart of their faith. The Holy Spirit, it had been believed from the beginning, guided Christ's one, holy, Catholic and apostolic Church. The denial of Church authority by prominent Catholic theologians and by legions of clergy and religious, accompanied by sweeping changes in worship services and disciplinary practices, left millions of Catholics dazed and angry. *Humanae Vitae* compounded matters by making a majority of Catholics in America and elsewhere in the West aware of their personal doubts about the supreme and infallible wisdom of Rome.

The price for abandoning authority and tradition and embracing the world has long been known to be expensive for Christian churches. Jewish scholar Will Herberg, speaking before a national convention of Catholics belonging to the Newman Apostolate, criticized many Catholic intellectuals for urging the Church to "slough off its old ways and bring itself up to date by adjusting itself to the spirit of the age." Herberg declared, "I say just the opposite: in all that is important, the Church must stand firm in its witness to the truth that is eternal and unchanging; it needs no updating.... If it is to remain true to its vocation, it must take its stand against the world, against the age, against the spirit of the age—because the world and the age are always, to a degree, to an important degree, in rebellion against God."[15] Similarly, National Council of Churches official Dean M. Kelley argued, in *Why Conservative Churches Are Growing*, that "reasonable," "tolerant," "relevant," and undemanding churches die because they fail to offer the spiritual rigor, the religious authority, and the supernatural emphasis people need. But too few Catholic leaders paid attention.[16]

After the 1960s, the decline in the number of clergy and religious and seminarians was dramatic. The number of Catholic sisters per 10,000 Catholics in the United States, for example, fell from 39.4 in 1965 to 18.1 in 1990. The looming priest shortage had less to do with defections than with the dearth of young men pursuing vocations.[17] At the same time, there was a serious drop in religious commitment among most Catholic laity, as measured by church attendance, frequency of confession, participation in church activities, financial contributions, and even daily prayer. Sociologists Roger Finke and Rodney Stark have concluded, "Recent declines in the vigor of American Catholicism reflect one more cycle of the sect-church process whereby a faith becomes a mainline body and then begins to wilt."[18]

Most Catholics were thoroughly assimilated into the secular culture by the 1970s and 1980s, being prosperous and well educated, having small families, and generally placing their individual judgment above that of the Church. In 1974, a national survey showed that only 12 percent of Catholics would acknowledge the Pope as having the right to "mandate issues of birth control."[19] In the late 1980s, three in four Catholics told pollsters they were more likely to rely on their own consciences than on papal teachings.[20] By the early 1990s, Americans were more likely to stray from the Catholic Church than from any other major religious group.[21]

Archbishop Sheen, of course, was fully aware of the turmoil plaguing the Church in the late 1960s. Though at all times staunchly defending the Second Vatican Council, he was displeased by certain developments he and many others had not anticipated when they voted for the historic documents that modernized the Church. As early as April 1966, Sheen expressed unhappiness with English translations of the Gospels, the Mass and the Missal, thinking them designed to please the least literate of Catholics.[22] In 1975, he expressed reservations about the liturgical experimentation going on as well as the lack of instruction available. "I say that the laity of this country are in an uproar against the want of religious teaching or catechetical training, both in the schools and in the pulpit."[23] He was highly critical of the abandonment of habits by religious. In a 1975 speech in Peoria, he began, "Most Reverend Bishop O'Rourke, Reverend Fathers, Recognizable Sisters, and friends."[24] In a letter to a mother superior, he quoted chapter and verse from Church documents showing that it was forbidden for religious to wear secular apparel.[25] In 1976, he wrote to John Cardinal Carberry of St. Louis, "As the sense of the Sacred diminishes, Sisters in pants distribute communion, while priests sit idle in the sanctuary. This 'option' results from a decay of the reverence for the Lord's Presence."[26]

Many new church buildings failed to win the archbishop's approval. "The ancient architecture was always using material things as signs of something spiritual. But today our architecture is flat, nothing but steel and glass, almost like a crackerbox. Why? Well, because our architects have no spiritual message to convey."[27] He was highly critical of modern theologians who refused to discuss sin, repentance, hell and Satan. "The demonic is always most powerful when he is denied."[28]

Sheen was appalled as well by the extremely casual clothes that people were beginning to wear to church on Sunday. The sight of people receiving the Eucharist without confession of serious sins, and dashing out of the Mass immediately after receiving the Host, left him sorrowful. He had no sympathy for the cries from the left that women be priests. "If the Lord wanted women to be priests, instead of symbolizing the Church," Sheen asserted, "He would have made His Immaculate Virgin Mother a priest."[29] The archbishop told one audience,

> *We have moved away from the standard of Christ to the standard of the world. We do not ask ourselves, "Does this please Christ?" but "Does this please the world?" So I will dress and act in such a way that I will not be separate from the world; I want to be with it. We marry this age, and we become a widow in the next one. We take on its verbiage, its fashions. This is one reason for so much instability in the church today: the sand on which we are walking is shifting. We've given up the rock which is Christ.*[30]

In his autobiography, Sheen declared that the confusion and agitation among Catholics following Vatican II were inevitable.

> *It is a historical fact that whenever there is an outpouring of the Holy Spirit as in a General Council of the Church, there is always an extra show of force by the anti-Spirit or the demonic. Even at the beginning, immediately after Pentecost and the descent of the Spirit upon the Apostles, there began a persecution and the murder of Stephen. If a General Council did not provoke the spirit of turbulence, one might almost doubt the operation of the Third Person of the Trinity over the Assembly.*[31]

In time, Sheen believed, the Church would cope with all the problems it faced, as it always had. Yet he had no illusions about the impact of radical social and ecclesiastical change. He said simply that he expected the Church to become smaller but more effective. He told television interviewer Bill Moyers in 1973, "We will become less and less. Those who influence society, as Toynbee says, belong to the creative minority."[32]

There were many things about the era as a whole that Fulton found objectionable. He was angered, for example, by *Roe v. Wade*, the Supreme Court decision of 1973 legalizing abortion on demand.

He once told Sister Marlene Brownett, "Marlene, in the future you will be known as a Catholic not because you defend, honor, and declare yourself as a follower of Christ, but because you defend LIFE!"[33] He told an audience in Philadelphia:

> *Notice that the heavenly messenger did not tell Mary that she would conceive a fetus. No! She would conceive and bear a Son, a person, a Child of the Most High God. It was inconceivable to her that because of her poverty, the overpopulation in Bethlehem, inadequate housing and the shame attached to the unusual nature of her conception that she would thwart the life within her, as some women do today. Life is sacred.*[34]

Sheen often excoriated the public's fascination with sex divorced from love and marriage, observing that "Sex in a human being is not the same as sex in a pig."[35] He found nothing new in the youth culture of the period, or in student radicalism. "All their plans for a revolutionary take-over of society were tried in the last forty years by youths who wore red shirts, brown shirts, and black shirts," he wrote.[36] Hippies were trying hopelessly to be monks without God, "Jeremiahs without Israel, prodigals without a father's house, an unpenitential society—opposing gurus of the concrete desert."[37] Sheen also preached against the widespread compassion expressed toward criminals, especially by judges "who, fearful of restraining a liberty turned into license, pardon the mugger and ignore the mugged."[38]

The increasing pragmatism of American life was a frequent Sheen target. He told Bill Moyers in a television interview of "a decline in justice, honor, decency, purity and the like." This, he believed, stemmed from the public's blindness toward natural law. "This country lacks an objective and a philosophy of life. In order to discipline oneself, one has to see a higher standard of values.... There is not a great deal of public virtue when pragmatism rules, because everything is decided by utility. And once utility takes over, then nothing is virtuous. If a thing is useful for me, then I will do it. If it is profitable for me, then I will do it."[39]

Christendom, thought Sheen, had come to an end. "Christendom is the political, economic, moral, social, legal life of a nation as inspired by the gospel ethic. That is finished. Abortion, the breakdown of family life, dishonesty, even the natural virtues upon which the supernatural virtues were based, are being discredited." But it was far from the end of Christianity.[40]

Sheen could not repress his basic optimism, and he saw the present as a challenge. He told Moyers: "These are wonderful times in which to be alive because 30 years ago, and in other days, when we were moral, when we had a spirit of work in the United States, not a spirit of sloth and avoiding responsibility, it was easy to be good, it was easy to be American, it was easy to be Christian. Today, it's hard. You're being tested." Using a favorite sentence of his from G. K. Chesterton, he continued, "Dead bodies float downstream— it takes a live body to resist the current. And that's why these are great days. They are struggle, and I love them."[41]

Sheen also expected that in a short time the country would right itself, abandoning secularism and hedonism and returning to the faith and objective moral standards it once had. In a newspaper column republished in *Children and Parents,* he cited sociologist Pitrim A. Sorokin, who argued that all societies revolve through a three-stage cycle: sensuality, disintegration, and morality. Sheen wrote, "We are presently on the eve of the third. All of us will live to see the reaction setting in."[42]

The archbishop believed that one of the forces leading to the restoration of righteousness was the law enforcement agencies of the nation, in particular the FBI. In Cleveland to celebrate a Mass for Law Day in May 1969, he told the special agent in charge of the Cleveland office that J. Edgar Hoover was one of the greatest men in the country, and again voiced his admiration for the work of the bureau. That was music to the exceedingly vain director's ears.

Sheen exchanged friendly letters with Hoover after his resignation from Rochester, and accepted an invitation to lead the annual FBI Men's Retreat in Faulkner, Maryland, in early 1970.[43] When he was hospitalized in February for a week, suffering from a severe cold and laryngitis, Hoover sent him a personal letter, saying, "I did want you to know that the thoughts and prayers of your friends in the FBI are with you, and we wish you a complete recovery." Sheen remained on the bureau's special correspondents list.[44]

In late 1969, David Frost interviewed Sheen on his national television program. The archbishop defended priestly celibacy, the Pope's stand against artificial birth control, and his own opposition to the Vietnam War. He agreed to back President Nixon in his effort to end hostilities in Vietnam. "Christian war is never justified," he said. A secular war may be necessary in defense of country, but "never, never an offensive war. I think we must begin to make wars against war."

Frost pressed Sheen on the birth control issue, raising the example of a married couple that did not want or dared not have more children. Would you advise the man and woman to stop making love? he asked. "I say to them," Sheen replied, "I am still convinced that this is not right, but under the circumstances you must trust in the mercy of God. And you continue to make love." Frost asked if the advice would extend to the continuance of love-making "with birth control." Perhaps Fulton took a deep breath before responding. He then said, "Yes, with birth control. . . . Believe me, this is a question of anguish." He continued, "And we must admit that there are cases that tear your heart out, and concessions are made to these people. No one ever lays the finger on them and says that this is a sin. Here is only a moral guide. This is the ideal. This is the law. Not all of us keep the law." In "anguish" cases, he said, "I sympathize with all these people with all of my heart. And so does the Church. And that was also the way the Holy Father concluded and he begged them over and over to trust in the mercy of God, and to abide in prayer."[45]

This was the only recorded instance in which Sheen modified his view of *Humanae Vitae*. The response also marks one of the extremely rare times in his life that Sheen took a position openly at odds with Church teaching. No doubt this is why he quickly added that the Pope and the Church itself empathized with those facing the thorny issue.

෴

ACCOMPANIED BY FR. Michael Hogan, Sheen traveled to Dublin in August 1971 to speak at the Carmelite Church. An estimated twenty-five million viewers throughout Europe saw the Mass, televised in color, which marked the seventh centenary of the Carmelites in Ireland.[46]

Sheen soon returned to Lourdes, again with Sister Marlene. She later recalled two others who sometimes accompanied Fulton to Lourdes. Fr. Vincent Nugent had lived with Sheen at the brownstone on Thirty-eighth Street and was a friend and secretary. He wrote for *Worldmission* and served as the Society's staff missiologist. Edward T. O'Meara, Sheen's longtime assistant and successor at the Society for the Propagation of the Faith, was also a loyal and trusted friend. According to Joan Sheen Cunningham, he was a "sounding board" for Fulton's sorrows over the years.[47] When Sheen returned to New York, Nugent and O'Meara were closer to him than any other priests.

Throughout the early 1970s, Sheen continued to travel, preach and write. In 1972, for example, he journeyed to Orange County, California, to preach at Robert Schuller's huge Garden Grove Community Church. The two thousand seats in the sanctuary and on the lawn were supplemented with four thousand folding chairs for those who came to hear Fulton Sheen's sermon. "The message he gave made a profound impression on my mind," Schuller said later, adding, "He was my friend."[48]

On August 7, 1973, the archbishop spoke before an enormous audience of Lutheran youth in the Houston Astrodome.[49] At seventy-seven years of age, he was away from home three weeks of every month. He still believed in a line he had written in 1939: "Burning the candle at both ends for God's sake may be foolishness to the world, but it is a profitable Christian exercise—for so much better the light!"[50]

In Boston for a three-hour Good Friday service in the Civic Auditorium, in March 1973, Sheen granted an interview to a *Boston*

Globe reporter that was unusually revealing. He talked about giving away almost everything he had earned over the years, some $10 million he said, "to the poor and the hungry and the forgotten people of the world." While his income remained in excess of six figures from writing, lecturing, and public appearances, he kept only a small amount, he said, to cover household expenses and hamburger. "I cook a lot of hamburger because the pleasure of eating it is never exceeded by the pain of washing the dishes." He had no housekeeper for his three-room apartment, he said, and the dusting didn't get done. "All of us came from dust, so I am reminded constantly about the dust to which I am returning."

Fulton spoke of his desire to return to television and of the resistance he faced from studio executives, whom he called "office dinosaurs." While the public would like to see another Sheen show, "The media of communications does not want the 'peace' of American minds disturbed by an ethical evaluation of our morals—the business of our family life, marriage, and the like."

The elderly archbishop impressed the reporter as being unusually spry and lively. He noted also that Sheen could not weigh more than 125 pounds, "a circumstance that lends an ascetic gauntness to his features." Fulton boasted of his continued tennis playing and his commitment to good health. "I have to keep fit physically because I preach a lot of retreats for priests and nuns. This is a task requiring that I talk a half-dozen times a day for 30 or 40 minutes, standing on my feet without notes. So my legs and my lungs must be kept strong, just as my mind must be kept alert."

Sheen spoke of his delight at being in Boston during Easter week. "I love Boston more than I do any other city because its people have a culture and refinement that sets them apart. One of my big regrets is that I wasn't born here."[51] There was little chance that the folks back in El Paso and Peoria would see the interview.

Later that year, Sheen was at the Friar's Club of California, participating in a banquet honoring his old rival for ratings, comedian Milton Berle, for his six decades in show business. The archbishop paid an extraordinarily warm tribute to his longtime friend. In his autobiography, published the following year, Berle quoted from the speech at length.[52]

That fall, Fulton returned to the Carmelite church in Dublin to preach and celebrate Mass. He was deeply impressed by the Carmelite Fathers; it was his third visit to the parish in five years.[53]

In early 1974, Sheen told a friend in Germany that during the first two months of the year, he would be traveling thirty thousand miles, giving retreats and lectures. He was also completing a book, *Those Mysterious Priests*.[54] That spring, Fulton wrote casually to Vincent and Marian Cahill, "I am giving a retreat in Oregon and then leave for several lectures throughout the country."[55] And yet, Sheen could tell one audience, "I've been a priest for fifty-five years, for which I thank God. I was doing much better thirty years ago in my own mind than I am now. Now I feel as if I have done so little."[56]

Many who observed this frail defender of the faith on his whirlwind tours must have wondered how long he could continue. The extraordinary energy he expended would have worn out healthy men fifteen years his junior. At times, there were signs that not all was well. In Albany, New York, in 1974, Sheen began hiccupping violently during an address to the chamber of commerce. The hiccupping continued to the point that Edwin Broderick, Fulton's former television director and now bishop of Albany, offered to take him to the local emergency room. Sheen refused, asking Broderick to call his brother Tom. Fulton flew into Manhattan and was met by his brother at the airport. He then spent the next three weeks in Lenox Hospital.[57]

Somehow, Sheen arranged another television series, this time with a public broadcasting station in Toledo, Ohio. In 1974 and 1975, he did thirteen "non-religious" half-hour programs, filmed in color, under the title *What Now America?* Rediscovered in the mid-1990s by Dan Morgan, a former announcer for Sheen's programs, the tapes show the deterioration of Fulton's telegenic presence.

The archbishop wore only regular clerical apparel on the series; even the pectoral cross was gone. The stage contained simply a blackboard and an American flag. The first program opened with

"Long time, no Sheen," and the audience response was more like a murmur than a laugh. The program was devoted to patriotism, and Sheen thundered on about moral deterioration, citing, inevitably, Toynbee's judgment about civilizations rotting from within. The second program was devoted to the subject of youth. Sheen's generalities were sweeping and at times highly questionable. The permissiveness that youth experienced, he contended, began on the date of the first atomic bomb explosion. At one point, he whipped out thick reading glasses to quote from a letter. At the conclusion of the talk, Fulton had to ask people behind the cameras how much time was remaining, and finding himself three minutes short, expressed his nervousness. Still, he was charming, articulate, and remarkably fit and attractive for a man of his age.

The series was offered free to Public Broadcasting System stations, and quickly disappeared.[58] The golden age of television was long over for Sheen. People now expected sex and violence in the media, not somber orations and corny stories. The two hottest programs in 1975 were *All in the Family,* which linked religion with ignorance and bigotry, and *Baretta,* an action-packed cop show.

In March 1975, as Sheen approached his eightieth birthday, he told a luncheon group at St. Bartholomew's Episcopal Church in Manhattan that he was praying daily to die within the next year. He did not wish to live beyond that point, he said, because he knew he could not work "at full capacity." He hoped he would die "on a feast of the Blessed Mother and in the presence of the Blessed Sacrament." Smiling, he added, "If I don't, God is going to be very embarrassed."[59]

The following month, the Catholic University of America awarded Sheen the President's Patronal Medal and an honorary degree. Both were awarded in a service at the National Shrine of the Immaculate Conception, where Fulton was celebrant of a Mass. In an interview, Fulton said he believed that women might one day be ordained as deaconesses in the Church. He also revealed that he had visited forty-two colleges and universities during the past three years. His popularity on campus, he added, had nothing to do with his antiwar stance. "At a talk I gave at UCLA, 80 percent of the questions were on prayer."[60] A few days later, Fulton flew to Ireland, where he gave eighteen sermons, and then to Lourdes.[61]

On his eightieth birthday, Fulton wrote to Vincent and Marian Cahill, "Yes, I am 80. It does not seem so, for the years have come to me on tiptoe without ever making me weary of working for the Lord."[62]

On May 17, Sheen was in Philadelphia to celebrate the twenty-fifth anniversary of Mary H. Downing's conversion. Downing, a technical writer, had been attracted to Sheen while listening to the *Catholic Hour* and became one of a multitude who received personal instruction. Sheen said it was the first time he had attended the anniversary of a conversion and hoped it would start a trend. (A couple attending the celebration asked to have their picture taken with the archbishop. He told the husband to stand next to him, and then he could tell others that Sheen was the first man ever to come between them. As the photo attests, everyone appreciated the joke.)

Attending the celebration was Mary Nordeman, a Philadelphia waitress whom Sheen had first befriended in the early 1950s when he noticed her regularly in the *Catholic Hour* audience. For the rest of Sheen's life, Nordeman sent him homemade cookies, in which he delighted, and spent three and a half years crocheting elaborate, fine lace for a magnificent alb worn by her hero.

Sheen referred to Downing and Nordeman as "the two Marys," and held them in great affection. Both received numerous Sheen letters over the years and were on hand for his installation in Rochester.[63]

In the summer of 1975, Fulton flew to the Philippines to give a retreat to local bishops.[64] On September 7, he preached before seventy-five thousand people attending a Holy Year Rally at the New Orleans Superdome.[65] Later that year, in Los Angeles, he presided and preached at a three-hour service. As usual, the sermon was delivered without notes, and Loretta Young thought the performance "thrilling." Afterward, the actress took Sheen to a party in Beverly Hills, where someone told the archbishop that he was getting better and better at his preaching. "I know it," he replied. "Isn't it marvelous?"[66]

The same year, Fulton returned home to El Paso and Peoria. He no doubt knew it was for the last time. In El Paso, he suggested to a cousin, Mrs. Clarys Cleary, that they walk down the main street and see the old Newton Sheen hardware store building. Despite an effort to restore the edifice as a tribute to the archbishop, the building had fallen into disrepair and was razed. His cousin Merle Fulton later noted that the house where Fulton's grandparents had lived was still there, "but that's about all. Time just about takes care of everything."[67]

When Sheen went to the Peoria airport to return to New York, he was all but unrecognized. The small, dapper figure was not someone most people in the airport knew much if anything about. One exception was a nun who walked up, gave him a kiss, and walked on without saying a word. Mrs. Cleary, with her cousin at the time, said later, "The young didn't know him, and the older people loved him so much they forgot convention." She had fixed her famous relative a lunch, and Fulton said goodbye to his youthful roots with a peanut butter sandwich in his pocket.[68]

In early 1976, three visitors from Rochester arrived at Fulton's apartment to discuss the Sheen Archives at St. Bernard's Seminary. Fr. Joe Brennan was rector of the seminary; Fr. Jaspar (Jack) Pennington, an Episcopal priest, was the librarian; and Matthew Paratore was a lecturer and public relations man for the seminary. The idea of a depository of all Sheen papers, books and artifacts had come from Pennington. Sheen had given away books and other materials to the library at St. Bernard's in 1969, and four years later Pennington and Sheen had agreed to create the Sheen Archives.[69] Now the trio was seeking further contributions.

Sheen brought out a beautiful Byzantine chalice, made in Russia in about 1802, saying that it could go to the seminary at his death. (Fulton donated it in 1979 to St. Patrick's Cathedral, calling it "the most precious possession of my life and the only one that matters to me.")[70] He then produced a large collection of photographs, "boxes and boxes," Brennan said later, and Pennington selected a few for immediate display. Eventually, the entire collection was designed to go to the archives.

Then Sheen showed the three visitors what Brennan later recalled as a "fairly fat" manila envelope, saying something like "Here is the real story about myself and Cardinal Spellman. I'm going to give it to you." (Paratore saw a few of the letters on a subsequent visit.) Brennan objected to the donation, saying that such documents were extremely delicate and should go through appropriate legal channels. The archbishop then telephoned Edythe Brownett, who apparently agreed with Brennan. Sheen decided not to hand them over. Still, Brennan left the meeting with the understanding that Sheen would will the documents, along with a large number of other things, to the archives.[71] (See the Author's Note for more on the documents and the Sheen Archives.)

In the course of the discussion, Pennington suggested that the model for the Sheen Archives be the meticulously organized and well-financed Thomas Merton collection. Sheen voiced extreme displeasure, and the matter was dropped. Pennington later learned from others that Sheen disliked Merton, the hero of many contemporary liberals.[72]

Pope Paul VI sent Sheen a personal letter on the twenty-fifth anniversary of his consecration to the episcopacy. The document noted the archbishop's many years of university teaching, his missionary activity, and his radio and television ministry.

> *In virtue of this, Venerable Brother, We wish to offer you Our heartfelt praise for each and every one of these, and to honor you and congratulate you for these and all your magnificent works. We greatly rejoice and give thanks to God for neither age nor state of health has impeded you, but always with a joyful spirit, with pastoral devotedness and good manners, even now you draw many men to Christ and to the Church; particularly to priests you have given spiritual admonition and help; to vast assemblages you have sown the truths of the Gospel.[73]*

A short time later, Archbishop Joseph L. Bernardin of Cincinnati wrote a similar letter of praise. "Who could begin to estimate the extent of mission awareness on behalf of The Society for the Propagation of the Faith? Who could begin to measure the influence you have had and continue to have on the lives of people through radio, television and the press? We can only marvel at the example of what one person can do."[74]

Fulton returned to Rochester on September 27, 1976, to give a talk at the formal dedication of the Archbishop Fulton John Sheen Archives at St. Bernard's Seminary. He was a bit nervous about how he would be received, but all went well.[75] The room was filled with Sheen tapes and books.[76] The talk began, characteristically, with self-deprecation, making the point, with humorous stories from his past, that he was undeserving of an archive. Levity aside, he went on to say that the materials collected for the archives could not alone explain their author. He continued:

> *Very often, when I go to Paris . . . I visit Carmes. It was an old Carmelite monastery, but after the French Revolution was converted into one of the dormitory buildings of the Institute Catholiques, and there is one room that I always visit. It's at the end of a corridor . . . and over the desk was carved a peephole. It was the room of the great preacher Lacordaire, and as he sat at that desk he could look through that peephole, and what did he see? He looked on the tabernacle—he looked on the Blessed Sacrament. It was that that made Lacordaire great.*
>
> *There is no complete explanation of Fulton J. Sheen in these books, in these tapes. You have to look for a secret from the outside, where knowledge is converted into wisdom, and that is done only at the feet of Christ and his Blessed Sacrament. So may all who enter this room be reminded of a peephole. Look through it, and you'll explain Fulton John Sheen.*[77]

After the festivities, Jaspar Pennington was shocked to hear several local priests, still angry about Sheen's administration of the diocese, privately condemning their former bishop "as the worst person around."[78]

Pennington discovered, as he carried on his single-handed and unfunded struggle to create a credible Sheen archive, that the archbishop was completely disorganized. When asked where all of his private correspondence was, Sheen said simply that he didn't keep track of such things. It had almost all been destroyed. Pennington pled with Sheen to find and save some things for the archives. He did, and the few documents that are available resulted from Pennington's plea. As for his publications, Pennington said Sheen "had no sense of copyrights."

During one visit to Sheen's apartment, Pennington asked him about a particular incident, suggesting that there might be a newspaper clipping on it. Fulton went to a closet and opened one of two footlockers filled with clippings. He plunged his hands into the clippings, scattering some around the floor, thinking perhaps that the right clipping could easily be found. These clippings, a lifetime collection, were not organized in any way. Pennington quickly took steps to transport the contents of the footlockers to Rochester.[79]

∾

TWO DAYS AFTER turning eighty-one, Sheen was in Las Vegas giving the main address before a crowd of over six thousand gathered in the Convention Center for a Bicentennial Celebration and Mass. The diocesan newspaper declared that Sheen "showed the flash and fire or oratorical brilliance which makes him an institution in his own time."[80] Then in August, Fulton preached at the International Eucharistic Congress in Philadelphia.[81] In March of 1977, he spoke to the Hibernian Society in Savannah, Georgia. And so on. At nearly eighty-two, he was still wed to his incredible schedule.

What kept him going? The average person might say "the applause." And there is surely some truth in that. Having tasted great fame, one may find obscurity pure torment. Jaspar Pennington thought that Sheen worried about his public image, fearing he was outdated and might be forgotten.[82]

But there was much more to Fulton Sheen than that. He was above all a supernatural man. He believed himself called by God to defend the faith and His Church, and to love the human race. It was not the urge for fame that required Sheen's daily Holy Hour, that brought him for decades to the homes of the poor and the sick, that took him to untold numbers of convents and monasteries to give retreats, that prompted him to counsel and instruct thousands of converts, that made him answer tens of thousands of letters with advice and prayer, that stirred his lifelong generosity, that compelled him to go to Africa to hold the hands of lepers, that drove him repeatedly to Lourdes and Fatima.

The books, the radio, the television, the well-reported sermons at St. Patrick's and elsewhere—they bore compensations for the ego, of course. There is truth in the "prima donna" image many continue to associate with Sheen. But the principal work of his life was not primarily about pride. He believed himself driven by the Holy Spirit, loved by a Savior, supported by a Holy Mother, inspired by the Vicar of Christ. And he would not stop, even slow down, until he was no longer capable of bearing the responsibilities he had long firmly believed were his. He would live intensely as long as possible.

In early 1977, Sheen granted an interview to the evangelical Protestant magazine *Christianity Today*. (Earlier in the year, he had been a guest of honor at the annual convention of evangelical broadcasters in Washington.) While he repeated many clichés, forged over a lifetime, he had, as always, something interesting to say, and he said it well.

Fulton thought the Catholic Church better off theologically and liturgically than in the past. Spiritually, however, "I do not think we are as good as we were twenty or thirty years ago." Part of the problem, he believed, was an overemphasis on social problems and an unwillingness to talk about personal sin. "Many feel that if they carry a banner for social justice they need not be concerned about their personal morality." He lamented the drift into narcissism and the flight from reason and systematic philosophy that character-ized the 1960s and 1970s. Still, he acknowledged that Thomism was no longer the exclusive approach to Catholic truth. "Today there is no reason why one should follow Aquinas more than Augustine. It is really a matter of philosophical taste. They are both viable and valuable." When asked about popular theologian Hans Kung, Ful-ton dismissed him as a twentieth-century Arian.

Sheen again voiced a strong interest in ecumenism. "I think the closer we get to Christ the closer we get to one another. That is why one feels very much at home with a real Christian. Our differences as Protestants and Catholics are lovers' quarrels." And he spoke highly of the evangelical theologian Francis Schaeffer. "His sum-mary of philosophical doctrines is one of the best that I have ever read, and I taught philosophy in graduate school for twenty-five years." Still, he had some misgivings about the charismatic move-ment and the "healing" evangelists then popular. As for the future, Fulton said simply, "I have taken a resolution all the rest of my life to preach nothing but Christ and him crucified."[83]

When his brother Tom died, Fulton was summoned to celebrate a Mass for family and friends. A distinguished and selfless physi-cian, and a much beloved father and friend, Tom had suffered from Alzheimer's disease and for some two years had been unable to carry on a conversation. The archbishop had paid a last visit to his brother, telling Halley Sheen, Tom's wife, that she was a saint for taking such good care of her husband during the ordeal.[84] Edythe Brownett said later that Fulton "deeply loved his brother and was very saddened by his death." She recalled the many times Tom and Halley had joined Fulton in New York for lunch, and stated a belief that the two brothers were "very close."[85] This view was not shared by one of Tom's daughters, Marie, who said she saw little of her uncle over the years, especially during her father's illness.[86]

Sister Marlene Brownett traveled with Fulton to Lourdes dur-ing the summer of 1977. He had slowed down a bit, she thought, but otherwise seemed normal. His nurse friend Cathy Yetman was

along. After Marlene returned to the United States, Fulton telephoned her to say he would soon be entering the hospital with a
cardiac problem.[87] While he had not suffered a heart attack, his
lungs were filling up with fluid and he was dying.

On July 15, at New York's Lenox Hill Hospital, Fulton under-
went open-heart surgery. He was the oldest person ever to undergo
that type of operation, and he required seventy pints of blood during the procedure.[88] A pacemaker was installed. Sheen's physician,
Marlene wrote later, was amazed when a priest came to the intensive care unit after surgery "and celebrated Mass at the foot of the
bishop's bed. Sheen sat up and at the consecration was able to move
his hands and pronounce the words as a concelebrant."[89]

In mid-August, prostate surgery was required. During the ordeal,
the Pope wrote twice and called once.[90] President Jimmy Carter
telephoned twice.[91] Terence Cardinal Cooke of New York and Mother
Teresa paid visits.[92] Sister Marlene was among the few allowed to
visit daily and worship with Sheen. Messages and gifts poured into
the hospital.[93] Fulton had the gifts passed out to other patients. After
his return home, the avalanche of good will continued, and he told
the doorman to bring him the cards and give away the gifts.[94]

Sheen remained hospitalized until early November. Edward T.
O'Meara wrote that throughout the recovery process, Sheen "retained
his youthful cheerfulness. Through long and painful days and nights
in an intensive care unit, there was never a lament or complaint;
always cheerfulness, always faith, always gratitude for the slightest
service."[95] O'Meara noted that one evening in the intensive care
unit, Sheen, barely conscious, overheard a nurse say that a man in
a nearby bed was dying. Unable to lift his hand, he raised a finger,
made the sign of the cross, and gave the unknown man conditional
absolution seconds before he died. A few months later, the widow,
who had seen the gesture, gave Fulton a Jewish medal in gratitude.[96]
O'Meara also wrote, "At my first concelebration of Mass with him
in his hospital room, he offered, with labored breath, an explanation of the Eucharist to a hospital attendant who had never before

witnessed a Mass." Fulton told O'Meara, "Woe to me if I do not preach the Gospel of Christ."[97]

Looking extremely gaunt but often flashing a smile, Fulton held a half-hour news conference upon leaving the hospital on November 3. "I was never afraid to die," he said, "because God is with me … wherever I go. At no time did I have any fear." His physician, Dr. Michael Bruno, said that the only thing now wrong with Sheen was "a lousy appetite. Once he starts eating, he'll look better." He also noted that the archbishop had already accepted several speaking engagements.[98]

In his first public appearance after surgery, Sheen received the Catholic Actors Guild Award.[99] Sheen had conducted the Actors Prayer Day for seven consecutive years at theaters around New York City. And, of course, he was being honored for his many years in the media. A large audience, a full orchestra (it was a dinner dance), Cardinal Cooke, Bishop O'Meara, Clare Boothe Luce, and a number of other distinguished guests were on hand to pay tribute to the archbishop. Actor Cyril Ritchard, president of the guild, made the introductions.

Sheen began his brief remarks by introducing the eight physicians who had, just days earlier, saved his life. With a voice slightly weakened by his ordeal, he proceeded to give a model talk, based on a pattern that had won the hearts and minds of audiences for decades: humor, self-deprecation, praise for his audience, a bit of theology, and a ringing conclusion with memorized verse. It was a stirring address that won prolonged applause.

Clare Boothe Luce's humorous remarks were almost as effective. Playing "the devil's advocate" against those who were already talking about canonization, she noted her longtime friend's sins: envy (he envied any clergyman who could carry a tune), covetousness (he coveted souls), anger (against those who were uncharitable and unkind toward others), a sort of reverse gluttony (he lived largely on canned pears), and sloth (he refused to read newspapers). Then, without tongue in cheek, she spoke of the "remarkable joy"

Sheen brought to life, and of his saintliness. She called him "my beloved archbishop."[100]

One observer who had known Sheen as a student at Loyola University in New Orleans, the *Philadelphia Inquirer* columnist Tom Fox, wrote that the most poignant moment of the evening occurred when young Andrea McArdle, who was starring in the Broadway play *Annie,* walked over to Sheen's table and sang "You Light up My Life." There wasn't a dry eye in the ballroom. "It seemed a most fitting tribute to Fulton J. Sheen, for he had brought light into so many lives in his years on earth."[101]

On Good Friday, nearly five months later, Sheen appeared at St. Agnes Church to deliver a two-hour talk on the seven last words of Christ. The church was packed (a newspaper photograph shows Edythe Brownett sitting adoringly in the front row), and some eight hundred persons stood outside listening over a public address system. Police closed off traffic between Lexington and Third avenues to accommodate them. Clare Boothe Luce, at Sheen's request, flew from her home in Hawaii to serve as lector. White-haired, she wore thick glasses, the result of an eye operation six years earlier. Recording star Robert White sang hymns. Sheen's speaking schedule was reported to be booked solid for two years.[102]

This was largely bravado, however, for most of the time Fulton was confined to his apartment, under doctor's orders to rest. He was writing his autobiography.

When his brother Al died, Sheen was too ill to attend the funeral. Al had been a successful corporate executive and was widely admired for his boisterous and fun-loving ways. He had married, and there were two daughters. After his first wife died, Al married Connie Kain, a widow, in 1961, with Fulton officiating. Years later, Connie Sheen described her husband as "brilliant," "charming," a man who "dearly loved parties." Heavy drinking accompanied those parties, and Al died of cirrhosis of the liver.[103]

Connie Sheen recalled several good times she had shared with her husband and Fulton. But she also observed, and could not explain, the reticence Al had toward his older brother. She thought that "underneath," Al "dearly loved the bishop," but he didn't show it. When asked about his famous sibling, Al would say, "Who? My physician brother Tom?"[104]

In September 1978, Fulton returned to the hospital and remained four months. While there, he consoled a seventy-seven-year-old man who was contemplating suicide and talked to him about the Catholic faith he had lost forty-five years earlier. After several hours, Sheen heard the man's confession and offered him the Eucharist from his bed. Fulton wrote later, "I had asked the Lord to let my sufferings do some good for some soul and He had answered the prayer."[105]

Sheen wrote to his cousin Mary Baker in January 1979, telling her that he had been flat on his back since September "from an abuse of my heart after an operation." He added, "I have no complaint whatever about my condition because I firmly believe that the Lord often puts us on our back so that we will keep looking up to heaven."[106]

Earlier that month, Fulton had appeared at the National Prayer Breakfast in Washington, D.C. He had accepted the invitation against the advice of his cardiologist, Dr. Bruno, who accompanied him to the event. Officials asked Billy Graham, who was present, to be ready to fill in should Sheen be unable to carry on. Graham wrote later, "Even as he made his halting way to the podium, I silently prayed that God would grant him the necessary physical and spiritual strength."

"Mr. President," Fulton began, turning toward the chief executive and his wife, "you are a sinner." Having everyone's undivided attention, he then pointed to himself and said, "I am a sinner." He looked around the huge ballroom at the sophisticated and influential spectators, and continued, "We are all sinners, and we all need to turn to God. . . ." Graham wrote, "He then went on to preach one of the most challenging and eloquent sermons I have ever heard."[107]

Jimmy Carter, who had often watched Sheen on television, wrote many years later, "It was a real pleasure and an unforgettable experience for me to meet him in person, and I especially appreciated his coming to the National Prayer Breakfast while I was president. With the possible exception of Billy Graham, Bishop Sheen was the most well-known and admired person there—including presidents and other dignitaries."[108]

In April, in terrible and constant pain, and with Dr. Bruno and a nurse sitting in the front row in case of an emergency, Sheen returned to St. Agnes Church on Forty-third Street to deliver his third consecutive Good Friday sermon. As Sheen was helped to the pulpit, Msgr. Eugene V. Clark, a spokesman for the Archdiocese of New York, told a reporter that the archbishop was determined to deliver the sermon "even if it cost his life." "He has always said that it would not be a bad place to die—in the pulpit," Clark said. "And he has made his peace with God. He's ready. He wants to die with his boots on." Dr. Bruno said later that Sheen was "a very heroic man." He had advised against the public appearance.

Sheen was thin; his hands trembled. The congregation gave him a burst of applause as he stepped into the pulpit. Fulton spoke about sacrifice and passion. "I've had a great deal of suffering in the 83 years of my life," he said. "There has been physical suffering. And other kinds . . . but as I look back over the years, I have never received the punishment I deserved. God has been easy with me. He has never laid on me burdens equal to my faith."

At one point, Fulton raised his hands dramatically to the congregation: "Show me your hands. Do they have scars from giving? Show me your heart. Have you left a place for divine love?" He turned and left the pulpit, trailed by his doctor, nurse and several friends.

"I have been coming to these services for many years," a keypunch operator told a reporter. "It is always an experience that cannot be described." A freelance filmmaker said of Sheen, "I do not think he will be back again. I think he knows that and he was saying goodbye."[109]

On his eighty-fourth birthday, the *New York Times* carried a story on the celebration by family, friends and well-wishers.[110] Fulton confided to Mary Baker, "Being eighty-four reminds me of the poem by W. B. Yeats: 'The years, like great black oxen, tread me down. And God, the Herdsman, goads them on behind. And I am trampeled by their tramping feet.' " He added, "As long as I live Christ is with me. When I die I will be with Him."[111]

Despite his weakness and pain, Fulton kept busy through the spring of 1979. In May, he was a surprise speaker at St. Patrick's Cathedral, then marking its hundredth anniversary, and received a standing ovation.[112] At the invitation of an old friend, Msgr. George A. Kelly, he attended the anniversary celebration of St. Monica's Church, a few blocks from his apartment, along with Cardinal Cooke. During Communion, Sheen and Kelly chatted about the parish. When called upon, Sheen repeated what he had just heard, awing the audience with his grasp of parish history, and continued with what Kelly called "a magnificent talk."[113]

Sheen's friend Rabbi Marc Tanenbaum helped arrange to land him a role as narrator in a biblical movie. He observed that Sheen, extremely gaunt, was unable to digest food. Film producer John Heyman brought him some chicken soup, which Fulton said later "saved my life!"[114] At the same time, the Society for the Propagation of the Faith was touting a new film of its own, *The Great Inheritance*, featuring Sheen as narrator.

In July, Fulton summoned the strength to travel to Twin Lakes, Wisconsin, to preside at the wedding of Diane Sheen, the daughter of his nephew Joseph Sheen Jr. Diane's brother, Fulton J. Sheen III, later remembered the archbishop looking old and frail as he walked toward the church. In the pulpit, however, "he shed twenty years." The sermon was on the Church as the Bride of Christ, and was "powerful—very, very good."[115]

Later that summer, Sheen filmed a half-hour program for a New York television station on the impending visit of Pope John Paul II. As always, he stood while speaking. During this general period, he instructed four converts and validated two marriages. "The horizontal apostolate may sometimes be just as effective as the vertical," he wrote.[116]

On the sixtieth anniversary of his ordination, Fulton celebrated Mass with Bishop Edward O'Meara, Fr. Vincent Nugent, Edythe

Brownett, and two others in the chapel at his apartment. In a tape-recorded homily (the microphone was on his chest, and the pace-maker's click is pronounced), Sheen reflected on what he called the three "mind periods" of his priesthood; it was, in large part, a brief account of what later appeared in his autobiography as chapter twenty-one, "The Three Stages of My Life." He spoke of the great peace he now enjoyed daily, having fully realized the supreme importance of Christ in his life, of the work he still wanted to do, and of his desire to die before the Blessed Sacrament on a Saturday or on a feast day of Our Lady. Still, he acknowledged, the exact day on which he died did not really matter, because he knew that he belonged to Jesus and the Blessed Virgin. Fulton hoped that when he appeared before the Lord, He would say, "Oh, I heard My mother speak of you."[117]

His physician had ordered him to stay in bed, but after his Holy Hour and Mass, Sheen put in a normal day's activity, reading widely and working on his autobiography.

Fulton intended his autobiography to be published by Double-day, a major publishing house that had brought out other Sheen books. He chose not to sign a contract because he did not want to be bound by a deadline. Doubleday assigned editor Patricia Kossmann to the project. A Catholic who had grown up watching Sheen on television, she quickly became friends with Sheen and visited him regularly at his apartment. Fulton enjoyed the company of a canary given to him in his illness, which he called simply "bird" or "birdie." He was amazed when Kossmann told him how to identify its sex.[118]

The archbishop and the editor worshiped together, and then Fulton would read aloud portions of the book he had recently written. "He was an actor," Kossmann recalled. She did not take notes or make tape recordings of what she heard. Sheen wrote everything out by hand and went over the text carefully before turning it over to a typist.[119] In late September, perhaps because he lacked the strength to write, he was dictating the autobiography, holding a crucifix in his hand.[120]

On October 2, St. Patrick's Cathedral was packed with people awaiting the arrival of Pope John Paul II. (Fulton had been overjoyed by the election of the Polish poet-philosopher.)[121] As Sheen entered, the congregation applauded loudly. When the new Pope made his entrance, the archbishop, led by his secretary and appearing "feeble," according to Edwin Broderick, made his way to the Holy Father in the sanctuary. Fulton fell to his knees. The Pope helped him to his feet, and the two men warmly embraced, amid thundering applause. When Sheen was later asked what John Paul II said to him, he replied, "He told me that I had written and spoken well of the Lord Jesus, and that I was a loyal son of the Church." Nothing could have been more pleasing, for that was what Fulton had tried to do and be all of his life.[122]

On returning to Rome, the Holy Father wrote a letter to Sheen formally commending him for six decades of active and fruitful priestly service. "And so with Saint Paul, 'I thank my God whenever I think of you; and every time I pray for . . . you, I pray with joy, remembering how you have helped to spread the Good News.' "[123]

Sheen replied with a lengthy, learned and extremely moving letter affirming his complete faith in the Vicar of Christ and his Church and telling of his delight in the present Pontiff. He also offered historical perspective to aid John Paul II as he grappled with the Cold War, the aftershocks of Vatican II, and the cultural revolution of what has been called the Dreadful Decade, 1965–1975. About every five hundred years, Fulton wrote, a crisis hits the Church. The first was the fall of Rome, and God raised up Gregory the Great. In about the year 1000, schism and corruption occurred, and God called upon Gregory VII, a holy Benedictine, to stop the scandal. Five hundred years later, the Reformation split Western Christendom, and God gave the Church Pius V to apply the reforms of the Council of Trent and generate missionary activity throughout the world. "Now we are in the fourth cycle of five hundred years, with two world wars in twenty-one years, and the universal dread of nuclear incineration. This time God has given us John Paul II, who has drawn the attention of the world to himself as no human being has done in history."[124]

Although Fulton assured the Pope that he was, quoting the Psalmist's promise, "Vigorous in old age like a tree full of sap," he knew the end was nearing rapidly. He spoke frequently to his friends of death, saying, "It is not that I do not love life; I do. It is just that I want to see the Lord. I have spent hours before Him in the Blessed Sacrament. I have spoken to Him in prayer, and about Him to everyone who would listen, and now I want to see Him face to face."[125]

As he labored over his autobiography, Fulton probed the eternal problem of pain and suffering, a topic he could not now escape. While he once thought that life was filled with accident (one recalls his World War II writings), Fulton had since become convinced that there were no accidents.[126] He learned gradually that "all sufferings come from either the direct or the permissive Will of God ... all trials come from the Hands of the Loving God." In his old age he prayed to be able to offer up his pain and suffering for the good of the souls of others, as Christ offered Himself for the sins of the world. The suicidal man whom he brought back to the Church in the hospital in 1978 was proof, Fulton believed, that God had answered the prayer. He wrote, "Now in the era of the Second Look, *I consider everything a waste except knowing Christ. Anything that is done or read or spoken or enjoyed or suffered that does not bring me close to Him makes me ask myself: why all this waste?*"[127]

Fulton would have appreciated the words of another Catholic writer, Flannery O'Connor, who had also gained wisdom from suffering: "Sickness before death is a very appropriate thing and I think those who don't have it miss one of God's mercies. Success is almost as isolating and nothing points out vanity as well."[128]

In his autobiography, Fulton expressed great remorse for his worldliness—his prosperity, vanity and ease. He particularly regretted his fine clothes, his Cadillacs, his love of clerical titles and privileges.

> *While many young priests sought ways to imitate the way I preached, was I inspiring anyone to imitate Christ in the daily carrying of His Cross? I knew it was not right. I knew I should*

be giving away more than I gave. I should have resembled more closely Christ, Who had nowhere to lay His head. I should have fled from some applauding mobs as the Lord fled from the enthusiasms at Capharnaum after the multiplication of bread; maybe I was like Peter, who at one point "followed the Lord far off."

There were no "great mortifications" in his life, he wrote.

Fulton wrote only in general terms about his trials inside the Church; he would not describe the persecutions that were heaped upon him for a decade by Spellman. "I have resolved in this book not to touch on any suffering that came to me from others," he explained. These were "impure" sufferings, not the "intense kind most directly related to the open-heart surgery and consequent complications in which I came to a new dimension of pain."

As Christians must when talking about eternal questions, Fulton stressed the positive. On the last page of the manuscript he was able to complete, he wrote about pain as an avenue to glory, of resurrection following death, of scars "that will make us rejoice that He gave us a 'thorn in the flesh.' " There were many gifts he had enjoyed: Christian parents, unusual opportunities for education, and so on. But "the greatest gift of all may have been His summons to the Cross, where I found His continuing self-disclosure."[129]

On December 4, Fulton made out his will. He asked that his funeral Mass be celebrated in St. Patrick's Cathedral, and that he be buried in Calvary Cemetery, the official cemetery of the Archdiocese of New York. He left small amounts of money to three friends—Bishop O'Meara, Fr. Nugent, and Fr. Michael Hogan—asking that each celebrate one Low Mass for his intention. He left all of his manuscript files, kinescopes and videotapes to the Sheen Archives in Rochester. And he made the Society for the Propagation of the Faith the recipient of all his publication rights. Bishop O'Meara was the executor of the will, and Sheen gave him a letter (never made public) distributing his personal property, such as rings, religious vestments and crosses.[130]

A few days later, Fulton telephoned his niece Joan Sheen

Cunningham, worried about his books. They needed to be sorted and rearranged, and more had to be given away.[131] When Vincent Cahill, the FBI agent Sheen had befriended years earlier, called, Fulton invited him to visit, adding, "I'd love to see you."[132]

On December 7, Tom and Yolanda Holliger, who lived in New Jersey, stopped at the apartment for a chat. On a previous visit, a few weeks earlier, Fulton had posed for a photograph with the couple and their six children. Reeda Holliger, Fulton's cousin from Peoria, called on December 8, and Sheen told her about the visit by her son and his wife and of the plans they were making for the Holligers' youngest child, Michael, to receive First Communion in his chapel. "Now Reeda," he said, "you'll come to New York for this and we'll have ice cream and cake after for all the kids and for everybody." When asked about his health, Fulton said, "Oh, I'm fine."[133]

On the morning of December 9, a young couple was with Sheen at Mass and listened as he practiced part of a Christmas homily he was preparing for Midnight Mass at St. Patrick's. He also wrote a letter to Ann O'Connor, his longtime friend in London, thanking her for a blanket she had sent. "My heart has to be elastic—otherwise it would break in gratitude for your friendship and gifts during the year."[134] Early that evening, he died. It was the day after the Feast of the Immaculate Conception. And Fulton was found in his chapel, before the Blessed Sacrament.[135]

∽

FOLLOWING A PRIVATE wake for family members and close friends, the body was officially received by Terence Cardinal Cooke at the Fifth Avenue entrance of St. Patrick's Cathedral on the evening of December 10. The coffin was placed in the main aisle during a short Scripture service to which the public was welcome.[136] Sheen's body was moved the next day to the Lady Chapel, where thousands filed by for two days between 7:00 A.M. and 9:00 P.M. Among those in attendance was actor Martin Sheen, who had taken his stage name from the bishop and had met him in 1965.[137] So many people touched Sheen's hand as they passed by that Cardinal Cooke feared it might break.[138]

Several family members stayed with the cardinal during these days. Joseph Sheen Jr. later recalled sitting next to Cooke in the dining room, when the cardinal pointed to a painting of a bishop (no doubt Archbishop John Hughes) on the wall and said, "He built it," meaning St. Patrick's Cathedral, "and your uncle filled it. That's why I want him buried under the altar."[139] And so it was that the archbishop was laid to rest in the huge cathedral in which he had preached for half a century. "He belonged there," said Sister Marlene years later. "That altar was his."[140] The remains of Sheen and Spellman were buried at opposite ends of the crypt.

Three Masses were held at St. Patrick's in Fulton Sheen's honor. The first, on December 11, was at the request of the Society for the Propagation of the Faith. Archbishop (newly named) O'Meara, who had succeeded Sheen as director, was the major concelebrant. Fr. Vincent Nugent gave the homily. The second Mass was on the following day at the cathedral, requested by the Diocese of Rochester; the chief concelebrant was Rochester's Bishop Matthew Clark. The major service occurred on December 13.

Four cardinals, forty-eight bishops, Governor Hugh Carey, and Mayor Ed Koch joined the thousands who packed St. Patrick's Cathedral for the 2:00 P.M. funeral Mass.[141] Sister Ann Edward of the Sisters of St. Joseph, who had taught Edythe Brownett literature in college and had become a good friend of Sheen's over several decades, later recalled the extraordinary length of the procession into the cathedral and the variety of clerical vestments, including Byzantine Rite, on display.[142] Representatives from many churches and faiths were on hand, including Billy Graham and Rabbi Marc Tanenbaum. Sheen had always remained a priest of the Diocese of Peoria, and his bishop, Edward W. O'Rourke, was a concelebrant. Several priests and relatives from the Peoria area were also there.[143]

Terence Cardinal Cooke was the chief concelebrant. Edythe Brownett was asked to read the lessons, but her shyness and her grief were such that she could not bring herself to do it. Her sister, Marlene, the only woman in the procession, took her place.[144]

Archbishop O'Meara, Sheen's friend for more than twenty years, gave the eulogy. It was based, he said, on the private tape recording made by Sheen in September, reflecting on his own life and times. O'Meara spoke of Fulton's daily Holy Hour, his unending intellectual curiosity, the firmness of his views ("he held no opinions lightly"), and his success as an educator, author, and radio and television performer. His service to the Society for the Propagation of the Faith received a special emphasis—"surely you are not surprised that both in life and in death he gave it his every earthly possession."

He spoke as well of the many converts Sheen had brought into the Church. One of them, he said, "spoke for all of them and summed up this gift of his at the finish of an instruction by leaping to her feet and, with clenched fists, shouting heavenward: 'O God, what a protagonist you have in this man!' " O'Meara believed that Sheen would have regarded his meeting with John Paul II at St. Patrick's as the apex of his career. He repeated the words the Pope had said to Sheen. He noted also Fulton's growing sense of faith and peace in his old age.

The archbishop concluded the brief sermon powerfully:

> *Last Sunday, at 7:15 P.M. God called Archbishop Fulton Sheen to himself by name. It was a moment known to God, and fixed by Him from all eternity, a call to perfect life and truth and love, a call to a life he will never tire of, that can never be improved, and which he can never lose.*
>
> *Dear friend, Archbishop Sheen, we are all better because you were in our midst and were our friend. We trust you to the care of your "Lovely Lady dressed in blue." We pray that Jesus has already said: "I've heard My Mother speak of you."*
>
> *Bye now, Fulton Sheen, and God Love You Forever!*[145]

Author's Note

*N*ot long after Fulton Sheen's funeral, Archbishop O'Meara began distributing the personal effects found in the apartment of the deceased, in accordance with the will and the letter Fulton had left with his friend. The Sheen Archives in Rochester received publications, letters, newspaper clippings, and some clerical vestments. Joan Sheen Cunningham received furniture, a statue of St. Michael the Archangel, and several photographs. She turned over materials in her possession— television tapes and a scrapbook of Sheen newspaper clippings started by Fulton's mother—to the archives, as Sheen had requested.[1]

Sister Ann Edward, who enjoyed talking with Sheen about poetry, received the rosary he had used on his television show and a well-worn book of poems that was in his prie dieu (prayer desk).[2] Convert Mary Downing received Sheen's red sash and the paten he used for his chalice.[3] Fr. Vincent Nugent wound up with what became six file boxes of Sheen materials, including letters, photographs, sermons, notes, passports, vestments, audio reels and films, and assorted memorabilia, all of which were later deposited in the archives of St. John's University in New York.[4]

Fulton's autobiography was not quite finished when he died. Within a week, O'Meara gave Patricia Kossmann a briefcase containing the autobiography and a handful of crucifixes Sheen carried around with him for distribution. The manuscript was mostly typed but included handwritten pages that were no doubt still awaiting further scrutiny. O'Meara asked Kossmann to get the book ready for publication by Doubleday. It appeared in September 1980 and did well financially. Rights were later sold to Ignatius Press, and the book remains in print.

The Society for the Propagation of the Faith was, and is, the Sheen Estate, receiving the royalties from Sheen publications. There were so many items involved, and copyrights to be renewed, and books falling in and out of print, that O'Meara employed Kossmann to be the estate's literary representative. In 1994, she became an editor at Liguori Press and began publishing collections of Sheen's writings. She said later that she cherished her friendship with the archbishop during the brief time they knew each other. "I've done what I've done because of Sheen."[5]

And what happened to the folder of Sheen-Spellman documents that Fulton offered to the Rochester archives in 1976 but decided at the last minute to retain? We do not know.

When Archbishop John O'Connor of New York entered his new office in 1983, he discovered a box with a warning that it was not to be opened. It seems clear that O'Meara took the Spellman-Sheen letters in Fulton's office to Cardinal Cooke, who prohibited access to them. O'Connor opened the box and examined some of the letters, which confirmed what he had heard about bad relations between Spellman and Sheen. The box was placed in the archives of the cardinal's residence.[6]

Several years later, O'Connor told historian Fr. Tom Shelley about the papers. Shelley then alerted Fr. John Tracy Ellis, the distinguished historian at the Catholic University of America. At some point, the cardinal assured Ellis that the letters would be made available for study to any scholar Ellis recommended.[7]

On June 20, 1990, Ellis wrote to O'Connor on behalf of Fr. Tom McSweeney, who was writing a doctoral dissertation on Sheen's rhetoric at the University of Maryland.[8] Five days later, O'Connor replied to Ellis, denying the request. He assured Ellis that the letters in question had no bearing on McSweeney's topic, and involved strictly "personal matters between Cardinal Spellman and Archbishop Sheen." In a handwritten note at the bottom of the letter, the cardinal wrote, "Sorry, John. The material is trivial—the stuff of yellow journalism only."[9]

No doubt a vital element in O'Connor's decision was John Cooney's *The American Pope: The Life and Times of Francis Cardinal Spellman,* published in 1984. It was a sensationalistic account of Spellman's life containing an unsubstantiated charge that the cardinal had been a homosexual. This author heard repeatedly from interviewees the hope that my book would be on a higher level than Cooney's. I had similar responses from those who had read D. P. Noonan's *The Passion of Fulton Sheen,* which appeared in 1972. Both books left some insiders leery of talking to anyone engaged in writing recent Catholic history.

The Vatican Library's practice of closing documents for many decades may have also been in O'Connor's mind when he chose not to open the Spellman-Sheen correspondence. One priest later remembered O'Connor talking about closing all archdiocesan documents for fifty years.[10] The archdiocesan archives of New York, under his leadership, were notorious for restricting access to papers. In a conversation with the author, Sister Marguerita Smith, longtime guardian of the archives, spoke harshly of Cooney's biography of Spellman.[11]

Ellis appealed Cardinal O'Connor's decision. On July 2 he wrote to O'Connor, spelling out the historical importance of the correspondence, pointing in particular to the desire to document the reason Sheen left television in 1957. He noted the dependence historians had on Cooney and Noonan, and his desire to go beyond unsubstantiated claims.[12] There was no reply.

At McSweeney's request, Tom Shelley quietly explored the Spellman papers in the archdiocesan collection, hoping to find relevant information. He reported to Ellis that he had found very little and that the best information must be in the packet of letters in the possession of the cardinal.[13]

In July 1991, McSweeney tried again, writing to O'Connor and pleading his case. Again, the cardinal greeted the letter with silence.[14]

That October, McSweeney and O'Connor were together in a television studio. The priest approached the cardinal, introduced himself, and described his efforts to gain access to the Spellman-Sheen
papers. O'Connor asked Msgr. James McCarthy, his secretary, to
give McSweeney his card, to set up an appointment, and said that
after "we" looked at the documents in question, O'Connor would
decide what could and could not be made available. A week later,
McSweeney telephoned McCarthy and made an appointment. Soon,
the date was postponed. And then McSweeney found that McCarthy
was consistently unavailable. A staff member reported to the young
priest that the documents in question could not be found.[15] Before
long, McCarthy told McSweeney that the letters had been sent to
Rome.[16] O'Connor later told this author that he had personally sent
the materials to Rome.[17]

A Vatican official, responding to a request by the author to the
cardinal secretary of state, reported in early 1999 that the Vatican
Secret Archives and the Archives of the Secretariat of State "contain
no documents of any importance concerning Archbishop Fulton J.
Sheen."[18] Perhaps the Vatican would prefer the documents to remain
secret. Perhaps the letters were never sent to Rome. The death of
Cardinal O'Connor in 2000 opens the door for further inquiry.

And what of the Sheen Archives in Rochester? They were first
housed in a single room at St. Bernard's Seminary. When the seminary closed in 1981, the collection was offered to the Catholic University of America. The necessary funds could not be raised, and
the Sheen materials were dumped into a work room in the seminary, where they remained for about a year.[19] The papers were not
guarded, and many items were taken. The Sheen papers then went
to the St. Bernard Institute (what was left of the seminary) of the
Colgate-Rochester Divinity School. Fr. William Graf, a concerned
and helpful local priest who was named archivist in 1988, said later,
"It was a mass of materials thrown into a couple of upper rooms."[20]

Fr. Sylvester Falcone, who headed the institute and served as
director of the archives for five years, said later that he was "saddened

very much" by the neglect of the Sheen collection. Bishops were too busy to pay attention to the past, he said, and Sheen failed to provide the funds necessary to preserve the archives. This was typical, Falcone said, of Sheen's failure to pay attention to details.[21] At one point, the papers of Sheen's friend Vincent Nugent were offered and rejected.[22] Funds have been lacking to add the papers of others associated with Sheen to the archives.

In 1996, the Sheen collection was moved to the diocesan offices, where it remains today. The St. Bernard Institute is the legal owner. The diocese, the sole source of financial support for the archives, provides less than $6,000 a year for its maintenance.[23]

The Sheen materials have received little professional attention and are seldom used.[24] The entire collection contains only two Holliger boxes of Sheen correspondence, and one of them contains Bishop O'Meara materials, no doubt forwarded by the Society for the Propagation of the Faith. (O'Meara reportedly left no papers.) The rest consists of films, tapes, some 2,700 books, newspaper articles, photographs, and assorted memorabilia. Except for the books, items are not catalogued. There is no complete record of accessions. Two efforts to create a bibliography of Sheen publications, a most formidable task, proved inadequate. The author created Appendix A for this book.

The Sheen collection is staffed by part-time workers and volunteers. Some materials have been placed outside the archives. In a large back room of the same building, entered through a boiler room, there is a shelf of framed photos and four dust-covered boxes of Sheen's vestments and academic robes and hoods. Graf has not opened the boxes. More items from the collection have disappeared in recent years.[25]

Jaspar Pennington, founder of the Sheen Archives, says he was "greatly distressed" by the fate of the collection. The Episcopal priest declared in July 2000: "No one in the Roman Church has ever cared about the archives."[26] Fr. Graf hopes that this long-time policy of neglect will one day soon be reversed.

◡

For someone growing up in the 1950s, as I did, it was virtually impossible not to know about Bishop Fulton J. Sheen. His television show was widely celebrated, and his books seemed to be everywhere. I lost track of him in subsequent decades and, perhaps like most people, linked him with President Eisenhower, Johnny Ray, and Joe McCarthy, part of an era long gone and little lamented.

Soon after becoming Roman Catholics in mid-1997, my wife and I noticed in Church literature that many continued to buy Sheen books and video and audio tapes. I was shocked to discover that a solid biography had yet to appear, and Kathie suggested that I undertake the assignment. The first step in this effort was to discover what others had written about the once prominent cleric.

The two most widely quoted books on Sheen are extremely similar to each other and were written by a disgruntled priest who was one of the very few people Sheen ever fired. Both books contain useful insights but are sometimes misleading and unreliable.[27] Only a single, unpublished doctoral dissertation has been written by a historian.[28] A Catholic priest, Myles P. Murphy, published a brief, shallow, and controversial hagiography in 2000.[29]

Sheen is mentioned only once in David J. O'Brien's *American Catholics and Social Reform: The New Deal Years,* and is coupled with the anti-Semitic rabble-rouser Father Charles Coughlin.[30] In William M. Halsey's *The Survival of American Innocence: Catholicism in an Era of Disillusionment, 1920–1940,* Sheen is dismissed as "the Catholic counterpart of Norman Vince Peale and Billy Graham," and his Thomism is rejected as "a vehicle for domination."[31] (Linking publications by Sheen and Peale can only be done by someone who reads no farther than book titles. *Peace of Soul* is to *The Power of Positive Thinking* what *The Taming of the Shrew* is to *I Love Lucy.*)

One would think that Catholic scholars today might pay more attention to Sheen. University of Notre Dame historian Jay P. Dolan, in *The American Catholic Experience: A History from Colonial Times to the Present,* calls Sheen, in a brief paragraph, a "true Catholic hero" for his achievements in the media. (The sole source cited for his comments on Sheen is an obituary from a Rochester, New York, newspaper.)[32] Georgetown University theologian Chester Gillis, in *Roman Catholicism in America,* calls Sheen "a spellbinding preacher" who "brought the message, and was the public face of Catholicism to a generation of Catholics and non-Catholics alike." (He cites no sources on Sheen and omits him from a series of biographical sketches of leading American Catholics, a list that includes liberal actor Martin Sheen and radical feminist theologian Rosemary Radford Reuther.)[33] Similar examples are difficult to find.[34] Jesuit historian Mark S. Massa of Fordham University dismisses Sheen in *Catholics and American Culture* as little more than a proponent of pop psychology, his Catholic fans being people moving into the affluent culture "where religious homogeneity, not difference, assured social acceptance."[35]

Two Protestant historians have been more sympathetic. Mark A. Noll, in *A History of Christianity in the United States and Canada,* presents a positive and knowledgeable, albeit brief, account of Sheen's life and times.[36] Martin J. Marty analyzes three of Sheen's books and looks at the impact of his television programs in *Modern American Religion,* vol. 3, *Under God, Indivisible, 1941–1960.* This examination is fair and provocative although terse and generally condescending.[37]

College textbooks also slight Sheen. John A. Garraty's extremely popular *The American Nation* doesn't mention him.[38] In a volume on America since 1945 by Dewey W. Grantham, Sheen is cited only once: his book *Peace of Soul* is linked with Norman Vincent Peale's *The Power of Positive Thinking* and both are relegated to the "cult of reassurance" and the "peace of mind" religion of the postwar years.[39] He is treated similarly by George Donelson Moss in *America in the Twentieth Century.*[40]

Sheen did not make the life of the historian easy. He destroyed almost all of the letters that passed across his desk in the course of his lengthy career. This attitude toward his correspondence is puzzling. He did not often give interviews, and it may be that he merely cherished his privacy. In 1946 he told a reporter that he would prefer not to have a story written about him, dismissing publicity as "artificial as rouge on the cheek. Doing the job is the important thing, even if you're a street cleaner."[41] He told another reporter, "Anything that I have comes from God. Glory be to God! Let that be my interview."[42]

Perhaps the solution to the puzzle is simply that in the course of a very busy life filled with travel and moving personal belongings from residence to residence, Sheen lacked the inclination to carry about a huge number of letters. How huge? In 1946 alone, he was writing between 150 and 200 letters a day.[43] In the early 1950s, according to Sheen, the television show was generating between 15,000 and 25,000 letters per *day*, and he tried to answer as many as his schedule allowed.[44]

In the late 1940s, Fulton showed an interviewer a notebook he kept, listing names of hundreds of letter writers and three or four words summarizing the contents of their letters. The letters themselves, generated by Sheen's radio programs, were discarded. Copies of the replies, often based on form letters, were apparently not made. Sheen did not keep complete records of his correspondence, he said. "It's not wise. This is God's work."[45]

Moreover, a friend who knew him in the 1960s and '70s noted that Sheen seemed not at all interested in his past. He did not act like an old man and was not given to reminiscence. He wanted at all times to be current—to read the latest books and articles; to be youthful and relevant.[46] When interviewed at seventy-seven, he said he could not even cite the number of the books he had written: "like Rousseau in the case of his children, I've abandoned each of them at birth. I've never bothered to keep count because, if I did, that would be relying on the past and I don't think any of us should rely on the past."[47]

In any case, Sheen letters and documents are to be found in a wide assortment of other manuscript collections. Scores of people who knew Sheen have been willing, often eager, to speak for the record. And Sheen's relatives have been extremely cooperative, providing me with an abundance of photographs and documents along with their recollections.

Acknowledgments

There are many people who, through their kindness and generosity, have assisted this project. The Lynde and Harry Bradley Foundation enabled me to take a year away from the classroom. The Historical Research Foundation provided research and travel funds. The Homeland Foundation funded my work for one summer. I am deeply indebted to Dr. Michael Joyce and William F. Buckley Jr. for their support and encouragement.

My research assistant, Chad Abel-Kops, was excellent in every way. Little did I know when I taught him historical methods as an undergraduate that he would mature into such a diligent and thorough pursuer of facts. John Shepherd, archivist at the Catholic University of America, was extraordinarily helpful. Fr. Joe Wilson provided both wisdom and knowledge in abundance.

Sheen family members were uniformly friendly and cooperative. Special thanks go to Joan Sheen Cunningham, Eileen Sheen Khouw, Anne Gevas, Joseph Sheen Jr., Mary Fulton Baker and Connie Sheen, who showered me with documents, photographs, genealogical charts, and memories. Friends of the late archbishop, including Sister Marlene Brownett, Vincent and Marian Cahill, Ann O'Connor, Mary Nordeman, Loretta Young and Ursula Faymonville were especially generous.

The late John Cardinal O'Connor provided access to the Francis Cardinal Spellman Papers in the Archdiocese of New York Archives. Dr. Timothy Meagher, archivist and museum director at Catholic University, helped me obtain departmental files on his campus. Fr. George J. Auger assisted my work with the papers of St.

Viator College. Fr. William Graf was my invaluable guide and mentor in Rochester, especially in the Sheen Archives. Fr. Robert McNamara, the historian of the Diocese of Rochester, provided information and wisdom. Monsignor Michael Wrenn was a wonderful host and adviser in New York. Monsignor Tom McSweeney assisted with documents and accounts of his own research efforts. Gregory Ladd, co-founder of the Archbishop Fulton John Sheen Foundation, the Rev. Theron Hughes, and Sharon Hefferen provided valuable interview leads. Blythe Roveland-Brenton explored the newly discovered Vincent Nugent Collection for me at St. John's University, New York.

The research materials for this book, open to all, have been deposited at the Marquette University Library. Dean of the Library Nicholas Burckel and historian Paul Prucha, S.J., of Marquette have been valuable friends for many years.

I am grateful in many ways to my editor, Peter Collier.

Above all, as always, I give thanks to Kathie.

APPENDIX A

Bibliography of Sheen Books, Booklets, Pamphlets and Anthologies

Books

1. *God and Intelligence.* London: Longmans-Green, 1925.

2. *Religion Without God.* London: Longmans-Green, 1928.

3. *The Life of All Living: The Philosophy of Life.* New York: The Century Co., 1929; also published in an abridged version with an altered subtitle by Popular Library, New York, 1929.

4. *The Divine Romance.* New York: The Century Co., 1930.

5. *Old Errors and New Labels.* New York: The Century Co., 1931.

6. *Moods and Truths.* New York: The Century Co., 1932.

7. *Way of the Cross.* New York: Appleton-Century-Crofts, 1932.

8. *The Philosophy of Science.* Milwaukee: The Bruce Publishing Co., 1934.

9. *The Eternal Galilean.* New York: Appleton-Century-Crofts, 1934.

10. *The Mystical Body of Christ.* New York: Sheed and Ward, 1935.

11. *Calvary and the Mass: A Missal Companion.* New York: P. J. Kenedy and Sons, 1936.

12. *The Moral Universe: A Preface to Christian Living.* Milwaukee: The Bruce Publishing Co., 1936.

13. *The Cross and the Beatitudes.* New York: P. J. Kenedy and Sons, 1937; also published the same year in an abridged version by Country Life Press, Garden City, New York.

14. *The Cross and the Crisis.* Milwaukee: The Bruce Publishing Co., 1938.

15. *The Rainbow of Sorrow.* New York: P. J. Kenedy and Sons, 1938; published in the same year by Garden City Books, Garden City, New York.

16. *Liberty, Equality and Fraternity.* New York: Macmillan, 1938.

17. *Victory over Vice.* New York: P. J. Kenedy and Sons, 1939.

18. *Freedom under God.* Milwaukee: The Bruce Publishing Co., 1940.

19. *The Seven Virtues.* New York: P. J. Kenedy and Sons, 1940.

20. *Whence Comes War.* New York: Sheed and Ward, 1940.

21. *For God and Country.* New York: P. J. Kenedy and Sons, 1941.

22. *A Declaration of Dependence.* Milwaukee: The Bruce Publishing Co., 1941.

23. *God and War.* New York: P. J. Kenedy and Sons, 1942.

24. *The Armor of God: Reflections and Prayers for Wartime.* New York: P. J. Kenedy and Sons, 1943. (An abridgement, titled *The Shield of Faith,* was published on the same day by the same publisher.)

25. *The Divine Verdict.* New York: P. J. Kenedy and Sons, 1943.

26. *Philosophies at War.* New York: Charles Scribner's Sons, 1943.

27. *Seven Words to the Cross.* New York: P. J. Kenedy and Sons, 1944.

28. *Love One Another.* New York: P. J. Kenedy and Sons, 1944.

29. *Seven Pillars of Peace.* New York: Charles Scribner's Sons, 1944.

30. *Seven Words of Jesus and Mary.* New York: P. J. Kenedy and Sons, 1945.

31. *Preface to Religion.* New York: P. J. Kenedy and Sons, 1946.

32. *Characters of the Passion.* Garden City, New York: Garden City Books, 1946. (Also published by P. J. Kenedy and Sons in 1947.)

33. *Philosophy of Religion: The Impact of Modern Knowledge on Religion.* New York: Appleton-Century-Crofts, 1948.

34. *Communism and the Conscience of the West.* Indianapolis: Bobbs-Merrill, 1948.

35. *Peace of Soul.* New York: McGraw-Hill, 1949.

36. *Lift up Your Heart.* New York: McGraw-Hill, 1950.

37. *Three to Get Married.* New York: Appleton-Century-Crofts, 1951.

38. *The World's First Love.* New York: McGraw-Hill, 1952. (An abridged version, titled *The World's Great Love: The Prayer of the Rosary,* was published in 1978 by Seabury Press, New York.)

39. *Way to Happiness.* New York: Maco Magazine Corp., 1953. (Republished the following year by Garden City Books, Garden City, New York.)

40. *Life Is Worth Living.* New York: McGraw-Hill, 1953+.

41. *Life Is Worth Living, Second Series.* New York: McGraw-Hill, 1954+.

42. *The Church, Communism, and Democracy.* New York: McGraw-Hill, 1954+.

43. *Life Is Worth Living, Fourth Series.* New York: McGraw-Hill, 1954+.

44. *The Life of Christ.* New York: Maco Magazine Corp., 1954.

45. *Way to Happy Living.* New York: Maco Magazine Corp., 1955.

46. *Thinking Life Through.* New York: McGraw-Hill, 1955+.

47. *God Love You.* Garden City, New York: Doubleday, 1955.

48. *Way to Inner Peace.* Garden City, New York: Garden City Books, 1955.

49. *Thoughts for Daily Living.* Garden City, New York: Garden City Books, 1956. (Also published in 1956 by Browne and Nolan, Dublin, Ireland.)

50. *Life Is Worth Living, Fifth Series.* New York: McGraw-Hill, 1957+.

51. *Science, Psychiatry and Religion.* New York: Dell, 1957+.

52. *Life of Christ.* New York: McGraw-Hill, 1958.

53. *Go to Heaven.* New York: McGraw-Hill, 1960.

54. *These Are the Sacraments.* New York: Hawthorn Books, 1962. (Revised edition published in 1964 by Doubleday, Garden City, New York.)

55. *The Priest Is Not His Own.* New York: McGraw-Hill, 1963.

56. *Missions and the World Crisis.* Milwaukee: Bruce Press, 1963.

57. *The Power of Love.* New York: Maco Magazine Corp., 1964. (Published in 1965 by Simon and Schuster, New York.)

58. *Walk with God.* New York: Maco Magazine Corp., 1965.

59. *Christmas Inspirations.* New York: Maco Magazine Corp., 1966. (Republished in 1984 as *Rejoice!* by Doubleday, Garden City, New York.)

60. *Footprints in a Darkened Forest: Vital Words for Today's Changing World.* New York: Meredith Press, 1967.

61. *Guide to Contentment.* New York: Maco Publishing Co, 1967.

62. *Lenten and Easter Inspirations.* New York: Maco Publishing Co., 1967. (Republished in 1984 as *Cross-Ways: A Book of Inspiration* by Doubleday, Garden City, New York.)

63. *Children and Parents.* New York: Simon and Schuster, 1970.

64. *Those Mysterious Priests.* Garden City, New York: Doubleday, 1974.

65. *That Tremendous Love: An Anthology of Inspirational Quotations, Poems, Prayers and Philosophical Comments.* New York: Harper and Row, 1967.

66. *Treasure in Clay: The Autobiography of Fulton J. Sheen.* New York: Doubleday, 1980.

(+ printed television talks)

Booklets

1. *The Way of the Cross.* New York: Appleton-Century-Crofts, 1932. (Also published by Our Sunday Visitor, Huntington, Indiana in 1932 and by Garden City Books, Garden City, New York in 1933.)

2. *The Seven Last Words.* New York: The Century Co., 1933.

3. *Jesus, Son of Mary.* New York: The Declan X. McMullan Co., 1947.

4. *The Fifteen Mysteries of the Rosary.* St. Paul: Catechetical Guide and Educational Society, 1951.

5. *Crisis in History.* St. Paul: Catechetical Guide and Educational Society, 1952.

6. *The True Meaning of Christmas.* New York: McGraw-Hill, 1955.

7. *Church of the Poor; or, the "Poor" Church.* New York: Mission, 1963.

Pamphlets

1. *The Lord's Prayer on the Cross.* Paterson, New Jersey: St. Anthony's Guild, 1936.

2. *Tactics of Communism.* New York: Paulist Press, 1936.

3. *Liberty under Communism.* New York: Paulist Press, 1936.

4. *Communism: The Opium of the People.* Paterson, New Jersey: St. Anthony's Guild, 1937.

5. *Communism Answers Questions of a Communist.* New York: Paulist Press, 1937.

6. *Communism and Religion.* New York: Paulist Press, 1937.

7. *The Way of the Cross for Our Enemies.* Paterson, New Jersey: St. Anthony's Guild, 1938.

8. *The Conversion of Heywood Broun: A Funeral Sermon Preached by Fulton J. Sheen.* New York: The Saint Paul Guild, 1939.

9. *What Can I Do?* Washington, D.C.: National Council of Catholic Men, 1942.

10. *The Christian Order and the Family.* New York: Catholic Information Society, 1944?

11. *The Moral Basis of Peace, Related to the Dumbarton Oaks Conference.* San Francisco: Monitor Press, 1945.

12. *East Meets West.* New York: Catholic Near East Welfare Association, 1946.

13. *The Ideological Fallacies of Communism,* with Solomon Andhil Fineberg and Daniel A. Poling. Washington, D.C.: HUAC pamphlet #97608, 1957.

14. *The World's Great Love: The Prayer of the Rosary.* New York: Seabury Press, 1978.

Catholic Hour Publications

1. *The Enrollment of the World.* New York: Paulist Press, 1928.

2. *The Divine Romance.* Huntington, Indiana: Our Sunday Visitor, 1930. (Published the same year as a book of the same title.)

3. *Manifestations of Christ.* Huntington, Indiana: Our Sunday Visitor, 1932.

4. *The Way of the Cross.* Huntington, Indiana: Our Sunday Visitor, 1932. (Published the same year as a booklet of the same title.)

5. *Seven Last Words.* Huntington, Indiana: Our Sunday Visitor, 1933. (Published the same year as a booklet of the same title.

6. *The Hymn of the Conquered.* Huntington, Indiana: Our Sunday Visitor, 1933.

7. *The Eternal Galilean.* Huntington, Indiana: Our Sunday Visitor, 1934. (Also published the same year as a book of the same title.)

8. *The Queen of Seven Swords.* Huntington, Indiana: Our Sunday Visitor, 1934.

9. *The Fullness of Christ.* Huntington, Indiana: Our Sunday Visitor, 1935.

10. *The Prodigal World: Social Reconstruction Is Conditioned upon Spiritual Regeneration.* Huntington, Indiana: Our Sunday Visitor, 1936.

11. *Our Wounded World.* Huntington, Indiana: Our Sunday Visitor, 1937.

12. *Freedom and Democracy: A Study of Their Enemies.* Huntington, Indiana: Our Sunday Visitor, 1937.

13. *Justice and Charity,* Part 1, *The Social Problem and the Church.* Huntington, Indiana: Our Sunday Visitor, 1938.

14. *Justice and Charity,* Part 2, *The Individual Problem and the Cross.* Huntington, Indiana: Our Sunday Visitor, 1938.

15. *Patriotism.* New Haven, Connecticut: Knights of Columbus, 1938.

16. *Cardinal Hayes: A Eulogy by Msgr. Fulton J. Sheen.* Huntington, Indiana: Our Sunday Visitor, 1938.

17. *Pius XI: A Eulogy by Msgr. Fulton J. Sheen.* Huntington, Indiana: Our Sunday Visitor, 1939.

18. *Freedom, Part One.* Huntington, Indiana: Our Sunday Visitor, 1939.

19. *Freedom, Part Two.* Huntington, Indiana: Our Sunday Visitor, 1939.

20. *Communism, Capitalism, and Property.* Huntington, Indiana: Our Sunday Visitor, 1939.

21. *Peace: The Fruit of Justice.* Huntington, Indiana; Our Sunday Visitor, 1940.

22. *The Seven Last Words and the Seven Virtues.* Huntington, Indiana: Our Sunday Visitor, 1940.

23. *War and Guilt.* Huntington, Indiana: Our Sunday Visitor, 1941.

24. *Freedom and Peace.* Huntington, Indiana: Our Sunday Visitor, 1941.

25. *Christ in Exile.* Washington, D.C.: The Bishops Relief Committee, 1941.

26. *Peace.* Huntington, Indiana: Our Sunday Visitor, 1942.

27. *The Crisis in Christendom.* Huntington, Indiana: Our Sunday Visitor, 1943.

28. *One Lord, One World.* Huntington, Indiana: Our Sunday Visitor, 1944.

29. *Friends.* Washington, D.C.: National Council of Catholic Men, 1944.

30. *You.* Huntington, Indiana: Our Sunday Visitor, 1945.

31. *The Seventh Word: The Purpose of Life.* Huntington, Indiana: Our Sunday Visitor, 1945.

32. *Easter.* Huntington, Indiana: Our Sunday Visitor, 1945.

33. *Love on Pilgrimage.* Huntington, Indiana: Our Sunday Visitor, 1946.

34. *The Holy Hour: Readings and Prayers for a Daily Hour of Meditation.* Huntington, Indiana: Our Sunday Visitor, 1946?

35. *Light Your Lamps.* Huntington, Indiana: Our Sunday Visitor, 1947.

36. *The Modern Soul in Search of God.* Huntington, Indiana: Our Sunday Visitor, 1948.

37. *The Love That Waits for You.* Huntington, Indiana: Our Sunday Visitor, 1949.

38. *The Rock Plunged into Eternity.* Huntington, Indiana: Our Sunday Visitor, 1950.

39. *The Woman.* Huntington, Indiana: Our Sunday Visitor, 1951.

40. *Life of Christ.* Huntington, Indiana: Our Sunday Visitor, 1952.

41. *The Prodigal World.* Huntington, Indiana: Our Sunday Visitor, 1952.

Anthologies by Others

1. *Sheed and Ward Samplers,* vol. 2, *Fulton Sheen.* New York: Sheed and Ward, 1936.

2. *The Fulton J. Sheen Treasury.* New York: Popular Library, 19??.

3. Frederick Gushurst and the staff of *Quote,* eds. *The Quotable Fulton J. Sheen.* Anderson, South Carolina: Drake House, 1967.

4. Bill Adler, ed. *The Wit and Wisdom of Bishop Fulton J. Sheen.* Garden City, New York: Doubleday, 1969.

5. *The Electronic Christian: 105 Readings from Fulton J. Sheen.* New York: Macmillan, 1979.

6. *A Fulton J. Sheen Reader.* St. Paul, Minnesota: Carillon Books, 1979.

7. *On Being Human: Reflections on Life and Living.* Garden City, New York: Doubleday, 1982.

8. Henry Dieterich, ed. *Through the Years with Fulton Sheen: Inspirational Selections for Each Day of the Year.* Ann Arbor, Michigan: Servant Books, 1985.

9. George A. Martin, Richard P. Rabatin, and John L. Swan, eds. *The Quotable Fulton Sheen: A Topical Compilation of the Wit, Wisdom, and Satire of Archbishop Fulton J. Sheen.* New York: Doubleday, 1989.

10. *From the Angel's Blackboard: The Best of Fulton J. Sheen: A Centennial Celebration.* Liguori, Missouri: Liguori/Triumph Books, 1995.

11. Beverly Coney Heirich, ed. *Mornings with Fulton Sheen: 120 Holy Hour Readings.* Ann Arbor, Michigan: Servant Books, 1998.

12. *Simple Truths: Thinking Life Through with Fulton J. Sheen.* Liguori, Missouri: Liguori/Triumph Books, 1998.

13. *In the Fullness of Time: Christ Centered Wisdom for the Third Millennium.* Liguori, Missouri: Liguori Publications, 1999.

APPENDIX B

Hints for Presenting a Talk

In 1979, while in a restaurant waiting for guests to arrive, Sister Ann Edward asked Archbishop Sheen for some hints about presenting a talk. As he spoke, she furiously took notes, adding numbers when she typed up the results:

1. Voice-tone: Plato recalls tone three or four days after hearing a talk. It's the *tonal* quality that strikes an audience.

2. When listening to a speaker, count the words on each breath. Indicate each word by a dash, and each pause by a stroke. If it's—/—/, it's dull, flat, stale.

3. Avoid a pulpit voice. Be natural. As Disraeli said, "There's no index of character as sure as the voice."

4. Learn [the] value of *pauses*. Never for their own sake, but for emphasis or to allow the thought to sink into the audience. They need time for digestion.

5. A whisper can have more value than a shout. Macaulay said of Pitt, "Even a whisper of his was heard in the remotest corner of the House of Commons."

6. If there's a commotion, disturbance, or latecomers, do not raise the voice; lower it and the audience will try to catch the whisper.

7. [The] audience is infallible in judging if a voice is artificial or natural.

8. Let [a] first sentence be interesting. Do not state the obvious, e.g. "Today we celebrate a 25th anniversary."

9. Only nervous speakers need water.

10. If brevity is the soul of wit, the secret of oratory is "know when to quit."

11. Before beginning, pause a few moments. As a mother cannot forget the child of her womb, we can't forget the child of our brain.

12. Start with a *low* voice.

13. Audience needs a come-on; feel superior, not timid or obsequious.

14. To begin with, have a story where *you* come out second best.

Summary

1. Talk naturally.

2. Plead vehemently.

3. Whisper confidentially.

4. Appeal plaintively.

5. Proclaim distinctly.

6. Pray constantly.

—Tell plot first. Homer did; Shakespeare did.

—Any emphasis needs time.

—All ears? Audience silent? Pause if they're not.

—Never state the obvious.

—Lungs full of air are resonant. (Ball on a fountain of water, bouncing.)

At that point, the guests arrived and Sheen's ten-minute presentation ended. A copy of these notes, with commentary by the note taker, is in the Ann Edward file.

Notes

Introduction

1. See "Top 100 Catholics" at www.catholic-internet.org/.

2. Matthew Bunson, ed., *2000: Our Sunday Visitor's Catholic Almanac* (Huntington, Indiana: Our Sunday Visitor, 2000), p. 391.

3. Gladys Baker, *I Had to Know* (New York: Appleton-Century-Crofts, 1951), p. 182.

4. *Peninsula Times-Tribune* (Palo Alto, California), 10 December 1979.

5. John Tracy Ellis, *Catholic Bishops: A Memoir* (Wilmington, Delaware: Michael Glazier, Inc., 1983), p. 84.

6. Quoted in John P. Gallagher, "Worth Watching," *Catholic New York*, 6 February 1992, p. 13.

7. James C. G. Conniff, *The Bishop Sheen Story* (New York: Fawcett Publications, 1953), p. 12.

8. See Mary Ann Watson, "And They Said 'Uncle Fultie' Didn't Have a Prayer ...," *Television Quarterly* 26 (1992), pp. 18–19.

9. George H. Gallup, *The Gallup Poll: Public Opinion, 1935–1971* (New York: Random House, 1972), pp. 1111, 1113, 1296, 1357, 1462.

10. Baker, *I Had to Know*, p. 182. See *New York Times*, 14 April 1941.

11. Fulton J. Sheen, *The Queen of Seven Swords*, 11th ed. (Huntington, Indiana: Our Sunday Visitor, 1948).

12. Three books traditionally cited as Sheen's should not be: *This Is the Mass* (1958), *This Is Rome* (1960), and *This Is the Holy Land* (1961). Sheen made minor contributions and posed for photographs, but the bulk of the writing was done by others; Sheen's name on the cover was designed to increase sales. Philip Caroman and James Walsh, eds., *The Fulton J. Sheen Sunday Missal* (New York: Hawthorn Books, 1961) had little to do with Sheen himself.

13. Henry Everett Malone, "The Radio-Preaching Art of Monsignor Sheen" (M.A. thesis, Catholic University of America, 1949), p. 55.

14. Fulton J. Sheen, *Communism and the Conscience of the West* (Indianapolis: Bobbs-Merrill, 1948), p. 59.

15. Ibid., pp. 107–8.

16. Fulton J. Sheen, *Way to Happiness: An Inspiring Guide to Peace, Hope and Contentment* (Staten Island, New York: Alba House, 1998), p. vii.

17. Editorial, "A Life Worth Living," *America*, 22 December 1979, p. 401.

18. Bob Considine, "God Love You," *Cosmopolitan*, July 1952, p. 98.

19. His own estimate. *Boston Evening Globe*, 29 March 1973.

20. Quoted in Editorial, *Mission Magazine*, Spring 1980, p. 1.

21. Mary Baker heard such speeches when she invited Sheen to speak before the Radcliffe Catholic Club. Mary Baker interview, 23 November 1999. All of my interviews are in my files; dates are provided only when more than one interview occurred. All files referred to in the notes are my own files, housed at Marquette University.

22. Fulton J. Sheen, *Friends* (Washington, D.C.: National Council of Catholic Men, 1944), p. 63.

23. Ibid., p. 73.

24. Fulton J. Sheen, *The Eternal Galilean* (New York: D. Appleton-Century, 1934), p. 62.

25. Sheen, *Communism and the Conscience of the West*, p. 79.

26. Fulton J. Sheen, *Peace of Soul* (Liguori, Missouri: Triumph Books, 1996), p. 259.

27. "Bishop Sheen Speaks Out," *Image*, a 1973 article, p. 18, in the Eileen Sheen Khouw file.

28. "Microphone Missionary," *Time*, 14 April 1952, pp. 72–74.

29. Donald F. Crosby, *God, Church, and Flag: Senator Joseph R. McCarthy and the Catholic Church, 1950–1957* (Chapel Hill: University of North Carolina Press, 1978), pp. 15–16.

30. David Caute, *The Great Fear: The Anti-Communist Purge under Truman and Eisenhower* (New York: Simon and Schuster, 1978), pp. 108–9, 123, 131.

31. Ellen Schrecker, *Many Are the Crimes: McCarthyism in America* (Boston: Little, Brown and Co., 1998), p. 74.

32. Richard Gid Powers, *Not Without Honor: The History of American Anti-communism* (New York: The Free Press, 1995), pp. 194, 250.

33. http://www.tvsaint.com. Cicarelli was dying of lung cancer and hoped that through ardent prayer, using Sheen as an intercessor, he would be cured. He died a short time later, but his five children pledged to carry on the canonization effort. *St. Petersburg Times,* 8 July 2000.

34. Homer Carey Hockett, *The Critical Method in Historical Research and Writing* (New York: The Macmillan Co., 1955), p. 51.

Chapter 1: A Successor of the Apostles

1. Jay P. Dolan, *The American Catholic Experience: A History from Colonial Times to the Present* (Notre Dame: University of Notre Dame Press, 1980), pp. 139–44, 302–3. Ireland exported priests and nuns to the United States well into the twentieth century. A single institution, All Hallows College of Dublin, supplied the New World with 1,500 priests between 1842 and 1902. See Roger Finke and Rodney Stark, *The Churching of America, 1776–1990: Winners and Losers in Our Religious Economy* (New Brunswick, New Jersey: Rutgers University Press, 1992), pp. 136–37.

2. Thomas C. Reeves, *The Life and Times of Joe McCarthy: A Biography* (Lanham, Maryland: Madison Books, 1997), pp. 1–3.

3. *Boston Post* reporters Ken Crotty and James Jones did a series of stories on Fulton J. Sheen and his family, published from 7 May to 18 May 1953. Their accounts, based on primary sources and interviews in Illinois, are extremely valuable. For genealogical information noted here, see *Boston Post,* 15 May 1953. On Melissa Robinson's probable heritage, see copy Fulton J. Sheen to Robert McNamara, 8 March 1977, given to me by Fr. McNamara and now in the Sheen Family file. I am also indebted to Anne Gevas, the Sheen family historian, who provided me with genealogies, photographs, personal recollections, and leads for interviews. See the Anne Gevas file.

4. Merle Fulton interview, 1 September 1999; Joan Cunningham interview, 4 October 1999; John E. Sheen interview; Sheen, *Treasure in Clay,* p. 7.

5. Thomas Sheen quoted in *PM Magazine,* 12 July 1940.

6. John E. Sheen interview; Merle Fulton interview, 1 September 1999.

7. Anne Gevas to the author, 7 March 2000, Anne Gevas file. For more on this, see the Anne Gevas file.

8. "Microphone Missionary," *Time,* 14 April 1952, p. 73; Kenneth Stewart, "Monsignor Fulton J. Sheen," *PM Magazine,* 23 June 1946, p. m8; Anne Gevas to the author, 24 November 1999, Anne Gevas file.

9. Anne Gevas obtained this information in documents from the Woodford County Clerk's office in Eureka, Illinois. Gevas to the author, 9 October 1999, Anne Gevas file.

10. One family account contends that Newt and his brother Andrew became Catholic again to help their hardware business in predominantly Catholic El Paso, Illinois. Anne Gevas to the author, 7 March 2000, Anne Gevas file.

11. Anne Gevas to the author, 7 March 2000, Anne Gevas file. Eva Marie married a man named Walsh. Joe Sheen, Fulton's brother, reached out to her at some point, and Eva attended Joe's funeral in 1955. Joan Cunningham interview, 4 October 1999. For more, see Anne Gevas file.

12. Mary Baker interview, 23 November 1999.

13. John E. Sheen interview; Joseph Sheen Jr. interview.

14. Merle Fulton interview, 1 September 1999.

15. Joan Cunningham interview, 4 October 1999.

16. *Boston Post,* 14 May 1953.

17. *Boston Post,* 7, 8 May 1953.

18. Fr. Lawrence P. Morrissey (pastor of St. Mary's Church) to the author, 23 August 1999, Sheen Family file.

19. *Boston Post,* 7 May 1953.

20. Sheen, *Treasure in Clay,* pp. 8–10.

21. Ibid., p. 8.

22. Copy, Fulton J. Sheen to Robert McNamara, 8 March 1977, courtesy of Fr. McNamara.

23. *Boston Post,* 8 May 1953.

24. Sheen, *Treasure in Clay,* p. 16; John E. Sheen interview; Joseph Sheen Jr. interview.

25. *Boston Post,* 15, 18 May 1953.

26. Dolan, *The American Catholic Experience,* pp. 243, 253.

27. Sheen, *Treasure in Clay,* p. 316.

28. Ibid., p. 8. Sheen also says, on page 10, that his middle name, John, was given him at confirmation. In fact, John Peter was his baptismal name. Lawrence P. Morrissey to the author, 23 August 1999, Sheen Family file. See *New York Times,* 27 October 1966 for the same account of the name change.

29. *Peoria Journal Star,* 12 December 1979; tape recording of Sheen homily, 20 September 1979, in the possession of Marlene Brownett. See also *Boston Post,* 7 May 1953; "Microphone Missionary," *Time,* p. 19. Sheen cousin Merle Fulton claims that Sheen changed his first name because neighborhood boys taunted him by using "P. J." as a racial epithet. Fulton refuses to elaborate, and I have been unable to verify the story. See Merle Fulton interview, 1 September 1999, and see him quoted in *Peoria Journal Star,* 11 December 1979. See also Lawrence P. Morrissey to the author, 23 August 1999, Sheen Family file.

30. Undated biographical statement on her father, Tom, by Eileen Khouw, received by the author on 3 December 1999, Eileen Sheen Khouw file; John E. Sheen interview; Catherine Sheen interview.

31. Sheen, *Treasure in Clay,* pp. 10–13.

32. *Boston Post,* 8 May 1953.

33. Sheen, *Treasure in Clay,* pp. 316–17. The *Boston Post* reporters in 1953 attributed this practice to the Brothers of Mary at the Spalding Institute. *Boston Post,* 11 May 1953.

34. George Weigel, *Witness to Hope: The Biography of Pope John Paul II* (New York: HarperCollins, 1999), p. 78.

35. Sheen, *Treasure in Clay,* p. 10.

36. John J. Delaney, *Dictionary of American Catholic Biography,* 1st ed. (New York: Doubleday, 1961), pp. 542–43.

37. Sheen, *Treasure in Clay,* p. 316.

38. Stewart, "Monsignor Fulton J. Sheen," p. m7.

39. Sheen, *Treasure in Clay,* p. 30. See also p. 331.

40. Joseph F. Sheen, "My Brother's Vocation," *Missionary Youth,* 1954, pp. 10–11.

41. Sheen, *Treasure in Clay,* p. 230

42. Ibid., p. 329.

43. Copy, Fulton J. Sheen to Robert McNamara, 8 March 1977, Sheen Family file.

44. Sheen, *Treasure in Clay,* p. 16.

45. Fulton J. Sheen, *Children and Parents* (New York: Simon and Schuster, 1970), p. 26.

46. Joseph F. Sheen, "My Brother's Vocation," p. 11.

47. Fulton J. Sheen, *Way to Inner Peace* (Staten Island: Alba House, 1998), p. 68.

48. Ibid., pp. 166–67.

49. Sheen, *Treasure in Clay*, p. 17.

50. Ibid., 18–20.

51. Joan Cunningham interview, 4 October 1999.

52. Sheen, *Children and Parents*, p. 80.

53. Fulton J. Sheen, *Life Is Worth Living, First and Second Series* (San Francisco: Ignatius Press, 1999), p. 49.

54. Sheen, *Treasure in Clay*, p. 350.

55. Sheen, *Communism and the Conscience of the West* (Indianapolis: Bobbs-Merrill, 1948), p. 149.

56. Catherine Sheen interview.

57. Ibid.

58. Reeda Holliger interview, 22 April 2000. Margaret Reeda Eibeck Holliger claims to be related to Fulton Sheen through Newton Sheen: her father and Newton, she says, were cousins. This cannot currently be substantiated. Fulton Sheen believed Reeda to be a cousin, however, and the two remained friends all of his life. I found the woman, at 98, extremely persuasive.

59. Sheen, *Treasure in Clay*, pp. 13–14.

60. Dolan, *The American Catholic Experience*, p. 292.

61. *Boston Post*, 13 May 1953. On the haberdashery, see an informal, unpublished history of Fulton J. Sheen and his brothers by Fr. Bernard Mulvaney, a colleague and friend of Sheen's at Catholic University. It is in the Saint Viator papers at the Provincial Offices of the Clerics of Saint Viator, Arlington Heights, Illinois.

62. *Boston Post*, 10 May 1953.

63. Sheen, *Treasure in Clay*, p. 14; *Boston Post*, 13 May 1953. A classmate, quoted in the *Boston Post* article, remembered Fulton as the star of the play *The Missing Bonds*.

64. *Boston Post*, 11 May 1953.

65. Ibid., 10 May 1953.

66. Ibid., 13 May 1953.

67. James C. G. Conniff, *The Bishop Sheen Story* (New York: Fawcett Publications, 1953), p. 21.

68. *Catholic Post*, 16 December 1979.

69. John E. Sheen interview.

70. Joan Cunningham interview, 4 October 1999. Fulton later noted that his father "could never read novels." Sheen, *Treasure in Clay*, p. 78.

71. Joseph Sheen Jr. to the author, 22 June 2000.

72. Sheen, *Treasure in Clay,* p. 18.

73. *Peoria Journal Star,* 12 December 1979; Merle Fulton interview, 1 September 1999. Cf. Sheen, *Treasure in Clay,* p. 30.

74. Sheen, *Treasure in Clay,* p. 172; *Catholic Post,* 16 December 1979.

75. Sheen, *Treasure in Clay,* p. 18.

76. See Conniff, *The Bishop Sheen Story,* p. 20.

77. George Auger to the author, 4 December 1999, enclosing Al's high school transcript from St. Viator, St. Viator file; Merle Fulton interview, 1 September 1999; Catherine Sheen interview. Fulton's uncle, attorney Daniel R. Sheen, was said to have contributed financially to Fulton's education beginning at St. Mary's. Michael Glazier and Thomas J. Shelley, eds., *The Encyclopedia of American Catholic History* (Collegeville, Minnesota: The Liturgical Press, 1997), p. 1285.

78. See "The Year of Reconciliation—1978," a publication of Olivet Nazarene College, which took over the St. Viator campus in 1938. It is available on the Internet. See also Adrien M. Richard, *The Village: A Story of Bourbonnais* (Bourbonnais, Illinois: Centennial Commission of the Village of Bourbonnais, 1975), pp. 72–74.

79. Richard McBrien, ed., *HarperCollins Encyclopedia of Catholicism* (New York: HarperCollins, 1995), p. 1309.

80. Dolan, *The American Catholic Experience,* p. 292.

81. *Annual Catalog, St. Viator College* (Bourbonnais, Illinois, 1913); Mulvaney manuscript. All of the St. Viator College records, including publications and student transcripts, are now at the Provincial Offices of the Clerics of Saint Viator. This collection will hereafter be cited as St. Viator Papers.

82. *The Viatorian* 34 (June 1917), p. 239.

83. Transcripts in St. Viator Papers.

84. "Microphone Missionary," pp. 73–74. An expanded version of this story is in Conniff, *The Bishop Sheen Story,* p. 24.

85. Sheen, *Treasure in Clay,* pp. 14–16.

86. *The Viatorian* 34 (June 1917), pp. 289, 291.

87. Ibid., pp. 239, 261, 289, 291–2.

88. Ibid., pp. 239, 262.

89. Ibid., p. 255.

90. *The Viatorian* 33 (January 1916), pp. 32–35; 34 (March 1917), pp. 122–25.

91. *The Viatorian* 34 (June 1917), pp. 239, 264.

92. Joseph F. Sheen, "My Brother's Vocation," p. 13.

93. Ibid., p. 11.

94. Joseph F. Sheen, *Treasure in Clay,* pp. 31–32. Cf. Fulton J. Sheen, *Guide to Contentment* (New York: Maco Publishing Co., 1967), p. 123.

95. Sheen, *Treasure in Clay,* pp. 32–34.

96. Copies of accounts found in the Diocesan Listings, box 6, file 7 in the archive of what is now the Saint Paul Seminary School of Divinity of the University of St. Thomas, in St. Paul, Minnesota.

97. Grazier and Shelley, eds., *Encyclopedia of American Catholic History,* p. 1246. At the close of 1916, there were 102 Roman Catholic seminaries in the United States with 6,898 seminarians. Finke and Starke, *The Churching of America, 1776–1990,* p. 139.

98. Kenneth J. Heineman, *A Catholic New Deal: Religion and Reform in Depression Pittsburgh* (University Park, Pennsylvania: Penn State University Press, 1999), p. 4.

99. Ruth Harris, *Lourdes: Body and Spirit in the Secular Age* (New York: Viking Penguin, 1999), pp. 15, 36, 283–85.

100. *National Catholic Register,* August 6–12, 2000, p. 4.

101. Eamon Duffy, *Saints and Sinners: A History of the Popes* (New Haven: Yale University Press, 1997), pp. 243–44, 246.

102. See the *Baltimore Catechism,* no. 3 (any edition), the answers to Questions 510, 511, 516. See also *Catechism of the Council of Trent for Parish Priests* (Rockford, Illinois: Tan Books, 1982), pp. 515–17.

103. See Dolan, *The American Catholic Experience,* pp. 334–38.

104. Ibid., pp. 303–4, 317–20; Duffy, *Saints and Sinners,* pp. 250–51.

105. William M. Halsey, *The Survival of American Innocence: Catholicism in an Era of Disillusionment, 1920–1940* (Notre Dame, Indiana: University of Notre Dame Press, 1980), pp. 16–17.

106. Ibid., pp. 139–42. Neo-Thomism was also employed by Anglo-Catholics (Anglicans favorable to Roman Catholicism) and several secularists, such as Robert Maynard Hutchins of the University of Chicago and his friend, philosopher Mortimer Adler. See Sydney E. Ahlstrom, *A Religious History of the American People* (New Haven: Yale University Press, 1972), p. 1012; Harry S. Ashmore, *Unseasonable Truths: The Life of Robert Maynard Hutchins* (Boston: Little Brown, 1989), pp. 158–64. Adler became a Roman Catholic in 2000 at the age of 97.

107. Dolan, *The American Catholic Experience,* pp. 386–87.

108. Charles R. Morris, *American Catholic: The Saints and Sinners Who Built America's Most Powerful Church* (New York: New York Times Books, 1997), p. 84.

109. Ibid., pp. 135, 242, 255.

110. Quoted in Philip Gleason, *Keeping the Faith: American Catholicism Past and Present* (Notre Dame, Indiana: University of Notre Dame Press, 1989), p. 102.

111. Quoted in Dolan, *The American Catholic Experience,* p. 351.

112. See Gleason, *Keeping the Faith,* pp. 99–106.

113. Morris, *American Catholic,* p. 133.

114. Halsey, *The Survival of American Innocence,* p. 49.

115. *The St. Paul Seminary Register* for 1918 and 1919, in the St. Paul Seminary Archives at the University of St. Thomas.

116. Sheen, *Treasure in Clay,* p. 20.

117. William Ferris interview; Edwin Broderick interview, 2 June 1999. See Fulton J. Sheen, *Preface to Religion* (New York: P. J. Kenedy and Sons, 1946), pp. 6, 164.

118. Sheen, *Treasure in Clay,* p. 20; Conniff, *The Bishop Sheen Story,* p. 29.

119. Joan Cunningham interview, 4 October 1999; Matthew Paratore interview; Mary Giaratanna interview; Joan Dalton interview, 16 December 1998; Hilary Franco interview, 19 March 1998.

120. Sheen, *Treasure in Clay,* p. 229.

121. Ibid., pp. 187–99. Cf. Joseph Bernardin, *The Gift of Peace: Personal Reflections by Joseph Cardinal Bernardin* (Chicago: Loyola Press, 1997), pp. 96–100.

122. Matthew Paratore interview.

123. Sheen, *Treasure in Clay,* p. 189.

124. Fulton J. Sheen, *The Holy Hour: Readings and Prayers for a Daily Hour of Meditation* (Washington, D.C.: National Council of Catholic Men, c. 1946), pp. 3, 5. See also Fulton J. Sheen, *God and War* (New York: P. J. Kenedy and Sons, 1942), pp. 27–28.

125. See copy, Sharen Darling to Chad Abel-Kops, 12 February 1999, St. Paul Seminary file; Rita Watrin, *The Founding and Development of the Program of Affiliation of the Catholic University of America: 1912 to 1939* (Washington, D.C.: Catholic University, 1966), pp. 11–12.

126. See the official statement by George A. Carton, 8 May 1978, Sheen Correspondence, box 30, Sheen Archives.

127. D. P. Noonan, *The Passion of Fulton Sheen* (New York: Dodd, Mead, 1972), p. 10; Sheen, *Treasure in Clay*, p. 187.

128. *Dallas Morning News*, 14 June 1967.

129. *Boston Post*, 8 May 1953.

Chapter 2: The Taste of Champagne

1. C. Joseph Nuesse, *The Catholic University of America: A Centennial History* (Washington, D.C.: Catholic University of America, 1990), pp. 6–34. The status quotation is on page 23.

2. Quoted in J. P. Dolan, *The American Catholic Experience: A History from Colonial Times to the Present* (Garden City, New York: Doubleday, 1985), p. 351.

3. Nuesse, *The Catholic University of America*, pp. 68–69.

4. Ibid., pp. 168, 190–92.

5. Ibid., p. 115.

6. Ibid., pp. 172–73.

7. The best source on Ryan is Francis L. Broderick, *Right Reverend New Dealer John A. Ryan* (New York: Macmillan, 1963).

8. Nuesse, *The Catholic University of America*, pp. 179, 212–13. Sheen's recollection of his two professors is in Sheen, *Treasure in Clay*, p. 22.

9. Nuesse, *The Catholic University of America*, pp. 110–11, 195.

10. William M. Halsey, *The Survival of American Innocence: Catholicism in an Era of Disillusionment, 1920–1940* (Notre Dame, Indiana: University of Notre Dame Press, 1980), p. 140.

11. Sheen, *Treasure in Clay*, pp. 22, 304.

12. Ibid., p. 256.

13. *Thirty-first Annual Commencement and Conferring of Degrees, June 16, 1920*, Catholic University of America Archives. CUA does not have formal records of the coursework completed by Sheen and Hart. Such information was often forwarded to the diocesan bishop sponsoring the student. There has been much confusion about the degrees bestowed on Sheen by CUA in 1920. Kathleen Riley Fields reports an S.T.D., a degree Sheen would never earn, in "Bishop Fulton J. Sheen: An American Catholic

Response to the Twentieth Century" (Ph.D. diss., University of Notre Dame, 1988), p. 4.

14. See Hart's obituary in *Washington Post and Times Herald*, 30 January 1959; CUA press release on Hart, 30 January 1959, Catholic University of America Archives. Veteran CUA philosopher Jude P. Dougherty, who took his doctorate under Hart, later described his mentor and colleague as "the most profound thinker" in the School of Philosophy, "saintly," and primarily "a street preacher, like Sheen." Jude P. Dougherty interview.

15. Sheen, *Treasure in Clay*, p. 91.

16. Gretta Palmer, "Why All These Converts? The Story of Monsignor Fulton Sheen," *Look*, 24 June 1947, p. 38.

17. Neo-Thomism continues to this day to receive papal endorsements. See Romanus Cessario, "Thomas Aquinas: A Doctor for the Ages," *First Things*, March 1999, p. 32.

18. Joseph Ratzinger, *Milestones: Memoirs 1927–1977* (San Francisco: Ignatius Press, 1997), p. 44.

19. *New York Herald Tribune*, 9 March 1959; Sheen, *Treasure in Clay*, p. 23.

20. Joan Cunningham interview, 4 October 1999; Eileen Sheen Khouw to the author, 12 December 1999, Sheen Family file.

21. Sheen Diary, 26 February 1922, Sheen Archives.

22. Fulton J. Sheen to S. Donohue, 14 September 1928, Patrick Cardinal Hayes Correspondence, New York Archdiocesan Archives; undated Eileen Khouw biographical statement on her father, Eileen Sheen Khouw file.

23. Sheen, *Treasure in Clay*, pp. 257–58; Sheen Diary, 4 February 1922.

24. Palmer, "Why All These Converts?" p. 40.

25. See the fine article on Louvain in Catholic University of America, *New Catholic Encyclopedia* (New York: McGraw Hill, 1967), vol. 8, pp. 1033–38; and Valentin Denis, *Catholic University of Louvain, 1425–1958* (Louvain: Catholic University of Louvain, 1958), pp. 28–29. Fulton later described seeing the ruined library and, later, a painting featuring the crucified Christ and Cardinal Mercier gazing upon the ruins. *The Rambler*, 29 January 1935, Rosemont College file.

26. Sheen, *Treasure in Clay*, p. 12.

27. Ibid., pp. 23–25.

28. Joseph Roddy, "A Talk with Bishop Sheen," *Look*, 27 January 1953, p. 38. The Fulton J. Sheen Papers at Catholic University contain seven hardback

notebooks filled with Sheen's lecture notes taken while at Louvain. Four are in French and three in English. The courses were: Introduction to Philosophy, Logic, Metaphysics, and Pragmatism. The notebooks were donated by Sheen in 1946.

29. Sheen, *Treasure in Clay,* p. 91. Cf. p. 12.

30. Ann O'Connor to the author, 31 May 2000; Ann O'Connor interview. In 1944, Fulton wrote to Ann, whom he always called Nora, "Please God I may be able to see you again next summer and what a joy it will be once again to have tea and cakes at Number 66. Nicer still will it be to hear you run down the stairs, for despite the passing of the years, to me you are still the same sweet little Irish girl that I met in the French church in that daydream of long ago." Copy, Fulton J. Sheen to Nora O'Connor, 7 December 1944, in O'Connor's possession.

31. Sheen, *Treasure in Clay,* pp. 270–72.

32. Sheen Diary, 1922, *passim.*

33. At about this same time, Fulton urged his brother Joe to get out of Peoria, travel to Chicago or New York, and go to law school. Three years from now, said Fulton sternly, he wanted to see Joe with a profession, a wife, and a child. Joe took his brother's advice and became a successful Chicago lawyer and family man. The letter is in the possession of Joseph Sheen Jr. Joseph Sheen Jr. interview.

34. *Dallas Morning News,* 13 June 1967.

35. Sheen Diary, 29 March, 1 April, 2 May 1922.

36. Sheen, *Treasure in Clay,* pp. 26–27.

37. Sheen Diary, 11 July 1922.

38. Sheen, *Treasure in Clay,* pp. 127–33.

39. Ibid., pp. 230–31.

40. Ibid., p. 27.

41. Copy, Alfred Wilder to Patrick G. D. Riley, 19 April 1999; Alfred Wilder to the author, 22 May 1999, Angelicum file. Father Wilder is dean of philosophy at the Angelicum. For more institutional documentation, see the Angelicum file.

42. Sheen, *Treasure in Clay,* p. 27.

43. See Johannes Beutler to the author, 15 February 2000. Fr. Beutler is vice-rector for academic affairs at the Gregorian. See the Gregorian file for further documentation.

44. William J. Hanford, "A Rhetorical Study of the Radio and Television Speaking of Bishop Fulton John Sheen" (Ph.D. diss., Wayne State University, 1965), p. 111.

45. Sheen, *Treasure in Clay*, p. 318.

46. Jan Drikie to Chad Abel-Kops, 23 February 1999, St. Edmund's College file. Fr. Drikie is an official at the Westminster Diocesan Archives in London.

47. Ann O'Connor interview. According to O'Connor, the idea of serving at Soho originated at a tea in her flat. Fr. Sheeron, a young curate at St. Patrick's, invited Sheen to the parish, to live and serve, after hearing the American complain of the cold he felt at the large French church in Leicester. See Sheen, *Treasure in Clay*, p. 52.

48. Tape recording of a speech before the Catholic Actors' Guild dinner, 12 November 1977, in the possession of Marlene Brownett; Sheen, *Treasure in Clay*, pp. 264–65.

49. On Knox, see the Ann O'Connor interview.

50. Sheen, *Treasure in Clay*, pp. 50–51.

51. *New York Herald Tribune,* 9 March 1959; Sheen, *Treasure in Clay,* pp. 25–26.

52. *New York Herald Tribune,* 9 March 1959.

53. Sheen, *Treasure in Clay*, pp. 27–28. Claude Troisfontaines to the author, 8 March 1999, Louvain file. This officially documents Sheen's academic record at Louvain.

54. The original document announcing the award, dated 4 June 1926, is in Sheen Correspondence, box 48, Sheen Archives.

55. Fulton J. Sheen, *God and Intelligence in Modern Philosophy: A Critical Study in the Light of the Philosophy of Saint Thomas* (London: Longmans, Green and Co., 1952), pp. 7–8, 17.

56. Ibid., pp. 21–22.

57. Ibid., pp. 27–28, 32.

58. Ibid., p. 41.

59. Ibid., p. 146.

60. Edward Sutherland Bates in *Commonweal,* 13 January 1926, pp. 264–65.

61. *America,* 19 June 1926, p. 238.

62. Halsey, *The Survival of American Innocence,* pp. 143–45.

63. Philip Gleason, *Keeping the Faith: American Catholicism Past and Present* (Notre Dame, Indiana: University of Notre Dame Press, 1989), p. 110.

64. Halsey, *The Survival of American Innocence,* p. 147.

65. Quoted in ibid., p. 149.

66. Sheen, *Treasure in Clay,* p. 28.

67. Henry Dieterich, ed., *Through the Year with Fulton Sheen* (Ann Arbor, Michigan: Servant Books, 1985), p. 180.

68. Reeda Holliger interview, 22 April 2000.

69. Sheen, *Treasure in Clay,* p. 318; James C. G. Conniff, *The Bishop Sheen Story* (New York: Fawcett Publications, 1953), pp. 31–32. In Conniff, the girl was ten, but the author heard the story second-hand. Sister Marlene Brownett, who later went to Lourdes three times with Sheen, heard Fulton tell the story on several occasions and believes it to be "absolutely true." Marlene Brownett interview, 24 February 2000.

70. Sheen, *Treasure in Clay,* pp. 41–42.

71. Ibid.

72. Ibid., pp. 276–77.

73. Ibid., p. 277.

74. Fulton Oursler, *Why I Know There Is a God* (Garden City, New York: Doubleday, 1950), pp. 144–50; Sheen, *Treasure in Clay,* pp. 41–42, 276–77.

75. *Boston Post,* 17 May 1953.

76. Ibid.

77. "Microphone Missionary," *Time,* 14 April 1952, p. 74. Cf. Sheen, *Treasure in Clay,* p. 42.

78. Sheen, *Treasure in Clay,* pp. 319, 322.

Chapter 3: A Catholic Philosopher for the New Age

1. Warren H. Willis, "The Reorganization of the Catholic University of America during the Rectorship of James H. Ryan (1928–1935)" (Ph.D. diss., Catholic University of America, 1971), pp. 1–2, hereafter referred to as the Willis dissertation.

2. Mimeographed pamphlet, "The Priests' University," box 2, folder 5, John T. McNicholas Papers, Catholic University of America Archives.

3. *The Tower,* 17 November 1926.

4. C. Joseph Nuesse, *The Catholic University of America: A Centennial History* (Washington, D.C.: Catholic University of America, 1990), pp. 234–35.

5. *Washington Post,* 19 September 1926.

6. See the testimony of Dean Coln, box 2, folder 4, John T. McNicholas Papers; *Translation of the Proposed Revision of the Constitutions of the Catholic University* (Washington, D.C.: Catholic University of America, 1925), pp. 13–14, Catholic University of America Archives.

7. Fulton J. Sheen to Edward A. Pace, 9 April 1931, Sheen personnel file, faculty records, Catholic University of America Archives.

8. Nuesse, *The Catholic University of America*, p. 200.

9. On the other hand, the dean of the law school and the head athletic coach each received $10,000. See the testimony of Professors Hugh T. Henry, Henry Schumacher, and Joseph T. Barron, box 2, folder 4, McNicholas Papers. See also Willis dissertation, p. 21.

10. Minutes of 28 February 1928, School of the Sacred Sciences Minutes, Catholic University of America.

11. Fulton J. Sheen to Edward A. Pace, 22 May 1929, Sheen personnel file, faculty records, Catholic University of America Archives.

12. *Journal of Religion* 9 (October 1929), p. 663.

13. *The Tower*, 9 March 1927.

14. Ibid., 1 November 1934.

15. Ibid., 8 December 1938.

16. *Washington Evening Star*, 2 January 1927.

17. This generality was based on a study of CUA catalogues from 1926 to 1950.

18. *Catholic Observer*, 13 January 1927.

19. Copy, Fulton Sheen to Mary Fulton Carr, 18 February 1928, Eileen Sheen Khouw file.

20. Ibid.

21. Copy, Fulton Sheen to Mary Fulton Carr, 20 November 1929, Eileen Sheen Khouw file.

22. See the Rosemont College file; interview with Sister Marlene Brownett, 24 February 2000; Mother Mary Christina, *Mother Mary Cleophas of the Society of the Holy Child Jesus, President of Rosemont College, 1939–1946* (Philadelphia: The Peter Reilly Co., 1950), pp. 78–79, 109–10; Mother Mary Eleanor, *His by Choice: The Sisters of the Holy Child Jesus* (Milwaukee: Bruce Press, 1960), pp. 7–10 (a preface by Sheen). The 19 December 1944 issue of the campus newspaper, *The Rambler*, contains a photograph of student Patricia Kennedy, a daughter of the former ambassador to Britain, Joseph P. Kennedy.

23. *The Universe* (London), undated 1928 issue in the Sheen Archives. On returning from Europe in September, Fulton found his brother Tom a job at St. Vincent's Hospital in New York. Fulton J. Sheen to S. Donohue, 14 September 1928; Sister M. Felicite to S. Donohue, 27 September 1928, Patrick Cardinal Hayes Papers, New York Archdiocesan Archives.

24. *New York World,* 9 December 1929.

25. An unidentified clipping, probably from early October 1929, in the Scrapbook Collection at the Catholic University of America Archives. Prof. John A. Ryan of the National Catholic Welfare Conference soon denounced Prohibition and President Hoover before the House Judiciary Committee. *Washington Post,* 27 February 1930.

26. *Washington Star,* 10 February 1930.

27. An unidentified clipping from December 1930 in the Scrapbook Collection at the Catholic University of America Archives.

28. Fulton Oursler, *Why I Know There Is a God* (Garden City, New York: Doubleday, 1950), p. 120.

29. Fulton J. Sheen to the Rev. Mother Prioress, 7, 17 November 1926; 8 January 1927, Sheen Correspondence, box 48, Sheen Archives.

30. Willis dissertation, pp. 228–32.

31. Nuesse, *The Catholic University of America,* p. 211.

32. Sheen, *Treasure in Clay,* pp. 43–44; copy, Faculty of Theology to Bishop T. J. Shahan, 11 January 1927, in School of the Sacred Sciences Minutes, Catholic University of America.

33. Minutes, special meeting of the full professors, 6 April 1927, Catholic University of America.

34. See the relevant documents in the Charles A. Hart file, Catholic University of America.

35. The original constitution of 1889 required the S.T.D. of both top officials. *Translation of the Constitutions, Catholic University of America* (Washington, D.C.: Catholic University of America, n.d.), pp. 7–8. The revised constitution of 1926 permitted the officials to have either the S.T.D. or a doctorate in Canon Law. *Translation of the Proposed Revision of the Constitutions of the Catholic University* (Washington, D.C.: Catholic University of America, n.d.), pp. 5, 7. Both publications are in the CUA Archives.

36. *General Information, 1927–1928* (Washington, D.C.: Catholic University of America, 1927), pp. 26, 92. In the previous year's publication, pages 26 and 97, Sheen was listed as S.T.B. and Ph.D.

37. *Courses of Study, 1928–1929* (Washington, D.C.: Catholic University of America, 1928), pp. 20, 22.

38. The document can be dated by the residence and the academic ranking listed on the sheet.

39. *The Tower,* 29 February 1929; *New York World,* 9 December 1929.

40. Robert Trisco to the author, 27 June 2000, Catholic University of America file. Fr. Trisco, an eminent scholar of American Catholicism, noted the D.D. degrees earned by Martin John Spalding (1810–72) and Michael Augustine Corrigan (1839–1902).

41. See a copy of the undated application and curriculum vitae (probably the early fall, 1928) in School of the Sacred Sciences Minutes, Catholic University of America. It appears to have been typed by Sheen himself.

42. See *Who's Who in America,* (Chicago: The A. N. Marquis Co., 1930–31), vol. 16, p. 1998.

43. "Interrogatories for Faculties of Theology, Canon Law and Philosophy" (1934), John T. McNicholas Papers.

44. The c.v. is in Sheen's personnel file, faculty records, CUA Archives.

45. Sheen had received the LL.D. degree at St. Viator's in 1929 and at Loyola University in Chicago in 1930.

46. *Ottawa News Review,* October 1942.

47. In Sheen's personnel file, faculty records, CUA Archives.

48. Ibid.

49. A copy of the luncheon program is in the Mary Baker Scrapbook, in the possession of Eileen Sheen Khouw.

50. In the "Articles about Sheen" drawer, Sheen Archives.

51. Willis dissertation, pp. 202–5; John Shepherd to the author, 7 July 2000, Catholic University of America file.

52. Page 45 of Sheen's autobiography, *Treasure in Clay,* contains a story that some may think sheds light on the question. Fulton claimed that when James H. Ryan became rector of CUA in 1928, he "insisted that all the professors in the School of Theology must have a Doctor of Divinity in order to keep up academic standards." A man being considered as Ryan's replacement had a Ph.D. from CUA, and now, wrote Sheen, the rector was requiring him to "go to Rome for further schooling to get a D.D. before being named to the School of Theology." This demand, Sheen claimed, was the origin of a serious rift between the theologians and philosophers and the rector.

This account is inaccurate. The incident occurred in 1929, a year after Fulton's D.D. suddenly appeared. The new rector, James H. Ryan, was attempting to raise the standards in the School of the Sacred Sciences over the heated objections of the theologians. John A. Ryan wanted Francis J. Haas, a former student, to be his successor in the position of moral theology. But Haas's doctorate, from CUA in 1922, was from the School of Philosophy, where he majored in sociology and minored in economics and social psychology. Ryan refused to appoint Haas on the ground of Article 68 of the 1926 Constitution, which required instructors of theology to have "the necessary academic qualifications including at least the Master's degree or Licentiate." Moreover, said the rector, Haas "has had no academic preparation nor experience in teaching moral theology." There was nothing in any of this involving the D.D. degree. Haas would be hired by CUA in 1937 to head the Department of Economics. Sheen, *Treasure in Clay,* p. 342; School of the Sacred Sciences Minutes, 1 June 1929, Catholic University of America; Nuesse, *The Catholic University of America,* pp. 307–11; William John Shepherd to the author, 27, 28 June 2000, Catholic University of America file.

53. "Microphone Missionary," *Time,* 14 April 1952, p. 74.

54. See Sheen, *Treasure in Clay,* pp. 42–46.

55. Ibid., pp. 343–45.

56. Willis dissertation, pp. 232–33.

57. Special Meeting of the Full Professors, 8 April 1929, School of the Sacred Sciences Minutes, Catholic University of America.

58. On Healy, see Willis dissertation, p. 230.

59. John A. Ryan to the Visiting Committee, 11 May 1931, McNicholas Papers.

60. See the minutes of the meetings of 19 May and 30 May 1930, School of the Sacred Sciences Minutes, Catholic University of America.

61. On Coln, see Willis dissertation, p. 229.

62. See the testimony of John A. Ryan, 13 May 1931, box 2, folder 4, McNicholas Papers.

63. Nuesse, *The Catholic University of America,* p. 254.

64. Copy, Franz J. Coln to Pietro Fumansoni-Biondi, 11 April 1931, box 2, folder 5, McNicholas Papers.

65. Willis dissertation, pp. 237–39.

66. See "Minutes of the Faculty of Philosophy, from October 4th, 1927, to June 7th, 1930," Catholic University of America. The first reference to

Sheen is in "Dissertations submitted April, 1930," p. 3. He was the major professor for a doctoral dissertation in philosophy.

67. The hearings are in box 2, folder 4, McNicholas Papers.

68. See Willis dissertation, pp. 245–47; Nuesse, *The Catholic University of America*, pp. 253–54.

69. On Schumacher, see Willis dissertation, p. 230. See the subcommittee report and copy, John A. Ryan to John T. McNicholas, 8 November 1931, box 2, folder 5, McNicholas Papers.

70. Copy, John A. Ryan to John T. McNicholas, 25 September 1931, box 2, folder 5, McNicholas Papers.

71. Fulton J. Sheen, *Philosophy of Science* (Milwaukee: The Bruce Publishing Co., 1934), p. 188.

72. Willis dissertation, pp. 118, 121.

73. The classroom, which seats thirty comfortably, is still used by campus philosophers and is little changed from the years Sheen used it.

74. Several of Sheen's annual faculty reports are in Sheen's personnel file in the CUA Archives.

75. In 1930, Rector Ryan ordered a controversial reorganization that merged the School of Philosophy in the Graduate School of Arts and Sciences and in the College of Arts and Sciences. After his departure, new university statutes were set in place that officially restored the School of Philosophy.

76. Kathleen Riley Fields, "Bishop Fulton J. Sheen: An American Catholic Response to the Twentieth Century" (Ph.D. diss., University of Notre Dame, 1988), p. 22; Report from Members of the Teaching Staff, for the academic year ended 30 June 1939, Sheen personnel file, CUA Archives.

77. Conversation with Monsignor Robert Paul Mohan, 15 June 2000.

78. See Sheen, *Treasure in Clay*, pp. 253–54; Chad Abel-Kops interview of Robert Paul Mohan, attached to the Robert Paul Mohan interview.

79. "Monsignor's Tenth," *Time*, 11 March 1940, p. 61. See Sheen, *Treasure in Clay*, p. 105.

80. Ibid., p. 254.

81. Willis dissertation, pp. 255–57.

82. Ibid., pp. 258–59; Nuesse, *The Catholic University of America*, pp. 280–81. Cf. Sheen, *Treasure in Clay*, pp. 46–47, where Fulton tells of a misperception by Ryan that led the rector and others to believe incorrectly that

Sheen was directly responsible for his removal. For perceptive commentary on Ryan, see John Tracy Ellis, *Catholic Bishops: A Memoir* (Wilmington, Delaware: Michael Glazier, Inc., 1983), pp. 25–28.

83. Robert Paul Mohan interview. In 1935, in a letter to Archbishop McNicholas, CUA Church historian Peter Guilday criticized Sheen and John A. Ryan for devoting too much time to outside activity. Peter Guilday to John T. McNicholas, 20 April 1935, Episcopal Visiting Committee file, McNicholas Papers.

84. I am indebted to my research assistant, Chad Abel-Kops, for this information, taken from CUA archival files and telephone books of the period. In 1936, Sheen invited both the rector and vice-rector to his home for dinner, a celebration of the anniversary of his ordination. Copy, Fulton J. Sheen to Patrick McCormick, 12 September 1936, Sheen personnel file, CUA Archives.

85. Copy, Fulton J. Sheen to Mary Baker, 14 July 1930, Mary Baker Scrapbook, Eileen Sheen Khouw file. He also reported taking some time off for golf.

86. Sheen, *Treasure in Clay,* pp. 51–58.

87. Sheen, *Treasure in Clay,* p. 78.

88. Hilary Franco interview, 19 March 1998.

89. Sheen, *Treasure in Clay,* p. 352.

90. Rev. Leo A. Foley in *The Tower,* 18 January 1980.

91. James C. G. Conniff, *The Bishop Sheen Story* (New York: Fawcett Publications, 1953), p. 26.

92. Robert Paul Mohan interview. An engineering student of the class of 1935 recalled how Sheen would often see him at a bus stop after 5:00 P.M. and offer him a ride home, knowing that he lived with his parents near Sheen. The professor was extremely friendly, and once told the young man how he had talked his way out of a speeding ticket in Delaware even though he was not wearing his Roman collar. William Schuyler Jr. interview, 6 April 1999.

93. Ann Edward to the author, 3 July 2000.

94. See Sheen, *Treasure in Clay,* p. 63; copy, Sheen to Mary Fulton Carr, 18 February 1928, Ellen Sheen Khouw file. Kathleen Riley Fields claims to have found correspondence between Sheen and Joseph McSorley pointing to 1927 instead of 1928. Fields dissertation, pp. 95, 102. I have been unable to verify this source.

95. See Fields dissertation, pp. 95–100.

96. See ibid., pp. 100–1; Thomas C. Reeves, *The Empty Church: The Suicide of Liberal Christianity* (New York: The Free Press, 1996), pp. 114–15.

97. Copy, John E. Elwood to Charles F. Dolle, 11 September 1929, National Council of Catholic Men Papers, CUA Archives.

98. Copy, Justin McGrath to Fulton J. Sheen, 4 January 1930, Sheen file, Press Department box, CUA Archives.

99. *Catholic News,* 19 April 1930.

100. See Sheen, *Treasure in Clay,* p. 64. In May 1930, an NCWC official reported to the apostolic legate, "If we had to pay for this [network programming], the cost would be about $1,500,000.00 a year." Copy, John J. Burke to Pietro Fumansoni-Biondi, 13 May 1930, "Information Media: Radio: Broadcasts: Catholic Hour, 1929–44" folder, NCWC Papers, CUA Archives.

101. *Boston Post,* 23 December 1933.

102. *Our Sunday Visitor,* 24 December 1933.

103. *Boston Post,* 3 May 1936.

104. *Catholic News,* 19 April 1930.

105. Ibid., 20 May 1933.

106. *Washington Post,* 15 March 1934. In his autobiography, Sheen said that he first approached Mann personally and made no mention of the radio broadcasts. Sheen, *Treasure in Clay,* p. 261.

107. *Boston Post,* 3 May 1936.

108. *Philadelphia Standard and Times,* 18 September 1931.

109. *The Universe* (London), 1 July 1932.

110. Ibid., 22 July 1932.

111. *The Tower,* 12 May 1932.

112. *New York Times,* 7 May 1933.

113. *The Tower,* 27 May 1937. See Joan Cunningham interview, 4 October 1999.

114. *Cleveland Press,* 25 September 1935.

115. Joseph Schrembs to Fulton J. Sheen, 25 May, 4 October 1935, Sheen Correspondence, box 48, Sheen Archives.

116. See for example the list of publications in the first pages of *Seven Pillars of Peace,* published in 1945 by Charles Scribner's Sons. The recycling of material and the haste with which it was done led to repetition within the same volume. In the 1931 *Old Errors and New Labels,* the same point,

using similar language, is made on pages 45, 83, 125, and 205; another point is made on pages 6, 77–79, 95, and 309.

The recycling would continue after Sheen left the radio. Newspaper columns were also collected and woven into the books, along with excerpts from earlier works and talks, and the result was sometimes awkward. In the later *Way to Inner Peace,* for example, similar points appear on pages 4, 18, 35–36, 54, 64–65; again on pages 127–28, 138–39, and 146; again on pages 135 and 156; again on pages 131–33 and 175; and again on pages 125–27, 189, and 192–93. In *Children and Parents,* we see similarities on pages 13 and 17, 24 and 26, 24 and 28, 57 and 61, 58 and 63, 84 and 91, 85 and 92, and 25 and 115.

117. Fulton J. Sheen, *The Life of All Living: The Philosophy of Life* (New York: The Century Co., 1929), p. 103.

118. *New York Herald Tribune,* 12 February 1934.

119. Ibid., 26 February 1934.

120. *New York Times,* 26 February 1934.

121. Ibid., 12 March 1934.

122. Ibid.

123. Ibid., 19 March 1934.

124. *Washington Evening Star,* 9 July 1934.

125. Sheen, *Treasure in Clay,* p. 335.

126. Patrick Hayes to Sheen, Sheen Correspondence, box 48. Bishop Edwin Broderick, who worked for Francis Cardinal Spellman for many years, claims that Spellman nominated Sheen. Perhaps, but at the time Spellman was a bishop in Boston, struggling to revive a debt-ridden parish in Newton Center, Massachusetts; a close relationship with Sheen seems unlikely. Edwin Broderick interview, 27 March 1999.

127. Telegram, Eugenio Pacelli to Sheen, 2 June 1934, Sheen Correspondence, box 48.

128. Eugenio Pacelli to Sheen, 27 December 1934 and 18 April 1938; Patrick Hayes to Sheen, 17 December 1935, Sheen Correspondence, box 48.

129. Sheen, *Treasure in Clay,* p. 92; D. P. Noonan, *The Passion of Fulton Sheen* (New York: Dodd, Mead, 1972), p. 20.

130. *New York Times,* 13 March 1934.

131. *Catholic News,* 24 July 1934.

132. Gladys Baker, *I Had to Know* (New York: Appleton-Century-Crofts, 1951), pp. 125–41; *New York Times*, 18 December 1957.

133. Edward T. O'Meara to Jean Jadot, 30 January 1976, Sheen Correspondence, box 30.

134. *New York Times*, 18 March 1935.

135. Ibid., 25 March 1935.

136. Ibid., 16 March 1936.

137. Ibid., 23 March 1936.

138. Ibid., 30 March 1936.

139. Ibid., 6 December 1937.

140. Charles R. Morris, *American Catholic: The Saints and Sinners Who Built America's Most Powerful Church* (New York: New York Times Books, 1997), p. 152.

141. Ibid., pp. 151–52; Jay P. Dolan, *The American Catholic Experience: A History from Colonial Times to the Present* (Notre Dame: University of Notre Dame Press, 1980), pp. 402–3.

142. Morris, *American Catholic*, pp. 403–4; David J. O'Brien, *American Catholics and Social Reform: The New Deal Years* (New York: Oxford University Press, 1968), pp. 179–80.

143. Ibid, pp. 182–84.

144. Ibid., pp. 192–211.

145. Sheen, *The Eternal Galilean*, pp. 54–55. Cf. *New York Times*, 14 March 1938.

146. Sheen, *Treasure in Clay*, pp. 82–84.

147. Sheen, *Seven Pillars of Peace*, pp. 54–55.

148. Fulton J. Sheen, *Footprints in a Darkened Forest* (New York: Meredith Press, 1967), p. 118. For other jabs at the New Deal, see Sheen, *Communism and the Conscience of the West*, pp. 129, 134, 148.

149. Fulton J. Sheen, *War and Guilt* (Huntington, Indiana: Our Sunday Visitor, 1941), pp. 138–39.

150. Fulton J. Sheen, *The Mystical Body of Christ* (New York: Sheed and Ward, 1935), pp. 72–75.

151. Ibid., pp. 241–43. The celebrated liturgical scholar Virgel Michel wrote a scathing review of the book in *Orate Fratres* 9 (18 April 1936), pp. 281–85, condemning it for everything from bad theology to typographical errors. Rumor had it that Michel also claimed privately that Sheen was guilty

of plagiarism in the book. The rumor was published in Kathleen Hughes, *The Monk's Tale: A Biography of Godfrey Diekmann* (Collegeville, Minnesota: The Liturgical Press, 1991), p. 105. It was no doubt the source of the alleged statement by Frank Sheed (the publisher was Sheed and Ward) that he would accept another Sheen book if the author would "agree to put the whole thing in quotation marks." Wilfrid Sheed, *Frank and Maisie: A Memoir with Parents* (New York: Simon and Schuster, 1985), p. 106. In fact, Sheed and Ward published a Sheen anthology in 1936 and a third book, *Whence Comes War,* in 1940. I have found no evidence of plagiarism.

Chapter 4: Battle Lines

1. For his later observations, see Fulton J. Sheen, *Pius XI: A Eulogy by Msgr. Fulton J. Sheen* (Huntington, Indiana: Our Sunday Visitor, 1939).

2. This topic is handled admirably in Kathleen Riley Fields, "Bishop Fulton J. Sheen: An American Catholic Response to the Twentieth Century" (Ph.D. diss., University of Notre Dame, 1988), p. 208. In a major biographical account of Sheen's life, published in 1941, we read: "In 1931 he agreed with Chesterton's praise of Mussolini . . ." *Current Biography 1941* (reprint, New York: H. W. Wilson Co., 1971), p. 784.

3. Charles R. Morris, *American Catholic: The Saints and Sinners Who Built America's Most Powerful Church* (New York: New York Times Books, 1997), pp. 238–39.

4. Gerald P. Fogarty, *The Vatican and the American Hierarchy from 1870 to 1965* (Collegeville, Minnesota: The Liturgical Press, 1982), p. 240.

5. *Wall Street Journal,* 30 December 1999.

6. Malcolm Muggeridge, *Chronicles of Wasted Time,* Chronicle 1: *The Green Stick* (New York: Quill, 1982), p. 244.

7. Ibid., p. 255.

8. Douglas Hyde, *Dedication and Leadership* (Notre Dame, Indiana: University of Notre Dame Press, 1966), pp. 16–23. Hyde later became a Catholic. He observes on page 21, "It is ludicrous to suppose that half-hearted Christians can conduct a fruitful dialogue with fully-dedicated Communists."

9. Stephane Courtois, et al., *The Black Book of Communism: Crimes, Terror, Repression* (Cambridge: Harvard University Press), pp. 204–7.

10. *Boston Post,* 2 May 1937.

11. *Cleveland Press,* 25 September 1935.

12. *National Catholic Register,* 14–20 March 1999.

13. Cohen's obituary in *Milwaukee Journal Sentinel,* 28 June 1995; Harvey Klehr, John Earl Haynes and Friorikh Igorevich Firsov, *The Secret World of American Communism* (New Haven: Yale University Press, 1995), pp. 217–24; John Earl Haynes and Harvey Klehr, *Venona: Decoding Soviet Espionage in America* (New Haven: Yale University Press, 1999), pp. 317–21.

14. E.g., *The (Brooklyn) Tablet,* 9 September 1939. Said Sheen, "The Press fell down completely reporting the Civil War in Spain, not only by misrepresenting facts now generally admitted, but also by concealing the truth."

15. See John David Valaik, "American Catholics and the Spanish Civil War, 1931–1939" (Ph.D. diss., University of Rochester, 1964), pp. 382–96.

16. Morris, *American Catholic,* p. 234.

17. Valaik, "American Catholics and the Spanish Civil War," p. 399.

18. *New York Times,* 10 January 1939.

19. *The Tablet,* 31 October 1936.

20. *The Tower,* 18 November 1937.

21. Gladys Baker, *I Had to Know* (New York: Appleton-Century-Crofts, 1951), p. 256.

22. Fields dissertation, p. 172.

23. Kenneth Stewart, "Monsignor Fulton J. Sheen," *PM Magazine,* 23 June 1946, p. m6.

24. *The Tablet,* 5 February 1944.

25. Fogarty, *The Vatican and the American Hierarchy,* p. 272.

26. John Cooney, *The American Pope: The Life and Times of Francis Cardinal Spellman* (New York: Times Books, 1984), p. 136. On Franco and the Church, see esp. Stanley G. Payne, *Fascism in Spain, 1923–1977* (Madison: University of Wisconsin Press, 1999), pp. 240–42, 254, 319, 327–28.

27. Harold E. Fey, "Catholicism Fights Communism," *Christian Century,* 3 January 1945, pp. 13–14.

28. *New York Times,* 10 December 1938.

29. Ibid., 28 February 1938. Sheen later broke with Anderson after she broadcast over Berlin radio and expressed anti-Semitism. Stewart, "Monsignor Fulton J. Sheen," pp. m6–7.

30. *New York Journal and American,* 10 January 1939. See Fields dissertation, pp. 177–78, for coverage of the controversy that swirled after Sheen's speech.

31. *New York Journal and American,* 10 January 1939.

32. Peter Berglar, *Opus Dei: Life and Work of Its Founder Josemaria Escriva* (Princeton, New Jersey: Scepter Publishers, 1994), p. 151.

33. Morris, *American Catholic,* pp. 234–36.

34. See Payne, *Fascism in Spain,* pp. 246–49, for one aspect of this estimate.

35. Quoted in D. P. Noonan, *The Catholic Communicators* (Huntington, Indiana: Our Sunday Visitor, 1990), p. 35.

36. *New York Times,* 4 December 1939.

37. *Boston Post,* 3 May 1936.

38. Noonan, *The Catholic Communicators,* pp. 26–28.

39. Minutes, Catholic Hour Executive Committee, 28 December 1933, p. 3; cf. Minutes, Catholic Hour Executive Committee, 15 January 1937, p. 11, National Council of Catholic Men Papers, Catholic University of America Archives. By October 1938, total Catholic Hour assets amounted to $5,455.54. Minutes, Catholic Hour Executive Committee, 23 November 1938.

40. *Providence Visitor,* 16 September 1937.

41. Mary Giaratanna interview. There seem to be no formal Catholic Hour financial records available today. Sheen's papers contain no such data.

42. Stacy V. Jones, "Msgr. Fulton J. Sheen," *Catholic Digest,* September 1946, pp. 82–83.

43. Joan Cunningham interview, 4 October 1999.

44. Joan Dalton interview, 16 December 1998; *New York Post,* 14 October 1955; Sister Marlene Brownett interview, 11 February 2000.

45. Joan Cunningham interview, 10 January 2000; Marlene Brownett interview, 11 February 2000; Thomas Holliger interview, 19 April 2000.

46. Marlene Brownett interview, 11 February 2000. In gratitude, the boy built a toy altar with a photo of Sheen in it. Fulton was startled and delighted when he saw it.

47. Fulton J. Sheen to Mrs. James McGranery, 11 February 1948, box 30, Personal Correspondence files, James McGranery Papers, Library of Congress. The McGranerys were among those who made financial donations to Sheen. See Fulton J. Sheen to "My dear Jim and Regina," 26 December 1949, box 30, Personal Correspondence files, James McGranery Papers.

48. Marlene Brownett interview, 11 February 2000; Vincent Hartnett interview. For a brief summary of Sheen's outlook on money and material

possessions, see Fulton J. Sheen, *Way to Happiness* (Staten Island, New York: Alba House, 1998), pp. 25–28, 141–44.

49. *Peoria Register,* 27 October 1940.

50. National Council of Catholic Men brochure in the Sheen Archives.

51. "Convert Specialist," *Newsweek,* 26 February 1940, p. 48.

52. Ibid.

53. *New York World-Telegram,* 22 May 1939.

54. Fulton J. Sheen, *The Conversion of Heywood Broun: A Funeral Sermon Preached by Bishop Sheen* (New York: The Saint Paul Guild, 1939), p. 11.

55. Sheen, *Treasure in Clay,* pp. 260–61; *The Tablet,* 23 December 1939; "Biography by Sheen," *Time,* 1 January 1940.

56. *Catholic Times,* 19 June 1936; *Irish Times,* 24 June 1936.

57. *The Tower,* 4 November 1937.

58. Ibid., 27 January 1938.

59. Ibid., 24 February 1938.

60. *Pittsburgh Catholic,* 3 March 1938.

61. Copy, Bruce Mohler to Miss Regan and Mr. Heffron, 25 April 1938, Sheen Correspondence, box 48, Sheen Archives.

62. *Ottawa News Review,* October 1942. This lengthy piece contains a summary of Sheen's career, obviously supplied by Fulton himself. The "corporation" may well have been the Washington Cadillac dealership discussed in *Treasure in Clay,* pp. 337–38. Here the reported proposal to the owner was "about one half of the profits every year."

63. *New York Times,* 12 March 1939.

64. *Nashville Banner,* 17 April 1939.

65. *Ottawa News Review,* October 1942.

66. Joseph Sheen Jr. interview.

67. National Council of Catholic Men brochure in the Sheen Archives.

68. *New York Herald Tribune,* 24 June 1937.

69. Joan Cunningham interviews, 4 October 1999, 21 October 1999.

70. Edwin Broderick interview, 27 March 1999.

71. John Tracy Ellis, *Catholic Bishops: A Memoir* (Wilmington, Delaware: Michael Glazier, Inc., 1983), p. 80.

72. D. P. Noonan, *The Passion of Fulton Sheen* (New York: Dodd, Mead, 1972), p. 102.

73. Yolanda Holliger interview, 19 April 2000.

74. Joe Hart interview.

75. Noonan, *The Passion of Fulton Sheen,* p. 19.

76. Matthew R. Paratore interview.

77. Fulton J. Sheen, *The Way of the Cross* (Garden City, New York: Garden City Books, 1932), unpaginated [pp. 18–19 counting from the first page of the introduction].

78. Fulton J. Sheen, *Three to Get Married* (New York: Dell, 1951), pp. 29–30.

79. *60 Minutes* transcript, vol. 2, no. 4, Tuesday, 28 October 1969, p. 3, Sheen Archives.

80. Sheen, *Treasure in Clay,* pp. 209–12.

81. Ibid., p. 325.

82. Sheen, *These Are the Sacraments* (New York: Hawthorn Books, 1962; rev. ed., Garden City, New York: Doubleday, 1964), p. 108.

83. Fulton J. Sheen, *Footprints in a Darkened Forest* (New York: Meredith Press, 1967), pp. 30–31.

84. Sheen, *Treasure in Clay,* pp. 192, 198.

85. Ibid., p. 190.

86. Ellis, *Catholic Bishops,* p. 81. Sheen had known Spellman, to some extent, as early as 1931. Ibid., p. 85.

87. Ibid., pp. 78–81.

88. *New York Daily News,* 29 January 1941.

89. Cooney, *The American Pope,* p. 71.

90. James C. G. Conniff, *The Bishop Sheen Story* (New York: Fawcett Publications, 1953), p. 31.

91. Eugenio Pacelli to Sheen, 27 April 1936, Sheen Correspondence, box 48, Sheen Archives. Pacelli also received $68,824 from Macaulay.

92. *New York Herald Tribune,* 16 January 1939. See Cooney, *The American Pope,* pp. 37–39.

93. Gretta Palmer, "Why All These Converts? The Story of Monsignor Fulton Sheen," *Look,* 24 June 1947, p. 40; T. J. Toolen to K. I. Jemison, 24 January 1959, Archdiocese of Mobile Archives.

94. Ellis, *Catholic Bishops,* p. 80.

95. *Catholic Week* (Birmingham, Alabama), 5 December 1941.

96. Jones, "Msgr. Fulton J. Sheen," p. 83.

97. Sheen, *Treasure in Clay,* pp. 105–6; *Catholic Week,* 25 June 1943.

98. *Catholic Week,* 12 May 1950; 21 October 1960. See T. J. Toolen to Sister M. Gonzaga, 7 March 1967, Archdiocese of Mobile Archives.

99. Katherine Crowley-York to the author, 11 August 2000, Margaret Yates file. Crowley-York and her sister, Mary Theresa Soyka, both contributed to this letter describing their mother.

100. Anne Charnley interview.

101. Ibid.

102. Mary Giarantanna interview.

103. Anne Charnley interview.

104. Ellis, *Catholic Bishops,* p. 81. The appointment, against the wishes of FDR, went to the archbishop of Milwaukee, Samuel A. Stritch. See Robert J. Gannon, *The Cardinal Spellman Story* (Garden City, New York: Doubleday, 1962), pp. 178–80.

105. A copy of the deed is in the Sheen Home file.

106. See John C. Murphy, "Frederick V. Murphy: The Catholic Architect as Eclectic Designer and University Professor," *U.S. Catholic Historian* 5 (Winter 1997), pp. 91–104. John C. Murphy is Frederick Murphy's son.

107. John C. Murphy to Chad Abel-Kops, 14 June 1999, Sheen Home file.

108. All documents and data are in the Sheen Home file.

109. Conniff, *The Bishop Sheen Story,* p. 10.

110. Copy, Fulton J. Sheen to Martin Work, 14 March 1951, Archdiocese of New York Archives. The radio program itself paid Fulton and the other speakers $25 a lecture and another $25 for travel. Conniff, *The Bishop Sheen Story,* p. 3.

111. Joan Cunningham interview, 4 October 1999, 10 January 2000; Sister Marlene Brownett interview, 11 February 2000.

112. Joseph Sheen Jr. interview.

113. *New York Post,* 14 October 1955.

114. Palmer, "Why All These Converts?" p. 40.

115. Sheen, *Treasure in Clay,* p. 338.

116. Sheen, *Moods and Truths,* p. 68.

117. Sheen, *The Eternal Galilean,* pp. 46–47.

118. Mary Giaratanna interview; Noonan, *The Passion of Fulton Sheen,* p. 20.

119. Jones, "Msgr. Fulton J. Sheen," p. 81.

120. Sheen, *Treasure in Clay,* pp. 337–38.

121. Anne Charnley interview.

122. Mary Giaratanna interview.

123. This was gleaned by Chad Abel-Kops, who researched the Hawthorne residence and spoke at length with its then current occupants.

124. Morris, *American Catholic,* p. 191.

Chapter 5: The Loss of God, the Beginning of Tyranny

1. *New York Times,* 16 March 1936.

2. Ibid., 11, 27 September 1936.

3. Ibid., 30 November 1936.

4. Ibid., 7 October 1936.

5. Minutes, Catholic Hour Executive Committee, 15 January 1937, p. 8, National Conference of Catholic Men Papers, Catholic University of America Archives.

6. *Catholic News,* 19 February 1938.

7. *The (Brooklyn) Tablet,* 26 February 1938.

8. E.g., ibid., 13 April 1940; *New York Journal-American,* 18 March 1941.

9. *New York Daily Mirror,* 13 March 1939.

10. Robert J. Gannon, *The Cardinal Spellman Story* (Garden City, New York: Doubleday, 1962), pp. 71–73.

11. See John Cooney, *The American Pope: The Life and Times of Francis Cardinal Spellman* (New York: Times Books, 1984), pp. 40–42.

12. Gannon, *The Cardinal Spellman Story,* pp. 87–88.

13. Ibid., p. 109.

14. Ibid., p. 159.

15. Gerald P. Fogarty, *The Vatican and the American Hierarchy from 1870 to 1965* (Collegeville, Minnesota: The Liturgical Press, 1982), pp. 259–66.

16. Gannon, *The Cardinal Spellman Story,* pp. 159–67, 170; Gerald L. Sittser, *A Cautious Patriotism: The American Churches and the Second World War* (Chapel Hill: University of North Carolina Press, 1997), pp. 110–12.

17. Cited in George Flynn, *Roosevelt and Romanism: Catholics and American Diplomacy, 1937–1945* (Westport, Connecticut: Greenwood Press, 1976), p. 110. "The Vatican is a sovereign state the same as Belgium, France and the United States, and President Roosevelt has merely sent his

representative from one sovereign state to another." *Memphis Press-Scimitar,* 26 April 1940. See Fulton J. Sheen, *Whence Comes War* (New York: Sheed and Ward, 1940), pp. 83–86, 91.

18. Quoted in Charles R. Morris, *American Catholic: The Saints and Sinners Who Built America's Most Powerful Church* (New York: New York Times Books, 1997), p. 240.

19. Sheen, *Treasure in Clay,* pp. 46, 231–32.

20. Joseph Sheen Jr. interview.

21. Sheen, *Treasure in Clay,* p. 232.

22. *New York Times,* 20 March 1939.

23. *The Tablet,* 9 September 1939.

24. Ibid., 10 April 1939.

25. Fulton J. Sheen, "Atheistic Communism: An Analysis of Its Philosophy and Application," *Our Sunday Visitor,* 16 April 1939.

26. *New York Times,* 23 April 1939.

27. Ibid., 20 May 1939.

28. Ibid., 30 August 1939.

29. Ibid., 2 December 1939.

30. Ibid.

31. Ibid., 11 December 1939.

32. Fogarty, *The Vatican and the American Hierarchy,* pp. 249, 273.

33. E.g., *The Tablet,* 9 September 1939; 13 April 1940.

34. *Boston Advertiser,* 7 April 1940.

35. *The Catholic Hour* received 300,000 requests for copies of Sheen's address on "Peace through Justice." *California Daily Bruin* (UCLA), 15 October 1940.

36. *The Tablet,* 18 May 1940.

37. *New York Times,* 12 February 1940.

38. *New York Herald Tribune,* 19 February 1940.

39. *New York Times,* 22 July 1941.

40. Anne Smith Charnley, who knew Sheen at this time, recalled that he had small luncheons after his Easter service at St. Patrick's, attended by his "little coterie" of friends. The McDonnells were prominent at these luncheons. "They may have given Sheen money and support. He was very well off." Anne Charnley interview.

41. D. P. Noonan, *The Passion of Fulton Sheen* (New York: Dodd, Mead, 1972), p. 99.

42. Ibid., pp. 99–100; *New York Times*, 14 July 1940. After twenty-three years of marriage, the Fords were divorced. A judge remarried Henry, who became a "lapsed" Catholic.

43. Loretta Young Louis interview. Young remembered Fulton saying "The only time you have is now. The eternal now." In 1949, Sheen gave a stirring radio address on the "Now Moment." Fulton J. Sheen, *The Love That Waits for You* (Huntington, Indiana: Our Sunday Visitor, 1949), pp. 73–79.

44. *Los Angeles News*, 14 October 1940; *Los Angeles Times*, 14 October 1940.

45. Fulton J. Sheen, *War and Guilt* (Huntington, Indiana: Our Sunday Visitor, 1941), p. 55.

46. *New York Times*, 14 April 1941.

47. Ibid., 18 May 1941.

48. "The Baccalaureate Sermon," *Notre Dame Alumnus*, June 1941, pp. 7–8, 20. Cf. *New York Times*, 10 March 1941.

49. G. Bromley Oxnam, "Msgr. Sheen and Clerical-Fascism," *Protestant Digest* 3 (June–July 1941), pp. 1–5.

50. Francis Talbot, S.J., in *Protestant Digest* 4 (August–September 1941), pp. 76–78.

51. See John Tracy Ellis, *American Catholicism*, 2nd ed. (Chicago: University of Chicago Press, 1969), p. 157. Cf. John Cooney, *The American Pope: The Life and Times of Francis Cardinal Spellman* (New York: Times Books, 1984), pp. 116–17.

52. *Memphis Press-Scimitar*, 26 April 1940. See Sheen, *Whence Comes War*, pp. 57–58.

53. Robert Moats Miller, *Bishop G. Bromley Oxnam, Paladin of Liberal Protestantism* (Nashville: Abingdon Press, 1990), pp. 437–39.

54. Kenneth Leslie in *Protestant Digest* 4 (August–September 1941), pp. 78–91.

55. Sheen, *War and Guilt*, p. 136.

56. Ibid., p. 138.

57. Cf. Sheen, *Whence Comes War*, pp. 49–52.

58. *Catholic News*, 19 February 1938.

59. Sheen, *War and Guilt*, pp. 123–31. Cf. Fulton J. Sheen, *For God and Country* (New York: P. J. Kenedy and Sons, 1941), pp. 33–48. This is an almost verbatim republication of the radio talk.

60. *Windsor Daily Star,* 6 October 1941.

61. *Columbus Register,* 17 October 1941.

62. *New York Times,* 17 November 1941.

63. Fogarty, *The Vatican and the American Hierarchy,* pp. 279–81.

64. *Ottawa News Review,* October 1942.

65. Copy, Jack A. Darrock to Fulton J. Sheen, 28 May 1942, Sheen Correspondence, box 48, Sheen Archives. In 1941, Sheen served as narrator of the "March of Time" film *The Story of the Vatican.* Shortly thereafter, he narrated the first sound film of the Solemn High Catholic Mass, *The Eternal Gift. New York World-Telegram,* 17 January 1942.

66. *Houston Chronicle,* 20 October 1943.

67. *Washington Post,* 3 January 1944.

68. *Youngstown Daily Vindicator,* 9 October 1943.

69. Richard Gid Powers, *Not Without Honor: The History of American Anticommunism* (New York: The Free Press, 1995), p. 182.

70. *Philadelphia Record,* 12 January 1944; *Knickerbocker News* (Albany, New York), 12 January 1944.

71. Kenneth J. Heineman, *A Catholic New Deal: Religion and Reform in Depression Pittsburgh* (University Park, Pennsylvania: Penn State University Press, 1999), p. 175.

72. Powers, *Not Without Honor,* p. 175.

73. *The Tablet,* 5 February 1944. See Fulton J. Sheen, *Seven Pillars of Peace* (New York: Charles Scribner's Sons, 1945), pp. 109–112.

74. Copy, D. W. Ladd to E. A. Tamm, 8 February 1944, Sheen FBI file. The contents of this file were obtained through the Freedom of Information Act.

75. Copy, Fulton J. Sheen to J. Edgar Hoover, 21 April 1944; J. Edgar Hoover to Fulton J. Sheen, 22 April 1944, Sheen FBI file.

76. *Catholic News,* 19 February 1938.

77. *Peoria Star,* 29 March 1943.

78. Merle Fulton interview, 1 September 1999.

79. Stories of Newt's last year are in the Sheen Descendant Story, Anne Gevas file.

80. Joan Cunningham interview, 4 October 1999.

81. Ibid.

82. See [Edward Hefferon], "Confidential Report, November 1, 1945," Office of General Secretary, "Information Media: Radio Broadcasts: Catholic Hour, 1945," NCWC Papers, Catholic University of America Archives. See also copy, Fulton J. Sheen to John W. Babcock, 1 November 1945; copy, Edward Hefferon to John W. Babcock, 8 November 1945; copy, Wilfrid Parsons to John F. Noll, 16 December 1945; copy, John F. Noll to Fulton J. Sheen, 31 December 1945; copy, John F. Noll to E. J. Hefferon, 31 December 1945; copy, Fulton J. Sheen to Paul F. Tanner, 12 January 1946; copy, Fulton J. Sheen to John F. Noll, 15 January 1946, NCWC Papers.

83. Cooney, *The American Pope*, pp. 112–13.

84. George A. Kelly interview, 4 January 1998.

85. Copy, Francis J. Spellman to "Your Excellency," 9 February 1942, Archdiocese of New York Archives. This letter was provided by Monsignor Tom McSweeney.

86. Gannon, *The Cardinal Spellman Story*, pp. 195–243.

87. Cooney, *The American Pope*, pp. 124–25.

88. Fogarty, *The Vatican and the American Hierarchy*, pp. 291–99.

89. Cooney, *The American Pope*, pp. 126–33; Gannon, *The Cardinal Spellman Story*, pp. 203–13.

90. Ibid., pp. 211–12, 240–41.

91. Ibid., p. 202.

92. Harold E. Fey, "Can Catholicism Win America?" *Christian Century*, 29 November 1944, p. 1378.

93. Gannon, *The Cardinal Spellman Story*, pp. 225–28.

94. *New York Times*, 27 March 1943.

95. There were later bombing incidents as well. See Fogarty, *The Vatican and the American Hierarchy*, pp. 295–306.

96. Gannon, *The Cardinal Spellman Story*, pp. 222–25, 245–48.

97. Sheen, *Whence Comes War*, p. 39. Cf. Sheen, *War and Guilt*, pp. 25–30, 73–74; Fulton J. Sheen, *God and War* (New York: P. J. Kenedy and Sons, 1942), pp. 30–38.

98. Sheen, *Whence Comes War*, pp. 44–45.

99. Sheen, *God and War*, p. 88.

100. Sheen, *Whence Comes War*, pp. 36, 45–54, 77–97. In a later wartime book, however, Sheen appeared much more charitable toward Protestants, writing, "The bad Catholic who gives no glory to God, and offends Him, is

heading for eternal loss. The non-Catholic who gives glory to God, according to the light of his conscience, is in his way to be saved." Sheen, *Friends* (Washington, D.C.: National Council of Catholic Men, 1944), p. 82.

101. Sheen, *Whence Comes War,* pp. 60–76.

102. Sheen, *God and War,* pp. 5–7, 81–82.

103. Fulton J. Sheen, *The Armor of God* (New York: P. J. Kenedy and Sons, 1943), pp. 16–18.

104. Sheen, *Seven Pillars of Peace,* pp. 76–86; *Danbury [Connecticut] News-Times,* 2 December 1944.

105. *New York Times,* 19 February 1945.

106. *San Francisco Examiner,* 19 April 1945.

107. Ibid.

108. Powers, *Not Without Honor,* pp. 182–83.

109. Cooney, *The American Pope,* pp. 204–7.

110. Sheen, *Treasure in Clay,* p. 230.

111. *New York Times,* 29 March 1939.

112. See Sheen, *Friends,* pp. 72–80. Cf. Sheen, *Seven Pillars of Peace,* pp. 21, 38–39.

113. Sheen, *War and Guilt,* p. 140.

114. Sheen, *War and Guilt,* p. 103.

115. Margherita Marchione, *Yours Is a Precious Witness: Memoirs of Jews and Catholics in Wartime Italy* (New York: Paulist Press, 1997), p. 150.

116. E.g., *New York Times,* 12 June 1955; Sheen, *Guide to Contentment* (New York: Maco Publishing Co., 1967), p. 73.

117. Quoted in Sittser, *A Cautious Patriotism,* p. 220.

118. *Rochester Democrat and Chronicle,* 15 October 1945. He continued to hold this view in 1952. See Fulton J. Sheen, *The World's First Love* (Garden City, New York: Image Books, 1955), pp. 231–32.

119. Sheen, *Communism and the Conscience of the West* (Indianapolis: Bobbs-Merrill, 1948), p. 215.

120. Ibid., p. 216. See pages 200–4 for a similar interpretation of World War I.

Chapter 6: Reaching Out

1. David J. O'Brien, *American Catholics and Social Reform: The New Deal Years* (New York: Oxford University Press, 1968), pp. 54–56, 217. Catholic

separatism, of course, also preceded the 1928 election. See Roger Finke and Rodney Stark, *The Churching of America, 1776–1990: Winners and Losers in Our Religious Economy* (New Brunswick, New Jersey: Rutgers University Press, 1992), pp. 138–39.

2. Harold E. Fey, "Can Catholicism Win America?" *Christian Century,* 29 November 1944, p. 378.

3. Charles R. Morris, *American Catholic: The Saints and Sinners Who Built America's Most Powerful Church* (New York: Times Books, 1997), pp. 174–75.

4. Ibid., p. 175.

5. On Marian piety during this period see Jay P. Dolan, *The American Catholic Experience: A History from Colonial Times to the Present* (Notre Dame: University of Notre Dame Press, 1980), pp. 384–86. Pre-Vatican II Catholicism in America is described memorably by Charles A. Fracchia in *Second Spring: The Coming of Age of U.S. Catholicism* (New York: Harper and Row, 1980), see esp. pp. 18–40. Fracchia stresses the solidarity of immigrants in a hostile environment as an ingredient in loyalty to the Church.

6. Kenneth J. Heineman, *A Catholic New Deal: Religion and Reform in Depression Pittsburgh* (University Park, Pennsylvania: Penn State University Press, 1999), pp. 6–7.

7. William B. Prendergast, *The Catholic Voter in American Politics: The Passing of the Democratic Monolith* (Washington, D.C.: Georgetown University Press, 1999), p. 115.

8. See John T. McGreevy, "Thinking on One's Own: Catholicism in the American Intellectual Imagination, 1928–1960," *Journal of American History* 84, no. 1 (June 1997), p. 120.

9. Ibid., pp. 121–24.

10. Gerard V. Bradley, "Legal Beagle: ECE's Best Friend May Be the Civil Law," *Fellowship of Catholic Scholars Quarterly* 22 (Fall 1999), p. 24.

11. For an excellent survey of these attacks, see McGreevey, "Thinking on One's Own," pp. 97–131. Niebuhr is quoted on page 98, Hook on page 128.

12. Paul Blanshard, *American Freedom and Catholic Power* (Boston: Beacon Press, 1950), p. 257.

13. Ibid., p. 302.

14. Ibid., pp. 206, 209. On page 103, Blanshard quoted a complaint by Fulton's favorite St. Viator College professor, Father William J. Bergan, to buttress his contention that most Catholic colleges were inferior.

15. McGreevey, "Thinking on One's Own," pp. 97–98, 120.

16. Robert J. Gannon, *The Cardinal Spellman Story* (Garden City, New York: Doubleday, 1962), p. 330.

17. Ibid., pp. 332–34.

18. *Boston Daily Globe*, 4 May 1945.

19. Fulton J. Sheen, *Communism Answers Questions of a Communist* (New York: Paulist Press, [1937]), pp. 7–13, 30.

20. *Boston Post*, 2 May 1937. Fulton learned years later that Communist leaders had arranged the dinner in hopes of winning him over to the party. Sheen, *Treasure in Clay*, p. 265.

21. *New York Times*, 12 October 1945; Louis Francis Budenz, *This Is My Story* (New York: McGraw-Hill, 1947), p. 164.

22. Louis Budenz to Fulton J. Sheen, 16 July 1964, Sheen Correspondence, box 48, Sheen Archives.

23. *Rochester Democrat and Chronicle*, 15 October 1945.

24. Sheen, *Treasure in Clay*, pp. 265–66; "Religion," *Newsweek*, 22 October 1945, pp. 99–100. For the full account by Budenz, see his *This Is My Story*, pp. 155–66, 332–51.

25. E.g., Herbert L. Packer, *Ex-Communist Witnesses: Four Studies in Fact Finding* (Stanford: Stanford University Press, 1962), pp. 121–77; Thomas C. Reeves, *The Life and Times of Joe McCarthy* (Lanham, Maryland: Madison Books, 1997), pp. 267–68, 275–77, 279–83, 305, 307, 327, 384–85, 388, 516.

26. Margaret R. Budenz to Fulton J. Sheen, 3 October 1978, Sheen Correspondence, box 30, Sheen Archives.

27. Reeves, *The Life and Times of Joe McCarthy*, p. 280, 653.

28. Sheen, *Treasure in Clay*, pp. 255–56; *New York Times*, 30 April 1969.

29. Bishop Edwin Broderick later described Algase as of moderate height, dark, and decidedly Jewish in appearance. He thought her extremely aggressive. When she entered a room, her abundant jewelry clanging, she would attempt to dominate whatever was going on. She was unpopular with both priests and laity, Broderick recalled. Edwin Broderick interview, 27 March 1999.

30. Ibid.

31. John Cooney, *The American Pope: The Life and Times of Francis Cardinal Spellman* (New York: Times Books, 1984), pp. 135–37; Gannon, *The Cardinal Spellman Story*, pp. 262, 388–89.

32. Gannon, *The Cardinal Spellman Story*, pp. 256–57, 268; *New York Times*, 4 August 1962.

33. Bricktop (Ada Smith), *Bricktop* (New York: Atheneum, 1983), pp. 220, 263.

34. Gretta Palmer, "Why All These Converts?" *Look,* 24 June 1947, pp. 39–40; *New York Times,* 2 January 1947.

35. Yolanda Holliger interview, 19 April 2000; copy, Fulton J. Sheen to Maria Goretti, 12 April 1966, Sheen Correspondence, box 48, Sheen Archives.

36. D. P. Noonan, *The Passion of Fulton Sheen* (New York: Dodd, Mead, 1972), p. 92.

37. In fact, the Kreislers were "reconverted." Both had been baptized Catholics, had lapsed into secularism, and were brought back to the Church by Sheen in 1947. Sheen also remarried the couple. *New York Times,* 1 April 1947. See Amy Biancolli, *Fritz Kreisler: Love's Sorrow, Love's Joy* (Portland, Oregon: Amadeus Press, 1998), pp. 80, 183–208, 212–13.

38. Sheen, *Treasure in Clay,* pp. 258–60.

39. Biancolli, *Fritz Kreisler,* pp. 313–15, 330, 343. See *New York Times,* 20 January 1962.

40. Quoted in Sylvia Jukes Morris, *Rage for Fame: The Ascent of Clare Boothe Luce* (New York: Random House, 1997), p. 315.

41. Clare Boothe Luce, "The 'Real' Reason, Part One," *McCall's,* February 1947, p. 132.

42. Sheen, *Treasure in Clay,* p. 264. For reminiscences of the tragic incident that brought the two together, see Fulton Sheen to Clare Boothe Luce, 12 January 1972, Sheen Correspondence, box 30, Sheen Archives.

43. Clare Boothe Luce, "The 'Real' Reason, Part Three," *McCall's,* April 1947, p. 88.

44. Sheen, *Treasure in Clay,* p. 264.

45. Luce, "The 'Real' Reason, Part Three," p. 85.

46. Luce, "The 'Real' Reason, Part One," p. 118.

47. John A. O'Brien, in *Winning Converts: A Symposium on Methods of Convert Making for Priests and Lay People,* ed. John A. O'Brien (New York: P. J. Kenedy and Sons, 1948), p. 59.

48. Luce, "The 'Real' Reason, Part Three," pp. 85–86. See Clare Boothe Luce, "Under the Fig Tree," in *The Road to Damascus: The Spiritual Pilgrimage of Fifteen Converts to Catholicism,* ed. John A. O'Brien (Garden City, New York: Doubleday and Co., 1950), pp. 213–30.

49. Edwin Broderick interview. This was perhaps especially true with the prominent. A rather typical convert later described her first session in

the confessional with Sheen on the day he brought her into the Church. Mary H. Downing interview.

50. See Francis J. Weber, *His Eminence of Los Angeles, James Francis Cardinal McIntyre* (Mission Hills, California: St. Francis Historical Society, 1997), vol. 1, p. 52; vol. 2, pp. 512–13. McIntyre was his second choice. See John Tracy Ellis, *Catholic Bishops: A Memoir* (Wilmington, Delaware: Michael Glazier, Inc., 1983), p. 97. On her confession, see Clare Boothe Luce, "The Right Priest," *Information on Religion and the American Scene*, December 1947, pp. 549–50.

51. Gannon, *The Cardinal Spellman Story*, pp. 294–95; Weber, *His Eminence of Los Angeles*, vol. 1, p. 59.

52. Quoted in Noonan, *The Passion of Fulton Sheen*, p. 97.

53. Loretta Young Louis interview.

54. E.g., Clare Boothe Luce, "On the Right Approach," in *Winning Converts*, ed. O'Brien, pp. 60–70. Sheen brought Luce to Catholic University more than once to talk about the Catholic faith. See Robert Paul Mohan interview, 31 March 1999; *The Tower*, 25 April 1950.

55. E.g., Fulton J. Sheen to Clare Boothe Luce, n.d., box 43, Clare Boothe Luce Papers, Library of Congress. Sheen frequently failed to date his handwritten letters to Luce. The context often reveals the approximate date of writing, however. The letter cited here, written from the Roosevelt Hotel in New York, is probably from the late 1940s.

56. Fulton J. Sheen to Clare Boothe Luce, c. 1946, box 31, Luce Papers.

57. Cablegram, Fulton J. Sheen to Clare Boothe Luce, 20 August 1949, box 33, Luce Papers.

58. Fulton J. Sheen to Clare Boothe Luce, c. 1949, box 33, Luce Papers.

59. Fulton J. Sheen to Clare Boothe Luce, 1967, box 40, Luce Papers.

60. Fulton J. Sheen to Clare Boothe Luce, n.d., box 43, Luce Papers.

61. Gretta Palmer, "Escaping from an Atheist's Cell," in *The Road to Damascus*, ed. O'Brien, pp. 43–55; Gladys Baker, *I Had to Know* (New York: Appleton-Century-Crofts, 1951), pp. 164–66, 171.

62. Fulton J. Sheen to Clare Boothe Luce, c. late 1940s, box 43, Luce Papers.

63. Palmer, "Why All These Converts?" *Look*, 24 June 1947, pp. 38, 40.

64. Copy, memorandum, D. M. Ladd to J. Edgar Hoover, 29 October 1948, FBI file. See Noonan, *The Passion of Fulton Sheen*, p. 94. Bentley converted in 1950. *New York Times*, 4 December 1963. On Bentley and Larsen, see Reeves, *The Life and Times of Joe McCarthy*, pp. 211, 290–95. The best

source on Larsen is Harvey Klehr and Ronald Radosh, *The Amerasia Spy Case: Prelude to McCarthyism* (Chapel Hill: University of North Carolina Press, 1996). See also the obituary in *Washington Post*, 4 May 1988. Sheen visited Larsen at his home at least once. Larsen had previously been twice married, and this blocked his application for baptism. A daughter, Linda, was baptized in the third grade and remains a devout Catholic. Her father was admitted into the Church on his death bed, his two earlier wives having died. Chad Abel-Kops interview with Thelma E. Larsen (the third wife), 30 March 2000; Chad Abel-Kops interview with Linda Tannever, 2 April 2000, Emmanuel Larsen file.

65. "How to Win a Convert," *Time*, 12 July 1948, pp. 60–61. Cf. Fulton J. Sheen, "Thoughts on Convert Making," *Information on Religion and the American Scene*, February 1947, pp. 51–52. This was reprinted in O'Brien, ed., *Winning Converts*, pp. 153–57. In the early 1950s, Sheen played a role in converting actress Virginia Mayo, who later remembered Sheen as "intelligent, humble, pleasant. It was wonderful to know him." See Virginia Mayo interview. See also "Microphone Missionary," *Time*, 14 April 1952, p. 73.

66. Joan Dalton interview, 16 December 1998. In the early 1950s, television tapes were substituted for audio tapes. Converts would see five of these tapes before meeting the bishop. The young women who ran the television tapes for converts were jokingly called "disk jockeys." Edwin Broderick interview, 27 March 1999.

67. Dickson Terry in *St. Louis Post-Dispatch*, 31 March 1947.

68. Mary H. Downing interview.

69. Kenneth Stewart, "Monsignor Fulton J. Sheen," *PM Magazine*, 23 June 1946, p. m9.

70. Sheen, *Peace of Soul*, pp. 53–54, 224. See also pp. 241, 259–80. See Sheen, *The Mystical Body of Christ*, pp. 306–8, and Sheen, *The Seven Virtues*, pp. 60–64.

71. Fulton J. Sheen, *Preface to Religion* (New York: P. J. Kenedy and Sons, 1946), pp. 17, 26–27, 33, 36–37, 57, 148, 195.

72. Sheen, "Thoughts on Convert Making," p. 51.

73. Daniel G. Reid, ed., *Dictionary of Christianity in America* (Downers Grove, Illinois: InterVarsity Press, 1990), pp. 97–98.

74. William Ward Ayer, "Romanism's Pied Piper: A Gospel-Eye View of the Roman Catholic Church's Top Propagandist—Msgr. Fulton J. Sheen," *United Evangelical Action*, 1 August 1948, pp. 3–4; 15 August 1948, pp. 3–4, 6.

75. Gannon, *The Cardinal Spellman Story,* pp. 366–68; copy, Francis Spellman to Ruth B. Shipley, 24 March 1948, Sheen Correspondence, box 48, Sheen Archives.

76. Gannon, *The Cardinal Spellman Story,* pp. 367–68.

77. Ibid, p. 368.

78. Sheen Travel Diary, 24 April 1948. The diary is in the Sheen Archives. It was clearly typed by Sheen from notes no longer available.

79. Gannon, *The Cardinal Spellman Story,* p. 368.

80. *Honolulu Star-Bulletin,* 24 April 1948.

81. Sheen Travel Diary, 26 April 1948.

82. Ibid., 28 April; *Sydney Herald,* 28 April 1948.

83. *The Sun* (Sydney), 27 April 1948; *Daily Mirror* (Sydney), 27 April 1948.

84. *The Register* (Sydney), 16 May 1948; *The Sun* (Sydney), 28 April 1948.

85. Fulton J. Sheen to Clare Boothe Luce, 5 May 1948, box 32, Luce Papers.

86. Sheen Travel Diary, 2, 3, 4 May 1948.

87. Ibid., 6 May 1948.

88. Ibid.

89. Ibid., 8 May 1948; unidentified copy of a Melbourne newspaper story of 8 May 1948 in ibid.

90. Ibid.

91. Ibid., 9 May 1948.

92. Ibid., 10 May 1948.

93. Gannon, *The Cardinal Spellman Story,* p. 367.

94. See Sheen, *Treasure in Clay,* p. 134.

95. Sheen Travel Diary, 12 May 1948. In his account of the speech in his autobiography, Sheen, obviously consulting his diary, changed the comment slightly to omit the reference to cardinals. Sheen, *Treasure in Clay,* pp. 135–36.

96. Sheen Travel Diary, 14 May 1948. Here, and for the entries of several days following, one can see Sheen's editing of the diary in his own hand. Perhaps another typed copy was to be made. Perhaps he was preparing the diary for publication. If so, it may be that publication was cancelled after the fall-out between Sheen and Spellman, only a little more than two years away.

97. Gannon, *The Cardinal Spellman Story,* p. 369.

98. Sheen Travel Diary, 20 May 1948.

99. Ibid., 23 May 1948.

100. *The Straits Times,* 22 May 1948.

101. Sheen Travel Diary, 25 May 1948.

102. Ibid.

103. Ibid., 28 May 1948. In his autobiography, Sheen altered a story recorded in his diary to create a greater comic effect; it involved Cardinal Spellman eating a lamb's eye offered to him at a dinner. Compare Sheen, *Treasure in Clay,* p. 133 with Sheen Travel Diary, 28 May 1948.

104. Sheen Travel Diary, 27 May 1948. "They came away feeling that they had 'shared in reflected glory' and also by their own admission, that they had learned, through the inmates, 'what the priesthood should be.'" *Manila Bulletin,* 31 May 1948. See also *Manila Times,* 31 May 1948, for Sheen's reflections on the leprosarium visit. Cardinal Spellman said he was "privileged" to give Benediction for the ambulatory lepers. Gannon, *The Cardinal Spellman Story,* p. 370.

105. Loretta Young Louis interview.

106. Noonan, *The Passion of Fulton Sheen,* pp. 4–6. See Sheen, *Walk with God,* pp. 56–57, 82–83.

107. Sheen Travel Diary, 31 May 1948.

108. Bullitt also thought FDR guilty of appeasement at Yalta. See Edward R. Stettinius, *Roosevelt and the Russians* (New York: Doubleday and Co., 1949), pp. 5–6.

109. Sheen Travel Diary, 3 June 1948; Sheen, *Treasure in Clay,* pp. 139–40.

110. Sheen Travel Diary, 3 June 1948.

111. Ibid., 7 June 1948; Sheen, *Treasure in Clay,* p. 141.

112. *Tokyo Stars and Stripes,* 8 June 1948.

113. Sheen Travel Diary, 8 June 1948.

114. Cf. Sheen, *Treasure in Clay,* pp. 141–42.

115. Sheen Travel Diary, 9 June 1948. Sheen was not present for a private interview with the emperor. See Gannon, *The Cardinal Spellman Story,* p. 373.

116. *Catholic News,* 19 June 1948. Sheen carefully followed his diary when writing his autobiographical account of this part of the trip. Sheen, *Treasure in Clay,* pp. 142–43.

117. Sheen Travel Diary, 9 June.

118. Ibid. The last entries are undated. Following the typed version of the diary are examples of notes taken in Sheen's hand.

119. Noonan, *The Passion of Fulton Sheen*, p. 52.

120. Sheen, *Treasure in Clay*, p. 146.

Chapter 7: Global Thinking

1. Sheen, *The Life of All Living*, p. 117. See also Sheen, *Religion Without God*, pp. 48–59, 250–52.

2. Sheen, *Old Errors and New Labels*, pp. 207–8.

3. *New York Times*, 10 March 1947.

4. Ibid., 20 July 1947.

5. Ibid., 2 July 1947.

6. Ibid., 6 July 1947. Brill noted that the New York Psychoanalytic Institute had prepared an official response to Sheen and that the *New York Herald Tribune* had published it. The *New York Times* did not.

7. Ibid., 22 July 1947.

8. Fanny Sedgwick Colby, "Monsignor Sheen and Mrs. Luce," *American Scholar* 17 (Winter 1947–48), pp. 35–38.

9. *Texas Catholic War Veterans*, November 1947. Sheen's speech was apparently tape recorded and published verbatim.

10. Sheen, *Peace of Soul*, pp. 123, 125–27, 136–37, 188.

11. Ibid., pp. 84–86, 89. See pp. 112–13, 146.

12. Ibid., p. 89.

13. Ibid., pp. 7, 42, 49–50, 67–68, 79–80, 91–94, 134–35, 141–43, 181. The quotation is on p. 102.

14. Ibid., p. 204. For more on Sheen and Freudian psychoanalysis, see Fulton J. Sheen, *The World's First Love* (New York: Image Books, 1956), pp. 113–14; Fulton J. Sheen, *These Are the Sacraments* (New York: Hawthorn Books, 1962), pp. 68–70 (a clear example of how Sheen recycled materials over the decades).

15. Donald F. Crosby, *God, Church, and Flag: Senator Joseph R. McCarthy and the Catholic Church, 1950–1957* (Chapel Hill: University of North Carolina Press, 1978), pp. 9–12, 16–22.

16. Ibid., p. 14.

17. Ibid., pp. 24–25.

18. Letter of 12 January 1943 to J. Edgar Hoover; Hoover to the letter writer, 2 February 1943, FBI file. As is the common practice, many of these documents found in the FBI files have names and dates blacked out.

19. Copy, D. M. Ladd to E. A. Tamm, 8 February 1944, FBI file.

20. Copy, Fulton J. Sheen to J. Edgar Hoover, 21 April 1944; copy, J. Edgar Hoover to Fulton J. Sheen, 22 April 1944, FBI file.

21. *Washington Times-Herald,* 25 March 1946. Hoover's query is handwritten on the article. Copy, memorandum, K. W. Dissly to D. M. Ladd, 27 March 1946; copy, memorandum, D. M. Ladd to J. Edgar Hoover, 25 March 1946, FBI file.

22. *Washington Times-Herald,* 25 March 1946. In 1947, Buckles was working for Congressman Sabath. He resigned over salary and working conditions. Copy, Harold H. Buckles to Matthew J. Connelly, 30 September 1947, Harry S. Truman Library. There is no record of any subversive activity on his part. *New York Times,* 9 June 1953.

23. Mary Jude Yablonsky, "A Rhetorical Analysis of Selected Television Speeches of Archbishop Fulton J. Sheen on Communism, 1952–1956" (Ph.D. diss., Ohio State University, 1974), p. 37.

24. Unidentified clipping dated 7 November 1946; copy, memorandum, Lou Nichols to M. A. [undecipherable], 4 May 1953, FBI file.

25. Copy, memorandum, D. M. Ladd to J. Edgar Hoover, 29 October 1948, FBI file.

26. Copy, memorandum, Edward Scheidt to J. Edgar Hoover, 14 May 1947; J. Edgar Hoover to Fulton J. Sheen, 28 May 1947, FBI file.

27. Copy, memorandum, J. Edgar Hoover to SAC, Washington, 20 April 1948; copy, memorandum, Guy Hottel to J. Edgar Hoover, 30 April 1948, FBI file.

28. Sheen, *Communism and the Conscience of the West,* pp. 17–23.

29. Crosby, *God, Church, and Flag,* pp. 13–14.

30. Sheen, *Communism and the Conscience of the West,* pp. 125–26, and Preface. He did, however, urge voters to judge candidates "on moral grounds," as "Contemporary history proves that modern political leaders, devoid of a moral inspiration and relying solely on a mass basis, prove ineffectual in time of crisis as did the Kerensky regime and the Weimar politicians." Ibid., p. 125.

31. *New York Times,* 18 April 1949.

32. The review was dated 20 April 1948, FBI file. On March 30, Sheen had delivered the opening prayer for the House of Representatives, stressing America's faltering relationship with God and urging House members to spend at least thirty minutes a day in prayer. *U.S. Congressional Record,* 80th Cong., 2d Sess. (Washington, D.C.: U.S. Government Printing Office, 1948), pp. 3701–2.

33. *New York Times,* 2 May 1949.

34. Ibid., 26 June 1949.

35. Thomas C. Reeves, *The Life and Times of Joe McCarthy* (Lanham, Maryland: Madison Books, 1997), pp. 268, 477–85, 488–91.

36. *New York Times,* 26 July 1949. On the Spellman-Roosevelt fracas, see Robert J. Gannon, *The Cardinal Spellman Story* (Garden City, New York: Doubleday, 1962), pp. 314–21. The quotation is on page 318. Historian John Tracy Ellis learned from James A. Farley, FDR's former postmaster general, that Pius XII expressed disapproval of Spellman's attack on the First Lady. Ellis thought that Spellman's apologetic trip to meet Mrs. Roosevelt may have stemmed from the Pope's displeasure. John Tracy Ellis, *Catholic Bishops: A Memoir* (Wilmington, Delaware: Michael Glazier, Inc., 1983), p. 93.

37. On Spellman's vital role in the appointment, see Gannon, *The Cardinal Spellman Story,* p. 145; copy, [Spellman] to Count Enrico Galeazzi, 11 August 1955; copy, Spellman to Sheen, 17 April 1961, Francis Cardinal Spellman Papers, Archdiocese of New York Archives; copy, Pietro Fumansoni-Biondi to Fulton J. Sheen, 20 September 1950, Fulton J. Sheen Collection, St. John's University Archives, Jamaica, New York.

38. Fulton J. Sheen II interview, 10 April 2000.

39. *The Tower,* 27 September 1950.

40. Ibid.

41. Sheen, *Treasure in Clay,* p. 106.

42. George A. Kelly interview, 4 January 1998; Francis J. Weber, *His Eminence of Los Angeles, James Francis Cardinal McIntyre* (Mission Hills, California: St. Francis Historical Society, 1997), vol 1, pp. 64–71; Gannon, *The Cardinal Spellman Story,* pp. 144–45; John Cooney, *The American Pope: The Life and Times of Francis Cardinal Spellman* (New York: Times Books, 1984), p. 248; Ellis, *Catholic Bishops,* pp. 97–99. Later, Spellman successfully recommended his own successor. Ibid., pp. 105–6.

43. Gannon, *The Cardinal Spellman Story,* p. 144.

44. Gannon, *The Cardinal Spellman Story,* p. 145; George A. Kelly interview, 4 January 1998. McDonnell, who had waited eleven years to be promoted to bishop, now had the right of succession to the bishop of Wheeling.

45. D. P. Noonan, *The Passion of Fulton Sheen* (New York: Dodd, Mead, 1972), pp. 21–22.

46. Sheen's photograph was used in campus promotional literature published in the year 2000.

47. Joan Cunningham interview, 2 April 2000.

48. James C. G. Conniff, *The Bishop Sheen Story* (New York: Fawcett Publications, 1953), p. 28.

49. Edythe Brownett interview.

50. Joan Cunningham interview, 2 April 2000.

51. Joan Cunningham interview, 21 October 1999; Marie Minnick interview, 4 October 1999.

52. Joan Cunningham interview, 9 November 1999.

53. Ibid; Edythe Brownett interview.

54. Edythe Brownett interview; Marlene Brownett interview, 11 February 2000.

55. Tom and Yolanda Holliger interview, 19 April 2000.

56. Eileen Sheen Khouw to the author, 30 October 1999, Eileen Sheen Khouw file.

57. Marlene Brownett interview, 11 February 2000; Sheen inscription to Marlene on the inside page of The Maryknoll Fathers, eds., *Daily Missile of the Mystical Body* (New York: P. J. Kenedy and Sons, 1957) in Marlene Brownett file.

58. Edythe Brownett interview; Marlene Brownett interview, 11 February 2000. See also Eileen Sheen Khouw to the author, 30 October 1999, Eileen Sheen Khouw file; Joan Cunningham interview, 9 November 1999; Edwin Broderick interview, 2 June 1999.

59. Noonan, *The Passion of Fulton Sheen,* p. 105.

60. Mary Baker interview, 13 November 1999.

61. Minutes of the Thirty-second Annual Meeting of the Bishops of the United States, November 1950, National Catholic Welfare Conference Papers, CUA Archives.

62. Sheen, *Treasure in Clay,* p. 110.

63. Conniff, *The Bishop Sheen Story,* p. 30. See also Marie-Jose Willimann interview, 28 August 1999. Cf. Wilfred Sheed, *Frank and Maisie: A Memoir with Parents* (New York: Simon and Schuster, 1985), pp. 243–46. This superficial and nasty account was written by an admittedly "abrasive" man, the son of a famous religious writer and publisher, who was dismissed in part for writing a novel while on the Society's payroll.

64. Noonan, *The Passion of Fulton Sheen,* p. 107.

65. Ross, "The Many Roles of Bishop Fulton J. Sheen," *New York Post,* 14 October 1955.

66. Noonan, *The Passion of Fulton Sheen,* p. 80.

67. Edythe Brownett interview. The numbers came from the Society, and Fulton used them on speaking tours. See, for example, *The Irish Catholic,* 10 July 1969.

68. Consodine, " 'God Love You,' " *Cosmopolitan,* July 1952, p. 97.

69. Conniff, *The Bishop Sheen Story,* p. 30.

70. I am greatly indebted to Marlene and Edythe Brownett for giving me both a World Mission Rosary and a God Love You medal.

71. Marlene Brownett, Edythe's younger sister, typed Sheen's "God Love You" columns at times, often from tape recordings made by her employer. Marlene Brownett interview, 11 February 2000.

72. Monica Yehle, "A Word from the Editor," *Mission,* Spring 1995, p. 8.

73. Consodine, " 'God Love You,' " p. 97.

74. *New York Post,* 14 October 1955; Office of the General Secretary files; Minutes, Administrative Board, NCWC, 11 November 1945, National Catholic Welfare Conference Papers, CUA Archives.

75. See Fulton J. Sheen, *The Woman* (Huntington, Indiana: Our Sunday Visitor, 1951), pp. 45, 50, 55, 60–61, 68, 73.

76. Copy, memorandum, Most Rev. Robert E. Lucey to Francis Spellman, 4 April 1951, Spellman Papers.

77. Copy, [Francis Spellman] to Enrico Galeazzi, 11 August 1955, Spellman Papers.

78. Copy, Fulton J. Sheen to Amleto Giovanni Cicognani, 15 May 1951, Fulton J. Sheen Collection, St. John's University Archives.

79. Fulton J. Sheen II interview, 10 April 2000.

80. Copy, Fulton J. Sheen to Amleto Giovanni Cicognani, 15 May 1951, Fulton J. Sheen Collection, St. John's University Archives; *New York Times,* 25 May 1951.

81. Copy, J. Edgar Hoover to Fulton J. Sheen, 14 September 1950; copy, Fulton J. Sheen to J. Edgar Hoover, 13 July 1951, FBI file.

82. *New York Times,* 23 May 1951.

83. Fulton J. Sheen II interview, 10 April 2000.

84. Noonan, *The Passion of Fulton Sheen,* p. 49.

85. Sheen Correspondence, box 48, Sheen Archives.

86. Unsigned, internal biography prepared by the FBI in mid-1953, Sheen file, FBI files. This raises the question: Did the FBI know that Sheen did not earn a second doctorate from a Roman institution, as he claimed? We do not know. The unnamed author, however, credits Sheen with a "D.D."

87. Matthew Paratore interview. See also Joan Dalton interview, 16 December 1998.

88. Rev. Patrick W. Collins to the author, 17 January 2000. Cf. Noonan, *The Passion of Fulton Sheen,* p. 49.

89. Edwin Broderick interview, 27 March 1999.

90. Hilary Franco interview, 26 October 1999.

91. Sheen, *Treasure in Clay,* p. 92.

92. Copy, telegram, Francis Spellman to Fulton J. Sheen, ? June 1951, Fulton J. Sheen Collection, St. John's University Archives. The stamp on the Spellman telegram is not entirely legible, but the month and year are clear, and the document is together with two other congratulatory telegrams dated June 9 and June 10. Blythe Roveland-Brenton interview.

93. On June 7, Spellman attended the funeral of Dennis Cardinal Dougherty in Philadelphia. Three days later, he said Mass at St. Patrick's Cathedral and presided at a ceremony marking the departure of 27 priests and two brothers for lifetime mission posts around the world. On June 12, he presided at the graduation exercises of Manhattan College, receiving an honorary degree. *New York Times,* 8, 9, 10 June 1951. The ceremony and the graduation exercise were surely in Spellman's appointment book long before the announcement of Sheen's consecration was made by the Vatican.

94. Noonan, *The Passion of Fulton Sheen,* p. 49.

95. Hilary Franco interview, 26 October 1999.

96. Edwin Broderick interview, 27 March 1999; Gannon, *The Cardinal Spellman Story,* p. 145; copy, Francis Cardinal Spellman to Fulton J. Sheen, 17 April 1961, Spellman Papers.

97. Fulton J. Sheen II interview, 10 April 2000. See a 1953 FBI biography of Sheen, FBI file. This account erroneously calls the nephew Fulton Sheen III.

98. *New York Times,* 12 June 1951. The photo of Sheen, wearing a tall miter and accompanied by a Vatican official, appeared in the *New York Times* on June 17. On Piazza, see George A. Kelly interview, 4 January 1998.

99. Fulton J. Sheen II interview, 10 April 2000. The often-cropped photograph of Sheen and the Pope is presented in full in Noonan, *The Passion of Fulton Sheen,* following page 88. It shows the military personnel, Fulton J. Sheen II (the young civilian on his knees in front) and several other guests present.

100. Conniff, *The Bishop Sheen Story,* p. 30; the 1953 FBI biography of Sheen, FBI file.

101. Sheen, *Treasure in Clay,* p. 93.

102. Vincent W. Jeffers to Francis Cardinal Spellman, 2 February 1952; Francis Cardinal Spellman to Fulton J. Sheen, 7 February 1952, Spellman Papers.

103. Fulton J. Sheen to Francis Cardinal Spellman, 8 February 1952, Spellman Papers.

104. Edwin Broderick interview, 27 March 1999.

105. Ibid.

106. *Boston Post,* 7 May 1953; *Catholic Post,* 22 September 1985.

Chapter 8: The Television Man of the Year

1. Edwin Broderick interview, 27 March 1999.

2. "Microphone Missionary," *Time,* 14 April 1952, p. 72.

3. John P. Keating, "Bishop Sheen: Purple Passage to the Church," *Catholic World,* April 1954, p. 6.

4. James C. G. Conniff, *The Bishop Sheen Story* (New York: Fawcett Publications, 1953), pp. 7, 9–11; Sheen, *Treasure in Clay,* p. 69.

5. Edwin Broderick interview, 27 March 1999.

6. Harriett Van Horne, "The Bishop versus Berle," *Theater Arts* 35 (December 1952), p. 95; Conniff, *The Bishop Sheen Story,* pp. 15–16.

7. Ibid., p. 15.

8. Edwin Broderick interview, 27 March 1999.

9. Marlene Brownett interview, 11 February 2000. For many years, it will be recalled, Trigger had served as the broker of goods sent to Sheen by admiring *Catholic Hour* listeners.

10. See Sheen, *Treasure in Clay,* pp. 69–70.

11. Ibid., p. 70. Cf. Conniff, *The Bishop Sheen Story,* p. 14, where the number is lower.

12. Joseph Roddy, "A Talk with Bishop Sheen," *Look,* 27 January 1953, p. 38.

13. Sheen practiced his Italian regularly with his chauffeur, Mario Ascari. Marlene Brownett to the author, 27 July 2000. Sheen, *Treasure in Clay,* p. 70.

14. Sheen and Ravaud worked together for about seven years. Sheen then hired her at the Society for the Propagation of the Faith, where she remained briefly until she was married. Sheen married the couple and later baptized their four children. Ravaud said she loved Sheen's "dynamism" and remembered him as a "wonderful man." Marie-Jose Willimann interview, 28 August 1999.

15. Edwin Broderick interview, 27 March 1999.

16. Quoted in Mary Ann Watson, "And They Said 'Uncle Fultie' Didn't Have a Prayer...," *Television Quarterly* 26 (1992), p. 3.

17. Conniff, *The Bishop Sheen Story,* p. 15.

18. Tim Taylor, "Fulton Sheen: Verities on TV," *CUE,* 22 November 1952, p. 20.

19. Sheen, *Treasure in Clay,* pp. 72–73.

20. Hilary Franco interview, 19 March 1998. Sheen and Hershfield, a star of radio's "Can You Top This?" had been friends for several years. See the photo of the two swapping jokes in *Catholic Week,* January 1948.

21. Van Horne, "The Bishop versus Berle," p. 65.

22. Ibid; Sheen, *Treasure in Clay,* p. 68.

23. "Sheen on TV Screen," *Life,* 24 March 1952, p. 92.

24. Edwin Broderick interview, 27 March 1999. Frank Bunetta was also Gleason's television director. Still, Fulton denied that he was a comedian. He said, "I do not go in for humor deliberately. I never tell a joke as a joke. I may use it to illustrate a point, but it is purely incidental." See Conniff,

The Bishop Sheen Story, pp. 5–7. For samples of Sheen's favorite jokes, see Sheen, *Treasure in Clay,* pp. 297–308.

25. "Sheen on TV Screen," p. 92.

26. Quoted in Watson, "And They Said 'Uncle Fultie' Didn't Have A Prayer...," p. 19.

27. Conniff, *The Bishop Sheen Story,* p. 4.

28. Loretta Young Louis interview.

29. For the topics and a sample of his humor, see Fulton J. Sheen, *Science, Psychiatry and Religion* (New York: Dell, 1962), pp. 7, 121, 145.

30. Ibid., pp. 45, 150–58.

31. See Will Herberg, *Protestant, Catholic, Jew: An Essay in American Religious Sociology* (Chicago: University of Chicago Press, 1983), pp. 46–56; Thomas C. Reeves, *Twentieth-Century America: A Brief History* (New York: Oxford University Press, 2000), pp. 158–60.

32. "Microphone Missionary," p. 72. Sheen did not surpass Berle in the television ratings, as is sometimes claimed. Du Mont's handful of affiliate stations could not compete effectively against the networks. See Watson, "And They Said 'Uncle Fultie' Didn't Have a Prayer...," p. 19.

33. Milton Berle, with Haskel Frankel, *Milton Berle: An Autobiography* (New York: Delacorte Press, 1974), p. 285. See Roddy, "A Talk with Bishop Sheen," p. 41. On 11 June 1952, Sheen appeared on Berle's telethon for the Damon Runyon Memorial Fund, making what a critic called "a gracious and pleasing speech praising the comic." *Variety Television Reviews,* vol. 4, *1951–1953* (New York: Garland Publishing, Inc., 1989), reviews for 11 June 1952.

34. Editorial, "Victory in Washington—and Sheen," *Christian Beacon,* 17 April 1952, pp. 1, 8.

35. John Tracy Ellis, *American Catholicism,* 2nd ed. (Chicago: University of Chicago Press, 1969), p. 125.

36. Martin E. Marty, *Modern American Religion,* vol. 3, *Under God, Indivisible, 1941–1960* (Chicago: University of Chicago Press, 1996) pp. 417–18. See Herberg, *Protestant, Catholic, Jew,* pp. 153–66.

37. Ellis, *American Catholicism,* p. 129.

38. *New York Times,* 21 April 1952.

39. Ibid., 28 April 1952.

40. Mary Jude Yablonsky, "A Rhetorical Analysis of Selected Television Speeches of Archbishop Fulton J. Sheen on Communism, 1952–1956"

(Ph.D. diss., Ohio State University, 1974), pp. 57–58. In the first *Life Is Worth Living* series, 6 of the 26 talks dealt with communism; in the second series, 8; in the third series, 7; in the fourth series, 8; and in the fifth series, 3. Ibid., pp. 34–36.

41. Robert J. Gannon, *The Cardinal Spellman Story* (Garden City, New York: Doubleday, 1962), p. 350.

42. Donald F. Crosby, *God, Church, and Flag: Senator Joseph R. McCarthy and the Catholic Church, 1950–1957* (Chapel Hill: University of North Carolina Press, 1978), pp. 132–39, 158–63, 187–88, 200–5.

43. Thomas C. Reeves, *The Life and Times of Joe McCarthy* (Lanham, Maryland: Madison Books, 1997), p. 670.

44. John Cooney, *The American Pope: The Life and Times of Francis Cardinal Spellman* (New York: Times Books, 1984), pp. 223–25. Bishop Edwin Broderick thinks the friendship between the two has been exaggerated for the purpose of linking the cardinal with Cohn's homosexuality. Cohn was a good friend of Edward "Ned" Spellman, the cardinal's nephew. "Roy would come occasionally to lunch with Ned," Broderick says. Spellman and Cohn were "only acquaintances." Edwin Broderick interview, 2 June 1999.

45. Crosby, *God, Church, and Flag*, pp. 242–51, *et passim.*

46. Ibid., p. 251.

47. See Reeves, *The Life and Times of Joe McCarthy*, pp. 674–75, *et passim.*

48. Gannon, *The Cardinal Spellman Story*, p. 348.

49. *New York Times*, 29 January 1950.

50. Fulton J. Sheen, *Crisis in History* (St. Paul, Minnesota: Catechetical Guild Educational Society, 1952), pp. 26, 30–31, 37, 40, 46–47, 55–57.

51. Undated memo, FBI file.

52. At Fritz Kreisler's suggestion, Sheen had taken organ lessons. His first teacher was famed swing organist Ethel Smith. Fulton acknowledged her prowess on the instrument but said that her instructional ability was weak. He then turned to a young friend, Yolanda Tomaiuoli, who was dating a cousin. She was an accomplished musician who would go on to earn a doctorate in music at Columbia University. Tomaiuoli said later that Fulton "could play some" but that "his musical talents were limited." In the late 1950s and early 1960s, he played an electric Hammond on the main floor of his building for personal enjoyment, occasionally displaying his skill to friends. Yolanda Holliger interview, 19 April 2000; Vincent Cahill interview; Joan Cunningham interview, 2 April 2000.

53. Vincent Cahill interview; "Memories of Marian T. Cahill Regarding Bishop Fulton J. Sheen [July 2000]," Vincent Cahill file. Cahill said that Sheen did not know he was an FBI agent when they first met. The compassion shown by Sheen was "strictly personal." Thereafter the two did not talk much about the bureau. Cahill did not know that Sheen and J. Edgar Hoover were friends.

54. Vincent Cahill interview.

55. Henry Dieterich, ed., *Through the Years with Fulton Sheen: Inspirational Selections for Each Day of the Year* (Ann Arbor, Michigan: Servant Books, 1985), p. 177. The woman died in October 1970. Copy, Fulton J. Sheen to Mary Nordeman, 28 October 1970, Mary Nordeman file. See Marlene Brownett to the author, 22 August 2000, Marlene Brownett file.

56. *New York Times*, 4 September 1952.

57. *Catholic Standard*, 10 October 1952.

58. *New York Times*, 22 October 1952; Sheen, *Treasure in Clay*, p. 66. Spellman said in May 1955 that Sheen was making $13,000 per broadcast. Perhaps that sum doubled when the program moved to ABC later that year. Copy, Francis Spellman to Enrico Galeazzi, 11 August 1955, Francis Cardinal Spellman Papers, Archdiocese of New York Archives.

59. Sheen, *Treasure in Clay*, p. 66.

60. Copy, Francis Spellman to Enrico Galeazzi, 11 August 1955, Spellman Papers.

61. *New York Times*, 22 October 1952; copy, memorandum, Gertrude Algase to Joseph F. McKee, 30 April 1955, Spellman Papers.

62. *New York Times*, 22, 26 October 1952.

63. Ibid, 21 July 1953.

64. Edwin Broderick interview, 27 March 1999.

65. Sheen, *Treasure in Clay*, pp. 66–68.

66. Ibid., p. 300; Watson, "And They Said 'Uncle Fultie' Didn't Have a Prayer," p. 19.

67. Thomas Holliger interview, 19 April 2000.

68. Conniff, *The Bishop Sheen Story*, p. 8.

69. *New York Times*, 22 February 1953.

70. Ibid., 30 April 1953.

71. Ibid., 9 November 1953.

72. Ibid., 27 October 1953.

73. Milton Berle, *B.S. I Love You: Sixty Funny Years with the Famous and Infamous* (New York: McGraw-Hill, 1988), p. 195.

74. Sheen, *Treasure in Clay*, p. 74.

75. For several memorable excerpts, see Sheen, *The World's First Love*, pp. 54–55, 59, 65.

76. See Ibid., pp. 19–28, 113, 181. An assortment of excerpts from glowing reviews appears on the Image Books edition published in 1956. The book club list is also presented here.

77. Conniff, *The Bishop Sheen Story*, pp. 30–31.

78. See Richard Gid Powers, *Secrecy and Power: The Life of J. Edgar Hoover* (New York: The Free Press, 1987), pp. 308–13, 317–23, 488–92.

79. *Milwaukee Journal*, 18 March 1988.

80. Ibid.

81. Copy, memorandum, C. L. Trotto to Mr. Clegg, 11 June 1953, FBI file.

82. Copy, J. Edgar Hoover to Fulton J. Sheen, 5 May 1953; copy, Fulton J. Sheen to J. Edgar Hoover, 19 May 1953, FBI file.

83. Copy, J. Edgar Hoover to Fulton J. Sheen, 12 June 1953, FBI file. A copy of the speech is in the file.

84. Copy, J. Edgar Hoover to Fulton J. Sheen, 15 June 1953; memorandum, Mr. Jones to Mr. Nichols, 29 June 1953, FBI file.

85. Copy, Fulton J. Sheen to J. Edgar Hoover, 29 June 1953, FBI file.

86. Copy, Fulton J. Sheen to J. Edgar Hoover, 25 August 1953, FBI file.

87. Copy, memorandum, SAC, New York to J. Edgar Hoover, 20 January 1954; memorandum, J. Edgar Hoover to SAC, New York, 25 February 1954, FBI file.

88. Copy, L. B. Nichols to Mr. Tolson, 9 March 1956, FBI file; *Catholic Standard*, 23 March 1956.

89. Copy, Fulton J. Sheen to J. Edgar Hoover, 19 February 1958, FBI file.

90. Copy, The Executives Conference to Mr. Tolson, 9 September 1954, Special Service Contacts file, FBI file.

91. Copy, J. Edgar Hoover to all SACs, 7 October 1954, FBI file.

92. Copy, memorandum, SAC, NYC to J. Edgar Hoover, 9 January 1967, FBI file. It appears in this letter that Sheen was being recommended to the Buffalo FBI office for similar duties.

93. *Buffalo Courier-Express*, 28 June 1967; copy, J. Edgar Hoover to Fulton J. Sheen, 30 June 1967, FBI file.

94. Copy, Charles G. Cusick to J. Edgar Hoover, 1 May 1969, FBI file.

95. See Sheen, *Science, Psychiatry and Religion,* pp. 148–49.

96. Fulton J. Sheen, "Pius XII," *Look,* 23 August 1955, p. 31.

97. Press release, 11 February 1955, University of Notre Dame Archives.

98. *Washington Star,* 30 May 1955.

99. John J. Fink, "A Memory," *Our Sunday Visitor,* 23 December 1979.

100. "Mass in English," *Jubilee,* October 1955, pp. 7–10.

101. *Boston Pilot,* 19 November 1955.

102. Robert F. McNamara, *The Diocese of Rochester in America,* 2nd ed. (Rochester: Diocese of Rochester, 1998), p. 512.

103. "The Two Marxes," *Time,* 9 May 1955, p. 70.

104. John E. Sheen interview, 28 August 1999; Joan Cunningham interviews, 4 October 1999, 3 May 2000.

105. Joseph Sheen Jr. interview. The ring now belongs to Sheen's son, Don, who proudly showed it to the author at the Sheen family picnic, 29 July 2000 in St. Charles, Illinois.

106. Copy, memorandum, Gertrude Algase to Joseph F. McKee, 30 April 1955; copy, Joseph F. McKee to Gertrude Algase, 5 May 1955; copy, memorandum, Gertrude Algase to Francis Cardinal Spellman, 24 June 1955, folder 9, Society for the Propagation of the Faith Papers, Spellman Papers.

107. John Tracy Ellis, *Catholic Bishops: A Memoir* (Wilmington, Delaware: Michael Glazier, Inc., 1983), p. 80. Ellis says that the sum came from Sheen's television broadcasts, but that must have been a slip on his part.

108. Edythe Brownett interview.

109. Copy, Vincent W. Jeffers to Francis Cardinal Spellman, 17 November 1955, Spellman Papers.

110. Interview with Edwin Broderick, 27 March 1999.

Chapter 9: Backed up Against the Cross

1. George A. Kelly interview, 4 January 1998.

2. Edwin Broderick interview, 27 March 1999.

3. John Cooney, *The American Pope: The Life and Times of Francis Cardinal Spellman* (New York: Times Books, 1984), p. 251.

4. Copy, Francis Spellman to Angelo Dell'Acqua, 2 May 1955; memorandum in Edward E. Swanstrom to Francis Spellman, 31 May 1955, Francis Cardinal Spellman Papers, Archdiocese of New York Archives.

5. Edwin Broderick interview, 27 March 1999.

6. Copy, Francis Spellman to Fulton J. Sheen, 26 May 1955, Spellman Papers.

7. Copy, Francis Spellman to Enrico Galeazzi, 2 June 1955 (two letters), Spellman Papers.

8. Copy, Francis Spellman to Joseph P. Kennedy, 1 July 1955, Spellman Papers.

9. Copy, Francis Spellman to Pietro Fumansoni-Biondi, 1 July 1955, Spellman Papers.

10. Pietro Fumansoni-Biondi to Francis Spellman, 8 July 1955, Spellman Papers.

11. Copy, Francis Spellman to Enrico Galeazzi, 11 August 1955, Spellman Papers.

12. Copy, Francis Spellman to Pietro Fumansoni Biondi, 16 August 1955; unnamed Vatican official to Spellman, 18 August 1955, Spellman Papers.

13. Copy, Pietro Fumansoni-Biondi to Francis Spellman, 30 October 1956, Spellman Papers.

14. John Tracy Ellis, *Catholic Bishops: A Memoir* (Wilmington, Delaware: Michael Glazier, Inc., 1983), p. 82.

15. Ibid., pp. 82–83; D. P. Noonan, *The Passion of Fulton Sheen* (New York: Dodd, Mead, 1972), p. 82.

16. See Noonan, *The Passion of Fulton Sheen,* pp. 81–82; Cooney, *The American Pope,* pp. 255–56. In 1974, Sheen told Fr. Patrick Collins of the meeting in Rome between Pius XII, Spellman, and himself, and of the Pope's decision in his favor. Patrick Collins to the author, 17 January 2000, Patrick Collins file.

17. Fulton J. Sheen form letter of 25 July 1957, box 131, office files, James McGranery Papers, Library of Congress.

18. Cooney, *The American Pope,* pp. 248–49.

19. Noonan, *The Passion of Fulton Sheen,* p. 82.

20. Ibid., p. 80; Hilary Franco interview, 19 March 1998; Edwin Broderick interview, 27 March 1999. See the Robert Neville columns in *New York Post,* 30 April, 5 June 1958.

21. Noonan, *The Passion of Fulton Sheen,* pp. 78–79; Robert F. McNamara interview with historian Florence D. Cohalan, 27 February 1989, Robert F. McNamara Papers, Sheen Archives; Sebastian Falcone interview; Robert Neville column in *New York Post,* 30 April 1958.

22. *New York Times,* 19 October 1957; "The Bishop's First Duty," *Newsweek,* 28 October 1957, p. 59.

23. Tim Brooks and Earle Marsh, *The Complete Directory to Prime Time Network TV Shows (1946–Present),* 6th ed. (New York: Ballantine Books, 1995), p. 595.

24. See interviews with Robert Paul Mohan, Mary Baker (28 October 1999), Joan Cunningham (4 October 1999), Loretta Young Louis, and Yolanda Holliger (19 April 2000).

25. Ellis, *Catholic Bishops,* p. 81.

26. Richard Conniff interview.

27. Copy, Fulton J. Sheen to Nicholas T. Elko, 23 September 1966, Sheen Correspondence, box 48, Sheen Archives.

28. James C. G. Conniff, *The Bishop Sheen Story* (New York: Fawcett Publications, 1953), p. 22.

29. Noonan, *The Passion of Fulton Sheen,* p. 80.

30. Fulton J. Sheen, *Life of Christ* (New York: Doubleday, 1990), p. 21.

31. Ibid., pp. 20–21.

32. For a solid review, noting Sheen's references to communism in the volume, see *New York Times,* 19 October 1958. The book was translated into several languages and is still in print.

33. Robert Paul Mohan interview.

34. Michael C. Hogan interview, 13 January 1999.

35. Sheen, *Life of Christ,* pp. 9–10.

36. Copy, Fulton J. Sheen to Marlene Brownett, dated 1959 by the recipient, Marlene Brownett file.

37. See *New York Times,* 27 March 1960.

38. Sheen, *Treasure in Clay,* pp. 153–67. For more on Karsh, see Noonan, *The Passion of Fulton Sheen,* pp. 108–9. For contemporary impressions of his trip, see copy, Fulton J. Sheen to Marlene Brownett [1961], Marlene Brownett file. Sheen had a prayer card made of the photograph of himself with the lamb.

39. Copy, J. Edgar Hoover to Fulton J. Sheen, 30 September 1957, FBI file. A transcript of the taped speech is included in the file.

40. *New York Times,* 15 November 1957.

41. Ibid., 26 February, 2 March 1958.

42. Robert Neville in *New York Post,* 30 April, 5 June 1958.

43. *New York Times,* 18 August 1958.

44. Sheen's *Curriculum Vitae,* 1966, p. 5, Sheen Archives.

45. See copy, Fulton J. Sheen to King Baudouin, 22 September 1959; copy, Fulton J. Sheen to Elizabeth Hapsburg, 23 September 1959, 28 October 1960; Fulton J. Sheen to King Baudouin, 28 October 1960, Sheen Correspondence, box 48.

46. Marlene Brownett interview, 24 February 2000.

47. *New York Times,* 18 June 1956.

48. Francis J. Weber, *His Eminence of Los Angeles, James Francis Cardinal McIntyre* (Mission Hills, California: St. Francis Historical Society, 1997), vol. 2, pp. 384–85.

49. Philip Gleason, "What Made Catholic Identity a Problem?" in *Faith and the Intellectual Life: Marianist Award Lectures,* ed. James L. Heft (Notre Dame, Indiana: Unversity of Notre Dame Press, 1996), pp. 92–96.

50. Sheen, *Footprints in a Darkened Forest,* p. 249.

51. Ibid.

52. Sheen, *Treasure in Clay,* pp. 233–36. On one of the two occasions Fulton helped consecrate missionary bishops, he wrote to friends, "Today, I stood next to the Holy Father for five hours as co-consecrator of 14 bishops, eight of whom were black, one was Japanese. It was a soul-stirring experience." Copy, Fulton J. Sheen to "My Dear Friends [Vincent and Marian Cahill], n.d., Vincent Cahill file.

53. Sheen, *Treasure in Clay,* p. 234; Noonan, *The Passion of Fulton Sheen,* pp. 140–41.

54. Gladys Baker had introduced Ralli to Sheen. The physician died in 1968. Yetman worked for Dr. Wilbur J. Gould, a prominent throat expert. She was well known and much loved by people in show business. Yetman continued to look after Sheen until his death. She died of cancer in 1990. Marlene Brownett to the author, 1, 2 July 2000. On Yetman, see also the Ann Edward interview. See also a copy of a loving statement by actress Angela Lansbury, which was read at the nurse's funeral, in the Ann Edward file. A photo of Yetman is in the Marlene Brownett file.

55. Sheen, *Treasure in Clay,* p. 149.

56. "Argentina," *Time,* 31 October 1960, p. 28; copy, Fulton J. Sheen to King Baudouin, 28 October 1960, Sheen Correspondence, box 48.

57. See Thomas C. Reeves, *A Question of Character: A Life of John F. Kennedy* (New York: The Free Press, 1991), pp. 31–32, 57, 190–93.

58. See ibid., pp. 70, 165, 186, 215, 272; Cooney, *The American Pope*, pp. 265–73.

59. Sheen, *Treasure in Clay*, p. 294.

60. *New York Times*, 26 November 1960. For a photograph of Sheen and six Suk women, see "His Greatest Love," *Mission*, Spring 1995, pp. 10–11. On page 12, the year for the trip to Kenya is erroneously given as 1957.

61. Sheen, *Treasure in Clay*, pp. 150–51.

62. Ibid., p. 151.

63. Copy, Fulton J. Sheen to Clare Boothe Luce, undated, box 212, Clare Boothe Luce Papers, Library of Congress.

64. Sheen, *Treasure in Clay*, pp. 151–52.

65. See Hilary Franco interview, 19 March 1998; Matthew Paratore interview; Edwin Broderick interview, 27 March 1999.

66. Fulton Sheen to Francis Spellman, 12 April 1961; copy, Francis Spellman to Fulton Sheen, 17 April 1961; Joseph A. Burke to Francis Spellman, 19 April 1961; G. P. Agagianian to Francis Spellman, 22 April 1961, Spellman Papers.

67. Eileen Sheen Khouw interview.

68. Noonan, *The Passion of Fulton Sheen*, p. 116. The talk, or at least portions of it, had earlier been featured on *Life Is Worth Living*. See "The Psychology of the Irish," in Sheen, *Life Is Worth Living: First and Second Series*, pp. 119–25.

69. Eleen Sheen Khouw interview.

70. Vincent A. Yzermans, ed., *American Participation in the Second Vatican Council* (New York: Sheed and Ward, 1967), p. 7.

71. Sheen, *Treasure in Clay*, pp. 283–84.

72. Yzermans, *American Participation in the Second Vatican Council*, p. 7.

73. Ibid., p. 525.

74. Sheen, *Treasure in Clay*, p. 284.

75. Ibid., pp. 293–94.

76. John F. Quinn, "The Man JFK Didn't Understand," *Crisis*, October 1999, p. 33.

77. Sheen, *Treasure in Clay*, p. 282.

78. Ibid., p. 285.

79. Ibid., p. 293.

80. Ibid., p. 289.

81. *New York Times,* 22 October 1962.

82. Ibid.

83. Yzermans, *American Participation in the Second Vatican Council,* pp. 4–12.

84. Ibid., pp. 7–10.

85. Sheen, *Treasure in Clay,* p. 293.

86. Copy, Fulton J. Sheen to Marlene Brownett, 8 November 1962, Marlene Brownett file.

87. Sheen, *Treasure in Clay,* p. 288.

88. Sheen, *Footprints in a Darkened Forest,* p. 250.

89. *New York Times,* 17 June 1963.

90. Sheen, *Treasure in Clay,* pp. 236–37.

91. Monsignor Eugene Clark quoted in Cooney, *The American Pope,* p. 265.

92. Sheen, *Footprints in a Darkened Forest,* p. 248. See Noonan, *The Passion of Fulton Sheen,* pp. 118–19, for earlier commentary.

93. *Washington Star,* 5 October 1974.

94. Eileen Sheen Khouw interview. Cf. Loretta Young Louis interview.

95. All subsequent quotations from council documents are from *The Sixteen Documents of Vatican II and the Instruction on the Liturgy with Commentaries by the Council Fathers* (Boston: Daughters of St. Paul, n.d.).

96. Yzermans, *American Participation in the Second Vatican Council,* pp. 26–27, 34, 43–45, 56–57.

97. *New York Times,* 1 May 1964.

98. See Mark A. Noll, *A History of Christianity in the United States and Canada* (Grand Rapids, Michigan: Wiliam B. Eerdmans Publishing Co., 1992), pp. 452–53.

99. Sheen, *Treasure in Clay,* p. 360.

100. Yzermans, *American Participation in the Second Vatican Council,* pp. 401–6.

101. *The Sixteen Documents of Vatican II,* pp. 322–23, 331.

102. Copy, Fulton J. Sheen to Clare Boothe Luce, undated but probably 1963 (and filed in the wrong box in the Library of Congress collection), box 212, Luce Papers.

103. *The Sixteen Documents of Vatican II,* pp. 350, 359; Yzermans, *American Participation in the Second Vatican Council,* pp. 449–57.

104. Yzermans, *American Participation in the Second Vatican Council*, pp. 521–35; *The Sixteen Documents of Vatican II*, pp. 461–512. The Society for the Propagation of the Faith soon published the address of November 9 as a pamphlet titled "The Mission World." The language there is very slightly altered from that given by Yzermans.

105. P. David Finks, "Crisis in Smugtown: A Study of Conflict, Churches, and Citizen Organizations in Rochester, New York, 1964–1969" (Ph.D. diss., Union Graduate School of the Union for Experimenting Colleges and Universities, 1975), p. 182. Hereafter referred to as Finks dissertation.

106. *The Sixteen Documents of Vatican II*, pp. 513–624. In 1964, Sheen advised a pharmacist not to sell a drug if it was used for "direct contraception." The birth control pill, he continued, was the most popular form of direct contraception, and he advised: "There has not been sufficient experimental evidence concerning how much it operates within the laws of nature itself, and also how much the motive would destroy a good purpose. These are questions which will be decided when more scientific evidence is available." Copy, Fulton J. Sheen to James Connors, 23 April 1964, Sheen Correspondence, box 48.

107. Yzermans, *American Participation in the Second Vatican Council*, pp. 202–3.

108. Ibid., pp. 210–12.

109. Ibid., p. 548.

110. Ibid., p. 580; *The Sixteen Documents of Vatican II*, pp. 256–59.

111. Quoted in Robert McClory, "When Wrong Turns out to Be Right," *U.S. Catholic*, May 1999, p. 12. See numbers 42, 54, 55 and 77 in Pius IX's "Syllabus of Errors."

112. See Thomas J. Shelley, " 'What the Hell Is an Encyclical?': Governor Alfred E. Smith, Charles C. Marshall, Esq., and Father Francis P. Duffy," *U.S. Catholic Historian* 15 (Spring 1997), pp. 87–107.

113. See the comment by Cardinal Cushing, a campaigner for the declaration, in Yzermans, *American Participation in the Second Vatican Council*, p. 623. For the full story, see pp. 617–64. Sheen is quoted on p. 637. See Fulton Sheen's Vatican II papers at the Sheen Archives.

114. *The Sixteen Statements of Vatican II*, pp. 383–402.

115. Sheen, *Treasure in Clay*, pp. 290–92.

116. Cooney, *The American Pope*, pp. 287–94; John Tracy Ellis, *American Catholicism*, 2nd ed. (Chicago: University of Chicago Press, 1969), pp. 191–92.

117. Cooney, *The American Pope,* pp. 286–87.

118. Copy, Fulton J. Sheen to M. Berenice, 31 January 1966, Sheen Correspondence, box 48.

119. Two letters, Fulton J. Sheen to Clare Boothe Luce, c. 1949, box 33, Luce Papers.

120. Copy, Fulton J. Sheen to Albert R. Zuroweste, 21 February 1966, Sheen Correspondence, box 48.

121. Copy, Fulton J. Sheen to Vincent Sheil, 1 August 1966, Sheen Correspondence, box 48.

122. George A. Kelly, *The Battle for the American Church Revisited* (San Francisco: Ignatius Press, p. 1995), pp. 65–70.

123. Sheen left the films of the series to the Sheen Archives in Rochester, New York. Officials there made a deal to reproduce and sell the films on videotape as a fund-raising device. See copy, Kathleen R. Fields to Anthony Zito, 24 February 1987, Catholic University of America Archives.

124. *New York Times,* 8 November 1966; Sergio Pignedoli, "Guest Editorial," *Worldmission,* Fall 1969, pp. 4–5.

125. Conniff, *The Bishop Sheen Story,* p. 2.

126. *New York Times,* 15 December 1966.

127. This is the opinion of his niece, Joan Sheen Cunningham, and it seems likely. Joan Cunningham interview, 23 May 2000.

128. Cooney, *The American Pope,* pp. 301–5.

129. Ibid., p. 305.

130. Joan Cunningham interview, 4 October 1999.

131. Thomas J. Shelley, "Slouching Toward the Center: Cardinal Francis Spellman, Archbishop Paul J. Hallinan and American Catholicism in the 1960s," *U.S. Catholic Historian* 17 (Fall 1999), pp. 24–25.

132. Andrew Apostoli interview, 28 October 1999. Sheen told Fr. Michael Hogan, his secretary in Rochester, that he had been given a choice. Hogan had the impression that Sheen was required to go somewhere. Michael C. Hogan interview, 13 January 1999. See also Matthew Paratore interview. Cf. *New York Times,* 8 November, 15 December 1966.

133. Patrick Collins to the author, 17 January 2000, Patrick Collins file.

134. See Robert F. McNamara, *The Diocese of Rochester in America, 1868–1993,* 2nd ed. (Rochester, New York: Diocese of Rochester, 1998), pp. 423–26, for Kearney's pre-Rochester history.

135. Confidential source. See also William Graf interview, 23 June 1999. On Casey, see McNamara, *The Diocese of Rochester*, pp. 487–89, 517–19. Casey left the diocese in May.

136. *New York Times*, 27 October 1966.

137. Ibid., 8 November 1966.

138. Copy, Fulton J. Sheen to Thomas K. Gorman, 29 November 1966, Diocese of Dallas Papers.

139. *New York Times*, 12 December 1966.

140. George A. Kelly interview, 4 January 1998.

Chapter 10: Exile

1. Robert McNamara, *The Diocese of Rochester, 1868–1968* (Rochester: Diocese of Rochester, 1968), p. 183.

2. *New York Times*, 8 November, 16 December 1966; McNamara, *The Diocese of Rochester*, p. 470.

3. McNamara, *The Diocese of Rochester*, pp. 477–78.

4. Ibid., pp. 472, 477, 499.

5. Ibid., pp. 483–84.

6. Ibid., pp. 510–12.

7. Ibid, pp. 515–16.

8. P. David Finks, "Crisis in Smugtown: A Study of Conflict, Churches, and Citizen Organizations in Rochester, New York, 1964–1969" (Ph.D. diss., Union Graduate School of the Union for Experimenting Colleges and Universities, 1975), p. 7.

9. See *New York Times*, 25, 26, 27, 28, 29 July 1964.

10. Joseph P. Brennan interview.

11. *New York Times*, 29 July 1964.

12. Finks dissertation, p. 92.

13. McNamara, *The Diocese of Rochester*, pp. 497–508.

14. Ibid., pp. 498–99, 507

15. Matthew Paratore interview. On the strictness at St. Bernard's, see William Graf interview, 24, 26 May 1999. Graf was a graduate.

16. William Ferris interview.

17. Robert Vogt interview, 25 June 1999.

18. McNamara, *The Diocese of Rochester,* pp. 512, 523.

19. Rev. Albert Joseph Mary Shamon, *The Bishop Sheen We Knew* (Oak Lawn, Illinois: CMJ Associates, 1997), p. 5.

20. William Graf interview, 23 June 1999.

21. Joseph P. Brennan interview.

22. Copy, notes, Robert F. McNamara interview with John F. Duffy, 11 March 1987, McNamara file.

23. McNamara, *The Diocese of Rochester,* p. 426.

24. *New York Times,* 15 December 1966.

25. Joe Hart interview; McNamara, *The Diocese of Rochester,* pp. 525–26.

26. Sheen wrote to Luce, "Your presence at the Installation was a natural grace, which made both you and me pleasing to Rochester." Copy, Fulton J. Sheen to Clare Boothe Luce, undated but clearly early 1967, Clare Boothe Luce Papers, Library of Congress.

27. Copy, Robert McNamara notes on the service, Robert McNamara file.

28. *New York Times,* 16 December 1966.

29. William Ferris interview.

30. *New York Times,* 16 December 1966.

31. Shamon, *The Bishop Sheen We Knew,* p. 5.

32. Copy, Robert McNamara notes on the service.

33. Pamphlet, "Guest List, Installation of Most R. Fulton J. Sheen, Ph.D., D.D., Bishop of Rochester, December 15, 1966," Mary Baker Scrapbook, in the possession of Eileen Sheen Khouw; McNamara, *The Diocese of Rochester,* p. 526.

34. *New York Times,* 16 December 1966.

35. McNamara, *The Diocese of Rochester,* p. 527.

36. Shamon, *The Bishop Sheen We Knew,* p. 9.

37. Sheen, *Treasure in Clay,* pp. 172, 176–77.

38. Shamon, *The Bishop Sheen We Knew,* pp. 8–11.

39. Pius XII may have let Sheen choose his successor. Sheen had met O'Meara in 1956 at a meeting in St. Louis. He "sensed" qualities in the young man that prompted him to bring O'Meara to New York as his assistant at the Society. *New York Times,* 18 February 1967. Joan Cunningham said later that Sheen and O'Meara were good friends, and that O'Meara was a fre-

quent "sounding board" for the bishop's frustrations while in Rochester. Joan Cunningham interview, 23 May 2000.

40. Michael C. Hogan interview, 13 January 1999.

41. Ibid; William Graf interview, 24 June 1999; Shamon, *The Bishop Sheen We Knew*, p. 11.

42. Michael C. Hogan interview.

43. William Graf interview, 24 June 1999.

44. Ibid.

45. Joseph P. Brennan interview.

46. Shamon, *The Bishop Sheen We Knew*, p. 19.

47. McNamara, *The Diocese of Rochester*, pp. 528–29; William Graf interview, 23 June 1999; Finks dissertation, pp. 136, 170–78. See also pp. 54–55, 80–83, and 99 of the Finks dissertation.

48. McNamara, *The Diocese of Rochester*, p. 536; Joseph P. Brennan interview; Finks dissertation, pp. 180–81.

49. Finks dissertation, pp. 138–40.

50. Ibid., p. 151.

51. See copy, Clare Boothe Luce to Fulton J. Sheen, 3 January 1967, Luce Papers.

52. "Roman Catholics," *Time*, 10 February 1967, pp. 47–48.

53. Copy, Clare Boothe Luce to Fulton J. Sheen, 3 January 1967.

54. Copy, Fulton J. Sheen to Thomas K. Gorman, 29 November 1966, Diocese of Dallas Papers.

55. Copy, J. Edgar Hoover to Fulton J. Sheen, 4 November 1966; copy, Fulton J. Sheen to J. Edgar Hoover, 10 November 1966; copy, memorandum, SAC, NY to J. Edgar Hoover, 9 January 1967; copy, Mildred Stegall to Cartha DeLoach, 5 June 1967; Cartha DeLoach to Mildred Stegall, 8 June 1967; copy, J. Edgar Hoover to Fulton J. Sheen, 30 June 1967; *Buffalo Courier-Express*, 28 June 1967; copy, memorandum, SAC Buffalo to J. Edgar Hoover, 18 October 1967, FBI file.

56. Fulton J. Sheen, *Cross-Ways: A Book of Inspiration* (Garden City, New York: Doubleday, 1984), p. 75. This is a later edition of the 1967 book.

57. Shamon, *The Bishop Sheen We Knew*, p. 20.

58. McNamara, *The Diocese of Rochester*, pp. 529–30.

59. Ibid., pp. 530–31.

60. William Graf interview, 23 June 1999.

61. McNamara, *The Diocese of Rochester,* p. 532; Joseph P. Brennan interview. See Sheen, *Treasure in Clay,* pp. 174–75. The bishop of Rochester was the chancellor of the Board of the Seminary, with the authority to hire and fire. One of Sheen's most popular appointees was the British convert and ex-communist writer Douglas Hyde. Sebastian Falcone interview.

62. *New York Times,* 15 September 1967.

63. Shamon, *The Bishop Sheen We Knew,* p. 25.

64. William Graf to the author, 1 June 2000; copy, notes, Robert F. McNamara interview with Joseph P. Brennan, 28 May 1977, McNamara file.

65. McNamara, *The Diocese of Rochester,* p. 532.

66. Shamon, *The Bishop Sheen We Knew,* p. 14; McNamara, *The Diocese of Rochester,* p. 533.

67. McNamara, *The Diocese of Rochester,* pp. 533, 556.

68. Ibid., p. 533; Michael C. Hogan interview.

69. *New York Times,* 24 July 1967.

70. Shamon, *The Bishop Sheen We Knew,* p. 11.

71. Ibid., pp. 18–19; *New York Times,* 7 August 1967; Sheen, *Treasure in Clay,* pp. 177–78.

72. Sheen, *Treasure in Clay,* p. 174; Shamon, *The Bishop Sheen We Knew,* pp. 16–17.

73. *New York Times,* 14 February 1967.

74. McNamara, *The Diocese of Rochester,* p. 535.

75. *New York Times,* 23 February 1967; *New York Daily News,* 16 December 1979.

76. McNamara, *The Diocese of Rochester,* pp. 534–35.

77. Shamon, *The Bishop Sheen We Knew,* p. 13.

78. Ibid., p. 26.

79. *New York Times,* 16 September 1967.

80. Sheen press release, 30 July 1967, cited in Kathleen Riley Fields, "Bishop Fulton J. Sheen: An American Catholic Response to the Twentieth Century" (Ph.D. diss., University of Notre Dame, 1988), pp. 461–62.

81. John Cooney, *The American Pope: The Life and Times of Francis Cardinal Spellman* (New York: Times Books, 1984), pp. 306–8.

82. *New York Times,* 29 October 1969. In January 1968, Bobby Kennedy and his wife, braving a snowstorm, took a cab from Buffalo to hear Sheen talk about the war and to discuss the issue with him. Michael C. Hogan interview.

83. Editorial, "Catholic Bishop Wants Troops Withdrawn from Vietnam," *Christian Century,* 16 August 1967, p. 1036.

84. McNamara, *The Diocese of Rochester,* pp. 535–36.

85. Ibid., pp. 536–37.

86. William Graf interview, 23 June 1999.

87. Michael C. Hogan interview; McNamara, *The Diocese of Rochester,* p. 546.

88. Ibid., pp. 544–45. Shamon later gave the credit to Fr. Gerald T. Connor. Shamon, *The Bishop Sheen We Knew,* pp. 29–33.

89. McNamara, *The Diocese of Rochester,* p. 546.

90. William Graf interview, 24 June 1999.

91. Andrew Apostoli interview, 28 October 1999.

92. McNamara, *The Diocese of Rochester,* p. 540.

93. *New York Times,* 7 August 1967.

94. Finks dissertation, p. 211.

95. *New York Times,* 8 October 1967.

96. McNamara, *The Diocese of Rochester,* p. 539.

97. *New York Times,* 15 October 1967.

98. Copy, Fulton J. Sheen to Marlene Brownett, dated by Brownett as 27 October 1967, Marlene Brownett file.

99. Thomas J. Shelley, "Slouching Toward the Center: Cardinal Francis Spellman, Archbishop Paul J. Hallinan and American Catholicism in the 1960s," *U.S. Catholic Historian* 17 (Fall 1999), p. 23.

100. *New York Times,* 3 December 1967.

101. Copy, Fulton J. Sheen to Clare Boothe Luce, 28 December 1967, box 40, Luce Papers.

102. Copy, Fulton J. Sheen to Clare Boothe Luce, undated, box 43, Luce Papers.

103. Shamon, *The Bishop Sheen We Knew,* pp. 13–14, 18, 26.

104. McNamara, *The Diocese of Rochester,* pp. 540–41; William Graf interview, 23 June 1999; Joe Hart interview; Michael C. Hogan interview.

105. *New York Times,* 2 March 1968. The *Times* reported erroneously that the church was used by 2,000 people.

106. William Graf to the author, 28 May 2000. Sheen had two other motives in donating the parish. He thought the diocese owned too much property and should begin getting rid of some of it. The possible imposition of taxes on church property was also considered. Copy, Robert F. McNamara interview with Dennis W. Hickey and James M. Moynihan, 7 March 1970, Robert F. McNamara file.

107. On the Board of Consultors, see William Graf to the author, 14 August 2000, in McNamara file. Later, with a new Code of Canon Law, the Priests' Council became the Board of Consultors (CIC #502). Ibid.

108. Copy, Robert F. McNamara interview with Dennis W. Hickey and James M. Moynihan, 7 March 1970.

109. Thomas Henseler interviews, 28 July, 1 August 2000. See *Peoria Journal Star*, 15 December 1967; 20, 25, 26 February 1968. Fr. Henseler has two Sheen letters that pertain to this event, both expressing his fond memories of his nine months as a curate and of his love for the people of St. Patrick's Church. The bishop later sent Fr. Henseler a gift of two previously unpublished photographs of himself taken by Karsh. They remain in Henseler's possession.

110. Copy, Robert F. McNamara interview with Dennis W. Hickey and John M. Moynihan, 7 March 1970.

111. Ibid; McNamara, *The Diocese of Rochester*, pp. 547–48.

112. *New York Times*, 28 February 1968.

113. Ibid, 2 March 1968.

114. Michael C. Hogan interview.

115. Sheen, *Treasure in Clay*, p. 180.

116. Copy, Robert F. McNamara interview with Dennis W. Hickey and John M. Moynihan, 7 March 1970.

117. McNamara, *The Diocese of Rochester*, pp. 548–49; Finks dissertation, pp. 185–212; editorial, *Rochester Democrat and Chronicle*, 4 March 1968.

118. Francis J. Weber, *His Eminence of Los Angeles, James Francis Cardinal McIntyre* (Mission Hills, California: St. Francis Historical Society, 1997), vol. 2, pp. 416–37, 593–602.

119. Copy, Robert F. McNamara interview with Dennis W. Hickey and John M. Moynihan, 7 March 1970.

120. *New York Times*, 4 March 1968.

121. McNamara, *The Diocese of Rochester*, p. 549.

122. *Rochester Democrat and Chronicle,* 4 March 1968.

123. McNamara, *The Diocese of Rochester,* p. 549.

124. Patrick Collins to the author, 17 January 2000, Patrick Collins file.

125. Sheen, *Treasure in Clay,* pp. 176, 180, 183.

126. Finks dissertation, p. 184.

127. Copy, Robert F. McNamara interview with Dennis W. Hickey and John M. Moynihan, March 7, 1970.

128. McNamara, *The Diocese of Rochester,* pp. 546–47. In 1998, the foundation opened Brentland Woods, a 51-unit apartment facility for the elderly in Henrietta, New York. See http://www.nynewswire.com/brentland.htm.

129. Sydney E. Ahlstrom, *A Religious History of the American People* (New Haven: Yale University Press, 1972), p. 953.

130. *New York Times,* 22 July 1968.

131. Ralph M. McInerny, *What Went Wrong with Vatican II: The Catholic Crisis Explained* (Manchester, New Hampshire: Sophia Institute Press, 1998), pp. 102–3 *et passim.*

132. *New York Times,* 16 October 1969.

133. Warren Hinckle, "Left Wing Catholics," *Ramparts,* November 1967, pp. 15–16, 23–24.

134. *L'Osservatore Romano,* 11 April 1968.

135. Sheen, *Treasure in Clay,* p. 229.

136. E.g., Sheen, *Old Errors and New Labels,* pp. 287–89; Sheen, *Friends,* pp. 20–21; and James C. G. Conniff, *The Bishop Sheen Story* (New York: Fawcett Publications, 1953), pp. 17–18; Eileen Sheen Khouw interview,

137. D. P. Noonan, *The Passion of Fulton Sheen* (New York: Dodd, Mead, 1972), pp. 134–35.

138. *Washington Star,* 16 January 1969.

139. Sheen, *Treasure in Clay,* pp. 237–38.

140. Robert F. McNamara to the author, 6 June 2000, McNamara file.

141. McNamara, *The Diocese of Rochester,* pp. 542–43. Full details are in Robert F. McNamara, "Ecumenism and the Rochester Center for Theological Studies," *Rochester History* 52 (Fall 1990), pp. 11–17.

142. See Finks dissertation, pp. 209–12.

143. [Fulton J. Sheen], "Sit down quickly and write fifty," (n.p., [1969]), [p. 6], in the possession of Mary Nordeman.

144. Sheen, *Treasure in Clay,* pp. 184–85. The assistantship was announced on 15 July 1976. The Vatican's letter informing Sheen is in Sheen Correspondence, box 30, Sheen Archives.

145. Confidential source. According to this source, Hogan was selected by Sheen to be one of his auxiliary bishops. Vatican officials, seeing three names on Sheen's list, chose two, omitting Hogan. When Sheen resigned, he handed Paul VI an envelope containing the name of the man he wanted to be his successor. This was Sheen's revenge on Rome's officialdom.

146. *New York Times,* 16 October 1969.

147. Shamon, *The Bishop Sheen We Knew,* p. 28.

148. Transcript, *60 Minutes,* 28 October 1969, Sheen Archives. Several Rochester priests wrote letters to Sheen expressing their deepest gratitude for his three years in the diocese. Bishops from around the Church also praised his good works. See the Fulton J. Sheen Collection, St. John's University Archives, Jamaica, New York.

Chapter 11: Frail Defender

1. Robert McNamara, *The Diocese of Rochester, 1868–1968* (Rochester: Diocese of Rochester, 1968), pp. 554–55.

2. Sheen, *Treasure in Clay,* pp. 177–78.

3. Copy, Fulton J. Sheen to Clare Boothe Luce, 12 January 1972, Sheen Correspondence, box 30, Sheen Archives.

4. Joan Cunningham interview, 4 October 1999.

5. Rev. Albert Joseph Mary Shamon, *The Bishop Sheen We Knew* (Oak Lawn, Illinois: CMJ Associates, 1997), pp. 27–28.

6. Copy, Friends of the Sheen Archives publication, c. 1976, CUA Archives.

7. Jaspar Pennington interview.

8. Joan Cunningham interview, 4 October 1999.

9. Matthew Paratore interview.

10. Copy, Fulton J. Sheen to Mr. and Mrs. Vincent Cahill, 10 December 1969, Vincent Cahill file.

11. Sheen, *Treasure in Clay,* p. 183.

12. See George A. Kelly, *The Battle for the American Church* (New York: Doubleday, 1979), pp. 63–65, 221–33, 261–85, 332–33; Kelly, *The Battle for the American Church Revisited* (San Francisco: Ignatius Press, 1995), pp. 63–89.

13. Quoted in Kelly, *The Battle for the American Church Revisited,* p. 54.

14. James Hitchcock, *Catholicism and Modernity: Confrontation or Capitulation?* (New York: Seabury Press, 1979), pp. 8, 55.

15. Quoted in Roger Finke and Rodney Stark, *The Churching of America, 1776–1990: Winners and Losers in Our Religious Economy* (New Brunswick, New Jersey: Rutgers University Press, 1992), p. 258.

16. Dean M. Kelley, *Why Conservative Churches Are Growing: A Study in Sociology of Religion* (Macon, Georgia: Mercer University Press, 1986), esp. pp. 158–79. See also Wade Clark Roof and William McKinney, *American Mainline Religion: Its Changing Shape and Future* (New Brunswick, New Jersey: Rutgers University Press, 1987), pp. 86–87, 95–96, 111, 160–61, 178–85.

17. Between 1978 and 1997 there were 21,850 who left the priesthood, the greater part being in Europe, with 9,699 exiting. During that same period, 144,357 priests died. By 1995, the average age of priests worldwide was 54.6 years, and of bishops, 66.49. ZENIT press release, 25 January 2000.

18. Finke and Stark, *The Churching of America,* pp. 255–65. The quotation is on page 261.

19. Quoted in ibid., p. 269.

20. George Gallup Jr. and Jim Castelli, *The People's Religion: American Faith in the 90s* (New York: Macmillan Publishing Co., 1989), p. 99.

21. Barry A. Kosmin and Seymour P. Lachman, *One Nation under God: Religion in Contemporary American Society,* 1st ed. (New York: Harmony Books, 1993), pp. 217, 256.

22. Copy, Fulton J. Sheen to Paul J. Hallinan, 22 April 1966, Sheen Correspondence, box 48, Sheen Archives.

23. Copy, Fulton J. Sheen to Robert F. McNamara, 23 December 1975, Robert McNamara file.

24. Patrick W. Collins to the author, 17 January 2000, Patrick Collins file.

25. Copy, Fulton J. Sheen to Mother Elizabeth Mary [Mother General of the Sisters of the Holy Child Jesus], 6 January 1977, Sheen Correspondence, box 30.

26. Copy, Fulton J. Sheen to John Joseph Carberry, 3 September 1976, Sheen Correspondence, box 30.

27. Henry Dieterich, ed., *Through the Year with Fulton Sheen* (Ann Arbor, Michigan: Servant Books, 1985), p. 148.

28. Ibid., p. 173.

29. *Catholic Standard and Times,* 12 August 1976.

30. Dieterich, ed., *Through the Year with Fulton Sheen*, pp. 26–27. This is largely a collection of speech excerpts delivered in the 1970s.

31. Sheen, *Treasure in Clay*, pp. 292–93. Cf. Giuseppe Alberigo, "The Christian Situation after Vatican II," in *The Reception of Vatican II*, ed. Giuseppe Alberigo, John-Pierre Jossua and Joseph A. Komonchak (Washington, D.C.: Catholic University of America Press, 1987), pp. 1–24.

32. "Bishop Sheen Speaks Out," *Image*, a 1973 article, p. 18, in the Eileen Sheen Khouw file.

33. Marlene Brownett to the author, 6 June 2000, Marlene Brownett file.

34. *Catholic Standard and Times*, 12 August 1976.

35. Sheen, *Guide to Contentment*, p. 38. Cf. Sheen, *Children and Parents*, pp. 88–94.

36. Sheen, *Children and Parents*, pp. 100–1, 106.

37. Ibid., p. 108.

38. Sheen, *Guide to Contentment*, pp. 105–6.

39. "Bishop Sheen Speaks Out," p. 17.

40. Dieterich, ed., *Through the Year with Fulton Sheen*, p. 18.

41. Ibid., p. 18. Cf. Sheen, *Walk with God*, pp. 37–38.

42. Sheen, *Children and Parents*, p. 119. Cf. Sheen, *Footprints in a Darkened Forest*, pp. 146–49.

43. Copy, J. Edgar Hoover to Fulton J. Sheen, 16 October 1969; copy, Fulton J. Sheen to J. Edgar Hoover, 22 October 1969; copy, memorandum, C. F. Downing to Mr. Conrad, 19 August 1969, FBI file.

44. Copy, J. Edgar Hoover to Fulton J. Sheen, 12 February 1970, FBI file.

45. *Catholic Virginian*, 19 December 1969.

46. Unidentified clipping of 6 August 1971, in the possession of Ann O'Connor.

47. Marlene Brownett to the author, 6 June 2000, Marlene Brownett file; Joan Cunningham interview, 23 May 2000.

48. Sheen appeared three times at the Crystal Cathedral. See a copy of the 1980 Robert Schuller pamphlet discussing Sheen in Marlene Brownett file.

49. Marlene Brownett to the author, 5 September 2000, Marlene Brownett file. This information was gleaned from a Sheen date book in the possession of Edythe Brownett. According to Marlene Brownett, there is only one such volume extant.

50. Quoted in Beverly Coney Heirich, ed., *Mornings with Fulton Sheen: 120 Holy Hour Readings* (Ann Arbor, Michigan: Servant Books, 1997), p. 46.

51. *Boston Post,* 29 March 1973.

52. Milton Berle, with Haskel Frankel, *Milton Berle: An Autobiography* (New York: Delacorte Press, 1974), p. 325.

53. Brochure announcing Sheen's coming appearance at the church on September 30 to October 3, 1973, in the possession of Ann O'Connor. See *The Irish Catholic,* 10 July 1969.

54. Copy, Fulton J. Sheen to Klaus Mund, 24 January 1974, Ursula Faymonville file.

55. Copy, Fulton J. Sheen to Mr. and Mrs. Vincent Cahill, 30 April 1974, Vincent Cahill file.

56. Dieterich, ed., *Through the Year with Fulton Sheen,* p. 26.

57. Edwin Broderick interview, 27 March 1999.

58. *Washington Star,* 20 July, 5 October 1974. The series is currently for sale on two video cassettes.

59. April 1975 update of the Associated Press biography, in Sheen Miscellaneous file.

60. *Washington Star,* 17 April 1975.

61. Copy, Fulton J. Sheen to Mary Fulton Baker, 15 April 1975, Eileen Sheen Khouw file.

62. Copy, Fulton J. Sheen to "My Dear Friends," 8 May 1975, Vincent Cahill file.

63. Copy, Fulton J. Sheen to Mary Nordeman, 14 February 1958; 18 December 1969, Mary Nordeman file; Mary H. Downing interview; Mary Nordeman to the author, 9 August 2000, Mary Nordeman file; assorted historical materials in Mary Nordeman's possession.

64. Copy, Edward T. O'Meara to Jan Jadot, 30 January 1976, Sheen Correspondence, box 30.

65. Marlene Brownett to the author, 5 September 2000, Marlene Brownett file.

66. Loretta Young Louis interview.

67. *Peoria Journal Star,* 12 December 1979.

68. *Catholic Post,* 16 September 1979.

69. Jaspar Pennington interview. See the statement "Sheen Archives" in the pamphlet "Archbishop Fulton John Sheen Special Collections Room," 27 September 1976, CUA Archives.

70. Copy, Fulton J. Sheen to Terence Cooke, 3 July 1979, Sheen Correspondence, box 30.

71. Interviews with Joseph P. Brennan and Matthew R. Paratore; Jaspar Green Pennington, ed., *The Sheen Archives: An Address by His Excellency the Most Reverend Fulton John Sheen* (Rochester, New York: Press of the Good Mountain, May 1978), introduction.

72. Jaspar Pennington interview. Sheen, however, had written a glowing review of Merton's autobiographical *The Seven Storey Mountain,* published in 1948.

73. Copy, Paul VI to Fulton J. Sheen, 8 May 1976, Sheen Correspondence, box 30.

74. Copy, Joseph L. Bernardin to Fulton J. Sheen, 2 June 1976, Sheen Correspondence, box 30.

75. Jaspar Pennington interview.

76. For a list of the initial contributions, see "Archbishop Fulton John Sheen Special Collections Room," 27 September 1976, CUA Archives.

77. Pennington, ed., *The Sheen Archives, passim.*

78. Jaspar Pennington interview.

79. Ibid. When in Peoria for the last time, earlier that year, Fulton told his nephew Joseph Sheen Jr. that he possessed nothing to document his early years. Joe had inherited a large collection of clippings and photographs from his father, and he gave it to Sheen. Fulton donated those materials to the Sheen Archives. This gift was the source of several photographs that later appeared in *Treasure in Clay.* Joseph Sheen Jr. conversation with the author, 29 July 2000.

80. *The Monitor,* 20 May 1976.

81. *Catholic Standard and Times,* 12 August 1976.

82. Jaspar Pennington interview.

83. "Bottom-Line Theology: An Interview with Fulton J. Sheen," *Christianity Today,* 3 June 1977, pp. 8–11.

84. Marie Minnick interview; Eileen Sheen Khouw to the author, 20 August 2000, Eileen Sheen Khouw file.

85. Edythe Brownett interview. Eileen and Marie Sheen later praised their father for his brilliance, integrity, humility, sense of humor, selfless devotion to the ill, and his sterling qualities as a father. "All the kids really loved him," said Marie. "We all thought he was perfect," said Eileen. Marie Minnick interview; Eileen Sheen Khouw interview. For a good contem-

porary article on Tom Sheen, see Sidney Fields, "Only Human," *New York Daily Mirror,* 23 December 1954. For a publication by the physician, see "Thomas N. Sheen, M.D.," *Bulletin of the New York Academy of Medicine* 37 (August 1961), pp. 573–77. Other materials are in the Eileen Sheen Khouw file.

86. Marie Minnick interview.

87. Marlene Brownett interview, 24 February 2000.

88. Sheen, *Treasure in Clay,* p. 345. Priests and religious were later asked to replace hospital blood supplies. *Catholic Standard,* 15 December 1977.

89. Marlene Brownett to the author (June 2000), Marlene Brownett file.

90. Copy, telegram, Edward O'Meara to Jean Villot, 16 July 1977; copy, mailgram, Edward T. O'Meara to Jean Villot, 14 August 1977; Jean Villot to Edward T. O'Meara, 17 August 1977, Sheen Correspondence, box 30.

91. *New York Daily News,* 4 November 1977.

92. Sheen, accompanied by Marlene and Edythe Brownett and Cathy Yetman, once visited Mother Teresa while she was in her order's Harlem convent on 145th Street in New York. Mother tried to persuade Yetman to join her in Venezuela. Cathy was tempted, but the bishop interjected, "We need her here." Marlene Brownett to the author, 1 July 2000, Marlene Brownett file.

93. *SHCJ News,* October 1977, p. 7.

94. Joan Cunningham interview, 4 October 1999.

95. Copy, form letter, Edward T. O'Meara to "Dear Friend of the Missions," November 1977, Marlene Brownett file. Sheen said later, "I suffered pain that I didn't know even existed, pain that was no longer outside of me, pain that possessed me, like an ocean overwhelming me. And outside of virtue, that's the only educator in the world." *Archbishop Fulton J. Sheen, Malcolm Muggeridge: A Conversation, May 1979* (New York: The National Committee of Catholic Laymen, 2000), p. 4. See also pp. 22–23.

96. Sheen, *Treasure in Clay,* p. 346; *Catholic News,* 25 August 1977. See copy, *Mission* magazine article signed by Edward T. O'Meara in Sheen Correspondence, box 30.

97. See copy, *Mission* magazine article signed by O'Meara. At the Mass on August 24, after Sheen had been moved to a private room from intensive care, Sister Marlene Brownett renewed her vows. Bishop Edward O'Meara and Fr. Vincent Nugent, were on hand. They as well as Sheen had been present at Marlene's first and final professions in 1962 and 1967. *SHCJ News,* October 1977, p. 7.

98. *New York Daily News,* 4 November 1977.

99. Sheen, *Treasure in Clay,* p. 341.

100. A tape recording of the event, which I heard, is in the possession of Marlene Brownett. For Brownett's comments on Actors Prayer Day, see Marlene Brownett to the author, 26 July 2000, Marlene Brownett file. On Sheen's disgust toward newspapers, see Dieterich, ed., *Through the Year with Fulton Sheen,* p. 184.

101. *Philadelphia Inquirer,* 13 December 1979.

102. *New York Daily News,* 25 March 1978.

103. Connie Sheen interviews, 5, 7 January 2000; Catherine Sheen interview.

104. Connie Sheen interview, 5 January 2000.

105. Sheen, *Treasure in Clay,* p. 348.

106. Copy, Fulton J. Sheen to Mr. and Mrs. Chet Baker, 31 January 1979, Eileen Sheen Khouw file.

107. Billy Graham, *Just As I Am: The Autobiography of Billy Graham* (San Francisco: HarperSanFrancisco, 1997), p. 693. Fulton wrote to Vincent and Marian Cahill, "I went to Washington last week for the Presidential Prayer Breakfast, accompanied by my good doctor. It was wonderful to be able to do it, and quite an experience as I had been on bed-rest for some four months. Now I will need another some months to recuperate from this journey." Copy, Fulton J. Sheen to the Cahill family, 23 January 1979, Vincent Cahill file.

108. Jimmy Carter to Chad Abel-Kops, 15 June 2000, Jimmy Carter file.

109. *Newsday,* 14 April 1979.

110. *New York Times,* 9 May 1979.

111. Copy, Fulton J. Sheen to Mr. and Mrs. Chester Baker, 3 June 1979, Eileen Sheen Khouw file.

112. *New York Times,* 13 May 1979.

113. George A. Kelly interview, 4 January 1998.

114. *New York Daily News,* 16 December 1979.

115. Fulton J. Sheen III interview, 16 September 1999.

116. *New York Daily News,* 21 September 1979; Sheen, *Treasure in Clay,* p. 350.

117. Sheen homily, 20 September 1979, in the possession of Marlene Brownett.

118. Patricia Kossmann interview.

119. Ibid; Patricia Kossmann to the author, 27 June 2000.

120. Sheen homily, 20 September 1979, in the possession of Marlene Brownett.

121. Matthew Paratore interview.

122. Edwin Broderick interview, 27 March 1999; copy, Robert Paul Mohan speech, 30 January 1980, attached to the Mohan interview; Sheen, *Treasure in Clay,* pp. 354–55.

123. Sheen, *Treasure in Clay,* p. 242.

124. Ibid, pp. 243–49.

125. Ibid., p. 354.

126. See Sheen, *The Love That Waits for You,* p. 78, a 1949 publication.

127. Sheen, *Treasure in Clay,* pp. 344–49. Cf. Sheen, *The Eternal Galilean,* pp. 214–19, a similar statement from the younger Sheen.

128. Sally Fitzgerald, ed., *The Habit of Being* (New York: Vintage Books, 1980), p. 163.

129. Sheen, *Treasure in Clay,* pp. 334–50.

130. The will is in the Sheen Archives. Edythe Brownett was one of the three witnesses who signed the document.

131. Joan Cunningham interview, 4 October 1999.

132. Vincent Cahill interview. Cahill had donated blood following Sheen's operation.

133. "Airplanes and Almond Joys: A Family Remembers Fulton Sheen," *Mission,* Spring 1995, p. 5; Reeda Holliger interview.

134. Copy, Fulton J. Sheen to Nora [Ann] O'Connor, n.d., postmarked 10 December 1979, in O'Connor's possession.

135. Joan Cunningham interview, 28 August 2000. Marlene Brownett noted later, "It was the feast of Juan Diego who was a devotee of Our Lady of Guadeloupe. So, in a certain sense he did die, as he had hoped, on a sort of feast of Our Lady." Marlene Brownett to the author, 5 September 2000, Marlene Brownett file.

136. Press release, Archdiocese of New York, in Archdiocese of New York Archives; "December 1979," a statement sent to the author by Marlene Brownett, in the Marlene Brownett file.

137. Copy, Martin Sheen to Sister Ann Edward, 8 August 1989, Ann Edward file.

138. Joseph Sheen Jr. interview.

139. Ibid.

140. Marlene Brownett interview, 11 February 2000.

141. *New York Times,* 14 December 1979.

142. Ann Edward interview.

143. *Peoria Journal Star,* 11 December 1979.

144. Marlene Brownett interview, 11 February 2000.

145. Sheen, *Treasure in Clay,* pp. 351–55.

Author's Note

1. Joan Cunningham interview, 4 October 1999.

2. Ann Edward interview.

3. Mary H. Downing interview. Some may have received items not listed in Sheen's letter. The gift to Mary Downing, for example, might well have come from Edythe Brownett. Eileen Sheen, on the other hand, received nothing.

4. See Blythe Roveland-Brenton to the author, 17, 22 August 2000, Vincent Nugent file. Blythe was the interim university archivist. Nugent suffered from severe Alzheimer's disease, and the Sheen materials, found in his room, were sent to St. John's by Vincentian Community officials. See John W. Carven to the author, 11 August 2000, Vincent Nugent file. Documents from this collection are cited in this biography as being in the Fulton J. Sheen Collection, St. John's University Archives, Jamaica, New York.

5. Patricia Kossmann interview.

6. John Cardinal O'Connor interview; Tom McSweeney interview.

7. Copy, Tom McSweeney to John P. Meier, 1 March 1992, Tom McSweeney file.

8. Copy, John Tracy Ellis to John Cardinal O'Connor, 20 June 1990, Tom McSweeney file.

9. Copy, John Cardinal O'Connor to John Tracy Ellis, 27 June 1990, Tom McSweeney file.

10. Sebastian Falcone interview.

11. Marguerita Smith interview. She noted that Cooney had not worked in the Spellman papers at the archives. The new Archives and Heritage Center that opened in the fall of 2000 at Dunwoodie allowed scholars access to many collections, including the Spellman papers, hitherto closed except by special permission. Linda Chmielewski interview.

12. Copy, John Tracy Ellis to John Cardinal O'Connor, 2 July 1990, Tom McSweeney file.

13. Copy, Tom Shelley to John Tracy Ellis, 8 July 1990; copy, Tom Shelley to John Tracy Ellis, 12 October 1990, Tom McSweeney file.

14. Copy, Tom McSweeney to John Cardinal O'Connor, 22 July 1991, Tom McSweeney file; Tom McSweeney interview.

15. Copy, Tom McSweeney to John P. Meier, 1 March 1992, Tom McSweeney file.

16. Tom McSweeney interview.

17. John Cardinal O'Connor interview. See John Cardinal O'Connor to the author, 19 June 1998, Archdiocese of New York file.

18. See Don Raffaele Farina to the author, 1 September 1998; Bishop G. B. Re to the author, 13 January 1999, Vatican file.

19. See copy, John B. Brady to Edmund D. Pelligrino, 27 March 1981; copy, C. Joseph Nuesse to Edmund D. Pelligrino, 6 April 1981; copy, C. Joseph Nuesse to Frank E. Lioi, 25 June 1981; copy, John B. Brady to C. Joseph Nuesse, 30 June 1981, CUA Archives.

20. William Graf interview, 23 June 1999.

21. Sebastian Falcone interview.

22. William Graf to the author, 10 August 2000 in Sheen Archives file; John W. Carven to the author, 11 August 2000, Vincent Nugent file.

23. William Graf to the author, 12 July 2000. The Sheen collection contains more documentation about the creation of the archives and efforts to obtain additional Sheen materials.

24. Historians are indebted, however, to the work of Kathleen Riley Fields, who organized the materials in the early 1980s for her doctoral dissertation on Sheen. See Kathleen Riley Fields, "Bishop Fulton J. Sheen: An American Catholic Response to the Twentieth Century" (Ph.D. diss., University of Notre Dame, 1988), pp. 516–27.

25. William Graf interview, 23 June 1999; Connie Derby interviews of 23, 24 June 1999.

26. Jaspar Pennington interview.

27. D. P. Noonan, *Missionary with a Mike: The Bishop Sheen Story* (New York: Pageant Press, 1968); *The Passion of Fulton Sheen* (New York: Dodd, Mead, 1972). On Daniel P. Noonan's dismissal, see Raymond Kupke interview, 24 March 1999. Msgr. Kupke, archivist of the Diocese of Paterson, New

Jersey, also shared a portion of Noonan's personnel file with me. See the D. P. Noonan file.

28. Kathleen Riley Fields, Ph.D. dissertation. There have been several dissertations from the field of mass communications, and one was published: Christopher Owen Lynch, *Selling Catholicism: Bishop Sheen and the Power of Television* (Lexington: University Press of Kentucky, 1998).

29. Myles P. Murphy, *The Life and Times of Fulton J. Sheen* (Staten Island, New York: Alba House, 2000). Kathleen Riley Fields objected strongly and publicly to Murphy's frequent use of her dissertation without giving it credit. See her commentary on the Amazon.com web page for Murphy's book.

30. David J. O'Brien, *American Catholics and Social Reform: The New Deal Years* (New York: Oxford University Press, 1968), p. 191.

31. William M. Halsey, *The Survival of American Innocence: Catholicism in an Era of Disillusionment, 1920–1940* (Notre Dame: University of Notre Dame Press, 1980), pp. 156–59.

32. Jay P. Dolan, *The American Catholic Experience: A History from Colonial Times to the Present* (Notre Dame: University of Notre Dame Press, 1980), p. 393.

33. Chester Gillis, *Roman Catholicism in America* (New York: Columbia University Press, 1999), p. 229.

34. Perhaps this is an example of how Catholic academics have internalized the anti-Catholicism of mainstream intellectual culture. See Matthew L. Lamb, "Will There Be Catholic Theology in the United States?" *America*, 26 May 1990, pp. 523–34. However, the author of the doctoral dissertation on Sheen, a graduate of Notre Dame University, assured this writer, "certainly that is not true of many professors and colleagues of mine." Kathleen L. Riley to the author, 6 March 2000.

35. Mark S. Massa, *Catholics and American Culture: Fulton Sheen, Dorothy Day, and the Notre Dame Football Team* (New York: Crossroad, 1999), p. 101. See also p. 41.

36. Mark A. Noll, *A History of Christianity in the United States and Canada* (Grand Rapids, Michigan: William B. Eerdmans, 1992), pp. 507–9.

37. Martin E. Marty, *Modern American Religion,* vol. 3, *Under God, Indivisible, 1941–1960* (Chicago: University of Chicago Press, 1996), pp. 89–94, 322–26.

38. John A. Garraty, *The American Nation: A History of the United States,* 8th ed. (New York: HarperCollins, 1995).

39. Dewey E. Grantham, *Recent America: The United States since 1945,* 2nd ed. (Wheeling, Illinois: Harlan Davidson, 1998), p. 179.

40. George Donelson Moss, *America in the Twentieth Century,* 3rd ed. (Upper Saddle River, New Jersey: Prentice Hall, 1997), p. 365.

41. Kenneth Stewart, "Monsignor Fulton J. Sheen," *PM Magazine,* 9 June 1946, p. m7.

42. *The Rambler* (Rosemont College), 7 June 1943.

43. Stewart, "Monsignor Fulton J. Sheen," p. m8.

44. Fulton J. Sheen, *Treasure in Clay: The Autobiography of Fulton J. Sheen* (San Francisco: Ignatius Press, 1993), p. 66.

45. Henry Everett Malone, "The Radio-Preaching Art of Monsignor Sheen" (M.A. thesis, Catholic University of America, 1949), pp. 15–16.

46. Matthew Paratore interview.

47. *Boston Globe,* 29 March 1973.

Interviews

These individuals have kindly provided information about Fulton J. Sheen.

Fr. George J. Auger
Fr. Joseph P. Brennan
Bishop Edwin Broderick
Edythe Brownett
Sister Marlene Brownett
Marian Cahill
Vincent Cahill
Anne Charnley
James C. G. Conniff
Laura Chmielewski
Joan Cunningham
Joan Dalton
Sister Connie Derby
Prof. Jude P. Dougherty
Mary II. Downing
Sister Ann Edward
Fr. Sebastian Falcone
William Ferris
Msgr. Hilary Franco
Merle Fulton
Ann Gevas
Mary Giaratanna
Fr. William Graf
Fr. Joe Hart
Fr. Paul Hartman
Fr. Patrick Hayes
Fr. Thomas Henseler
Fr. Michael C. Hogan
Reeda Holliger

Tom Holliger
Yolanda Holliger
Msgr. George A. Kelly
Eileen Khouw
Patricia Kossmann
Msgr. Raymond Kupke
Gregory Ladd
Loretta Young Louis
Virginia Mayo
Fr. Robert McNamara
Msgr. Tom McSweeney
Marie Minnick
Msgr. Robert Paul Mohan
Fr. Lawrence Morrissey
Mary Nordeman
Ann O'Connor
John Cardinal O'Connor
Matthew R. Paratore
Rev. Jaspar Pennington
Fr. Paul Prucha
Prof. Patrick Riley
Blythe Roveland-Brenton
Sister Marguerita Smith
William Schuyler
Catherine Sheen
Connie Sheen
Fulton J. Sheen II
Fulton J. Sheen III
Dr. John E. Sheen

Joseph Sheen Jr.
Fr. Robert Trisco
Robert Vogt
Marie-Jose Willimann

Index